ANIMAL

The author provides an insight into how crimes against animals contain not only legal, but also moral, gendered and cultural dimensions. This book will be a very important contribution to the study of animal abuse and will fill a gap for many green criminologists and others studying this field.

Ragnhild Sollund, University of Oslo, Norway

This book brilliantly synthesizes studies of criminal typology of offender types to those entities and individuals who commit animal harm worldwide across species, domestic and wild, to develop a green criminological agenda that recognizes animal harm as social harm and provides greater protection for all animals to promote the public good.

Joan Schaffner, George Washington University, USA

Angus Nurse highlights the destructive implications of Government policies that simultaneously weaken anti-cruelty regulations while relying on a punishment-as-deterrence approach to criminal justice policy. He makes a convincing case for an end to official complacency towards cruelty to animals, and the need for a holistic, multi-faceted approach to tackle animal harm.

Dan Lyons, Centre for Animals & Social Justice and
University of Sheffield, UK

GREEN CRIMINOLOGY

Series Editors:

Michael J. Lynch, *University of South Florida, USA*
Paul B. Stretesky, *University of Colorado, Denver, USA*

Now two decades old, green criminology – the study of environmental harm, crime, law, regulation, victimization, and justice – has increasing relevance to contemporary problems at local, national, and international levels. This series comes at a time when societies and governments worldwide seek new ways to alleviate and deal with the consequences of various environmental harms as they relate to humans, non-human animals, plant species, and the ecosystem and its components. Green criminology offers a unique theoretical perspective on how human behavior causes and exacerbates environmental conditions that threaten the planet's viability. Volumes in the series will consider such topics and controversies as corporate environmental crime, the complicity of international financial institutions, state-sponsored environmental destruction, and the role of non-governmental organizations in addressing environmental harms. Titles will also examine the intersections between green criminology and other branches of criminology and other areas of law, such as human rights and national security. The series will be international in scope, investigating environmental crime in specific countries as well as comparatively and globally. In sum, by bringing together a diverse body of research on all aspects of this subject, the series will make a significant contribution to our understanding of the dynamics between the natural world and the quite imperfect human world, and will set the stage for the future study in this growing area of concern.

Other titles in this series:

Eco-global Crimes
Contemporary Problems and Future Challenges
Edited by Rune Ellefsen, Ragnhild Sollund and Guri Larsen

Animal Harm
Perspectives on Why People Harm and Kill Animals

ANGUS NURSE
Birmingham City University, UK

LONDON AND NEW YORK

First published 2013 by Ashgate Publishing

2 Park Square, Milton Park, Abingdon, Oxon OX14 4RN
711 Third Avenue, New York, NY 10017, USA

Routledge is an imprint of the Taylor & Francis Group, an informa business

First issued in paperback 2016

British Library Cataloguing in Publication Data
Nurse, Angus.
  Animal harm : perspectives on why people harm and kill
  animals. -- (Green criminology)
  1. Animal welfare. 2. Animal welfare--Psychological
  aspects. 3. Animal welfare--Moral and ethical aspects.
  4. Animal welfare--Law and legislation.
  I. Title II. Series
  364.1'87-dc23

Library of Congress Cataloging-in-Publication Data
Nurse, Angus.
  Animal harm : perspectives on why people harm and kill animals / by Angus Nurse.
      p. cm. -- (Series green criminology)
  Includes bibliographical references and index.
  ISBN 978-1-4094-4208-0 (hardback) 1. Animal welfare--Law and legislation.
  2. Animals--Law and legislation. 3. Animal rights. 4. Wildlife conservation--Law
  and legislation. I. Title.
  K3620.N87 2013
  179'.3--dc23

                                                                    2012029814

ISBN 978-1-4094-4208-0 (hbk)
ISBN 978-1-138-24991-2 (pbk)

Contents

Preface

This book is based on more than 10 years' research into crimes against animals, primarily on wildlife crime. Yet it remains a work in progress and considerably more needs to be done before we fully understand those who 'willingly' kill, injure or harm animals and the various reasons why they do so. From the outset it should be made clear that this is not an animal rights book. While inevitably it includes some discussion of animal rights concepts, and debates concerning the legal protection of animals, its focus is illegal activity directed towards animals based on *current* law and the prohibitions contained therein, rather than on any notion of what the law should be or the case for legal personhood for non-human animals.

There are many excellent books that cover different aspects of animals' legal status. Singer's (1975) *Animal Liberation* is perhaps the classic text on utilitarianism and makes a case for animals to have legal protection or rights, on the grounds that humans and animals have equal interest in avoiding suffering. Regan's (1983) *The Case for Animal Rights* distinguishes legal rights from moral rights but effectively argues that animals should be granted the same (or similar) rights to humans because they have value. Steven Wise's *Rattling the Cage* (2000) raises persuasive arguments about legal personhood for animals and the need for fundamental legal rights of bodily integrity and liberty, and identifies the inadequacy of current law and judicial practice in providing for effective animal rights whether directly or indirectly. While I agree with many of the points made by these and other authors who make the legal and moral case for animal rights, my research interest is (and has been) animal harm as an aspect of criminal behaviour, and as a distinct and often neglected area of green criminology.

The study of animal rights and species justice considers animal abuse and suffering, and the development and nurturing of respectful relationships. Yet animal harm is rarely looked at as a distinct aspect of criminality, even within the species justice sub-category of green criminology researchers frequently examine animal abuse, wildlife crime and animal welfare as distinct and separate subjects. However, while there are different behaviours on display in various aspects of animal crime, my contention is that the animal offender exists as a distinct type of criminal, but can also be categorized according to his specific behaviour and type of offending. Law enforcement efforts in the animal law arena often ignore this reality and frequently treats all animal offenders as if they were the same, but so too do campaigners and activists. I contend that this perspective is flawed.

This book does not however suggest that animal abuse and animal offenders can be easily categorized as a homogenous type but instead takes a holistic approach to evaluating the reasons why people injure, harm or kill animals including the ethical and value judgements they make towards animals and the neutralizations and justifications that are provided for their actions. Rather than considering individual issues such as cruelty, smuggling of endangered wildlife or killing of protected wildlife as unconnected, it covers the whole remit of animal crimes and different aspects of animal cruelty, abuse, commercial exploitation and environmental harms associated with animals.

Selection of Topics

Although inevitably there is some bias towards the types of animal crime prevalent in the United Kingdom (UK) where much of the original field research and policy analysis took place, this book is international in scope; its topics having been selected to incorporate discussion of the international context of animal harm and its universality, taking into account the influence of cultural differences on specific activities. While a central theme of the book is the influence of masculinities on animal harm, given that animal abusers, killers of wildlife, and wildlife traders are predominantly male, it must be acknowledged that the extent to which male power and notions of masculinity influence, or are an excuse for, animal harm varies considerably. The public policy response to offending also varies between jurisdictions such that in some countries, certain animal harm activities are tacitly endorsed despite being theoretically unlawful and prohibited by statute, while in others seemingly 'minor' offences are disproportionately targeted by enforcement agencies.

This book seeks to understand these cultural differences and explore the different aspects of animal harm. In doing so it explores a range of activities, including: the abuse of domestic animals and animal cruelty, the commercial killing and exploitation of animals, the illegal trade in wildlife, sport and trophy hunting, and traditional fieldsports (or blood sports as animal activists and environmentalists might contend). In examining these issues it explicitly considers the links between animal harm and other offending including the links to human violence.

I said at the beginning that this is a work in progress. I should also say that the term 'animal harm', used throughout this book, was deliberately chosen as shorthand for a range of animal activities, which includes cruelty, causing injury, death, torture or exploitation of animals. The term 'animal' is also used throughout not because of any preference for this term above 'non-human animal' or 'companion animal' (which is used where appropriate), but because this is the term used consistently in legislation and the book's focus is animal harm that persists *despite* legislation that prohibits it. While broad in scope it is not intended to be comprehensive as this would require a much longer book; thus there are undoubtedly some animal harm activities that should perhaps be discussed but which have not been included, either for reasons of space or because they are the subject of current research incomplete at the time of writing. Any errors or omissions are my own and reflect the current state of the research into animal harm which, in my view, does not currently occupy the position it deserves within academia or policy discourse.

Angus Nurse
Birmingham City University, UK

Acknowledgements

This book would not have been possible without the support and assistance of several colleagues whose enthusiasm and constructive criticism has assisted greatly in refining many of the original ideas. Diane Ryland and Daniel Mills, colleagues at the University of Lincoln, helped develop some of the ideas through questioning some aspects of the work when it was being discussed as part of other research work. Reece Walters, formerly of the Open University and now with Queensland University of Technology, helped considerably in developing the final stages of the original research agenda, commenting favourably yet critically on some aspects. Matthew Cremin and David Wilson, colleagues at Birmingham City University, who commented on some of the original research which formed the basis of this book's wildlife aspects, provided invaluable constructive criticism of the early drafts of some material which appears here in its final reader-friendly form after their assessment of its 'raw' research form. Nic Groombridge of St Mary's University College Twickenham, who also examined some of the original wildlife crime research updated here, was also extremely helpful in providing insight into masculinities research. Thanks are also due to Caryl Jones for her proof reading and critical questioning which helped considerably in refining my communication of the book's more challenging ideas.

Ashgate's *Green Criminology* series is an important step forward in embracing animal harm as part of green criminology and in developing green criminology as a distinct discipline. I am especially grateful to the editors for their support for this project.

List of Acronyms

ADI	Animal Defenders International
ASPCA	American Society for the Prevention of Cruelty to Animals
AWIS	Animal Welfare Information Service
BCTF	Bushmeat Crisis Task Force
CITES	The Convention on International Trade in Endangered Species of Wild Fauna and Flora
CPS	Crown Prosecution Service
EAP	East Asia and Pacific
EIA	Environmental Investigations Agency
EPA	Environmental Protection Agency
EU	European Union
HSUS	Humane Society of the United States
IATA	International Air Transport Association
IFAW	International Fund for Animal Welfare
ILO	International Labour Organization
IUCN	International Union for the Conservation of Nature
NGO	Non-Governmental Organization
PETA	People for the Ethical Treatment of Animals
RSPB	Royal Society for the Protection of Birds
RSPCA	Royal Society for the Prevention of Cruelty to Animals
SAR	South Asia Region
SSPCA	Scottish Society for the Prevention of Cruelty to Animals
TCM	Traditional Chinese Medicine
TRAFFIC	The World Conservation Monitoring Body (CITES trade monitors)
UDAW	The Universal Declaration on Animal Welfare
UNESCO	The United Nation's Educational, Scientific and Cultural Organization
WCMS	World Federation of Chinese Medicine Societies
WCS	Wildlife Conservation Society
WEN	Wildlife Enforcement Network
WSPA	World Society for the Protection of Animals
WWF	World Wide Fund for Nature

Case Study Index

Chapter 1
Introduction

What makes people harm, injure, or kill animals?

The aim of this book is to answer that question through an evaluation of the reasons why people harm, inflict injury on, torture or kill animals and why they take them from the wild or use them in 'sports' which ultimately result in the animal's death. It considers the ethical and value judgements individuals and groups make about animals and the acceptability of harm caused to animals, as well as the neutralizations and justifications that are used to justify action towards animals that society generally finds unacceptable. The aim of this book is to situate animal abuse, wildlife crime, the illegal trade in wildlife and other unlawful activities directed at animals firmly within green criminology, where perspectives on species justice consider the responsibility man owes to other species as part of broader ecological concerns.

The book's origins are in research into wildlife crime conducted since 2000 (and which is ongoing) and which initially identified that while criminal justice policy generally treats all wildlife offenders as if they are rational actors motivated primarily by profit, the reality is that a variety of motivations and behaviours go to make up wildlife crime and various forms of animal abuse. In effect, this book attempts to outline the characteristics of the animal offender, dealing specifically with criminality and criminal behaviour involving animals. The book uses the term 'animal harm' (defined more explicitly in Chapter 2) to cover a range of activities directed at animals but which inevitably result in some form of harm whether physical or psychological. Analysis of animal harm provides for in-depth analysis of criminality and criminal behaviour in a variety of different ways. Attitudes towards animals both on the part of the offenders who harm them and the society which punishes, or in some cases allows the harm to continue, reveal much about tolerance for different forms of violence within society, sympathy towards the suffering of others, the capacity for empathy (Beetz 2009), or an inclination towards violence or other forms of antisocial behaviour (Linzey 2009). As a result, animal harm has importance as an area of study both in its own right as a particular type of crime, and as part of mainstream criminology. However the central contention of this book is that animal harm and offending against animals is a distinct type of criminality, albeit one that has many dimensions, and needs to be seen as such by criminologists, criminal justice policymakers and legislators, although as this chapter will outline, in practice, legislation already reflects differences in types of animal harm.

This chapter provides an overview of the legal protection of animals (domestic and wildlife), discussing both core concepts in international animal/wildlife protection law and the principles behind national laws. Before considering the specific types of animal harm (and their causes) discussed elsewhere in this book, the chapter examines the nature of animal protection legislation and the ethical and policy perspectives that define animal abuse and wildlife crime as illegal activity prohibited by law. It sets out the scope of the book as dealing with animal abuse and wildlife crime as a *combined* topic notwithstanding the differences in criminality inherent in specific animal harm activities discussed throughout the book. White's (2008) green criminology notion of animal rights and species justice deals with animal abuse and suffering, although a distinction should be made between crimes involving and impacting on animals in the wild, and animal cruelty offences that mainly involve domesticated or farmed animals. There is considerable academic literature on animal abuse (e.g. Felthous and Kellert 1987, Conboy-Hill 2000, Henry 2004, Linzey 2009), in particular on how animal abuse can be an indicator of future offending or antisocial behaviour personality disorders. This book's focus is *illegal* animal harm, i.e. activities already prohibited by legislation whether directly or indirectly. But rather than there being cohesive animal harm legislation a range of legislation has been enacted to address multiple animal harm problems incorporating principles of conservation, animal protection, animal welfare, animal cruelty and the commercial exploitation of animals. Animal harm might be prohibited under any of these legislative categories and the distinction between companion animal abuse, which is often associated with other relationships (i.e. human ones) within the family or wider domestic environment, and the abuse or exploitation of wild animals is an important one which is explored further.

Animal Harm as Green Criminology

Although now recognized as a legitimate field of study, one potential difficulty for green criminology is in framing harms to the environment (incorporating environmental criminology and ecological justice) as a distinct area of study somehow separate from other criminological concerns. As Peelo and Soothill identify, criminology 'appears as a relatively dull subject in which data and theory are used to unpick all that people of "common sense" know to be obvious truths about the state of crime in Britain and America today' (2005: ix). Yet green criminology at its best attempts to both challenge and indeed overturn many common-sense notions of crime to reveal and challenge the reality of harms with wider social impact and negative consequences for the environment and human relations. In the specific context area of human–animal relationships and species justice, green criminology is uniquely placed to promote news ways of thinking about our attitudes towards and exploitation of animals as an integral part of mainstream criminal justice, albeit one worthy of dedicated study as a distinct aspect of criminality.

White contends that 'there is no green criminological *theory* as such' (2008: 14) but there is instead a green 'perspective' which explicitly considers environmental issues (broadly construed) as part of criminology. However, within green criminology there are a set of theories relating to human–animal interactions which explore different aspects of animal harm and ecological justice. When taken together these theories coherently theorize that criminality negatively impacting on animals and their environments is of importance not only because such criminality reveals much about human behaviour but also because of its wider social impact. The implication of the green perspective is that harm to animals causes harm to wider human society.

Benton suggests that 'it is widely recognized that members of other animal species and the rest of non-human nature urgently need to be protected from destructive human activities' (1998: 149). Contemporary notions of justice must, therefore, extend beyond traditional human ideals of justice as a punitive or rehabilitative ideal, to incorporate shared concepts of reparative and restorative justice between humans and non-human animals and an obligation on human societies to minimize the harm caused to both their human and non-human residents. An effective criminal justice system arguably needs to provide justice for all 'citizens' whether human or 'nonhuman animal' (Donaldson and Kymlicka 2011) and to incorporate wider notions of citizenship in considering the impacts of criminality. In doing so the idea of justice requires expansion to consider the nature and consequences of criminal behaviour and different types of crime not just on human society, but also to the wider environment and to non-humans. However, within species justice discourse, there are different perspectives on the nature and causes of animal abuse and the importance of animal interests when compared with human interests (Singer 1975, Regan 1983, Linzey 2009). These differences are reflected both in animal protection legislation and in the criminal justice response to different aspects of animal harm.

Social theorists and theologians argue that man's dominant position on the planet necessitates living in harmony with the environment and 'non-human' animals (Singer 1975, Benton 1998, Linzey 2009). Thus violence and cruelty towards animals makes society poorer because it demeans us as individuals and increases the acceptance of violence within society. Within the animal rights literature there are complex arguments about the moral imperative to respect and promote animal welfare and the consequences of cruelty to animals for society. Criminologists (e.g. Benton 1998, Beirne 1999, White 2007) have also recognized the link between environmental and animal protection laws and the development or improvement of society. Increased acceptance of environmental concerns and better animal protection and welfare standards make society better by extending social justice principles beyond human concerns. Criminological research also indicates a link between animal cruelty and violence towards humans (Linzey 2009), primarily indicating that animal abuse is a precursor to human violence but also identifying violence towards animals as indicative of antisocial characteristics within human relationships. Promoting good animal welfare and preventing cruelty towards animals thus benefits society not only by preventing possible future violence towards humans, but also in protecting and improving society by positively influencing our co-existence with animals and the environment and developing a strongly institutionalized protection of universal civil liberties based on respect for and humanity to others.

Yet the reality is that much animal harm remains legal and indeed is positively provided for in legislation. Debates in theology, criminology and the study of animal law which consider the rights of animals and the moral wrong of inflicting harm on other sentient beings are not yet truly reflected in any form of universal animal protection legislation. Instead, in law animals are protected only in certain circumstances and from certain activities (Radford 2001, Zimmerman 2003, Schaffner 2011), primarily according to human interests, or at best where animal interests happen to coincide with human ones. While the principle argument for providing animals with legal rights is utilitarianism and recognition of the fact that animals as sentient beings can suffer (see Bentham 1789, Singer 1975) and that suffering in animals often causes humans to suffer, the concept of legal rights for animals has yet to be widely accepted by legislators and policymakers (see, for example, Wise 2000, Sunstein and Nussbaum 2004, Scruton 2006, Ascione 2008) although the need for improved standards of animal welfare and anti-cruelty statutes has been largely accepted by legislators around the world and incorporated into a range of legislative measures. Drawing on Jeremy Bentham's ideas that animals deserved equal consideration Singer, in *Animal Liberation* (1975), argued not that animals have rights, but that humans and animals have equal interest in avoiding suffering and so humans should apply equal consideration to animals, making moral choices that try to avoid animal suffering wherever possible. Crucially Singer does not argue that all animals should be treated equally and thus accepts that animals of different species have different interests. However, the principle of utilitarianism is that we should make our lives as free from cruelty as possible and avoid inflicting pain and suffering on animals and humans alike. For utilitarianism the benefit of animal welfare is its contribution to an ethical society which tries to minimize pain and suffering wherever and however they occur. Singer's utilitarianism thus provides that animal welfare contributes to the improvement of society and the public good by being a core philosophy that lessens violence in society, leads to a more moral society but, crucially, it does not seek to prohibit all uses of animals where society might benefit from the use (e.g. animals used for food and arguably some forms of animal research) if appropriate welfare standards are maintained. Animal law broadly incorporates this view, providing a framework for the continued use of animals where beneficial to human interests, while prohibiting actions that either conflict with or are incompatible with acceptable use or contravene socially constructed notions of acceptable behaviour commensurate with the use of animals. Initially, then, it could be argued that animal harm is legislated against primarily where it impacts on human animal use, although as this chapter progresses this initial definition proves inadequate.

Principles of Animal Law

From the outset it should be made clear that the animal harm discussed in this book relates to *illegal* activity rather than any wider notion of harm caused to animals which constitutes a moral wrong. Even though some moral dimensions of animal harm are discussed throughout the text, the primary focus is on behaviour already prohibited by the law according to the legalist perspective of crime which Situ and Emmons (2000: 2) define as

> The strict legalist perspective emphasizes that crime is whatever the criminal code says it is. Many works in criminology define crime as behaviour that is prohibited by the criminal code and criminals as persons who have behaved in some way prohibited by the law.

In short, the strict legalist view is that crime is whatever the criminal law defines it as being by specifying those actions prohibited under the law. For example the shooting of wild peregrine falcons (a protected species under UK wildlife law) would be a crime in the UK while the shooting of red grouse (during the 'open' season) would not be as UK law recognizes as legitimate the shooting of birds considered to be 'game', allowing them to be lawfully shot subject to certain conditions. Comparable legislative provisions exist in the United States, Canada and many other countries where game shooting is a lawful activity subject to state control through public law, and a regulatory regime which seeks to control numbers of birds and animals shot primarily through licensing and permit systems. This identifies one of the problems of a purely legalistic approach towards animal harm, that of the inconsistent manner in which the law deals with different animals; defining some forms of animal harm as permissible under the law, while prohibiting others. Non-governmental organizations (NGOs) and animal activists often consider this approach to animal legislation to be hypocritical, revealing the central dichotomy of animal legislation to be the conflict between human and animal interests with animal interests almost always being a secondary consideration. An alternative approach to animal legislation sometimes advocated by activists is the social legal perspective which argues that some acts, especially by corporations, 'may not violate the criminal law yet are so violent in their expression or harmful in their effects to merit definition as crimes' (Situ and Emmons 2000: 3). This approach 'focuses on the construction of crime definitions by various segments of society and the political process by which some gain ascendancy, becoming embodied in the law' (Situ and Emmons 2000: 3).

While the criminal justice system focuses solely on those acts that are prohibited by the criminal law, definitions of crime also need to consider how criminal acts manifest themselves and to consider those acts not yet defined as crimes but which go against the norms of society. Lynch and Stretesky, for example, explain that from an environmental justice perspective a green crime is an act that '(1) may or may not violate existing rules and environmental regulations; (2) has identifiable environmental damage outcomes; and (3) originated in human action' (Lynch and Stretesky 2003: 227). They explain that while some green crimes may not contravene any existing law, where they result in or possess the potential to result in environmental and human harm, they should be considered to be crimes. This is an important issue in animal harm because much campaigning activity is aimed at extending the remit of the criminal law to encompass activities that are currently legal but which NGOs, their supporters and animal activists consider should be made unlawful. Although much animal legislation is not intended as criminal law, frequently it is only through the use of the criminal law and its enforcement mechanisms that animal harm can be addressed where environmental protection measures prove inadequate. The social legal perspective provides a mechanism through which contemporary concerns about animal harm and the abuse of animals which is revealed by animal activists and others could be integrated into legislative policy.

Animal legislation serves multiple purposes and is intended to address a variety of human activities considered harmful towards animals, although arguably animal law is primarily aimed at preserving human interests. Schaffner defines animal law as 'legal doctrine in which the legal, social or biological nature of nonhuman animals is an important factor' (2011: 5). The notion of animals as property has frequently dictated the extent to and manner in which animals receive legal protection and influences legal definitions of animal welfare (Lubinski 2004). Broom, in his foreword to Radford's book *Animal Welfare Law in Britain* (2001), compares the treatment of animals as property in most early legal systems to the treatment of slaves, servants and even wives as possessions. This view persists in a number of legal systems (including in the UK's groundbreaking *Animal Welfare Act 2006*) providing the 'owner' of an animal with the means to seek redress for damage to their 'property' while limiting protection of the animal to its value as property. While some animal welfare and anti-cruelty laws are designed to protect human investment in property, Broom argues that the view of domestic and other animals as sentient beings that deserve respect is a natural social progression 'in the wake of a similar developing view that persons of other nations, creeds, or colours and women had such qualities' (Radford 2001: Foreword). Wise (2000) also argues strongly that legal rights for animals are a natural progression of human evolution, societal development and enlightened thinking. The nature of animal law is, however, diverse and goes beyond providing animal protection or regulating ownership to consider issues of trade, contract, tort, criminal law, charity law and several other areas the legal principles of which are not covered in detail by this book. Animal law does, however, provide a clear framework for defining the illegal animal harm that is the subject of this book.

International Animal Law

International law sets out the obligations on states in respect of legal standards. The primary international law mechanisms are treaties and conventions (Schaffner 2011). Yet at present there is no binding international treaty for the protection of animals and thus no clear international legal standard on animal protection. Instead, it is down to individual states to decide the content of their animal protection laws either through public or private law mechanisms, which either consider animals to be worthy of state protection and public enforcement of animal harm (via public law) or as property subject to civil law allowing individuals rather than the state to resolve potential animal harm problems (via private law). Thus levels of animal protection vary from country to country or even on a regional basis where municipal authorities have law-making powers (e.g. state or province laws within the United States, Canada and Australia) dependent on the legislative approach taken and the extent to which cultural perspectives on animal harm are incorporated into legislation.

Quinney's idea of crime as a social construction identified that acts defined as crime are, for the most part, behaviours undertaken by relatively powerless social actors (Quinney 1970). But the response to these actions and the way that knowledge and understanding of them is collected, collated and disseminated by different groups determines our understanding of crime. Animal harm is thus a social construction influenced by social locations, power relations in society and the need to both promote and protect specific ideological positions on animals by legislators and policymakers. Western conceptions of animal rights and the growing perception of a need for the legal personhood of animals to be part of law are not universally shared and thus western conceptions of animal harm cannot easily be incorporated into international law. Brown Weiss (1993) identified that until the 1960s environmental issues were viewed as state concerns and there was a lack of appreciation of the need for international environmental agreements. The *Convention on International Trade in Endangered Species of Flora and Fauna 1973* (CITES) was one of the first and oldest international legal agreements on environmental issues; it provided a framework for future wildlife and animal protection measures (Zimmerman 2003). While CITES was preceded by the 1946 *International Convention for the Regulation of Whaling*, the text of the whaling convention makes it clear that it was intended to 'provide for the proper conservation of whale stocks and thus make possible the orderly development of the whaling industry'. The whaling convention thus has trade and exploitation of whale stocks as its basis rather than being an international conservation or animal protection measure. While CITES (discussed further below) facilitates the use of animals by allowing wildlife trade under certain conditions through a permit system it also contains provisions clearly prohibiting use of endangered species and providing for criminal enforcement of any breach of its provisions. Rather than being pure international animal protection legislation CITES is conservation, management and trade legislation combined, which regulates a trade in animals and provides protection only in respect of the most vulnerable wildlife whose trade it prohibits. An unintended consequence of CITES is that by allowing a legal framework for trade in wildlife it facilitates the illegal trade and associated harm discussed in Chapter 8. Zimmerman (2003) describes CITES as successful, but as Schaffner (2011) contends, animal law is diverse and inconsistent and laws that are supposed to protect animals interests frequently do not. While a significant piece of international animal legislation, CITES has not yet fulfilled the role of international animal protection legislation although efforts have been made to implement such a measure.

A Universal Declaration of Animal Rights was presented to the United Nation's Educational, Scientific and Cultural Organization (UNESCO) in 1978 which included, among other things proposals for:

- The introduction of legal animals rights similar to human rights principles including the right to live, right to freedom, right to home (for wild animals), freedom from cruel or inhumane treatment and freedom of expression rights.
- Minimum standards of animal welfare and freedom from cruelty for companion animals.
- Governmental responsibilities for animal rights and animal welfare.
- The outlawing of animal experimentation.

Although the proposed convention failed to achieve widespread international agreement, it was significant in introducing the idea of an international law mechanism that would allow animals to command the respect of law as a matter of public debate. Subsequent efforts at such an international measure include the April 1988 Committee on the Convention for the Protection of Animals' proposal for an *International Convention for the Protection of Animals* which included measures on transportation of animal, methods of taking wildlife, care of exhibited wildlife and protection from cruel treatment. It is, however, worth noting that in 1982 the UN General Assembly adopted a World Charter for Nature which contains the following five principles of conservation:

1. Nature shall be respected and its essential processes should be unimpaired.
2. Population levels of wild and domesticated species should be at least sufficient for their survival and habitats should be safeguarded to ensure this.
3. Special protection should be given to the habitats of rare and endangered species and the five principles of conservation should apply to all areas of land and sea.
4. Man's utilization of land and marine resources should be sustainable and should not endanger the integrity or survival of other species.
5. Nature shall be secured against degradation caused by warfare or other hostile activities.

In principle, the UN Charter provides a mechanism for protecting animals from harm by providing a conservation framework that would prevent animal harm through species protection measures. In practice implementation of the Charter relies on national animal protection legislation although Sections 21–24 of the Charter provide authority for individuals to enforce international conservation laws that could provide animal protection and has been used by NGOs as a basis on which to conduct direct action to prevent animal harm (Roeschke 2009).

At the time of writing (early 2012), the World Society for the Protection Animals (WSPA), supported by other NGOs, is also pursuing a campaign for a Universal Declaration on Animal Welfare (UDAW) to be adopted by the United Nations. The proposal currently has in excess of two million signatures and its main principles are to provide for legal respect for animals welfare, obligations on member states 'to prevent cruelty to animals and to reduce their suffering' (Article IV) and an improvement in the effectiveness of existing member state legislation to protect animals (WSPA 2011).

The UDAW is significant in shifting the international law debate away from animal rights and legal personhood for animals and towards animal cruelty and the different aspects of animal harm this book discusses. The preamble to the UDAW recognizes that most states currently have some form of anti-cruelty or animal welfare law; thus Article VI of the UDAW seeks to improve practices and capacity-building using national and international law. As this chapter outlines, animal cruelty is already recognized as an appropriate subject for legislative intervention such that many states' anti-cruelty statutes already contain provisions aimed at addressing various aspects of criminality demonstrated by animal abuse (Nurse 2011, Schaffner 2011) and inherent in animal harm. As a result, an effective international animal cruelty treaty is likely more achievable than an animal rights one, a legal measure which has historically been resisted in part due to conflicting perspectives on the need for legal animal rights and how they might be achieved (Wise 2000, Rollin 2006). But legal animal rights have also been resisted on grounds of the likely impact that legal animal rights would have on private and commercial rights which rely on humans retaining animal property rights (Wise 2000). However international animal cruelty laws could by extension incorporate other aspects of animal harm while leaving scope for individual states to reflect appropriate cultural and commercial requirements within national laws. The derogation procedures operated by the European Union as part of its legal operating procedures that allow states to negotiate opt-outs from having to apply certain legislative measures, and the system of state legislatures, which allow for local/regional legislation, in the United States provide appropriate models. These types of procedure allow states a 'margin of appreciation' in the implementation of legislation where it is necessary to make changes or not fully apply legislation where this is necessary to fit state's circumstances.

Despite the lack of general international protection for animals, and thus the lack of a coherent international standard for animal harm, there are a number of provisions in international law relating to the conservation, management and trade in wildlife. CITES (mentioned earlier) regulates the trade in endangered species of wildlife by creating different levels of protection for wildlife in trade and introduces a wildlife trade tariff system which clarifies the legality of trading in specific wildlife and creates a framework for regulatory enforcement. The convention:

- Prohibits international commercial trade in the most endangered or vulnerable species which are listed in Appendix 1 of CITES.
- Allows commercial trade in species listed in Appendix II of CITES subject to the granting of export permits or re-export permits.
- Allows commercial trade in species listed in Appendix III of CITES subject to granting of export permits, re-export permits or possession and inspection of the required certificates of origin.

Criticisms of CITES include the claim that it allows trade in wildlife despite the evidence that wildlife trading is not sustainable and that animal harm is intrinsic to some aspects of the wildlife trade (Zimmerman 2003). There is also evidence that a vast illegal trade exists alongside the legal one (Lowther et al. 2002) and, as Chapter 8 discusses, criminality causing animal harm has developed within the CITES system. The wildlife trade is also plagued by weak enforcement when compared to other forms of transnational crime, making it an attractive diversification for organized crime seeking to maximize existing trade routes and criminal networks, and to develop new revenue streams (Roberts et al. 2001, Nurse 2011). CITES does, however, attempt to control the wildlife trade and its schedules and regulatory regime allow for identification of animal harm where non-compliance with the relevant CITES legislation occurs.

At a European level there are also treaties which provide general protection for animals, protection for animals during international transport and when transported for slaughter, and protection for animals kept as farm animals and as companion animals. For example the 1979 *Convention on the Conservation of European Wildlife and Natural Habitats* (the Bern Convention 1979) requires all Council of Europe states to promote national policies and enact legislation that conserves wildlife and wild animals. Article 7 of the convention requires the regulation of wildlife exploitation while Article 8 specifically prohibits 'indiscriminate' means of capturing and killing wildlife. The convention thus provides a Europe-wide legislative framework for monitoring and eliminating certain aspects of animal harm and requires national legislation across Europe that prevents indiscriminate animal killing. There are also regulations governing the use of animals in scientific procedures in the form of *Directive 2010/63/EU on animal experimentation*. The focus of these international efforts is primarily to provide minimum standards for animal welfare and to prevent practices that might amount to animal cruelty. These principles are developed further in national laws.

National Animal Protection Laws

The lack of coherent international protection for animals leaves animal protection primarily within the remit of national legislatures. A majority of states have adopted laws for dealing with animal issues although the perennial problem of animal law enforcement is lack of resources or lack of political will to provide for effective enforcement in those areas where human and animal interests conflict. Significantly, the lack of international legislation means that there is no international standard by which the effectiveness of animal legislation can be judged, although the ethical and theoretical frameworks of the animal rights, species justice and utilitarianism schools provide a benchmark for national legislation. A central issue is whether national legislation provides for effective protection for wild animals and prevents suffering and cruelty to companion animals or at least provides for an effective law enforcement and judicial response when animal cruelty occurs. However the content of law-making on animal issues is determined partly by whether a country is a common law jurisdiction or a private law one. Wise (2000) argues that the mechanistic application of precedent and rules in some legal systems means that legal personhood for animals remains unlikely, while the consideration of contemporary social context applied by the common law means that it is possible for common law judges to interpret legislation in a way that actively protects animals. While most common law judges are precedent judges, changes in legislation and policy to incorporate contemporary perspectives on animal protection and animal welfare have had the effect, in the European Union at least, of providing for legislation that gives limited rights to animals in the sense of requiring that their needs must be actively considered and that a failure to do so which causes either physical or psychological distress constitutes unlawful harm. This contrasts slightly with the historical focus on causing unnecessary suffering according to a subjective notion of what constitutes *necessary* suffering to an animal. Thus, a wider conception of animal harm is beginning to emerge within legislation and provides an additional level of legal protection.

National legislation however requires effective enforcement to provide for coherent animal protection and at state level inadequate resources and a lack of political will to provide for effective animal protection can have the negative effect of marginalizing even those laws which appear effective on paper. The reality of many state animal law regimes is that they are either dealt with as animal control measures in respect of feral or semi-wild animals (Schaffner 2011), as conservation management measures in respect of wild animals and as cruelty or welfare measures and property law in respect of companion animals. The result of such approaches is that animal harm is seen as being outside of mainstream criminal justice and is frequently enforced by the agricultural, conservation, environmental or health departments rather than the mainstream criminal justice ones. The consequence of this is that animal harm is at best regarded as a fringe criminal justice issue. Even where there are dedicated enforcement agencies such as the US and Canadian Fish and Wildlife Services and the UK's Wildlife Crime Officers network, integration with mainstream criminal justice is rarely achieved (Kirkwood 1994, Lowther et al. 2002) and except in certain specific circumstances (Linzey 2009) the link between animal harm and other forms of crime is under-explored. National laws do, however, provide a means through which animal harm can be defined within each state's specific social context. As Chapter 2 identifies, various definitions of animal harm exist within the legislative prohibitions on animal cruelty and wildlife crime and a coherent notion of what behaviour constitutes animal harm can only be achieved by considering how it is socially constructed and enshrined in legislation. Thus defining animal harm requires active consideration of the prohibitions contained in various national anti-cruelty, conservation management, wildlife protection and wildlife trade laws. That such laws conflict between and sometimes within states does not make the task any easier for those seeking to clarify or justify new animal laws and determine the level of protection afforded to animals against harmful human acts.

Anti-Cruelty Laws

Green criminology contends that the welfarist approach to animals allows for their exploitation provided that any suffering caused to them is not unnecessary (Ibrahim 2006). Anti-cruelty statutes predominantly seek to define what constitutes unnecessary suffering, and by implication clarify the limits of necessary suffering and required standards of humane animal treatment. Anti-cruelty statutes do not, however, incorporate a rights-based approach to animals and distinguish legal rights from moral rights (Regan 1983) while identifying that although animals do not formally have rights not to suffer or live free from human interference, the harmful effects of that human interference can be minimized or at least should not be excessive. White argues that 'an animal welfare perspective is one that views nonhuman animals as being part of a web of relationships involving humans and the biosphere' (2008: 22–3). Thus within the context of species justice discourse appropriate standards of animal welfare that incorporate a prohibition on cruelty, or at least its regulation, recognize that while there may be a right for humans to use animals, there is also an obligation to minimize inflicting pain and suffering in doing so. Regan (1983) noted that poor standards of treatment and welfare are sometimes 'justified' on the basis that the victims are not fully aware and thus lack possession of legal rights and the capability to exercise the appropriate rights. However it could be argued that harms done to animals are analogous to harms to children by virtue of both groups being unable to fully exercise their rights thus they are susceptible to harm (Regan 1983), in which case either both are acceptable or both should be prohibited. Anti-cruelty statutes are less concerned with rights and more concerned with acceptable forms of behaviour and treatment of the vulnerable but crucially are allied to perspectives that consider the reduction of cruelty is necessary both to enforce acceptable societal standards, and to ensure that animal working and companion animal lives are as productive and healthy as possible, especially where a companion animal might be considered part of the family (Kean 1998). Some adherents of animal rights theories argue that it is only through providing animals with rights that animal abuse and cruelty would be ended yet the anti-cruelty provisions of US and EU legislation already creates a framework to reduce animal cruelty and provide for enforcement of this aspect of animal harm. Thus while animals may continue to be discriminated against and suffer harm because they are considered (by some) to be inferior (White 2008), Tannenbaum has argued that the anti-cruelty provisions in state legislation 'create[s] legal duties to non-human animals. They therefore afford legal rights to nonhuman animals' (1995). It should be noted however that there are problems with enforcing these rights and there are numerous limitations and exemptions. Frasch (2000) explains that the principle behind much anti-cruelty legislation is concern for the human actor and the wider community because denying animals rights and the subsequent cruelty and abuse that is permitted due to the absence of rights might lead to violence towards humans. However anti-cruelty legislation is both a response to changing societal attitudes towards animals and has also influenced societal attitudes towards animals such that animal harm as socially constructed is now much less tolerated than in previous generations.

Schaffner (2011) identifies the UK as having one of the strongest traditions of anti-cruelty laws. The focus of early legislative efforts to protect animals was the elimination of public animal cruelty. On 3 April 1800, Scottish MP, Sir William Pulteney, attempted to ban bull-baiting by introducing a Bill into the House of Commons. The Bill was met with hostility in the House and did not succeed. At the time of its introduction animal baiting was widespread, perfectly legal and had previously been a sport enjoyed by the aristocracy (although at the time of Pulteney's attempt at legislation it was considered to be a lower-class sport). A second Bill was introduced in 1802 and this too was defeated.

It was seven years before another attempt was made to protect animals in the form of Thomas Erskine's animal cruelty Bill presented to the House of Lords in 1809. Radford (2001) explains that the importance of Erskine's Bill was that it did not seek to ban a specific activity but instead aimed to provide general protection for animals. The Bill 'sought to make it a misdemeanour for any person, including the owner, maliciously to wound or with wanton cruelty to beat or otherwise abuse any horse, mare, ass, ox, sheep or swine' (Radford 2001: 37). Erskine's Bill failed and he withdrew his attempt to pursue it the following year when he was met with overwhelming hostility in parliament.

The first successful attempt to introduce animal protection legislation came 10 years later when Richard Martin, MP for Galway, introduced a Bill to prevent cruelty to cattle. The Bill passed through both Houses and received the Royal Assent on 21 June 1822. Radford explains that:

> It became an offence for any person or persons (therefore including the owner) wantonly and cruelly to beat, abuse, or ill-treat any horse, mare, gelding, mule,

ass, cow, heifer, steer, sheep, or other cattle. A prosecution was to be initiated by making a complaint on oath to a magistrate and, upon conviction, the magistrates were required to impose a fine of at least ten shillings, up to a maximum of five pounds. (Radford 2001: 39)

Following his success Martin tried to bring in a Bill to prohibit bull-baiting and dog-fighting and in 1824 tried to extend his 1822 Act to dogs, cats, monkeys and other animals. He was unsuccessful but his persistent campaigning on animal protection and his success in achieving the 1822 Act were to lead to further animal protection legislation. In 1835 Joseph Pease MP was successful in having extensive animal protection legislation passed. Pease's Act repealed and re-enacted Martin's Act, adding torture to the list of prohibited activities and extending protection to bulls, dogs and other domestic animals. Pease's Act was subsequently repealed by the *Prevention of Cruelty to Animals Act 1849*.

These initial attempts to prevent cruelty to animals mostly dealt with domestic animals or animals that were in some way under human control. Since these early efforts many pieces of legislation have been enacted in different jurisdictions that give protection to animals and which allow for enforcement action to be taken against prohibited cruelty. While Schaffner (2011) argues that EU anti-cruelty legislation is particularly strong, the common characteristics of anti-cruelty legislation are specifying which activities constitute cruelty and unacceptable animal harm. This is discussed further in Chapter 2.

Animal Welfare Laws

In defining animal harm, it is important to distinguish between animal cruelty and animal welfare. While Ibrahim's (2006) notion of a welfarist approach and humane treatment for animals is primarily aimed at preventing or reducing suffering, animal welfare laws have increasingly sought to recognize and define minimum standards of care and comfort for animals separately from the concerns with causing suffering that are the subjects of anti-cruelty statutes. Thus while anti-cruelty statutes may prohibit certain deliberate animal harm actions such as the kicking, crushing or stabbing of animals, animal welfare statutes may provide for such things as minimum standards of room or movement specifications for animals in factory faming operations and transport, or for food and water requirements. Such standards may, thus, acknowledge the necessity of a certain level of animal harm but seek to ensure its reduction rather than prohibition or provide for a level of comfort prior to slaughter. In the context of green criminology's species justice discourse, therefore, animal welfare legislation provides for the continued use and exploitation of animals but arguably provides for a limited rights mechanism within the confines of the animals-as-property perspective. Particularly in the western world, governments have increasingly sought to adopt minimum animal welfare standards through legislation. The EC Treaty, for example, contains the specific 'Protocol on Protection and Welfare of Animals' which obliges member states of the European Union and the EU institutions to pay full regard to the welfare of animals when formulating and implementing Community policies. Across Europe, animal welfare has growing stature in policy-making reflecting the interests of the public, policymakers and legislators in making animal welfare a core part of public policy. Such legislation frequently aims to make unlawful activities which cause or prolong the suffering of animals even while continuing the dominance of human interests over animal ones. Some who support good standards of animal welfare and anti-cruelty laws are not solely concerned with the actual harm to the animal, but are concerned about what such treatment indicates about the abuser and whether it indicates a propensity to violence that might ultimately lead to violence against humans. The progression thesis effectively requires a combination of two separate causal propositions: 1) those who abuse animals are more likely to commit interpersonal violence towards humans; and 2) those who commit interpersonal violence are more likely to have previously abused animals. In that regard, one important perspective often overlooked in the debate on animal welfare is that promoting good animal welfare and respect for animals has the 'tangible' benefit of preventing violence towards humans and antisocial behaviour that has a negative impact on society. This perspective has become an increasingly important consideration in US public policy where the FBI and other law enforcement agencies use animal cruelty as one indicator of possible further offending in dangerousness assessments (Brantley et al. 2009) and there has been much research on the link between animal cruelty and violence towards humans. In some US states, social services and other healthcare and social policy professionals are now involved in interventions designed to prevent juvenile offenders involved in animal cruelty offences from escalating to other forms of violence. The public policy objective pursued by such studies and policy interventions in the United States is that dealing with animal welfare offenders and strictly enforcing animal cruelty laws benefits society by preventing further crimes against society.

Theories relating to animals as property argue that animal welfare benefits those that have an investment in animals as property (including farmers, livestock producers and retailers) as healthier animals maximize return on their investment. There are, admittedly, economic arguments concerning the costs of pursuing high standards of animal welfare within a market place where organic and ethically sourced goods may attract a premium beyond the reach of many consumers. Yet food and health scares, the benefit to consumers (see below), and the progressive development of animal welfare legislation in various countries, indicate that the move towards higher animal welfare standards may be an inevitability for food and livestock producers. Arguably the public benefit is thus an industry more able to withstand consumer and EU legislative demand and contribute to the UK economy. Effective animal welfare legislation and a strong culture of ethical consumerism also benefits consumers who gain psychological well-being from buying ethically sourced, animal welfare compliant, goods. Effective animal welfare standards may also benefit human health as animals raised to high animal welfare standards are said to be more resistant to harmful pathogens, which could negatively impact on human health. While there are debates about the benefits to human health from organic foods and ethical farming, there is no doubt that animal welfare has become a mainstream issue in food consumption with brands such as Freedom Foods becoming established in the UK market and some evidence that consumers are prepared to pay more for ethically sourced foods promoting good standards of animal welfare.[1] Animals-as-property theorists also note that legislation concerning property has developed as society progresses so that whereas other human beings (e.g. children, slaves, wives) have previously been seen as property, societal development has resulted in legislation changing this position, providing protection and fundamental rights for each of these property groups and contributing to the improvement of society. Animal welfare legislation which provides welfare rights and standards for animals thus contributes to the culture of fundamental rights within society which benefits vulnerable groups.

Theorists from different perspectives within animal rights debates have identified that the reduction of animal cruelty, prevention of animal abuse and provision of equal consideration for animals and humans alike benefits society by creating a society that is increasingly cruelty free and where cruelty towards both non-human animals and humans is less likely to occur and is not tolerated when it does. In some respects this mirrors criminological *control* theory, which argues that some crime is prevented due to the formal and informal controls that operate within a community, so that crime which harms the community is not tolerated and the community actively engages with law enforcement agencies to prevent crime. Criminologists and law enforcement professionals have increasingly become interested in animal welfare issues (specifically animal abuse and animal cruelty) as a potential risk factor in violence towards humans. A variety of studies have identified that those who commit interpersonal violence are more likely to have previously abused animals such that in some US states professional agencies have begun to intervene with juvenile animal abusers to prevent any escalation in offending. Increasingly the link is also becoming accepted within other jurisdictions; in 2001 the Royal Society for the Prevention of Cruelty to Animals (RSPCA) and the National Society for the Prevention of Cruelty to Children (NSPCC) held their first joint conference in over 100 years to explore the links between child abuse and animal abuse, and subsequently the *First Strike Scotland* campaign was initiated to explore and address the links between animal abuse and family violence. In 2003 the UK's Royal College of Veterinary Surgeons provided

---

1   See for example Mintel's report *Attitudes Towards Ethical Food and Drink: Is Ethical a Profitable Route? – Ireland – February 2008*, which comments that food scares, animal welfare issues, environmental concern and health and well-being are the clear motivations behind Irish consumers' growing tendency to 'think before they eat'. The report indicated that consumers were willing to pay up to 20 to 30 percent more for ethically sourced foods (where they were able to do so).

guidance for vets on reporting animal abuse, and in 2009 Sussex Academic Press published a book on the links between animal abuse and violence towards humans. Criminal justice and social welfare agency intervention with animal abusers thus provides the tangible benefit of protecting the public from violent offenders and the harmful effects of crime. While this is currently an intangible benefit due to the lack of co-ordinated intervention or policy initiatives in different jurisdictions, there is considerable evidence that animal abuse is one of the risk factors in serious crime which should be considered in dangerousness assessments and crime prevention.

Wildlife Legislation

Discussions of wildlife crime often centre on a particular type of offence; usually that of wildlife trade and the trade in endangered species (see Holden 1998, Roberts et al. 2001). Beyond the trade issue, wildlife crime encompasses a range of different offences involving a diverse range of species, including badgers, birds, seals and small and large mammals.

Wildlife legislation is not a new phenomenon either in the UK or United States but has developed from a historical basis where animals were viewed as property (for example in the UK all wild deer were said to belong to the king in the Middle Ages and swans have been historically viewed as the property of Crown) to the creation of legislation giving animals some legal protection. Radford explains that:

> over the course of almost two centuries the law in Britain has been developed to provide greater protection for individual animals because society at large and public policy makers have recognized that the way in which each is treated matters ... The body of law which has built up over almost two centuries is, however, complicated and unwieldy, its form, substance, application, and effect can all be difficult to understand. (Radford 2001: viii)

Much wildlife legislation in both the UK and the United States has been developed as a result of the efforts of NGOs from a moral rather than criminal justice perspective, although US efforts which argue that the federal government has an obligation to protect wildlife and the environment are perhaps more subject to political influence and amendment dependent on who the incumbent of the White House is. This is an important factor on both sides of the Atlantic in identifying the importance (or lack of) attached to wildlife legislation by successive governments and has perhaps led to wildlife legislation being seen less as a criminal justice issue and more as an environmental or animal rights one.

Wildlife crime also encompasses a range of different criminal behaviour and different types of criminal act. In addition to the commercial and smuggling activities associated with wildlife trade, wildlife offences include a range of criminal activity that incorporates offences including: unlawful killing or wounding, robbery and theft, cruelty and aggravated assault, handling stolen goods, and deception or intent to profit from an illegal act.

A more extensive list of offences is discussed in Chapter 2, which defines animal harm, but these considerations illustrate the diverse nature of animal harm and the challenges facing statutory enforcers and NGOs in dealing with wildlife offences. Wildlife legislation seeks to provide for protection of wildlife by either prohibiting specific acts, and defining these prohibited acts within legislation, or by providing for general protection via legislative conditions that generally make it an offence to take birds or animals from the wild, trade in wildlife or disturb wildlife during the breeding season. However the extent to which such protections exist varies between wildlife and jurisdictions.

Contemporary Notions on Animal Harm Laws

While this book proposes a definition of animal harm in Chapter 2 and begins the process of defining the criminality exhibited by (and inherent to) different aspects of animal harm in Chapter 3, the basic question of 'what is crime' and in particular 'what is crime constituting animal harm' is one that has a complex answer.

At time of writing, NGOs in the UK and the United States are campaigning for improvements to animal harm laws and, specifically in the United States, are actively campaigning against governmental efforts to reduce the level of protection for some wildlife and to ensure levels of protection for native wildlife. Thus while NGOs in the UK are campaigning against the illegal persecution of birds of prey on shooting estates, their colleagues in the United States are fighting efforts by anti-bison ranchers to remove the last genetically pure bison from the lands of Montana and the threat that the federal government will remove federal protection from grey wolves by making amendments to the *Endangered Species Act 1973* (ENN 2012). The feared result of this latter move is that wolves will become a target species where they are perceived to compete with livestock or game in much the same way that some of the UK's birds of prey are perceived.

Such conflicts demonstrate the social construction of animal harm and the manner in which animal harm can be socially condoned (Cohn and Linzey 2009). The reality of animal protection law is that despite the ideal of a utilitarian approach to animals and animal protection (Singer 1975) there are inevitably some conflicts between animal interests and human interests and these conflicts are reflected in animal laws that provide some protection for certain animals while allowing the killing and use of others where human interests dictate that this is a priority. The Earthjustice and Defenders (United States) examples illustrate that such considerations are sometimes politically motivated and so the notion of species justice itself becomes not only socially constructed but subject to a political construction. Game shooting, while currently legal, has also been the subject of calls from some UK NGOs for it to be legislated against on moral grounds. Arguably this is a natural extension of the success in banning hunting with dogs in the UK with the passing of the *Hunting Act 2004* and perhaps represents a natural, incremental extension of animal protection that could someday naturally result in legal animal rights (Wise 2000). Yet the UK's Coalition Government has cautiously indicated that it might be open to repealing the *Hunting Act 2004* and the US Fish and Wildlife Service and federal government have shown that protection of native wildlife, even under the *Endangered Species Act 1973*, can be reversed. Thus the current social construction of illegal animal harm is one in which western governments are considering restricting its definition by allowing a wider range of species to be killed or at least creating the circumstances where this would be possible. In the case of wildlife crime, many activities that are classified as crimes today (such as bear-baiting, wild bird trapping, egg collecting and hunting with dogs) were previously lawful and it is mainly through pursuing campaigns on moral rather than legal grounds that animal protection groups have been able to persuade legislators to prohibit these activities (Kean 1998, Radford 2001). The definition of animal crime, therefore, includes not just legal but moral, gender and cultural elements as well as a range of different criminal types.

One theoretical explanation for crime is that of deviance, the idea that the individual involved in crime breaks away from the norm or ideal to act in an abnormal manner (i.e. the commission of a crime). Muncie and Fitzgerald (1994) explain that the deviant is one to whom the label of deviant is applied according to the rules of the society. Deviance is not, therefore, defined by the quality of the act the person commits but is a consequence of the application of the rules and sanctions to an offender (Becker 1963).

Theoretically, then, for crime to exist there must be not just deviance but also a social reaction. In the classification of crimes, there are many acts of deviance that will not be classified as crimes or may be classified as low level crimes not requiring official sanction. These classifications change over time and vary across cultures. Certainly egg collecting (defined as animal harm and part of wildlife crime) was a popular schoolboy pursuit during much of the twentieth century where the eggs of wild birds were taken for study but today is considered to be crime, attracting the attention of law enforcement professionals and action in the courts. White explains that 'when it comes to environmental harm, what actually gets criminalized by and large reflects an anthropocentric perspective on the nature of the harm in question' (White 2007: 41). The way in which environmental 'rights' are framed in law is determined by a range of strategic interests (political, cultural and even the interests of industry) and depends on which of a series of conflicting rights achieves prominence. School children are now taught the value of wildlife and principles of environmentalism and conservationism and egg collecting is no longer a socially condoned activity. Until recently hunting wild animals with dogs (and in particular fox-hunting) was legal in the UK, demonstrating that while it may have been the subject of deeply polarized debate between enthusiasts and opponents what was considered to be deviant behaviour by one group of people was viewed as perfectly normal by another group. Whether or not a person is considered to be deviant can, therefore, depend on the legal and cultural conditions of a society.

Some deviant acts are also officially sanctioned. The killing of badgers, for example, would be an offence under the UKs *Protection of Badgers Act 1992* (see Chapter 2) but a trial cull of 11,000 badgers to prevent bovine tuberculosis was carried out by the UK's Department for Environment, Food and Rural Affairs (DEFRA) between 1998 and 2006 (DEFRA and RSPCA websites) and there are concerns that it may be repeated. NGOs (RSPCA and NFBG) were opposed to the cull and might consider it to be a wildlife crime but as an officially sanctioned action it would not attract any law enforcement activity.

The social reaction to deviant behaviour also differs from group to group, not least among the criminals themselves. While it might be expected that those who commit criminal behaviours would think of themselves as criminal and have a criminal self-image, many do not. Gamekeepers caught poisoning or trapping wildlife or farmers and ranchers killing wolves might be unwilling to admit that they are criminals although they can easily admit and identify criminality in others such as poachers. They may deny that their actions are a crime, explaining them away as legitimate predator control or a necessary part of their employment or may accept that they have committed an 'error of judgement' but not a criminal act. Matza (1964) developed drift theory to explain how delinquents often accept a moral obligation to be bound by the law but can drift in and out of delinquency. He suggested that people live their lives fluctuating between total freedom and total restraint, drifting from one extreme of behaviour to another. While they may accept the norms of society they develop a special set of justifications for their behaviour which allows them to justify behaviour that violates social norms. These techniques of neutralization (Sykes and Matza 1957, Eliason 2003) allow delinquents to express guilt over their illegal acts but also to rationalize between those whom they can victimize and those they cannot. This means that offenders are not immune to the demands of conformity but can find a way to rationalize when and where they should conform and when it may be acceptable to break the law. As an example, for those offenders whose activities have only recently been the subject of legislation, the legitimacy of the law itself may be questioned, allowing for unlawful activities to be justified. Many fox-hunting enthusiasts, for example, strongly opposed the UK's *Hunting Bill* during its passage through parliament as being an unjust and unnecessary interference with their existing activity and so their continued hunting with dogs is seen as legitimate protest against an unjust law and is denied as being criminal (see Chapter 3 for a further discussion of criminality and offender rationalizations).

The nature of the criminal act in part determines how it is defined. At one end of the scale there may be the simple crimes of disaffected and 'deviant' youth. Litter, vandalism and petty theft carried out by bored or aggressive youngsters with too much time on their hands and a limited amount of life chances. Wilson (1985: 45) explained that delinquency was largely an expression of toughness, masculinity, smartness and the love of excitement by lower-class youth.

At this lower end of the criminal scale street-corner gangs and youths comprising mainly lower-class boys (and some girls) are in conflict with the laws of the middle class. Crime then becomes a matter of the haves versus the 'have-nots' with the latter reacting to assert their values against a society that imposed middle-class values upon them and to which they secretly aspire. In wildlife crime this is demonstrated by the actions of those offenders from predominantly working-class backgrounds and the lower end of the scale that Wilson describes. This lower end of the scale relates not just to the concept of low class or low level crime (i.e. relatively minor crime) but also to the social class of offenders. In particular, those individuals employed in the game-rearing, ranching and farming industries who commit animal offences, come predominantly from the working class. They are mainly the farmers, gamekeepers, beaters and under-keepers rather than the estate owners or managers; owner-managers in farming country are included but might define themselves as small businessmen rather than working class. Badger-baiters and badger-diggers are also predominantly from the lower class (Campaign for the Abolition of Terrier Work 2006 and evidence from case files) and even within hunting with dogs, terrier-men and those responsible for the kennels are disproportionately represented in offences whereas Masters of Foxhounds and those of higher social status might be the expected offenders as the 'leaders' of the hunts.

At the other end of the scale are the offences of rape, murder or crimes against the person, property or the state that are considered to be serious crime. These are crimes that cannot easily be explained as the actions of one or two deviant individuals or the minor criminal behaviour of a disaffected youth. One debate in criminological theory concerns how much of crime is committed by rational actors (Clarke and Cornish 2001, Eliason 2003). Does the offender actively choose to commit his crimes? Arguably some aspects of criminal offending (planning by serial killers, the laying of poisoned baits to kill birds of prey, for example) are subject to rationality but the ends are not. Criminological theory explains that some offenders are 'conditioned' towards being criminal while others are not and differing perceptions within societies may influence the nature of criminality. Eliason's (2003) research supported the application of neutralization theory, concluding that those who engaged in wildlife law violations in Kentucky fitted Sykes and Matza's (1957) model. But the full extent of an animal offender's decision-making and the extent to which rational choice played a part was outside the scope of his study.

The effect of societal perceptions of deviance is that the policy response to serious crime and the criminals involved in it is likely to be one of punishment rather than treatment, reflecting the outrage and sense of injustice felt by society against those who are unwilling to follow the rules adopted by society. Serious crimes will result in stiffer sentencing and have resources targeted at them while perceived minor offences may be dealt with by way of treatment or rehabilitation. One implication for animal harm given the social constructionist factors outlined in this chapter is that in some areas and jurisdictions it is not perceived as serious crime but instead as 'minor' or technical crime with action focusing on fines or minor sanctions. What this fails to do is to address the causes of animal harm or to provide for any effective rehabilitative or preventative measures, and as a result animal harm risks becoming a persistent factor of animal law. Indeed some jurisdictions may question whether animal harm should be classified as a crime at all, instead attempting to deal with animal harm as a civil issue or matter for NGOs. However this book contends that animal harm is crime and should be a matter for criminal justice policy.

The Importance of Studying Animal Harm

As an area of green criminology animal harm has importance beyond its consideration of species justice issues and levels of environmental or animal harm. White's notion of animal rights and species justice considers that the 'animal-centred discourse of animal rights' (2008: 21), while sharing some commonalities with environmental justice, is constructed primarily around utilitarian theory with a focus on minimizing suffering and pain. However this book contends that animal harm is of importance not primarily because of any focus on the number or nature of bird or animal suffering incidents and considerations of respectful treatment, but because of its scope to provide for a study of criminal behaviour, policing, NGO activity and environmental law enforcement. As a distinct area of 'green' criminology animal harm crime is an area of great significance in studying crime and criminal activity for a variety of reasons:

- While the number of animal incidents might be relatively small in comparison to mainstream criminality, the potential impact on certain animal species, in terms of the number of birds and animals killed and the effect on the spread of populations, is considerable. The loss of animals from the wild is also of concern because of the impact on biodiversity, and the difficulties in determining the consequences of such actions.
- Animal harm is an area of criminal justice where NGOs exert considerable influence on policy and also carry out operational law enforcement activities. In a number of jurisdictions the statutory authorities continue to rely on the support of voluntary organizations and so animal harm (and in particular wildlife crime) offers an opportunity to study the co-dependence between NGOs and statutory agencies in protecting animals.
- There is evidence that organized crime has begun to recognize that wildlife crime (one aspect of animal harm) is a 'soft option' where its traditional operations and transit routes can be utilized with a lesser risk of enforcement activity (see Lowther et al. 2002, South and Wyatt 2011).

- Animal harm provides an opportunity to study a distinct area of criminal behaviour and to determine what the abuse of companion animals and the exploitation and trading of wildlife might tell us about offenders and societal attitudes towards animals.
- Animal harm provides an almost unique opportunity to study a fringe area of policing and criminal justice outside of mainstream law enforcement concerns but inextricably linked to them.
- Animal harm provides an opportunity to study the application of environmentalism, animal rights, green criminology and perspectives on environmental justice across a wide area of animal offending.
- It is an emerging and expanding area of law, policy and green criminology with links to both criminal and international law.

In all of the above areas, animal harm is an important area of study where green criminology can significantly add to understanding of crime and justice; each area is discussed further below.

While the number of incidents of animal harm may be relatively small when compared to other areas of crime (especially serious crime) it is of importance to consider the effect that illegal activities can have on the populations of some of the world's rarest and most threatened birds, mammals and animals. One wildlife crime incident could, for example, involve a number of different birds or animals. For one bird, the red-backed shrike, the Royal Society for the Protection of Birds (RSPB) has said that egg collecting (where collectors remove viable eggs from nests in order to place them in their own collections) was partly responsible for the species becoming extinct as a breeding bird in the UK. In the past, illegal persecution of birds of prey through poisoning and other means has helped other species to become extinct. The red kite, for example, a native species in England, has been the subject of a reintroduction programme following its extinction as a breeding bird through persecution, but the reintroduced birds continue to suffer from illegal persecution. The RSPB considers that illegal persecution continues to affect the populations of wild birds of prey although it is difficult to produce conclusive trends. The Society states that:

> Whatever the true pattern the proven levels of continuing persecution are still very much a cause for concern and in respect of species such as red kite and hen harrier the situation remains critical to the extent that these species are actually endangered. Persecution also has detrimental effects on species such as golden eagle which is missing or occurs in reduced densities in some eastern parts of its range in Scotland. (RSPB 1998: 11)

Published studies (Bibby and Etheridge 1993, Etheridge et al. 1997, Sim et al. 2001) have also indicated that the hen harrier, a bird which is heavily persecuted on grouse moors, is absent as a breeding species from areas of suitable habitat as a result of persecution and the range of the buzzard in Scotland has also been restricted. Persecution of other reintroduced species such as wolves, bears and bison have also been recorded and US NGOs including Earthjustice and Defenders of Wildlife continue to raise concerns about ongoing threats to these species. Animal harm can, therefore, have a significant effect on populations of wildlife limiting the range of species to areas where persecution does not exist and reducing the population of species in some areas where it should be healthy.

Animal harm is also an interesting study of criminal behaviour itself. There are a variety of different types of offence within the broad area of animal harm such that not all offenders are motivated by money or even 'gain' from their criminal activity in the traditional sense of direct personal benefit. Yet there has been little research into the behaviour of animal offenders beyond the limited research undertaken into animal abuse and wildlife trafficking, nor has there been much evaluation of the different policies needed to address different types of animal harm. Instead, animal offenders are often treated as a homogenous group and policies aimed at dealing with animal harm do not appear to differentiate between the different types of offence and offender.

While some offenders may be motivated by economic concerns, either in the form of direct personal financial gain or the protection of commercial interests, analysis shows there are some offenders for whom the motivation is either a desire for power or control over a bird or animal, or a need to fulfil some behavioural trait in themselves. As in mainstream criminal justice, some animal offenders justify their activities by stating that animal harm is a victimless crime and that their activities should not really be considered as criminal. In this way, animal harm can be compared to the controversy over some other forms of deviance or criminality such as illicit drugs consumption or sex crime. The comparison is further advanced by the fact that, in some aspects of animal harm, offenders are otherwise law-abiding individuals, whose criminal behaviour in respect of animal harm is an aberration. Of course, this does not hold true for all animal offenders and there are, inevitably, those for whom animal crime is just another form of criminal activity or an extension of existing criminality. This is certainly true in wildlife trafficking and perhaps the involvement of organized criminal gangs in this form of crime together with the sums of money involved (see Chapter 8) accounts for the disproportionate level of attention paid to this form of crime. But this book contends that other forms of animal harm are of importance and critically evaluates the motivations and behaviours of animal offenders based on the available literature and the author's field research among NGOs and policymakers over a number of years. NGOs are especially important in shaping animal harm policy because the NGOs that have accepted (moral) responsibility for dealing with animal harm operate mainly from an environmental or animal welfare standpoint rather than a criminal justice or policing one. While this does not in any way impugn their effectiveness as campaigners or policy professionals it does raise questions about the integration of animal harm into mainstream criminal justice policy. NGOs act as policy advisors, researchers, field investigators, expert witnesses at court, scientific advisors, casework managers, and, in the case of a small number of organizations, prosecutors, playing a significant practical role in policy development and law enforcement (see the list of useful organizations contained in the Appendices). Acting together, NGOs also contribute greatly to the public debate on animal harm, generating considerable publicity for the issue and co-ordinating (and undertaking or funding) much of the research into specific aspects of animal harm and their effects. They can also develop public support for a range of policies influencing public policy and, in the current climate of economic crisis, are sometimes seen by government (at least in the west) as having responsibility for its implementation. NGOs are not usually the lead agency in criminal justice enforcement, but in animal harm there are NGOs that both assist the police and prosecutors and NGOs that actively detect and investigate crime and use their litigation power to challenge legislation and the effectiveness of government enforcement action. It is also an area where NGOs have traditionally collated information on the amount of animal crime that exists, often having a clearer idea of crime levels than the statutory enforcement authorities given the wide variance in recording practices and classifications of animal harm within police, customs and other official agencies. One consequence of this is that NGOs are often in a better position than the statutory authorities to determine the levels of animal harm, specify what the problems are and identify the required legislative and policy solutions, and to make the case for legislative change and increased resources. This gives NGOs a position of considerable influence in directing the law enforcement agenda to areas where they have a specific interest and where they have acquired considerable expertise. It also allows NGOs to be effective in raising public awareness of animal harm issues. In effect, animal harm allows for the study of 'private policing' in an area of criminal justice policy where a considerable amount of law enforcement activity is still carried out on a voluntary basis by private bodies such as the RSPCA's uniformed inspectorate (in respect of animal welfare crimes in the UK) and the American Society for the Prevention of Cruelty to Animals (ASPCA) and other state animal protection bodies in the United States. It is also an area where the hidden aspects of animal harm are revealed by the actions of bodies like the Environmental Investigations Agency (EIA) or Animal Defenders International (ADI) who carry out undercover investigations to expose animal cruelty, failures in legislation and the ineffectiveness of public enforcement. Whereas in some areas, such as street crime, police functions are being privatized with the introduction of private security patrols, community support officers and street wardens, animal harm is an area where the policing function has traditionally been carried out by NGOs and it is only recently that international policing bodies such as Interpol have begun to respond to the global nature of animal harm.

Animal harm is also of interest as a study of a 'fringe' area of criminal justice given its social construction as an animal welfare or environmental issue. In a range of jurisdictions the police and prosecutors still rely heavily on NGOs, and citizens also have come to understand and expect that NGOs like the Sierra Club, Defenders of Wildlife and Earthjustice will take action in the United States where the federal government fails to do so. Animal law enforcement in the UK is still carried out on a largely voluntary basis with the police and prosecutors relying heavily on the work of NGOs and volunteers to detect and prosecute animal offences. It is also true that many of those police officers who are involved in dealing with wildlife crime in the UK do so on a voluntary basis in addition to their other duties (Kirkwood 1994, Nurse 2003). Despite the publicity that animal harm cases often attract it is not a mainstream policing priority and so also offers a useful study of police classification of and attitudes towards crime (Reiner 2000), as the resources devoted to animal harm and the importance attached to it varies from (police) area to area and across different jurisdictions. Yet some aspects of animal harm (particularly wildlife crime) overlap with other crimes or can be compared to, for example, white-collar crime, which Percy (2002) describes as 'the corrupt practices of individuals in powerful positions'. In particular, those offences relating to the game-rearing industry (where protected wildlife is killed illegally to ensure economic benefit for the commercial operation sometimes alongside legitimate predator control) demonstrate the institutional motivation for committing offences together with the expertise that offenders may have compared to the relative lack of expertise exhibited by police and other enforcers. Very little co-ordinated law enforcement activity is directed at the fight against white-collar animal crime, except for the corporate environmental crime enforcement work carried out by the Environment Agency in the UK and the United States Environmental Protection Agency (EPA). Both organizations can only act as an industry watchdogs and take action after environmental abuse is discovered rather than having a positive crime prevention and law enforcement role. (Although it could be argued that the US EPA arguably monitors compliance with environmental regulations more proactively than its UK counterpart.)

Animal Harm as Species Justice

Animal harm also provides an opportunity to consider the social construction of species justice and the differences between rural crimes and urban concerns about criminal justice. Green criminology's focus on animal rights has been broadly embraced as an acceptable policy perspective yet the animal rights movement has arguably made little progress in achieving legal rights for animals (Donaldson and Kymlicka 2011). Various arguments are raised in environmentalism concerning why animals should be protected and environmental offenders and animal abusers should be punished but a distinction can be made between effective punishment for harm through the criminal justice system and the necessity of legal rights for animals. In effect, the species justice movement has become bogged down in theoretical arguments about animal rights that are regrettably unlikely to be resolved in the near future. But beyond the simple moral wrong of causing harm to animals and the need to safeguard nature for future generations, environmentalists and conservationists consider that the environment should be valued in economic terms and that man's impact on the environment and wildlife should be limited.

Arguably current legislation already does this. For all their faults, both CITES and the *International Whaling Convention* provide for an economic value to be placed on wildlife and the regulation of wildlife as a resource. Species protection concerns relating to the extinction of various species as a result of human interference and the need to conserve animals that will otherwise be driven to extinction are also already reflected in contemporary legislation which provides an additional level of protection for rarer or threatened species. Arguments raised in defence of animals, concerning the moral wrong of inflicting harm on other sentient beings (Bentham 1789, Singer 1975, Regan 1983), the need for legal rights for animals (Regan 1983, 2001, Wise 2000) and for increased standards of animal welfare, are also reflected in existing anti-cruelty legislation and in the specific wording of legislation which closely defines what amounts to cruelty or unacceptable behaviour towards animals.

Thus while debates persist in theology, criminology and the study of animal law concerning the rights of animals, the moral wrong of inflicting harm on other sentient beings, the relationship between man and non-human animals and the need for legal rights for animals and issues of animal abuse and increased standards of animal welfare to be addressed (see Wise 2000, Sunstein and Nussbaum 2004, Scruton 2006, Ascione 2008), animal legislation has already provided for all of these things. Of course that is not to say that the environmental justice and species justice concerns of green criminology have all been met, and indeed later chapters of this book show how what appears to be effective legislation on paper is often implemented through weak and ineffectual enforcement regimes that fail to address some crucial elements of animal harm. Yet a legislative and enforcement regime *does* exist and the environmental conservation, socio-legal and animal welfare literature often fails to consider the reasons why people commit crimes against animals and the measures needed to prevent offences and offending behaviour. Animal harm, however, provides an opportunity to consider criminal behaviour in relation to animals and to develop a theoretical basis for why individuals commit crimes involving animals and what mechanisms might be employed to address or reduce the incidence of these crimes and the criminal behaviour involved. This issue, often overlooked in green criminology, is directly considered by this book although no pretence is made that it provides a comprehensive solution.

As this chapter outlines, animal harm is subject to both national and international law, and, as such, is also of interest in studying the manner in which states adopt and enforce the limited global conventions that exist and implement animal protection into their national legal systems. The importance of animal harm is, thus, that it provides a unique area of study in the fields of law, NGO and pressure group policy-making and practice, policing and the interplay between statutory and voluntary/private policing, as well as criminology and criminal behaviour.

Conclusion

This book considers different dimensions of animal harm, specifically the various aspects of criminality and behaviour that constitute animal harm. While animals are generally protected under national law, the extent to which the law incorporates utilitarian ideals and provides for protection against specific animal harm activities varies on a species and a country level. Thus animal harm continues as a fact of society requiring law enforcement intervention to prevent a level of animal harm unacceptable to society. As a result, the criminal law is frequently used to address animal harm notwithstanding the reality that much animal protection legislation is not intended to be used for criminal purposes but was instead designed to allow the use (or exploitation) of animals where this is compatible with human interests.

Thus the position that exists across animal law is one that permits certain animal harm in accordance with a socially constructed perception of its benefits. Animals can be trapped, hunted, sold and killed subject to the conditions specified in law. While animal law creates a range of animal harm offences and explicitly provides for punishment of prohibited animal harm activities, Benton's (1998) notion of shared rights, Singer's (1975) view of animal interests being incorporated into utilitarian species justice policy and Donaldson and Kymlicka's (2011) idea of human-animal citizenship are not yet reflected in either international or national law regimes. Instead, animal law regimes, while seeking to achieve some protection of animals and limited recognition of animal rights, continually make animal interests secondary to human ones.

This book contends that animal harm's incorporation into green criminology is a necessary component of ecological and species justice. For animal rights activists and environmentalists, the cause of animal harm is often simply defined; those who injure or kill animals take pleasure in exercising power over others, have tendencies towards cruelty and inflicting pain and put their own desires over other considerations (Cohn and Linzey 2009), or they are simply evil; both exploiting and making animals 'weak precisely so they may treat them badly' (Rowlands 2009: 205). However the author's research into animal cruelty, wildlife crime and related offending indicates that while some animal harm is undoubtedly caused by those who enjoy exercising their power over others, including defenceless animals, the causes of animal harm are complex, varied, and not easily explained without considering in detail the precise nature of the specific type of animal harm and the circumstances in which it occurs. The role of not just the offender but also other actors involved in the events surrounding animal harm also must also be considered.

NGOs involved in animal harm and the criminal justice agencies that respond to wildlife crime generally discuss animal offences as if they are all committed by rational actors who might be deterred through appropriate sentencing and punishment regimes. However, the evidence that this is the case is often not coherently presented and criminological theory suggests that offenders have different motivations for their crimes meaning that not all individuals will turn to crime even where conditions dictate that this might be the expected response to social and other circumstances. The views of NGOs on the factors involved in wildlife offences and the reasons why animal crimes take place and previous research on the characteristics of offenders were considered in the author's research into wildlife crime to determine if it is possible to identify different types of wildlife offender and the policies needed to address each type of offender. These ideas are developed further here (see Chapter 3) and extended to cover other forms of animal harm. This aspect of the research is intended to assess the evidence for there being different types of offender that might respond differently to existing or proposed policy and sentencing approaches. Egg collectors, for example, who often spend thousands of pounds in pursuing their activities, might not be deterred by increased fines, simply seeing this as an increased cost of pursuing their 'hobby'. Those employed by the game-rearing industry might not be deterred by the threat of a prison sentence if the alternative is loss of a job and home, and organized crime may well be able to withstand even the most punitive of wildlife crime penalties given the scope of their transnational operations and profit base. Analysis of the available literature shows that no dedicated assessment of the different types of offender currently exists or is considered in policy development (except in limited cases and for specific offences) and so this book's analysis proposes new models (or classifications) for animal offenders.

This book contends that public policy's dogmatic insistence on treating all offenders as if they are all rational actors who choose to commit their offences is flawed. While it might be comforting to think of animal offenders as simply evil or lacking in empathy for their victims, the reality is that not all animal harm consciously views animals as the target of the criminal act, not all animal harm disregards the impact on animals and biodiversity of its actions, and social factors sometimes influence criminal behaviour. In the case of animal harm social factors can determine both to whom any harm is caused and the extent to which animals may suffer directly or indirectly as a result of any animal harm. While policy professionals and academics have embraced green criminology as a means of rethinking the study of criminal laws, ethics, crime and criminal behaviour (e.g. Lynch and Stretesky 2003, Beirne and South 2007, White 2008) green criminology has paid little attention to animal abuse, the related issue of wildlife crime and the specific behaviours of those who harm, injure and kill animals, while the focus of anti-cruelty statutes, animal welfare and wildlife law enforcement has primarily been on apprehension and punishment of offenders with little attention being paid to preventative measures, the rehabilitation of offenders or identifying the links with other more 'mainstream' criminal activity.

For criminologists there are some important questions to consider such as: what makes people kill animals? Is animal harm a gateway to human violence? What are the links between animal crime and other forms of offending? How should the illegal trade in wildlife be addressed? For policy professionals and legislators, an appropriate question to consider is: how does animal harm fit in with the overall criminal profile of the offender such that the criminal justice system can effectively deal with them?

This book contends that ecological crime discourse (which includes species justice) needs to distinguish between different types of animal abuse and different types of offender and it seeks to do so throughout the following pages. To begin with, Chapter 2 seeks to more clearly define what constitutes animal harm.

References

Ascione, F.R. (ed.) (2008). *The International Handbook of Animal Abuse and Cruelty: Theory, Research and Application*, Indiana: Purdue University Press.

Becker, H. (1963). *Outsiders: Studies in Sociology of Deviance*, New York: Free Press of Glencoe.

Beetz, A. (2009). Empathy as an Indicator of Emotional Development, in A. Linzey (ed.) *The Link Between Animal Abuse and Human Violence*, Eastbourne: Sussex Academic Press, 63–74.

Beirne, P. (1999). For a Nonspeciesist Criminology: Animal Abuse as an Object of Study. *Criminology*, 37(1), 1–32.

Beirne, P. and South, N. (eds) (2007). *Issues in Green Criminology: Confronting Harms against Environments, Humanity and Other Animals*, Devon: Willan.

Bentham, J. (1789 [1970]). *Introduction to the Principles of Morals and Legislation*, edited by J.H. Burns and H.L.A. Hart, London: Athlone Press.

Benton, T. (1998). Rights and Justice on a Shared Planet: More Rights or New Relations? *Theoretical Criminology*, 2(2), 149–75.

Bibby, C.J. and Etheridge, B. (1993). Status of the Hen Harrier *Circus cyaneus* in Scotland in 1988–89. *Bird Study*, 40, 1–11.

Brantley, A.C., Lockwood, R. and Church, A.W. (2009). An FBI Perspective on Animal Cruelty, in A. Linzey (ed.) *The Link Between Animal Abuse and Human Violence*, Eastbourne: Sussex Academic Press, 223–7.

Brown Weiss, E. (1993). International Environmental Law: Contemporary Issues and the Emergence of a New World Order. 81 *GEO. L.J.* 675, 677.

Campaign for the Abolition of Terrier Work (2006), *The Most Evil Bloodsport in the Country*. Available at www.diggingout.org [accessed 17 May 2008].

Clarke, R.V. and Cornish, D.B. (2001). Rational Choice, in R. Paternoster and R. Bachman (eds) *Explaining Crime and Criminals: Essays in Contemporary Criminological Theory*, Los Angeles: Roxbury, 23–42.

Cohn, P.N. and Linzey, A. (2009). Hunting as a Morally Suspect Activity, in A. Linzey (ed.) *The Link Between Animal Abuse and Human Violence*, Eastbourne: Sussex Academic Press, 317–28.

Conboy-Hill, S. (2000). *Animal Abuse and Interpersonal Violence*, Lincoln: The Companion Animal Behaviour Therapy Study Group.

Donaldson, S. and Kymlicka, W. (2011). *Zoopolis: A Political Theory of Animal Rights*, Oxford: Oxford University Press.

Eliason, S.L. (2003). Illegal Hunting and Angling: The Neutralization of Wildlife Law Violations. *Society & Animals*, 11(3), 225–43.

Etheridge, B., Summers, R.W. and Green, R.E. (1997). The Effects of Illegal Killing and Destruction of Nests by Humans on the Population Dynamics of the Hen Harrier *Circus cyaneus* in Scotland. *Journal of Applied Ecology*, 34, 1081–105.

Felthous, A. and Kellert, S. (1987). Childhood Cruelty to Animals and Later Aggression Against People: A Review. *American Journal of Psychiatry*, 144, 710–17.

Frasch, P.D. (2000). Addressing Animal Abuse: The Complementary Roles of Religion, Secular Ethics, and the Law. *Society & Animals*, 8(3), 331–48.

Henry, B.C. (2004). The Relationship between Animal Cruelty, Delinquency, and Attitudes toward the Treatment of Animals. *Society & Animals*, 12(3).

Holden, J. (1998). *By Hook or by Crook: A Reference Manual on Illegal Wildlife Trade and Prosecutions in the United Kingdom*, Sandy: RSPB/TRAFFIC/WWF.

Ibrahim, D.M. (2006). The Anti-Cruelty Statute: A Study in Animal Welfare. *Journal of Animal Law and Ethics*, 1(1), 175–203.

Kean, H. (1998). *Animal Rights: Political and Social Change in Britain since 1800*, London: Reaktion Books.

Kirkwood, G. (1994). *The Enforcement of Wildlife Protection Legislation: A Study of the Police Wildlife Liaison Officers' Network*, Leicester: De Montfort University.

Linzey, A. (ed.) (2009). *The Link Between Animal Abuse and Human Violence*, Eastbourne: Sussex Academic Press.

Lowther, J., Cook, D. and Roberts, M. (2002). *Crime and Punishment in the Wildlife Trade*, Wolverhampton: WWF/TRAFFIC/Regional Research Institute (University of Wolverhampton).

Lubinski, J. (2004). *Introduction to Animal Rights*, 2nd edn, Michigan: Michigan State University – Detroit College of Law.

Lynch, M.J. and Stretesky, P.B. (2003). The Meaning of Green: Contrasting Criminological Perspectives. *Theoretical Criminology*, 7(2), 217–38.

Matza, D. (1964). *Delinquency and Drift*, New Jersey: Transaction.

Muncie, J. and Fitzgerald, M. (1994). Humanising the Deviant: Affinity and Affiliation Theories, in Mike Fitzgerald, Gregor McLennan and Jennie Pawson (eds), *Crime and Society: Readings in History and Theory*, London: Routledge, 403–28.

Nurse, A. (2003). *The Nature of Wildlife and Conservation Crime in the UK and its Public Response, Working Paper No, 9*, Birmingham: University of Central England.

Nurse, A. (2011). Policing Wildlife: Perspectives on Criminality in Wildlife Crime. *Papers from the British Criminology Conference*, 11, 38–53.

Peelo, M. and Soothill, K. (2005). Introduction: Crime is Exciting but What of Criminology? in Moira Peelo and Keith Soothill (eds), *Questioning Crime and Criminology*, Cullompton: Willan Publishing, ix–xvi.

Percy, K. (2002). *Fighting Corporate and Government Wrongdoing: A Research Guide to International and U.S. Federal Laws on White-Collar Crime*, Austin: University of Texas at Austin School of Law.

Quinney, R. (1970). *The Social Reality of Crime*, Boston: Little Brown. Radford, M. (2001). *Animal Welfare Law in Britain*, Oxford: Oxford University Press.

Regan, T. (1983). *The Case for Animal Rights*, Berkeley: University of California Press.

Reiner, R. (2000). *The Politics of the Police*, Oxford: Oxford University Press.

Roberts, M., Cook, D., Jones, P. and Lowther, D. (2001). *Wildlife Crime in the UK: Towards a National Crime Unit*, Wolverhampton: Department for the Environment, Food & Rural Affairs/Centre for Applied Social Research (University of Wolverhampton).

Roeschke, J.E. (2009). Eco-Terrorism and Piracy on the High Seas: Japanese Whaling and the Rights of Private Groups to Enforce International Conservation Law in Neutral Waters. *The Villanova Environmental Law Journal*, XX(1), 99–136.

Rollin, B.E. (2006). *Animal Rights and Human Morality*, New York: Prometheus.

Rowlands, M. (2009). The Structure of Evil, in A. Linzey (ed.), *The Link Between Animal Abuse and Human Violence*, Eastbourne: Sussex Academic Press, 201–5.

Royal Society for the Protection of Birds (1998). *Land for Life: A Future for the UK's Special Places for Wildlife*, Sandy: RSPB.

Schaffner, J. (2011). *An Introduction to Animals and the Law*, New York: Palgrave Macmillan.

Scruton, R. (2006). *Animal Rights and Wrongs*, London: Continuum.

Sim, I.M.W., Gibbons, D.W., Bainbridge, I.P. and Mattingley, W.A. (2001). Status of Hen Harrier *Circus cyaneus* in the UK and the Isle of Man in 1998. *Bird Study*, 48, 341–53.

Singer, P. (1975). *Animal Liberation*, New York: Avon.

Situ, Y. and Emmons, D. (2000). *Environmental Crime: The Criminal Justice System's Role in Protecting the Environment*, Thousand Oaks: Sage.

South, N. and Wyatt, T. (2011). Comparing Illicit Trades in Wildlife and Drugs: An Exploratory Study. *Deviant Behavior*, 32, 538–61.

Sunstein, C.R. and Nussbaum, M.C. (eds) (2004). *Animal Rights: Current Debates and New Directions*, New York: Oxford University Press.

Sykes, G.M. and Matza, D. (1957). Techniques of Neutralization: A Theory of Delinquency. *American Sociological Review*, 22, 664–73.

Tannenbaum, J. (1995). Nonhuman Animals and the Law: Property, Cruelty, Rights, in A. Mack (ed.), *Humans and Other Nonhuman Animals*, Columbus: Ohio State University Press, 125–84.

White, R. (2007). Green Criminology and the Pursuit of Social and Ecological Justice, in P. Beirne and N. South (eds), *Issues in Green Criminology: Confronting Harms against Environments, Humanity and Other Animals*, Devon: Willan, 32–54.

White, R. (2008). *Crimes Against Nature: Environmental Criminology and Ecological Justice*, Devon: Willan.

Wilson, J.Q. (1985). *Thinking about Crime*, 2nd edn, New York: Vintage Books.

Wise, S.M. (2000). *Rattling the Cage: Towards Legal Rights for Animals*, London: Profile.

World Society for the Protection of Animals (2011). *Universal Declaration on Animal Welfare (Draft Text)*, London: WSPA.

Zimmerman, M.E. (2003). The Black Market for Wildlife: Combating Transnational Organized Crime in the Illegal Wildlife Trade. *Vanderbilt Journal of Transnational Law*, 36, 1657–89.

Chapter 2
The Nature of Animal Harm

This chapter seeks to define animal harm as discussed throughout the remainder of this book. While animal rights and species justice perspectives generally consider animal harm to mean animal abuse and suffering (White 2008) this book defines animal harm as broadly falling into two categories: animal abuse or cruelty, and wildlife crime. Rather than considering these two aspects of animal harm as being distinctly separate, the book takes a holistic approach to the concept of animal harm which incorporates these two separate aspects of animal activity. While the extent to which animal harm is considered part of the criminal law rather than a civil offence varies between acts and from jurisdiction to jurisdiction, this book's focus is on both elements of animal harm as criminal activity. As a result the term animal harm as used throughout this book encompasses a wide remit of animal abuse, cruelty and welfare offences involving companion animals, and the unlawful hunting and trapping of wildlife, the unlawful taking of animals from the wild and the commercial killing of protected animals and wildlife. Where the term is used, it refers to animal harm in this broad sense, although references are made to the individual aspects of animal abuse or cruelty or wildlife crime when discussing specific aspects of animal harm.

Beirne (1999) argues that animal cruelty should be drawn into the realm of criminological inquiry as it has importance on multiple levels:

1. animal cruelty may signify other actual or potential interpersonal violence;
2. animal cruelty is, in many forms, prohibited by criminal law;
3. violence against animals is part of the utilitarian calculus on the minimization of pain and suffering (the public good);
4. animal cruelty is a violation of rights; and
5. violence against animals is one among several forms of oppression that contribute, as a whole, to a violent society.

While the first two of Beirne's points are crucial to this book's focus on animal harm as criminality under current law, analysis of animal harm and its implications need to go beyond discussions of cruelty and animal rights to also incorporate wider criminal justice perspectives. Wildlife crime, considered to be one of the most prevalent and lucrative forms of crime after the trade in drugs (South and Wyatt 2011 and see also Chapter 8), does not always involve cruelty and can involve humane methods of trapping and utilizing wildlife, which, while being harmful to animals in one sense (the 'harm' of being forcibly removed from the wild, sometimes in a manner that causes temporary injury, and then being reduced into captivity), would not constitute cruelty by most legal definitions. Yet wildlife crime is frequently absent from green criminology's discussions of species justice and is arguably absent from South's initial discussions of green issues as encompassing 'the environment, animal rights and the symbiosis between human societies and ecological systems' (1998: 212).

While it is acknowledged that green criminology has developed considerably in the last 15 years or so to encompass a broader definition of species justice, the 'animals' aspects of green criminology discourse is still dominated by discussions of animal rights, legal personhood, and animal abuse and cruelty. Only a few scholars discuss wider definitions of animal harm in any detail and pay attention to issues such as wildlife crime (see for example, Beirne 1999, 2009, Nurse 2003, 2011, Wyatt 2009, 2011). Fewer still discuss wider notions of animal harm as being separate from animal rights and consider the importance of animal harm as a criminal justice issue outside of rights talk and the justification for legal rights for animals. Yet legal protection for animals and law enforcement and criminal justice action to address animal harm is possible within current legislative frameworks. Thus, animal rights and animal harm need not be inextricably linked, and from a criminological perspective it is possible to treat animal harm as a mainstream crime problem without necessarily pursuing an animal rights agenda. A new definition of animal harm as part of the ecological justice or species justice discourse is therefore needed to encompass South's (1998) notion of human–ecological symbiosis, to reflect legislative developments and to also recognize developments in the field of human–animal studies (Shapiro 2008) that have moved beyond potentially limiting discussions framed around animal rights.

As Chapter 1 identifies, much of the harm inflicted on animals is currently legal, whether as part of legitimate food production, the fashion industry, or permissible pest control (of varying types). Thus, criminologists, animal activists and policy-makers face challenges in precisely defining animal abuse and cruelty (Agnew 1998) and distinguishing between the lawful and unlawful. As a result, a variety of animal harm activities that would undoubtedly satisfy a moral or ethical definition of cruelty would not constitute unlawful animal abuse. While that does not diminish their importance either as areas of study or areas where policy should be changed, traditional criminology's focus on examining the workings of the existing criminal justice system and, in particular, how it can be improved is instructive in showing how green criminology might develop its species justice discourse. Applying both mainstream and green criminological perspectives to animal harm provides a means through which an understanding of this aspect of criminal behaviour can be assessed and it is in this regard that this book examines the issue of animal harm and animal offence criminality.

This chapter provides an overview of the type of illegal activity involved in animal harm and discussed in depth within the following chapters. It clarifies what constitutes unlawful animal abuse (cruelty) and wildlife crime, distinguishing between morally unacceptable and legally permissible behaviours in order to clarify this book's animal harm definition.

Defining Animal Abuse Offences

The legalistic definition of animal cruelty informs the distinction between animal abuse and wildlife crime. Animal abuse incorporates cruelty and animal welfare offences, primarily directed at domestic animals (for convenience sake throughout this chapter the term domestic animals will be used throughout this chapter to refer to both companion animals and farm animals) rather than animals living in a wild or semi-wild state (including stray and feral animals). Animal abuse may be either direct or indirect but the concept of causing 'unnecessary suffering' is central to legal definitions of animal abuse. This concept permeates much anti-cruelty law and defines this aspect of animal harm as primarily being abuse or cruelty deliberately inflicted on animals. However beyond the theoretical and ethical questions it raises about what constitutes 'necessary' and avoidable animal suffering (Linzey 2009) it also raises questions about the extent to which inflicting animal suffering is intentional, accidental or an integral part of some activities, even where steps might be taken to minimize animal harm.

As Chapter 1 indicates, anti-cruelty statutes generally attempt to define animal abuse, specifying which activities are prohibited and providing guidance to animal owners, investigators and prosecutors alike by explicitly categorizing animal abuse activities by including descriptors and definitions within legislation. There is, however, considerable variation even between different regions of the United States where state anti-cruelty acts adopt different definitions reflecting legislators' preferences or intentions towards animal protection. For example, Alaska's Anti-Cruelty Statute 11.61.140 defines animal cruelty as when a person 'knowingly inflict[s] severe physical pain or suffering; or with criminal negligence fails to care for an animal and causes its death or severe pain or prolonged suffering', while Massachusetts' General Laws Chapter 272–77 more expansively specifies cruelty to animals as when a person:

> overdrives, overloads, drives when overloaded, overworks, tortures, torments, deprives of necessary sustenance, cruelly beats, mutilates or kills an animal, or causes or procures such; and whoever uses in a cruel or inhuman manner in a race, game, or contest, or in training therefore, as lure or bait a live animal; inflicts unnecessary cruelty upon it, or unnecessarily fails to provide it with proper food, drink, shelter, sanitary environment, or protection from the weather, or cruelly drives or works it when unfit for labor, or wilfully abandons it, or carries it or causes it to be carried in or upon a vehicle, or otherwise, in an unnecessarily cruel or inhuman; or knowingly and wilfully authorizes or permits it to be subjected to unnecessary torture, suffering or cruelty of any kind.

In addition, Massachusetts has separate provisions relating to the *malicious* killing of an animal, which by implication does not include the above acts. In this case the law specifically makes it an offence where any person 'wilfully and maliciously kills, maims or disfigures any horse, cattle or other animal of another person, or wilfully and maliciously administers or exposes poison with intent that it shall be taken or swallowed by any such animal' (Massachusetts' Gen Laws Ch. 266-112). Other US states also distinguish between 'ordinary' animal abuse and malicious or wanton animal abuse which implies a greater level of severity in the abuse.

These and comparable definitions across anti-cruelty legislation identify *deliberate* physical harm as the essential element in animal abuse as defined by legislation. Schaffner comments that US anti-cruelty laws are primarily designed to 'protect animals from the intentional and gratuitous infliction of pain and suffering at the hands of humans' (2011: 22). Phrases like 'wilfully and maliciously', 'knowingly and recklessly' or 'intentionally' are commonly found in US and UK legislation, reflecting legislators' focus on acts of violence towards animals which has also dominated criminological attention in species justice discourse. This reflects theoretical debates about both the exercise of power over animals by man (Rollin 2006, Linzey 2009) and animal rights discourse concerning not only animals' rights not to suffer pain, but also the moral wrong of deliberate exploitation of animals by humans. Violent exploitation of animals and their status as defenceless victims are key to Conboy-Hill's definition of animal abuse as 'the deliberate or neglectful harm of animals which can include beating, starvation, slashing with knives, sodomy, setting on fire, decapitation, skinning alive amongst other actions' (2000: 1) and criminology's focus on deliberate, violent animal abuse perhaps reflects a focus on animal cruelty as an aspect of violent crime as a key criminological and social concern (Wise 2000, White 2008, Linzey 2009). However, a broader definition of animal abuse needs to also incorporate non-physical abuse and other non-violent yet harmful acts which constitute abuse. Ascione's definition identified animal abuse and cruelty as being 'socially unacceptable behaviour that intentionally causes unnecessary pain, suffering, or distress to and/ or death of an animal' (1993: 228). While this definition importantly incorporates the concept of 'distress' which, broadly construed, includes non-physical harm, its focus is still on *intentional* animal abuse which this chapter contends is only a limited part of animal harm, albeit an important one. Of equal importance are the unintentional or incidental animal harm activities that are, nevertheless, unlawful and require criminological attention. Neglect causing animal harm still has the potential to cause significant injury to animals and may be linked to other aspects of criminality that are worthy of attention.

Critical Perspectives on Defining Animal Abuse Activities

Agnew identified that animal cruelty occurs across a wide spectrum of activities 'including factory farming, animal experimentation, hunting and trapping, and the use of animals for entertainment purposes' (1998: 179). In principle, many of these activities, although objectionable, to some are ostensibly legal, although they may both directly or indirectly incorporate animal cruelty as operational practices. One could, for example, argue that factory farming for the fur and meat industries is inherently cruel because any action that results in the unnecessary death of an animal to serve human ends constitutes animal abuse. But within the confines of this book's focus on *unlawful* rather than *immoral* animal harm it is not the ends but rather the means, and compliance with the legalistic perspective on animal harm, which determines whether an action amounts to animal harm. Although Agnew's list of activities (above) contains several that are lawful dependent on the circumstances, they also link to activities that are inherently unlawful in that illegal animal abuse is an integral part of these activities even when the industry itself seeks to be law-abiding. To take another part of Agnew's assessment, animal abuse is most likely when individuals:

1. are unaware of the impact or consequences of their behaviour on animals;
2. do not consider their behaviour to be wrong; and
3. benefit from their abusive behaviour. (Agnew 1998: 182)

To this list I would add a fourth consideration, that of:

4. industry specific or cultural norms being such that even where individuals are fully aware of the impact or consequence of their behaviour on animals, cultural or institutional acceptance of animal harm exists such that any condemnation of animal harm is an externality.

Animal abuse thus includes inflicting cruelty either directly or indirectly, or failing to comply with statutory animal welfare standards such that an animal incurs harm, injury, suffering or distress, either by human act or omission. Discussion of each of Agnew's original list illustrates this qualification.

Factory Farming

In many jurisdictions, the factory farming industry is regulated by animal welfare legislation which specifies that humane standards of animal welfare should be observed and implemented wherever possible. Yet animal harm is an integral part of both the fur and meat industries where animals are routinely kept in inhumane conditions that do not effectively cater for their needs (PETA website 2012). While the end product of both industries is inevitably the killing of animals, inhumane or ineffective methods of killing are routinely found in inspections (Lawrence 2004) and constitute normal practice in the unregulated, poorly regulated or black market sections of each industry (Schlosser 2002). Strain (Merton 1968) and control theories (Hirschi 1969) explain the prevalence of inhumane killing methods and ineffective animal husbandry in industries where the desire for profit and the lack or effective regulation create environments where animal abuse is not only possible but becomes operationally acceptable as a means of maximizing profits (Paternoster and Simpson 1996). Green criminology and environmental justice discourse shows that where compliance with regulations constitutes an unacceptably high business expense, companies will seek to evade or ignore these costs (Situ and Emmons 2000, Walters 2007, Hinteregger 2008). In addition, poorly paid workers at the socio-economic 'lower' end of the fur and meat trades often lack either the training or motivation to effectively implement good standards of animal welfare as doing so may make their jobs considerably more difficult or indeed place them in the position of lacking sufficient skills to carry out those jobs. In the fashion skin trade for example People for the Ethical Treatment of Animals (PETA) found evidence of animals being skinned while still alive (2011) with poorly paid producers lacking knowledge of humane animal killing methods (discussed further in Chapter 8). The external condemnation of pressure groups like PETA and national and regional cruelty prevention agencies, while potentially having some effect by way of mobilizing public opinion, is largely ineffective against financial imperatives within the food and fur industries.

Animal Experimentation

Animal experimentation, perhaps by its very nature, constitutes animal abuse in a species justice sense as it involves deliberately inflicting harm on animals. Yet again, this form of animal cruelty is lawful in many countries; theoretically being controlled by legislation that specifies which activities are permissible and which are prohibited. Generally animals can be experimented on by recognized scientific bodies or those holding the required permits in accordance with local regulatory requirements. Experimentation is subject to controls contained within legislation which may include codes of practice, outlining the relevant conditions to be followed, or specifying that animal experimentation facilities are subject to inspection by regulatory authorities. The acceptability of such activities is determined by the wording of *current* law in a particular jurisdiction, social habits and social and economic circumstances. A specific example of this is provided for in the UK's anti-vivisection case law. In 1895 in *Re Foveaux* [1895], 2 Chancery, 501, the court of appeal accepted an anti-vivisection trust as being charitable because its aims were considered to be of public benefit. However, in 1948 in *National Anti-Vivisection Society v. IRC* [1948] Ch 31, 47, the House of Lords denied the anti-vivisection cause charitable status with one judge, Lord Wright, indicating that the test of public benefit could vary from generation to generation as the law successively grew more 'tolerant'. This decision clarified that while the benefits to society from an activity like vivisection or testing on animals might be contested on moral grounds, the benefits should be interpreted in light of contemporary social knowledge of the practice. If, for example, a government allows testing on animals due to the 'possible' medical benefits of doing so, an anti-cruelty charity seeking to outlaw the practice may be in conflict with this perceived benefit and their efforts ignored. Thus practices like toxicology testing on animals, vivisection and genetic testing constitute animal abuse when they are carried out unlawfully (i.e. not in accordance with any required regulation and safeguards or where the testing is an unlicensed activity) but although such activities may involve pain and suffering, they would not constitute illegal animal abuse if conducted in accordance with current legislation. Regan (2007: 121) argues that those who argue for the benefits of animal experimentation 'conveniently ignore the hundreds of millions of deaths and the uncounted illnesses and disabilities that are attributable to reliance on the "animal model" in research' and this definition does not comment on the acceptability of animal experimentation or the suffering it causes. The ethical considerations of animal experimentation are, however, outside of the legalistic definition which concerns itself primarily with the lawfulness of an activity and whether public policy has permitted the activity to be positively legislated for. Comparing the experimentation on the seriously mentally retarded children of Willowbrook State Mental Hospital to experimentation on animals, Regan noted that poor standards of treatment and welfare are sometimes 'justified' on the basis that the victims are not fully aware and thus lack possession of and capability to exercise the appropriate rights. However in his comparison of the human and animal experiments, Regan also suggested that 'logically we cannot claim that harms done to the children violate their rights, but the harms done to these animals do not' (2007).

Hunting and Trapping

Hunting and trapping activities are discussed in further detail in Chapter 5 but raise specific concerns both about the animal abuse involved in taking animals from the wild and the level of criminality inherent in hunting and trapping activities. While legal hunting exists and is generally regulated through permit systems and oversight by government environmental or conservation departments there are concerns about the extent of illegal animal abuse associated with hunting. Webster (2000) argued that hunted animals (i.e. those chased by mounted hunts and packs of dogs) suffer stress of a kind that would meet the definition of illegal animal abuse by causing unnecessary suffering which is contained in UK legislation and in many US anti-cruelty statutes. While this is hotly contested by hunt supporters (All Party Parliamentary Middle Way Group and Veterinary Association for Wildlife Management 2009), persistent evidence is produced that hunted animals do not always die in humane ways and that considerable unnecessary suffering can be involved. Fox et al. (2005) concluded that many animals are merely wounded in shooting incidents and the UK's All Party Parliamentary Middle Way Group and Veterinary Association for Wildlife Management also concluded that while a direct hit by a marksman would cause instantaneous death 'shooting is intrinsically fallible, even if undertaken properly'. This is because inexpert or opportunistic shots may cause protracted suffering by wounding (2009). In addition, illegal practices are inextricably linked to the more commercialized forms of hunting such that illegal persecution of protected birds of prey has consistently been proved to linked to the shooting industry in the UK and illegal killing of seals is linked to the fisheries industry (Wilson et al. 2007). In addition Eliason (2003) found evidence that US hunting and angling regulations are almost routinely ignored by hunters who challenge their legitimacy. Other studies have found that rural hunting communities consider hunting and killing of wildlife to be their right irrespective of legislation (Bristow 1982, Pash 1986), and enjoy the challenge of outwitting enforcement agencies who they not only see as outsiders seeking to impose controls on their way of life, but actively engage with as the enemy (Forsyth and Marckesc 1993). The trapping methods used in hunting are also prone to abuse and contribute to animal cruelty because their effectiveness is frequently not monitored. While a number of humane traps are now available for hunting and trapping purposes, animals are still left to die when traps maim rather than kill outright and non-target species are often killed unlawfully when indiscriminate methods of hunting are used (House of Commons 2012).

Animals Used for Entertainment

The use of animals for entertainment encompasses a range of activities from the use of animals in circuses and zoos, through to the use of animals in television advertisements. Although both lawful and unlawful forms of animal use in entertainment exist, animal abuse has been associated with both, identifying animal harm as an integral aspect of different forms of animal use in entertainment.

In the circus and zoo world, animal abuse has been identified as integral to the training and care methods used. In its 1996–98 survey of UK circuses, Animal Defenders International (ADI) found that 'day-to-day violence towards animals in the circus industry is both accepted, and commonplace. Violence was used both during training sessions and to move animals about whilst feeding' (2003: 3). In its 2003 and 2005 investigation of animals in Portugese circuses, ADI found animals enduring 'severe confinement in deprived and unnatural environments, a lack of enrichment, inadequate diets, and physical abuse. We also noted animals displaying disturbed behaviour – such as pointless repetitive movements – which indicate severe stress' (2005: 3). The abuse of animals in circuses and zoos is linked to their status as commodities rather than consideration of animals as performers or participants. Melfi (2009) identified that in practice animal welfare standards are based on 'myth and tradition' rather than being scientifically validated. As a result, despite legislation specifying the need for good standards of animal welfare, the actual standards employed in the animal entertainment industry will be determined by practical considerations, not least of all the cost-benefit analysis involved in employing/implementing appropriate standards of animal welfare. Draper (2011) identified the very nature of the circus world as being an obstacle to ensuring good standards of welfare given that 'circuses move site every one or two weeks, and each site may differ radically in size, amenities and infrastructure' (2011: 26). Thus the facilities available to ensure good animal welfare standards are not consistently available and, in addition, ingrained practices may influence whether animal abuse occurs. The ADI research concluded that violence towards animals was used as a legitimized form of control across the circus world. Thus not only is severe confinement an issue with animals only being released from confinement in order to train and perform (ADI 2005) but in addition, 'violence in the training and control of animals is a regular occurrence and part of the circus culture' (2005: 9) so that it is used as an incentive for animals to learn and perform tricks, as a method of punishment when mistakes are made and as a tool to enforce obedience. The lack of any regular inspection regime is hampered by the travelling nature of the circus although poor standards of animal welfare and use of cruelty as an obedience and training tool are also found in the zoo and wildlife park industries (Green 1999). While a number of countries have now banned the use of animals in circuses, including Austria and Costa Rica, Singapore (India has a prohibition limited to some specific species and there are bans in some municipal jurisdictions in Australia and New Zealand) in those countries where they continue to be used, concerns are frequently raised about animal cruelty. Concerns also remain about the use of cruelty and negative reinforcement through force to train animals used in television advertisements (although some monitoring provisions exist in the United States and UK where NGOs monitor the treatment of animals used in entertainment).[1]

In addition to the ostensibly legal uses of animals for entertainment, a number of manifestly illegal activities continue to take place. Although made illegal in Britain in 1893 (1895 in Scotland), dog-fighting and cock-fighting continue in secrecy today in both the UK and the United States. Mott (2004) reported that in the United States family companion animals were being stolen and used as bait to test a fighting dog's instinct, with the result that large numbers of family animals were found maimed or killed. Dog-fighting has been a felony in all US states since 2008 yet evidence exists that it remains popular in low-income and ethnic minority areas. Evidence also exists of illegal dog-fighting in many parts of the world and it is considered widespread in Russia and parts of South Africa while being legal in some developing world countries. Both dog-fighting and cock-fighting are considered to be sports by adherents and are highly organized events with their own subculture attached to them. Fights are specially organized and bets placed on the outcome of the events by supporters and spectators. Anecdotal and primary evidence obtained both in the UK and the United States suggests that large sums of money are placed in bets and that the illegal gambling that takes place is an integral part of the activity and the culture that surrounds it (Hawley 1993, Saunders 2001, Nurse 2009).

Cock-fighting and dog-fighting are activities primarily based around directly observing animals inflicting pain on each with wagers placed on the outcome. Thus such sports directly engage in animal harm via animal cruelty. In the UK there is also some small overlap between those involved in illegal dog-fighting and those involved in illegal badger crime where dogs are set upon badgers with the precise goal of determining how much punishment a dog can take and which is the stronger of the two animals. Such activities are highly organized forms of animal

---

1   As of January 2012 the UK government's position is that it will pursue or work towards a ban on animals in circuses but in the meantime will implement a licensing system.

harm (discussed again and in more detail in Chapters 3 and 5) where a premium is attached to the levels of animal cruelty involved. Dogs undergo brutal training regimes to develop a taste for blood and flesh, and training regimes involving treadmills are sometimes used to develop muscle strength. Staffordshire Bull Terriers and American Pit Bull terriers are popular fighting dogs and are prized for their violent nature by their owners, often violent individuals themselves. The League Against Cruel Sports (LACS) provides the following overview of dog-fighting in the UK:

> Dog fights are illicitly organized (often by hardened criminals) usually at night time in outbuildings, barns, lock-ups and derelict premises away from or hidden from public view. The fighting 'pit' itself is a makeshift ring usually around fourteen feet and marked in two halves across the middle with a 'scratch line'. It may be carpeted for grip and enclosed by low boards. Each of the two owners set their dogs into the pit (often accompanied by themselves) and encourage the dogs to attack each other with shouts of 'seize him/shake him' etc. Fights are gruelling and may be of a long duration (often over an hour) usually resulting in serious injuries being suffered by one or both dogs. The loser may be killed outright. If one of the dogs turns away from the other, the 'referee' will call the fight off for twenty-five seconds. The dog will then be given 15 seconds to cross the scratchline and 'mouth' (bite) the other dog. If the dog fails to do this, or surrenders to its opponent by rolling over and offering its throat or belly, it will have lost the fight. (LACS website policy documents)

Good fighting dogs can change hands for sums in excess of £1,000 each in the UK and 'champion' dogs for several thousands of pounds, with large sums of money often being placed in bets on the outcome of each fight (Nurse 2009). The Animal Legal Defense Fund (ALDF) commented that NFL football star Michael Vick's dog-fighting operation 'housed and trained over 50 pit bull dogs, staged dog fights, killed dogs, and ran a high stakes gambling ring with purses up to $26,000' (2011). The operation was considered to be violent and bloody and made use of high security measures to avoid detection by law enforcement (ALDF 2011).

The nature of badger-baiting, cock-fighting and dog-fighting is such that it is very difficult to estimate how regularly the activities occur and how many animals are involved. Whereas some other forms of blood sport, such as hare coursing (lawful in the UK until recently) could be carried out lawfully and in the open, badger-baiting, cock-fighting and dog-fighting have long been unlawful, socially unacceptable underground activities and are carried out in secret and in specific locations. LACS (2000) states that 'the undercover world of cockfighting is most prevalent in the Midlands, East Anglia and the West Country and is very hard to penetrate thus making it difficult to prosecute those involved', and the same is true of other such illegal activities. However Operation Gazpacho, a three-year nationwide police and RSPCA investigation into illegal dog-fighting in the UK, found evidence of dog-fighting rings across the UK and was considered a success in interrupting the activities of several gangs (Carter 2005).

Summarizing Animal Abuse

Animal abuse then involves the direct or indirect inflicting of injury or harm on an animal. Such harm could be either physical or psychological but consists either of abuse by virtue of failing to provide adequately for a companion animal's needs, or of cruelty or mistreatment of an animal that results in or directly causes injury. Such animal abuse may be carried out as a consequence or incidental result of a lawful activity but the definition used and discussed throughout this book notes that any cruelty or abuse defined as unlawful is animal harm irrespective of the otherwise lawfulness of the activity or the intentions of the person committing the act. Thus accidental injury to an animal that nevertheless would constitute unlawful harm to a protected animal would be covered by this definition. The distinction is, however, made between animal abuse (cruelty) and wildlife crime as different aspects of animal harm. While it is undoubtedly true that wild animals suffer from cruelty, the second part of the animal harm definition that will now be discussed relates to those activities predominantly targeted at animals living in the wild.

What is Wildlife Crime?

Official classifications of wildlife crime vary from jurisdiction to jurisdiction with some (such as the United States) focusing predominantly on wildlife trade and environmental crimes such as pollution or habitat destruction while others include wider notions of crime in rural areas which affect criminals. In part the definitions of wildlife crime used in each jurisdiction reflect the types of crimes that occur within the country and this determines both the legislation which is enacted and the policies developed to deal with specific wildlife crime problems. This section explains the nature of wildlife crime and definitions of wildlife crime used within this book, and the different types of wildlife crime and criminality that occur across different jurisdictions within the broad definition of animal harm.

The author conducted field research into wildlife crime in the UK between approximately 2000 and 2008 and inevitably draws on some of that research in this discussion. To provide a brief context: the legislative position in the UK is one in which most native wildlife is protected by virtue of the *Wildlife and Countryside Act 1981* and the *Countryside and Rights of Way Act 2000*. In addition the *Hunting Act 2004* prohibits hunting of live mammals with dogs (similar but separate legislation exists in Scotland and Northern Ireland). Thus the UK has an established wildlife protection regime that operates alongside its animal welfare one. However much of the legislative development in the UK has been driven by those NGOs that still play a significant role in developing public policy on wildlife crime and in some cases still have a significant enforcement role. Thus different policy perspectives are pursued in respect of game offences and poaching, habitat destruction and pollution, offences involving domestic animals and animal welfare and cruelty offences. The role of NGOs also differs according to the types of crime as does the relationship between NGOs and policymakers. For example, game offences are considered to be effectively policed because the UK has strong game and anti-poaching legislation and there is good co-operation between the police and game-rearing staff over poaching. Thus game-rearing staff provide an effective monitoring force for poaching offences and regularly report these crimes (which directly affect their livelihoods) to the police, but the same is not true of wildlife offences such as bird of prey persecution where game-rearing staff are often suspects and may be in conflict with the police and conservationists over how they should be dealt with. This policy environment also creates a potential conflict over what constitutes criminality in wildlife crime in a domestic law sense although this book proposes a broad definition of wildlife crime to fit within its definition of animal harm.

Defining Wildlife Crime

Differing perspectives on wildlife crime exist in the policy and academic literature (Lowther et al. 2002, Nurse 2009, 2011, South and Wyatt 2011) although wildlife crime has frequently been taken to mean wildlife *trafficking* as the perceived most prevalent form of wildlife crime (Lowther et al. 2002, Wyatt 2009, South and Wyatt 2011). However, removal from the wild and sale of wildlife is only one aspect of wildlife crime which may involve harm to or direct killing of wildlife, removal from the wild, or the possession, sale or exploitation of wildlife.

While animal cruelty is sometimes clearly defined within wildlife crime, more complex and less clearly relevant definitions of crime exist. A crime may be an act (or failure to act) that is proscribed by statute or (in the UK) by the common law as a public wrong and so is punishable by the state. Radford explains that 'in respect of a great many criminal offences it is not enough for the prosecution to prove that the defendant committed the proscribed act; it must also demonstrate that they were culpable by reference to their state of mind at the time of the offence' (2001: 222). As a general rule, for an individual to be convicted of a crime the jury (or magistrate) must be convinced of three elements:

1. *actus reus*, that the act took place, can be verified and that a condition of illegality existed;
2. *mens rea*, i.e. that the state of mind of the offender was such that a condition of moral blameworthiness or culpable intentionality existed;
3. the absence of a defence (or the existence of a defence that can be nullified).

Determining that the conduct of the individual can be shown to have resulted in the commission of an offence and that a condition of illegality exists is sometimes problematic as, for example, legal predator control methods can sometimes be used illegally within game rearing but proving this to be the case is problematic. A further issue to consider is the requirement that for a crime to exist theoretically *actus rea* and *mens rea* must be present (Ryan 1998). In animal law *mens rea* (effectively 'guilty mind') is often indicated by use of terms such as 'intentionally', 'recklessly', 'maliciously' or 'wantonly' unless it is a crime of strict liability where the offender's intent may not be an issue. But generally the prosecution must demonstrate beyond reasonable doubt not only that the offender committed the offence but also 'that he knew what he was doing and was aware, or should have been aware of the likely outcome of his act or omission' (Radford 2001: 222). Some crimes are serious wrongs of a moral nature (e.g. murder or rape) while others may interfere with the smooth running of society (such as parking offences or litter) but are of a less serious nature and, as Lynch and Stretesky (2003) observe, the moral dimension of environmental harm and species justice is sometimes a factor in how such crimes are viewed by the public and NGOs.

Wildlife crime, however, is provided for in US and UK law as a means of protecting wildlife either from trade or from other forms of exploitation. For the purposes of defining animal harm, wildlife crime involves those acts which are a clear breach of existing legislation (whether national or international) and requires that the condition of illegality (referred to above) exists, rather than the term applying to those acts which are a perceived moral wrong but which are not yet subject to legislation. Some forms of predator or pest control, for example, are currently lawful in England and Wales and so despite current campaigns for them to be made unlawful, would not be covered by this definition as current wildlife crimes (although predator control activities may be subject to censure by NGOs).

Given the frequent difficulties of proving *mens rea* in wildlife crime cases the state of mind of the offender merits some discussion as a factor in animal harm. For the purposes of the criminal law, the general state of mind of the offender must fit into one of the following categories:

1. intention,
2. recklessness,
3. negligence.

The specific wording of some offences, as discussed elsewhere in this book, makes it difficult to prove intent to commit a crime and the fact that many wildlife crimes may not be witnessed also makes it difficult for prosecutors to demonstrate recklessness. In the *Wildlife and Countryside Act 1981*, for example, there is an offence of 'intentionally' disturbing the nest of a wild bird while it is in use or being built. While it might be relatively easy to prove that a person committed (the offence of) disturbance or was reckless as to the risks that his actions might cause to wild birds at the nest, it would be difficult to prove that the actual 'intent' of the individual's actions was to cause disturbance to the wild bird. In such a case the very wording of the *Wildlife and Countryside Act 1981* would make it difficult to establish that the crime had been committed.

It should also be noted, however, that some wildlife crimes are offences of strict liability that do not require the condition of *mens rea*. The UK's *Wildlife and Countryside Act 1981* makes possession of the eggs of a wild bird an offence irrespective of whether *mens rea* can be established, although there is a defence if the accused can prove that the eggs were taken other than in contravention of the legislation (i.e. prior to September 1982). In practice this means that a person commits an offence simply by possessing the eggs and the onus is on the accused to prove their possession is lawful rather than being on the prosecution to prove (beyond reasonable doubt) that they possess them unlawfully.

The definition of wildlife crime can be further clarified by considering the individual elements of: wildlife, wildlife law and the actions of the offender who commits the offence.

Definition of Wildlife

Defining wildlife crime requires consideration of what constitutes affected 'wildlife'. Definitions in the UK's *Wildlife and Countryside Act 1981* and the US *Endangered Species Act 1973* are concerned primarily with naturally occurring wildlife. The goal of such legislation is to protect the indigenous wildlife of a nation state or those species that are recognized as existing in a wild state either by virtue of their migratory patterns or as a result of becoming established in a wild state as happens with some escaped or accidentally released animals which develop sustainable breeding colonies. The definition of 'wildlife', therefore, includes any, bird, animal, mammal or reptile which is resident in or a visitor to a nation state, in a wild state or is a non-native bird, animal, mammal or reptile which is subject to that state's legislation by virtue of its conservation status. It does not, therefore, include non-native species or captive-bred species except where the law specifically classes these as being wildlife. Wildlife for the purposes of wildlife crimes does, however, include the possession or sale of those non-native species that are recognized as wildlife when incorporated into a state's endangered species legislation as a means of implementing CITES prohibitions on trade in animals that might be taken from the wild and subsequently traded.

Legislative Provisions

For an act to be considered a wildlife crime it must in some way contravene existing legislation (whether national or international). An act such as the taking of a wild bird from the wild and reducing it into captivity, for example, is prohibited by the *Wildlife and Countryside Act 1981* in the UK and by the *Endangered Species Act 1973* in the United States (for certain species) and thus would constitute a crime as defined by UK and US statute. The taking of a captive-bred bird such as a

European Eagle Owl, however, is not an offence prohibited by UK *wildlife* law as it relates to a captive bred bird rather than a wild bird as defined by the *Wildlife and Countryside Act 1981*. Thus while this would be an offence of property theft under other legislation and any cruelty to the bird would most likely be covered under the UK's animal welfare and anti-cruelty statutes, it does not constitute wildlife crime. (Ironically the penalties may be more severe under property legislation and might even be taken more seriously once the property rights and criminal theft are invoked.) Poaching or game offences are also not generally included in UK wildlife laws involving as they do birds and animals reared for the game industry or considered to be legitimate game animals that can be killed or taken, rather than wildlife, the taking of which is prohibited. However this is not always the case and Eliason (2003), in analysing hunting violations, defines these as wildlife crime in the United States in a way that they are not in the UK. Thus in defining wildlife crimes a careful understanding of the legislation may be needed before a conclusion can be drawn.

Wildlife Offender

A wildlife offender can be either an individual who profits or benefits in some way from the wildlife crime, or a corporation or organization that profits from the crime in some way. The 'profit' or 'benefit' to the offender is not necessarily a financial one. Collectors of wild birds' eggs, for example, are not known to sell their eggs to profit from their activity but instead are primarily interested in collecting the eggs of wild birds for personal enjoyment (Nurse 2011). Indeed, in some cases, egg collectors spend considerable sums of money in pursuing their activities, including purchasing special equipment to pursue their 'hobby'. Crimes for which there is no offender, such as the accidental destruction of wild birds' nests during the building of a bypass, would not be considered a wildlife crime or incorporated into the definition of animal harm.

For an act to be considered to be a wildlife crime, therefore, the act must:

- be something that is proscribed by legislation;
- be an act committed against or involving a wild bird, animal, reptile or mammal native to or a visitor to a country in a wild state; and
- involve an offender who commits the unlawful act.

What constitutes a wildlife crime can therefore be further clarified by creating and applying the following definition to this aspect of animal harm:

A wildlife crime is an unauthorised act or omission that violates national or international wildlife or environmental law and is subject to criminal prosecution and criminal sanctions, including cautioning by the police. A wildlife crime may involve harm or killing of wildlife, removal from the wild, possession, sale or the exploitation of wildlife.

As mentioned above, some NGOs also include a definition of wildlife crime based on moral values which can be seen in campaigns to make unlawful activities like hunting with dogs (recently made unlawful), shooting of game species or the use of snares. While these activities are not caught by the above definition used in this research, the calls for changes to legislation to criminalize these activities are relevant in showing the views of NGOs towards existing wildlife legislation and wildlife crimes.

Perspectives on Laws Protecting Wildlife

Across a range of jurisdictions, laws protecting wildlife are complex and fragmented. Rather than there being one piece of legislation protecting native wildlife, there is a vast range of statutes and subordinate legislation that protect indigenous wildlife.

On the launch of its new Wildlife Crime Intelligence Unit, the National Criminal Intelligence Service (NCIS) gave the following explanation of wildlife crime legislation in the UK:

> Wildlife crime encompasses a wide range of offences. Much of UK law in relation to wildlife crime is shaped by international regulations. The 1973 *Convention on International Trade in Endangered Species of Wild Flora and Fauna* (CITES) regulates international trade in endangered species. It prohibits trade of around 800 species, and controls the trade of around a further 23,000 species. CITES is implemented in the European Union (EU) by the *European Union Wildlife Trade Regulations* (EUWTR), which deal with imports and exports of wildlife and wildlife trade products to and from the EU, as well as trade within the EU and both between and within individual member states. In addition, there are offences and penalties established in UK law by the *Customs and Excise Management Act 1979* (CEMA) and the *Control of Trade in Endangered Species (Enforcement) Regulations 1997* (COTES). The *Wildlife and Countryside Act 1981* (WCA) was recently amended by the *Countryside and Rights of Way Act 2000* in England and Wales (CRoW), although the offences remain similar. Birds and other scheduled animal species are protected from prescribed killing methods, there is a prohibition on the taking or possessing of certain species, or parts or derivatives of them (such as birds' eggs), a prohibition on the uprooting of scheduled plant species and a general offence of introducing non-native plant or animal species. (NCIS 2002: 3)

The NCIS definition highlights the fact that wildlife is subject to a legislative regime that involves several statutes and definitions of criminal activity. Within the UK and United States alone, legislation has been enacted at species level with such pieces of legislation as the *Protection of Badgers Act 1992* and the *Deer Act 1991* in the UK and the *Endangered Species Act of 1973* and

Marine Mammal Protection Act of 1972 in the United States. There has also been general legislation protecting a wide range of wild animals and mammals, such as the UK's *Wildlife & Countryside Act 1981* and the *Wild Mammals (Protection) Act 1996*. Legislation has also been enacted to implement international wildlife protection legislation. For example, the wild bird provisions of the *Wildlife and Countryside Act 1981* were intended to implement the 1979 *EC Directive on Wild Birds* and give protection to all forms of native wild birds (with certain exceptions for pest control and agricultural purposes). In addition to this, wildlife offences can also be caught by other forms of legislation aimed at regulating commercial activities or creating offences in relation to other activities such as the import and export of prohibited items, including wildlife (covered in the UK by the *Customs and Excise Management Act 1979* (CEMA) and COTES Regulations which implement CITES).

An explanation of the main types of wildlife crime committed and main classifications of offences follows.

The Nature of Wildlife Offences

Following on from definitions of wildlife crime it is important to discuss the nature of wildlife offences given that discussions of wildlife crime often centre on a particular type of offence, usually that of wildlife trade and the trade in endangered species (see Holden 1998, Roberts et al. 2001). Beyond the trade issue, wildlife crime encompasses a range of different offences involving a diverse range of species, including: badgers, birds, seals and small and large mammals.

Wildlife crime also encompasses a range of different criminal behaviour and different types of criminal act. In addition to the commercial and smuggling activities associated with wildlife trade, wildlife offences include the following types of criminal activity:

• unlawful killing or wounding;
• robbery (taking from the wild of a protected species);
• disturbance of a protected species;
• cruelty and animal welfare offences;
• unlicensed (and unlawful) gambling;
• damage to property;
• illegal poisoning and unlawful storage and/or use of pesticides;
• theft and handling 'stolen' goods;
• deception;
• fraud and forgery;
• criminal damage (of protected sites);
• firearms-related offences.

A number of these offence types are offences of a 'type' that fall within the standard definitions of crime adopted by justice departments and generally incorporated into official crime statistics. Their inclusion here is for illustrative purposes only and to establish that within the remit of wildlife crime, a range of criminal activities are committed with consequences for the wildlife that are subject to these activities. Some are officially recorded and some are not, so how they are treated differs in official statistics and across jurisdictions according to the legislation in place. The killing or wounding of a person, for example, would automatically be recorded by the justice agencies broadly falling within a category of *Violence Against the Person* (an umbrella term that includes a wide range of offences including: homicide, threat or conspiracy to murder, wounding, and common assault) and as such is included in most official crime statistics as a measure of crime. However, the killing or wounding of a wild bird, animal or mammal, though violent and even where prohibited by law, would not be considered within the general classification of crime within the official crime statistics and would not be recorded except in those jurisdictions where statistics on animal crimes are collated and published.

Beyond the full range of individual offences that might be committed, wildlife offences fall into the following broad categories:

- killing, taking or possessing a wild bird;
- killing, taking or possessing a wild animal or mammal;
- trade in wildlife (alive or dead);
- trade in endangered species;
- taking or possession of wild birds' eggs.

These offences are individually discussed in more detail below.

Killing, Taking or Possessing a Wild Bird

The killing, taking or possession of wild birds is an offence in a range of jurisdictions where legislation is designed to protect wild breeding birds or to protect wild birds considered to be at risk. In the United States, for example, peregrine falcons were placed on the endangered list managed under the *Endangered Species Act of 1973* while in the UK the *Wildlife & Countryside Act 1981* (as amended by the *Countryside and Rights of Way Act 2000*) gives basic protection to all native UK wild birds and prohibits their killing, except for those species that are legally classed as pest species. Birds such as magpies and crows, for example, may be killed or taken for certain specified pest control purposes, and at specified times, such as for the protection of other birds or to prevent damage to crops or other agriculture (*Wildlife & Countryside Act 1981*). Pest control provisions in UK legislation also allow Canada geese and pigeons to be killed in public parks and open spaces to prevent perceived threats to public health that are caused by their droppings. The Act defines open and closed seasons for the killing or taking of these pest species and birds may not be taken during the closed seasons.

The offences involved in the killing or taking of birds also include the commercial exploitation of birds and the killing of birds to preserve commercial interests. Birds of prey, for example, are often killed on grouse moors, near pheasant release pens or farms, and in the UK a number of gamekeepers have been convicted of offences relating to bird of prey persecution. Some of these offences involve the use of prohibited means of taking birds such as poison or the use of pole, spring or cage traps. The persecution of protected birds of prey is considered by the conservation NGOs to be deliberate criminal activity perpetrated by those who know their actions are prohibited by law (see for example Etheridge et al. 1997, RSPB 2002).

For example, in October 2002 the RSPB, commenting on the fate of birds involved in the project to reintroduce red kites into the UK, observed that:

> A recent study of the release scheme in northern Scotland looked at the fate of 248 red kites fitted with wing tags between 1989 and 1998. From post-mortems on 24 recovered dead birds, 13 were confirmed as being poisoned. From the total number of missing wing-tagged birds it is estimated that as many as 93 birds, a staggering 37% of the total may have been illegally poisoned. Similar work for the release scheme in southern England has suggested around 10% of the red kites are falling victim to illegal poison. (RSPB 2002: 5)

Birds of prey are considered to be a threat to the populations of game birds such as grouse and pheasants and evidence exists to support the NGOs' belief that gamekeepers continue to kill the birds despite the fact that they now enjoy legal protection in the UK (Etheridge et al. 1997). Birds of prey are also taken from the wild to supply the trade in birds of prey for falconry where they can fetch large sums of money. There is also some anecdotal evidence to suggest that birds are taken for the taxidermy trade. In addition to birds of prey, some smaller birds, mainly finches, are taken to supply the trade in caged birds (this is discussed further below).

The possession of a wild bird, alive or dead, is an offence under UK wildlife legislation. There are some exemptions that allow the possession of injured wild birds for the purpose of rehabilitation but, in general, the onus rests on an individual in possession of a wild bird to show that it has come into his possession by lawful means. Barn owls, for example are common road casualties and figures released to coincide with the 1998 wildlife and roads symposium suggested that 3,000 barn owls are killed on the roads each year (WWF 1998). Research for the UK Post Office (Which 2008) reinforced this, suggesting that an estimated 20,000 urban foxes, and as many as 10 million birds (including three million pheasants and 3,000 barn owls) are killed on the UK's roads each year (Which 2008).

Killing, Taking or Possessing a Wild Animal or Mammal

In addition to the above offences relating to wild birds, similar offences relate to wild animals and mammals. This is perhaps the broadest range of offences, incorporating offences against badgers, seals, and other animals or mammals as the following sections discuss.

Badger Crime   The National Federation of Badger Groups (NFBG, now called the Badger Trust) says that thousands of badgers are killed illegally in Britain each year. A range of different offences fall within the broad remit of badger crime, including badger-baiting, snaring, lamping and shooting and poisoning which all account for badger deaths. NFBG figures listed on the Federation's website state that 'an estimated 10,000 badgers are killed every year by badger baiting and digging' (NFBG 2000) and WWF has reported 47,000 badgers killed on the roads each year (WWF 1998). In June 2002 the NFBG also published a report that stated that 'a large number of badgers are snared in Britain, despite this being illegal. In addition, an analysis of snaring incidents dealt with by the RSPCA showed that of 246 animals found caught in snares, 103 were badgers' (NFBG 2002: 2).

Although often spoken of together, badger-digging and badger-baiting are two separate and distinct types of offence (although it is often the case that badger-baiting follows on from badger-digging). Badger-digging involves the 'digging out' and removal of a badger from its sett, often for its later use in badger-baiting. Badger-baiting is a separate type of offence in which fighting dogs are set upon a badger. Baiting of captive animals such as bears, bulls and badgers became illegal in 1835 but badger-baiting and digging have never been totally eradicated and remain popular underground activities in the UK. For adherents the protracted battle between badgers, which can withstand considerable punishment, and dogs, can be an exciting and bloody spectacle. The League Against Cruel Sports (LACS) provides the following description of badger digging:

> These days, baiting is carried out in two ways. Firstly, at the sett from which the badgers have been dug. Badger diggers send specially trained terriers to attack badgers in their underground setts, and then dig through the tunnel roof to expose the fight – ending when the badger is bludgeoned to death with a spade. The badger is then usually buried in the sett – sometimes together with the body of the dog fatally injured in the battle. Alternatively, the animal is captured and removed from its sett and forced to fight for its life against a pack of snapping and snarling terriers. (LACS 2000)

Anecdotal evidence suggests that one of the primary reasons for badger-baiting, and similar 'fighting sports' like hare coursing, cock-fighting and dog-fighting is the gambling that accompanies the event (Naturewatch 2007). In relation to badger-baiting, LACS has commented that the bravery and 'gameness' of the dogs is what the adherents of the 'sport' find attractive (2000). Badger-baiting is a predominantly UK practice that takes place across rural areas where badgers live, although there are baiting hotspots in the north of England.

Trade in Wildlife (Alive or Dead)

The trade in wildlife, alive or dead, is generally prohibited by state legislation with certain exceptions and where subject to a regulatory regime. Legislation such as the UK's *Wildlife & Countryside Act 1981* (and its wildlife or wildlife trade protection equivalents in other jurisdictions) prohibits the sale of wild birds or animals alive or dead except where it can be shown that the bird or animal was sold other than in contravention of the legislation. Common provisions in legislation concerning wildlife trade are that the wildlife in question is of a type that can be sold if it can be determined that the bird or animal, even though it may be of a species classed as wildlife, was captive-bred and the relevant trade regulations are complied with. In cases where animals have died of natural causes or have been killed other than in contravention of the legislation the sale of the dead animal is frequently permitted. However there are usually regulatory controls which require the seller to obtain permits or health certificates in order to legitimize the sale.

However the ability to sell wild species under the guise of captive breeding is where animal harm frequently takes place. In the UK, small birds such as finches can be legally sold only if they are fitted with government-approved close-rings and bred from parents lawfully in captivity. However the RSPB (2002) reports that 'there is a ready market in the UK for trapped wild finches with many species fetching £40 or more on the black market. It has also been shown that some of the finches trapped in the UK are exported to other European countries such as Malta' (RSPB 2002: 22). Evidence thus exists to suggest that an illegal trade in birds such as finches exists alongside the legal trade in these species. In the case of larger animals required for theme parks and as pets there is evidence of a black market in exotic animals but also of birds and animals consistently being taken from the wild to supply consumer demand. Such activities frequently involve illegal trapping and transport methods and poor standards of animal care as well as the sale of animals that may not be suited for their end purpose as captive animals. There is scope to make a distinction between the general trade in wildlife that involves legitimate traders and distributors who seek to circumvent legislation and regulatory controls and the trade in endangered and rarer species which is subject to CITES controls (and relevant national legislation). The former generally involves 'lesser' forms of animal harm in respect of its focus on procuring birds and animals for sale to ordinary consumers while avoiding the regulatory regime. The latter involves organized crime (South and Wyatt 2011) and large-scale activity primarily by criminal gangs who have clear links to other offences such as drugs. Because of the large amounts of money that can be generated from rare species of wildlife, the trade in endangered species is considered to be a significant problem.

Trade in Endangered Species

When discussing wildlife crime in the media, academic and policy focus often centres on the illegal trade in wildlife and most notably the trade in endangered species. The trade involves both native and non-native species which can be traded either in contravention of a state's wildlife legislation or in contravention of regional or international wildlife legislation. For example, within the United States and UK, domestic legislation (the *Endangered Species Act 1973* and COTES respectively) classifies some native wildlife as endangered, thus falling within the remit of wildlife crime. For example, a number of UK birds of prey are classed as endangered by the European Union and are given protection by the European Union Regulations that implement CITES. Many of these species are traded in the UK (subject to the Regulations) and offences of unlawful trade have long been the target of organisations like TRAFFIC, the RSPB, Worldwide Fund for Nature (WWF) and HM Customs & Excise. The exact extent of the trade in endangered species is difficult to quantify as it is not routinely monitored, although the sale of all native species of birds of prey and owls is controlled by the EU CITES Regulation and COTES. The RSPB explains that of the 46 reported incidents in 2004 involving the taking, sale and possession of live or dead wild birds, '16 related to the possession, sale or taking of live birds of prey' (RSPB 2005: 7). However, with the rare species, it is not the absolute number of incidents that is the main area of concern. The small number of birds that make up some populations means that any wildlife trade can sometimes be detrimental to the species' survival. Wildlife and Countryside Link reinforce this point as follows:

> The illegal trade in wildlife presents a serious threat to the survival or conservation of many endangered species. The value of a particular specimen is usually related to its scarcity, so a vicious circle operates through this illegal trade: as a species becomes more endangered, so its price increases, as do the financial rewards for smugglers. High rewards, and the low risks of detection and punishment, have made the illegal wildlife trade attractive to criminals.
>
> Although some offenders are either linked directly or indirectly with legitimate trade networks, there is increasing evidence that more organized crime elements are becoming engaged in the most lucrative areas of the illegal wildlife trade. Existing smuggling routes used by serious organized crime groups for their trade in other illegal commodities (such as small arms, drugs and humans) can be readily used for additional profitable products – such as wildlife. (Wildlife and Countryside Link 2002: 2)

Taking or Possession of Wild Birds' Eggs

The taking or possession of wild birds' eggs is prohibited under UK law (and in several other jurisdictions) but the practice still continues. Egg collectors appear at nest sites and simply take the eggs of wild birds for their own private collections. Where an egg is viable, the collector will drill a small hole in the egg and flush out the contents to leave the hollow shell of the egg intact. This can then be displayed in a glass case or cabinet alongside other eggs. Possession of eggs is an offence of strict liability in the UK and the onus of proof rests on anybody in possession of eggs to show, on the balance of probabilities, that their possession is lawful.

Conclusions on Animal Harm

Given the different activities involved, the different species which are subject to animal harm and variations in legislative approach to different animals, this chapter concludes that a broad definition of animal harm is required. Rather than discussing animal abuse and wildlife crime as separate activities this book's discussion of animal harm encompasses a definition of animal harm as being:

> Animal harm is any unauthorized act or omission that violates national or international animal law whether anti-cruelty, conservation, animal protection, wildlife or general law that contains animal protection provisions (including the protection of animals as property) and is subject to either criminal prosecution and criminal sanctions, including cautioning and disposal by means other than a criminal trial or which provides for civil sanctions to redress the harm caused to the animal whether directly or indirectly. Animal harm may involve injury to or killing of animals, removal from the wild, possession or reducing into captivity, or the sale or exploitation of animals or products derived from animals. Animal harm also includes the causing of either physical or psychological distress.

While this definition is perhaps lengthy it nevertheless reflects the composite nature of animal harm as comprising of various activities whether direct or indirect and as affecting both companion animals and wildlife. Crucially, it also reflects the fact that companion animals and wildlife are affected differently by animal harm and that the different types of animal harm activities involve different and distinct types of criminality. It therefore concludes that animal harm is defined by its behavioural traits as much as by whether animal abuse, cruelty or other forms of exploitation are involved and that criminological examination of animal harm requires developing a broad definition of animal harm.

References

Agnew, R. (1998). The Causes of Animal Abuse: A Social-psychological Analysis. *Theoretical Criminology*, 2(2), 177–209.

All Party Parliamentary Middle Way Group and Veterinary Association for Wildlife Management (2009). *Hunting, Wildlife Management and the Moral Issue* [unspecified publication details].

Animal Defenders International (2003). *Animals in UK Circuses*, London: Animal Defenders International.

Animal Defenders International (2005). *Stop Circus Suffering: Animal Circuses in Portugal*, London: Animal Defenders International.

Animal Legal Defense Fund (2011). *Animal Fighting Case Study: Michael Vick*, Cotati, CA: ALDF. Available at http://www.aldf.org/article.php?id=928 [accessed 29 January 2012].

Ascione, F.R. (1993). Children who are Cruel to Animals: A Review of Research and Implications for Developmental Psychopathology. *Anthrozoos*, 4, 226–7.

Beirne, P. (1999). For a Nonspeciesist Criminology: Animal Abuse as an Object of Study. *Criminology*, 37(1), 1–32.

Beirne, P. (2009). *Confronting Animal Abuse: Law, Criminology, and Human-Animal Relationships*, Lanham: Rowman & Littlefield.

Bristow, A.P. (1982). *Rural Law Enforcement*, Boston: Allyn & Bacon.

Carter, H. (2005) Man Jailed after Admitting Dogfights, *The Guardian Online*, 17 May 2005. Available at http://www.guardian.co.uk/uk/2005/may/17/animalwelfare.world?INTCMP=SRCH [accessed 10 January 2012].

Conboy-Hill, S. (2000). *Animal Abuse and Interpersonal Violence*, Lincoln: The Companion Animal Behaviour Therapy Study Group.

Draper, C. (2011). Wild Animals in Travelling Circuses: The Circus Has Still Not Left Town. *Journal of Animal Welfare Law*, Autumn/Winter, 25–6.

Eliason, S.L. (2003). Illegal Hunting and Angling: The Neutralization of Wildlife Law Violations. *Society & Animals*, 11(3).

Etheridge, B., Summers, R.W. and Green, R.E. (1997). The Effects of Illegal Killing and Destruction of Nests by Humans on the Population Dynamics of the Hen Harrier Circus cyaneus in Scotland. *Journal of Applied Ecology*, 34, 1081–105

Forsyth, C.J. and Marckesc, T.A. (1993). Thrills and Skills: A Sociological Analysis of Poaching. *Deviant Behavior*, 14(2), 157–72.

Fox, N.C., Blay, N., Greenwood, A.G., Wise, D. and Potapov, E. (2005). Wounding Rates in Shooting Foxes (Vulpes vulpes). *Animal Welfare*, 14(2), 93–102.

Green, A. (1999). *Animal Underground*, New York: Public Affairs/Perseus Books.

Hawley, F. (1993). The Moral and Conceptual Universe of Cockfighters: Symbolism and Rationalization. *Society and Animals*, 1(2).

Hinteregger, M. (2008). *Environmental Liability and Ecological Damage in European Law*, Cambridge: Cambridge University Press.

Hirschi, T. (1969). *Causes of Delinquency*, Berkeley: University of California Press.

Holden, J. (1998). *By Hook or by Crook: A Reference Manual on Illegal Wildlife Trade and Prosecutions in the United Kingdom*, Sandy: RSPB/TRAFFIC/WWF.

House of Commons (2012). Select Committee on Environmental Audit: Written Evidence Submitted by Animal Aid. London: The Stationery Office. Available at http://www.publications.parliament.uk/pa/cm201213/cmselect/cmenvaud/writev/140/wild35.htm [accessed 2 September 2012].

Lawrence, F. (2004). *Not on the Label: What Really Goes into the Food on Your Plate*, London: Penguin Books.

League Against Cruel Sports (LACS) (2000). *Dogfighting*, London: LACS.

Linzey, A. (2009), *Why Animal Suffering Matters: Philosophy, Theology and Practical Ethics*, Oxford: Oxford University Press.

Lowther, J., Cook, D. and Roberts, M. (2002). *Crime and Punishment in the Wildlife Trade*, Wolverhampton: WWF/TRAFFIC/Regional Research Institute (University of Wolverhampton).

Lynch, M.J. and Stretesky, P.B.M. (2003). The Meaning of Green: Contrasting Criminological Perspectives. *Theoretical Criminology*, 7(2), London: Sage.

Melfi, V. (2009). There are Big Gaps in Our Knowledge, and Thus Approach to Zoo Animal Welfare: A Case for Evidence-based Zoo Animal Management. *Zoo Biology*, 28, 574–88.

Merton, R.K. (1968). *Social Structure and Social Theory*, New York: Free Press.

Mott, M. (2004). U.S. Dog-Fighting Rings Stealing Pets for 'Bait', *National Geographic News*. Available at http://news.nationalgeographic.com/news/2004/02/0218_040218_dogfighting.html [accessed 20 January 2012].

National Federation of Badger Groups (NFBG) (2000). *Tackling Illegal Persecution*, London: NFBG.

National Federation of Badger Groups (NFBG) (2002). *The Case for a Ban on Snares: A Report by the National Federation of Badger Groups*, London: NFBG.

Naturewatch (2007). *Fact Sheet on Cruelty to Badgers*, Cheltenham: Naturewatch.

NCIS (2002). *National Wildlife Crime Intelligence Unit Launched at NCIS* (NCIS Press Release), London: NCIS.

Nurse, A. (2003). *The Nature of Wildlife and Conservation Crime in the UK and its Public Response, Working Paper No 9*, Birmingham: University of Central England Birmingham, Faculty of Law and Social Sciences.

Nurse, A. (2009). Dealing with Animal Offenders, in A. Linzey (ed.) *The Link Between Animal Abuse and Human Violence*, Eastbourne: Sussex Academic Press, 238–49.

Nurse, A. (2011). Policing Wildlife: Perspectives on Criminality in Wildlife Crime. *Papers from the British Society of Criminology Conference*, 11, London: British Society of Criminology, 38–53.

Pash, P. (1986). Poacher Wars. *Illinois Department of Conservation: Outdoor Highlights*, 14(1), 3–9.

Paternoster, R. and Simpson, S. (1996). Sanction Threats and Appeals to Morality: Testing a Rational Choice Model of Corporate Crime. *Law and Society Review*, 30(3), 549–84.

People for the Ethical Treatment of Animals (2011). A Schocking Look Inside Chinese *Fur Farms*. Norfolk, VA: PETA. Available at http://features.peta.org/ChineseFurFarms/ [accessed 20 January 2012].

People for the Ethical Treatment of Animals (2012). *The Fur Industry*. Norfolk, VA: PETA. Available at http://www.peta.org/issues/animals-used-for-clothing/fur.aspx [accessed 20 January 2012].

Radford, M. (2001). *Animal Welfare Law in Britain*, Oxford: Oxford University Press.

Regan, T. (2007). Vivisection: The Case for Abolition, in P. Beirne and N. South (eds), *Issues in Green Criminology: Confronting Harms against Environments, Humanity and Other Animals*, Devon: Willan Publishing, 114–39.

Roberts, M., Cook, D., Jones, P. and Lowther, D. (2001). *Wildlife Crime in the UK: Towards a National Crime Unit*, Wolverhampton: Department for the Environment, Food & Rural Affairs/Centre for Applied Social Research (University of Wolverhampton).

Rollin, B.E. (2006). *Animal Rights and Human Morality*, New York: Prometheus.

Royal Society for the Protection of Birds (RSPB) (2002). *Birdcrime 2001: Offences against Wild Bird Legislation in 2001*, Sandy: RSPB.

Royal Society for the Protection of Birds (RSPB) (2005). *Legal Eagle, Issue 43, January 2005*, Sandy: RSPB.

Ryan, C. (1998). *Criminal Law*: 4th Edition, London: Blackstone Press.

Saunders, T. (2001). *Baiting the Trap: One Man's Secret Battle to Save Our Wildlife*, London: Simon & Schuster.

Schaffner, J. (2011). *An Introduction to Animals and the Law*, New York: Palgrave Macmillan.

Schlosser, E. (2002). *Fast Food Nation: What the All-American Meal is Doing to the World*, London: Penguin Books.

Shapiro, K. (2008). *Human Animal Studies: Growing the Field, Applying the Field*, Ann Arbor: Animals & Society Institute.

Situ, Y. and Emmons, D. (2000). *Environmental Crime: The Criminal Justice System's Role in Protecting the Environment*, Thousand Oaks: Sage.

South, N. (1998). A Green Field for Criminology? A Proposal for a Perspective. *Theoretical Criminology*, 2(2), 211–33.

South, N. and Wyatt, T. (2011). Comparing Illicit Trades in Wildlife and Drugs: An Exploratory Study. *Deviant Behavior*, 32, 538–61.

Walters, R. (2007). Crime, Regulation and Radioactive Waste in the United Kingdom, in P. Beirne and N. South (eds), *Issues in Green Criminology: Confronting Harms against Environments, Humanity and Other Animals*, Devon: Willan, 186–285.

Webster, J. (2000). Submission by John Webster, M.A., Vet M.B. (Cantab) 1963 PhD (Glasgow) 1996, University of Bristol School of Veterinary Science to the Committee of Enquiry into Hunting with Dogs.

Which (2008). Wildlife Crashes Injure 500 Motorists a Year, Which.co.uk. Available at http://www.which.co.uk/news/2008/03/wildlife-crashes-injure-500-motorists-a-year-133972/ [accessed 27 April 2008].

White, R. (2008). *Crimes Against Nature: Environmental Criminology and Ecological Justice*, Devon: Willan.

Wildlife and Countryside Link (2002). *Response to the Pre-consultation Paper: Review of Statutory Instrument 1997 No 1372 The Control of Trade in Endangered Species (Enforcement) Regulation 1997*, London: Wildlife and Countryside Link.

Wilson, S., Anderson, L. and Knight, A. (2007). *The Conservation of Seals Act 1970: The Case for Review*, Scotland: Seal Forum.

Wise, S.M. (2000). *Rattling the Cage: Towards Legal Rights for Animals*, London: Profile.

Worldwide Fund for Nature (1998). Wildlife and Roads: 47,000 Badgers Killed each Year, WWF. Available at www.wwf-uk.org/News/n_0000000217.asp [accessed 27 April 2008].

Wyatt, T. (2009). Exploring the Organization in Russia Far East's Illegal Wildlife Trade: Two Case Studies of the Illegal Fur and Illegal Falcon Trades. *Global Crime*, 10(1 & 2), 144–54.

Wyatt, T. (2011). The Illegal Raptor Trade in the Russian Federation. *Contemporary Justice Review*, 14(2), 103–23.

Chapter 3
Identifying Animal Offenders

This chapter analyses the criminological behaviour involved in animal harm, looking at the distinction between the behaviours of animal abusers and wildlife crime offenders. It also considers the techniques of neutralization employed by animal offenders to justify or deny culpability for their actions. There is considerable academic literature on animal abuse (e.g. Felthous and Kellert 1987, Conboy-Hill 2000, Henry 2004, Linzey 2009) and, in particular, on how animal abuse can be an indicator of future offending or antisocial behaviour personality disorders. However, green criminology has paid little attention to the cause of specific behaviours of animal abusers and wildlife offenders or the nature of offending behaviour across animal harm. Yet there is evidence that within specific aspects of animal harm such as animal abuse or wildlife crime, particular types of offenders exist, each driven by their own distinct motivations and carrying out specific offence types (Nurse 2011).[1] While the focus of animal harm law enforcement has primarily been on the apprehension and punishment of offenders, with little attention being paid to preventative measures or the rehabilitation of offenders, a blanket approach to animal harm that views all offenders as motivated by profit (in the case of wildlife crime) or the desire to inflict cruelty (animal abuse) may be inherently flawed. There is thus a need to closely define animal harm criminality.

This chapter explicitly examines offender behaviour, its causes and the policy response applying criminological theory and explanations of crime to animal harm and the behaviour of animal abusers and wildlife offenders. In doing so it develops a new typology of animal offenders as traditional, economic, masculinities, hobby, and stress offenders. It discusses the causes of their crimes, the role of the community in both allowing animal harm abuse to continue and in determining the public policy response to animal harm offenders. In considering animal harm's criminality, a distinction should be made between crimes involving and impacting on animals in the wild, and animal cruelty offences that mainly involve domesticated or farmed animals. Companion animal abuse, where animal 'ownership' is often a significant factor in a way that it is not with wildlife, is subject to different legislation (although which sometimes overlaps) and involves different types of offender to that of wild animal offending. As a result, this chapter recommends

---

1   The wildlife crime research that formed the basis of this chapter's early offender models was presented at the 2011 British Society of Criminology conference held at Northumbria University in July 2011. Feedback from that conference presentation was invaluable in the development of the final offender models discussed in this chapter.

new approaches to animal harm offending which recognize differences in offender behaviour, motivations and responses to law enforcement and punishment. It sets out a framework for how animal offenders are considered by mainstream criminal justice, arguing that a policy approach which adopts a uniform approach to dealing with wildlife crime and offending is inherently flawed and ineffective, a theme further developed later in the book.

Perspectives on Criminality in Animal Harm

Understanding the psychology of offenders, the economic pressures that affect them and the sociological and cultural issues that impact on behaviour greatly aids understanding of what needs to be done to address behaviours (Becker 1963) and the conditions that lead to animal harm. Some offences are motivated by purely financial considerations, some by economic or employment constraints (Roberts et al. 2001: 27) and others by predisposition towards some elements of the activity such as collecting; or exercising power over animals or by controlling others via the threat of harm to animals. Wildlife offences, for example, involve different elements, some incorporating the taking and exploitation of wildlife for profit (wildlife trade), others involving the killing or taking or trapping of wildlife either in connection with employment (bird of prey persecution) or for purposes linked to fieldsports (hunting with dogs).

Sykes and Matza's neutralization theory (1957) is a useful model for identifying the justifications used by offenders that gives them the freedom to act (and a post-act rationalization for doing so) while other theories explain why animal harm offenders are motivated to commit specific crimes. Animal offenders exist within communities, although there may not be a community about where the crimes take place or neighbours to exert essential controls on offending (especially in respect of wildlife offences which often take place in remote areas). Offenders may also live within a community or subculture of their own which accepts their offences, as many animal harm offences carry only fines or lower level prison terms which reinforce the notion of animal harm as 'minor' offences unworthy of official activity within mainstream criminal justice. In addition, Sutherland's (1973) differential association theory helps to explain the situation that occurs when potential animal abusers and wildlife offenders learn their activities from others in their community or social group (Sutherland 1973). For example, mature egg collectors in the UK argue that there is no harm in continuing an activity that they commenced legitimately as schoolboys. Examination of case files and newspaper reports on egg collecting confirm that new collectors continue to be attracted to the 'hobby' and learn its ways through interaction with more established collectors. Similarly, junior gamekeepers on shooting estates and ranchers or farmers coming into the profession (often from within the family) learn techniques of poisoning and trapping from established staff as a means of ensuring healthy populations of game birds for shooting or protecting livestock from predators. Awareness of the illegal nature of their actions leads to the justifications outlined by Sykes and Matza (1957) but the association with other offenders, the economic (and employment related) pressures to commit offences and the personal consequences for them should they fail are strong motivations to commit offences (Merton 1968).

Elsewhere, communities encourage the main learning process for criminal behaviour within intimate groups and association with others. In fox-hunting, youngsters are encouraged to hunt by their parents or other adult hunt members and at the conclusion of a successful hunt may be 'blooded' (smeared with the blood of the fox) as a sign of acceptance into the fox-hunting fraternity. This, in part, ensures that the traditional sport of fox-hunting will continue as new enthusiasts are taught the ways of the sport from a relatively early age. Many rural communities have strong traditions of hunting or fieldsports (see Chapter 5) which persist despite legislative attempts to control such practices, and within indigenous communities traditional hunting and animal harvesting practices survive legislative efforts (John et al. 1985), although exemptions contained within legislation sometimes allow traditional subsistence hunting to continue (see Chapter 6 for a further discussion).

Some offences are also crimes of masculinities involving cruelty to, or power over, animals, in some cases linked to sporting or 'hobby' pursuits, perceptions by the offender of their actions being part of their culture where toughness, masculinity and smartness (Wilson 1985) combine with a love of excitement. In the case of badger-baiting, badger-digging, hare coursing, dog-fighting and cock-fighting, for example, gambling and association with other like-minded males are factors and provide a strong incentive for new members to join already established networks of offenders.

The following section explores the type of criminality inherent in animal harm in more detail before developing new models of animal offenders, taking into account the specific characteristics of both animal abusers and wildlife offenders.

Identifying the Animal Offender

Past academic debate on crime has generally accepted that crime and criminality are predominantly male concerns (e.g. Groombridge 1996). This perhaps reflects the role of gender and predominance of male offenders in serious and violent crime and concerns over youth crime; in particular both the propensity towards violence of young males and the extent to which young males might become victims of crime (Norland et al. 1981, Campbell 1993, Flood-Page and Mackie 1998, Harland et al. 2005).

Considerations of why men commit the majority of crime, and certainly more crime than women, have taken into account biological explanations of crime and whether there are physiological reasons for men committing crime (Lombroso and Ferrero 1895, Worrall 2001). They have also considered whether the socialization of young men and the extent to which routes to manhood leave young men confused or anxious about what it means to be a man and whether this influences young males' criminality (Harland et al. 2005, Kimmell et al. 2005). Restrictive notions of masculinity dictate that many men are forced into roles as defenders and protectors of their communities (Harland et al. 2005) and are also encouraged to comply with the image of the 'fearless male' (Goodey 1997) and achieve the ideal of hegemonic masculinity (Connell 1995, Harland et al. 2005). Men are encouraged to reject any behaviour construed as being feminine or un-masculine or which does not conform to traditional masculine stereotypes and engage in behaviour (such as the 'policing' of other men) which reinforces hegemonic masculinity (Beattie cited in Harland et al. 2005).

Animal abuse is significantly influenced by masculinities, often involving the exercise of male power (frequently patriarchal) over other less powerful members of a family or community. The cruelty inflicted on animals, whether physical or psychological, illustrates stereotypical male behaviour such as the exercise of control through physical force, intimidation and coercion employed in other areas such as domestic abuse, spousal control or the disciplining of children (Browne 1993, Arkow 1996). Many wildlife crimes also involve appropriate male behaviours such as aggression, thrill-seeking or having an adventurous nature. Recklessness, thrill-seeking and assertiveness are conducive to committing wildlife crime in sometimes difficult and dangerous outdoor conditions, with a requirement to negotiate wildlife (e.g. dangerous species and adult wildlife protecting its young) and the attentions of law enforcement and NGOs. In addition, the outlet for aggression allowed by such crimes as badger-baiting and badger-digging, and hare coursing, and the opportunities for gambling related to these offences (and others such as cock-fighting) are likely to appeal to young men seeking to establish their identity and assert their masculinity and power over others. Such crimes by their very nature provide opportunities for men to engage in and observe violence, and to train animals (fighting cocks, dogs) that represent an extension of themselves and reinforce elements of male pride, strength, endurance and the ability to endure pain.

Wildlife offenders are predominantly male and occupy many of the predator control jobs in the game-rearing industry in the UK in which significant illegal killing of wildlife takes place. Men also dominate the farming, ranching and commercial fieldsports industries. Huntsman Julian Barnfield in his submission to the UK's Burns Inquiry on Hunting with Dogs observed that his job came with a 'tied' rent-free house without which his family could not live in the countryside (Burns et al. 2000). Gamekeepers and huntsmen are thus placed firmly in the male provider role and lack of success in predator control, and by inference a failure to perform adequately in the job, potentially leads to loss of the family home and the resultant feelings of inadequacy and damage to male pride and self-esteem. While masculinities may not be the cause of all animal harm, it is certainly a factor to be taken into account in some wildlife crimes and some companion animal abuse. Green criminologists and sociologists in the United States have established a discourse concerning the links between animal abuse and violence towards humans which informs analysis of wildlife offending. Conboy-Hill (2000) defines animal abuse as 'the deliberate or neglectful harm of animals and can include beating, starvation, slashing with knives, sodomy, setting on fire, decapitation, skinning alive amongst other actions' (Conboy-Hill 2000: 1). There are some similarities between this definition and the scope of animal harm considered by this book and, in particular, the prohibited methods of killing animals contained in US state anti-cruelty statutes and the UK's *Wild Mammals (Protection) Act 1996*. Ascione's (1993) definition of animal abuse and cruelty as being 'socially unacceptable behavior that intentionally causes unnecessary pain, suffering, or distress to and/ or death of an animal' (Ascione 1993: 228) incorporates the stabbing, burning and crushing offences contained within the *Wild Mammals (Protection) Act 1996* and the poisoning, trapping and shooting offences involving wild animals contained within the *Wildlife and Countryside Act 1981*. While the objective of much US research is to identify the relationship between histories of animal abuse and later violent offending, its consideration of the behaviour of offenders, their motivations and how they see themselves (mostly from self-reports of animal cruelty offences) is of relevance to UK wildlife offending. The increasing evidence of US research is that childhood abuse of animals is linked to later interpersonal violence (Felthous and Kellert 1987, Ascione 1993) and while not all wildlife crime involves violence or violent abuse, where it does occur it indicates that offenders may develop a tendency towards violence that manifests itself first in animal abuse but which could escalate into adult human violence. While not all individuals will necessarily go on to harm animals or become involved in the more violent types of wildlife crime (hare coursing, poisoning, badger-baiting, etc.), Beetz (2009) suggests that abuse which affects empathy may be a primary factor in determining what type of offender an individual becomes. In particular, close relationships with animals are thought to enhance empathy while violent attitudes towards animals can indicate a lack of empathy (Beetz 2009, Brantley 2009).

The evidence of animal abuse as indicator of violent inclinations specifically applies to wildlife crime (Flynn 2009, Nurse 2009, 2011). In particular, offenders engaged in thrill-seeking or 'sport' activities that involve the exploitation of wild animals are frequently motivated by the power that they gain over animals and justify their activities by denial of pain. Fox-hunting, fishing, deer-hunting or hare-coursing enthusiasts commonly argue that their quarry does not anticipate death and enjoys the chase (see, for example Burns et al. 2000, evidence submitted by the Morpeth and Curre Hunts). In addition, a belief in the widespread support for the activity, and a questioning of the legitimacy of those who wished to see it outlawed (Sykes and Matza 1957) persists among many of those who wish to continue to hunt with dogs. As just one example, the Ashford Hunt in its submission commented 'to criminalise an activity – such as foxhunting – in response to a campaign which itself is largely criminal sets a precedent which threatens all law abiding citizens whether they love foxhunting or loathe it' (Burns et al. 2000). The argument that the campaign against hunting was 'largely criminal' goes to the actions of Hunt Saboteurs and organizations like the Animal Liberation Front

(ALF), while at the same time ignoring the political legitimacy of organizations like LACS, Animal Aid and WWF. These and other NGOs (e.g. RSPB, RSPCA) are accepted within mainstream policy circles to such an extent that they are able to act as government and police advisors and their policy advice is actively sought. Yet by ignoring the actions of these socially acceptable NGOs and concentrating on those perceived as illegitimate or radical, the legitimacy of the campaign can be challenged (see Chapter 5 for a further discussion of resistance to NGO policy and legislative reform in animal harm).

As a causation of animal harm, the denial of injury is an important factor indicating not only that individuals do not see any harm in their activity but also confirming the view of animals as a commodity rather than as sentient beings suffering as a result of the individual's actions. Wise (2000) argues that the concept of inequality between humans and non-humans is central not just to the legal status of animals but also to how humans treat animals. The perception that certain animals do not feel pain allows offenders to commit their offences without considering the impact of their actions or feeling any guilt over them. In mainstream criminology, there is evidence that burglars and other offenders, when confronted by their victims in restorative justice conferencing, often express surprise that their victims have strong feelings about the crime and the actions of the offender (Shapland et al. 2007, Sherman and Strang 2007). As such, they do not readily see themselves either as criminals or causing harm by their criminality. Where a victim is unable to articulate their distress such feelings may be further legitimized by an offender.

Attitudes towards regulation are also an important factor in identifying the nature of animal harm, especially in wildlife offending. Eliason's (2003) assessment of poachers in Kentucky (which defined poaching as the illegal taking of wildlife resources and thus defined it as a wildlife crime rather than a game management offence) concluded that convicted poachers routinely employed neutralization techniques. These techniques included: denial of responsibility, claim of entitlement, denial of the necessity of the law, defence of necessity and recreation and excitement (Sykes and Matza 1957), both before and after engaging in illegal activity. Significant numbers of those interviewed by Eliason were aware that they were contravening regulations but considered that their breaches were minor or technical infringements that should not be subject to law enforcement attention. They often also denied the right of law enforcement officers to take action against them or contended that there were better uses of officers' time, i.e. enforcement action directed towards 'real' criminals.

The involvement of environmental and animal welfare NGOs without which offenders might not be apprehended provides an additional motivation for some individuals to commit animal harm. Different offenders may use different neutralizations and may also be subject to different motivations. By considering the different motivations and behaviours of offenders it is possible to determine if there are distinct types of animal offender, as follows.

Developing Offender Models

Ascione (2001) acknowledges the difficulties of classifying animal abuse, commenting that many attempts have been made to produce a typology of offenders and offending. A range of evidence informed the development of this book's new offender models relevant to animal harm over a number of years. Detailed interviews with UK and (selected) US NGOs and practitioners between 2001 and 2009 revealed specific problems experienced in investigating wildlife crime cases and clarified the reasons why NGOs and practitioners believe offenders commit wildlife crime within the context of their specialized view of wildlife offending (Denzin 2001). This research is referred to during this chapter. From the initial stages of the author's research, a provisional outline of wildlife crime offender characteristics developed which was subsequently refined following discussions with NGOs and practitioners. Further analysis of casework, policy documents, media reporting of various aspects of animal harm and secondary sources on animal abuse including the justifications given by offenders for their behaviour (via court transcripts, published interviews and research responses) also revealed much about determining factors in animal harm. As a result the initial outline typology of offenders was revised in 2011 and extended to incorporate the wider notion of animal harm explored by this book.

The analysis indicates that animal offenders broadly commit their crimes for the following *general* reasons:

1. profit (broadly construed) or commercial gain;
2. thrill or sport;
3. necessity of obtaining food;
4. antipathy towards governmental and law enforcement bodies;
5. tradition and cultural reasons.

While these are the primary motivations, ignorance of the law is also sometimes a factor, although not strictly a motivating factor, but more a justification or neutralization technique (Sykes and Matza 1957). Roberts et al. (2001: 27) surveyed 87 UK organizations about their perceptions to identify what NGOs considered to be the motivation for wildlife crime. Both this chapter's analysis and Roberts et al.'s research (2001) indicate that when asked NGOs accept that there may be different factors involved in motivating individuals to commit animal harm, even though this is not always reflected in their published policies which generally demonize all animal offenders as deviant or motivated by profit.

This chapter's analysis concludes that animal offenders (i.e. those committing animal harm as defined in this book) fall into five (relatively) distinct types, defined by their primary motivator. As a result, a new classification of offenders is developed by this chapter as follows:

a. **Traditional Criminals** – who derive direct (and sometimes personal financial) benefit from their crimes.
b. **Economic Criminals** – who commit wildlife crimes as a direct result of particular economic pressures (e.g. direct employer-pressure or profit-driven crime within their chosen profession). This category is distinguished from the previous category because of the specific, mostly legitimate, employment-related nature of their motivation to commit crime.
c. **Masculinities Criminals** – who commit offences involving harm to animals, exercising a stereotypical masculine nature both in terms of the exercise of power over animals and the links to sport and gambling. There is some link between these offences and low level organized crime.
d. **Hobby Criminals** – who commit those high status,[2] low level crimes for which there is no direct benefit or underlying criminal 'need' and for which the criminal justice reaction is disproportionate. These are distinguished from the previous category by the absence of harm/cruelty as a factor in the offences. The 'hobby' element is the primary motivator.
e. **Stress Offenders** – who commit offences involving animals as a direct consequence of their own victimization, often as a result of the exercise of force or masculine power upon them and their need to find a release for the stress this causes or as a result of being forced to commit animal harm by others. There is a direct link between these offences and the abuse of the offender whether physical or psychological.

Model A – The Traditional Criminal

Model A are traditional criminals whose crimes are committed to obtain direct personal financial benefit; the animal involved is simply a commodity through which this primary motivator may be achieved and might conceivably be substituted for any other type of activity such as car theft or burglary which provides similar benefit. Lea and Young argue that crime is antisocial not 'because of lack of conventional values but precisely because of it' given that the values of most 'working-class criminals' are conventional and involve individualism, competition and desire for material goods (Lea and Young 1993: 96).

Offenders that fit within Model A include: those who take wild bird chicks for breeding and subsequent sale as birds for falconry; those who deal in illegally killed wild birds or animals; and wildlife traffickers (rare or endangered species). This type of crime reflects the fact that some offenders' motivation reflects the absence of more acceptable means of wealth acquisition. Its offenders are involved in illegal activities not as any indirect consequence of (otherwise law-abiding) employment but who engage in particular activities as a direct means of achieving personal gain. Model A thus represents a rational choice offender, most likely

---

2 'High Status' in terms of the importance attached by enforcement bodies and the public to these crimes.

unaware of the full extent of the relevant animal legislation (except in some cases such as wildlife trafficking), but aware that their actions are unlawful in some way.

Rationalization and determination Opportunity (Clarke 1992) and an easy source of direct financial gain is one of the causes of Model A crime. Wildlife crime, for example, presents a low-risk, high-return option for the offender, with the potential to make thousands of pounds in a single transaction while the risks of detection, apprehension and punishment are slight in comparison to other offences. The relatively low stigma attached to some animal crimes (i.e. not widely categorized as 'serious' crime) allows offenders to rationalize their offending behaviour as harmless, technical or victimless offences. Traditional animal offenders also rationalize their crimes by viewing animals (and particularly wildlife which is not subject to property rights) as a resource which if they did not use somebody else would. They see their offences as, at best, minor crimes or crimes of a technical nature and are likely to be aware that enforcement of wildlife legislation is carried out predominantly by the voluntary sector and that penalties for animal crime are comparatively small.

Except in designated conservation areas or where threats have already been detected, wildlife resources are not closely monitored by the criminal justice agencies. Nor are they the subject of intensive crime prevention or target hardening initiatives in the way that other objects of criminal activity have been. Car thieves, for example, must negotiate alarms, immobilizers, theft registers and the likelihood that the owner will immediately inform police and insurance companies of the theft. In addition, industry-led target hardening and detection features are now a design necessity thus car theft carries with it dual risks of detection in the act of taking the car and in its subsequent sale or disposal. By contrast, the nests of wild birds are not routinely monitored (and only certain birds are required to be registered with the DEFRA under current UK legislation). With the exception of those rare species whose nests are monitored by NGOs or statutory conservation or enforcement authorities (such as the California condor), thefts of wild birds are not likely to be noticed immediately or directly notified to the police, unless observed by a member of the public or nest warden. The police response to such thefts and any subsequent sale of a wild bird is likely to be minimal providing a soft option for the offender wishing to make a quick and easy profit. The last dedicated survey of prices in the UK (Robinson 1991) indicated that birds of prey can sell for between several hundred and several thousands of pounds and the rarer the bird the greater the potential profit (Fox 2002) especially in the rare and exotic animal market (Green 1999).

Although the link between wildlife crime and organized crime is one that is discussed in more detail below, with particular emphasis on criminal gangs, there is also evidence of criminal gangs diversifying into wildlife crime using the same routes employed for trading in heroin and cannabis (e.g. Scottish Institute for Policing Research 2007, House of Commons Environmental Audit Committee

2008, Interpol 2010). A UK police representative interviewed for the author's wildlife crime research confirmed that:

> An organized criminal group will deal with anything that will make a profit and there [are] profits to be made from the trade in rare and endangered wildlife ...

> One particular area of interest is to determine where an organized gang might have established routes for the trade in various commodities. Where this is the case, it is possible for a gang to switch from one item, such as drugs, to another like wildlife. While the commodity may change the criminal activity doesn't. (Nurse 2011: 41)

Lea and Young (1993) cite crime as being likely in any community where community controls are insufficient to inhibit the behaviour of citizens. Although their focus was street crimes such as vandalism, the argument readily applies to 'traditional' animal harm where the lack of community is a factor. While it is not suggested that society considers animal harm to be acceptable, it is certainly true that an individual involved in the low level forms of animal harm typically committed by the traditional criminal will not be classified by society as a dangerous or serious criminal, although there are some groups vocal about the subject of animal harm such as NGOs and animal rights organizations who contend that they should be viewed as such. The exception is organized crime's involvement in illegal wildlife trafficking which is now widely accepted to be serious crime by enforcement agencies and governments (Interpol 2010).

The public policy response   Traditional animal harm criminals are treated much the same way as other criminals that fit within the classical model. The public policy response treats the offender as being a rational actor who chooses his course of action. The offender is considered to be sufficiently aware of the criminal nature of his actions that a deterrent approach might be effective. By raising the offender's level of awareness of the likely punishment, NGOs and criminal justice agencies hope to effect behavioural change. Publicity for convictions and the likely level of punishment is, therefore, an important part of the public policy response. In addition, as offenders are considered to be persistent offenders motivated entirely by profit and personal gain, moves towards a more punitive sentencing regime are advocated for the traditional animal offender.

Model B – The Economic Criminal

'Economic criminals' are primarily motivated by a range of economic and social pressures but the primary object is not (personal) financial benefit. This category includes those who commit animal harm during the course of their employment, as a result of direct and indirect pressure from their employers and others involved with their employment and livelihood. Examples include gamekeepers and others involved in (mostly legitimate) countryside sports, game-rearing or commercial fisheries, driven to their offending behaviour through employer interaction. This category also includes offences committed by a company or business in the conduct of an otherwise lawful business, often for commercial reasons, thus Model B is distinguished from Model A by the otherwise lawful operation of the Model B offender.

In Model B the offender's motivation comes in part from external pressures (e.g. an employer or a perception of market pressures) and in part from association with others within his sphere of employment or social circle who have also committed offences (Sutherland 1973). In the case of those involved in game-rearing, farming or ranching, for example, evidence from investigations suggests that gamekeepers are encouraged to kill otherwise protected birds, animals and mammals by employers. The objective is to ensure that large numbers of game are available for clients and retain the economic viability of the business. A well-stocked estate is essential to ensure successful shooting days and repeat customers and through internal, peer and employer pressure, gamekeepers are encouraged not to discriminate between those predators that are legal target species such as foxes (that can legally be shot) and birds of prey (protected at all times in the UK). Gamekeepers may otherwise be law-abiding individuals and will frequently co-operate with the police over other crimes such as poaching. Timber treatment staff and building and roofing contractors also feature amongst the offenders because the cost of conducting the necessary surveys to ensure that their construction work will not harm any animals present is not justified by the relatively low risk of apprehension, prosecution and conviction should they commit animal harm. The offender is most likely aware that his actions amount to offences under wildlife legislation but because of multiple pressures continues to commit offences. UK-based NGO the Bat Conservation Trust, for example, commented during the author's wildlife crime research that builders meant to survey for bats 'will get a survey done and will just try to wriggle out of it. They think "what's the fine going to be and what's the cost to me?" Often they will, just go ahead and do the work and take a chance anyway'.

The rationalizations used by offenders differ from those of the traditional criminal. Offenders argue that they are encouraged to commit the crimes for sound economic reasons. Moreover, they also argue that they should be allowed to control a wider range of animals than that permitted by current legislation in the interests of their business, denying the wisdom of the legislation under which they must operate. Efforts in the United States to remove legal protection from animals such as wolves, bears or bison that are considered to be competitors for food or a threat to livestock reflect this.

These offenders can be likened to white-collar criminals where 'successful business or professional people are apparently caught out in serious offences, quite often for behaviour which they did not expect to be treated as criminal, and for which it is quite difficult to secure a conviction' (Nelken 1994: 355). Nelken suggests that white-collar criminals are responsible people and that the crimes that they commit raise questions that are not posed by other types of criminal behaviour. Questions arise such as why do they do it when they have so much to lose; how likely are they to be caught; and what is the true level of crime in their area? These questions apply equally to Model B wildlife crimes, for example gamekeepers on grouse moors, who are employed to carry out lawful pest control, and who, in theory at least, stand to lose their jobs and homes if convicted (see below).

Such 'white-collar' wildlife offenders as gamekeepers, ranchers and fishermen act unlawfully in killing predators to protect game birds, livestock and fish stocks but continue to co-operate with the police over such incidents as poaching.

Rationalization and determination   Economic animal harm is directly related to outside pressures and lack of controls on offenders' activities. Crime is likely in any situation where an individual is encouraged to commit a crime for fear of losing his employment if he does not do so, providing a powerful motive for some animal harm and in particular wildlife crimes. The pressure to kill protected wildlife can either be direct or indirect; an employer directly informing the gamekeeper that birds of prey and other predators are to be controlled, or simply turning a blind eye to the activities of a gamekeeper who is regularly producing high levels of game for the estate. Evidence from case files also identifies that some new gamekeepers learn illegal techniques of predator control from other more senior staff. Recognition of the role of the employer in encouraging offences was reflected in the RSPB's 1991 attempt to introduce an amendment into the UK's *Wildlife and Countryside Act 1981* to make it an offence for any person to '*cause or permit*' another person to commit an offence. This was intended to reduce landowner pressure on staff to commit crime and create landowner liability (now partially implemented in the Scottish offence of 'vicarious liability' for wildlife crime).

In the case of companies, Situ and Emmons commented that: 'performance pressure, the estimated certainty and severity of punishment, and the crime facilitative culture at the level of the individual firm contribute to the probability of criminal participation' (2000: 60). Figures supplied by the Bat Conservation Trust (Childs 2003) reveal that in the UK, the majority of those convicted of bat-related offences were companies involved in otherwise lawful activities, pursuing unlawful means to achieve a legitimate business goal (i.e. profit) where strict adherence to bat conservation/protection legislation would impact negatively on the company's activities.

Economic offenders rationalize their unlawful activities as being the responsibility of others, including the employer who exerts pressure on them. Offenders thus deny culpability for their actions, argue that committing offences is a necessity of earning a living and providing for their family, that their crimes are victimless and of a technical or minor nature, and that the resources of the criminal justice agencies should be targeted towards 'real' and serious criminals.

In part these rationalizations are a defence mechanism against the perception (and campaigning) by NGOs that animal crime is serious crime justifying mainstream criminal justice agency attention, and demonstrate Sykes and Matza's (1957) neutralizations at work. That responsibility for animal law enforcement is largely outside the remit of mainstream criminal justice and is frequently the responsibility of NGOs provides justification for offenders to take chances in committing animal crime. Offenders are aware that the likelihood of getting caught and the likely fines if convicted potentially work in their favour. Generally it is not fear of punishment that deters offenders, but fear of apprehension (Siegal 2002, Carrabine et al. 2009) and, in the case of economic offenders, awareness of the likely punishment and small size of fines is a significant factor, as commercial interests frequently means that the potential punishment is obviated by the significant returns that can be achieved by ignoring, rather than complying with, wildlife laws. Commercial expediency thus provides a rationalization for the offences as to fully comply with the legislation costs money, delays projects and puts the company's profits at risk, while leaving the company at risk of competition from a company with a more 'flexible' attitude to wildlife legislation.

The public policy response   The public policy response to economic criminals is variable. Publicly, game-rearing estates in the UK have said that any gamekeeper convicted of a wildlife offence would be dismissed. NGOs however argue that this is not the case and that an offender can continue to commit offences without fear of any further sanctions being applied after conviction.

In some respects offences are detected and prosecuted primarily as a result of the efforts of the NGOs, according to the law enforcement detection and apprehension model, rather than as a result of any concerted effort by any statutory criminal justice agencies. For example Damania et al. (2008) identified that the enforcement regime is subject to a weak enforcement regime lacking in resources. In much wildlife protection where animals are targeted by smugglers NGOs are a vital component of enforcement action and without their efforts little could be achieved.

Model C – The Masculinities Criminal

Model C involves those offenders primarily motivated by power and notions of masculinity; such offences are seldom committed by lone individuals. In some of these crimes, the main motivation is the exercise of power allied to sport or entertainment; a link might also be made with organized crime and gambling. Such crimes, classed as crimes of masculinities, also include elements of cruelty or animal abuse of the kind, which is attracting the attention of law enforcement agencies in the United States (Clawson 2009). Examples include badger-digging, badger-baiting, cock-fighting and dog-fighting as well as some crimes that involve the 'sporting' killing or taking of wildlife. These activities should be distinguished from legitimate predator control activity permitted by national law; or the killing of animals to prevent the spread of disease, e.g. the badger culls that take place in the UK intended to prevent the spread of bovine tuberculosis. Evidence from the respective animal protection societies in Australia, the UK and the United States, and other monitoring or investigatory bodies like the ALDF and LACS, suggests that in these crimes, the offender is likely to derive some pleasure from his offence and this is a primary motivator, and there is a link between some of these crimes and other crimes of masculinities.

Rationalization and determination   Badger-baiting, cock-fighting, dog-fighting and hare coursing[3] are considered by some to be sports, although the inevitability of injury to the animals is significant. Anti-fieldsports NGOs conclude that it attracts a particular type of offender attracted by the harm to animals, the excitement and enthusiasm of causing such harm and engagement in the illegal activity (League Against Cruel Sports 1997: 20).

American research on animal-oriented crimes of the masculine, including cock-fighting and cock-fighting gangs, explains that: 'cockfighting can be said to have a mythos centered on the purported behaviour and character of the gamecock itself. Cocks are seen as emblems of bravery and resistance in the face of insurmountable odds' (Hawley 1993: 2). The fighting involved is 'an affirmation of masculine identity in an increasingly complex and diverse era' (1993: 1) and the fighting spirit of the birds has great symbolic significance to participants as does the ability of fighting and hunting dogs to take punishment in UK animal harm.

Masculine stereotypes can be reinforced and developed through offending behaviour (Goodey 1997) and are important factors in addressing offending behaviour which may sometimes be overlooked (Groombridge 1998). Animal offenders are predominantly male across most jurisdictions (exclusively so in the case of UK wildlife crime) and in the case of the more violent forms of animal offender exhibit distinctly masculine characteristics. The literature in the UK and public policy response is some way behind that of the United States in identifying a group of mostly young males involved in crimes of violence (albeit towards animals) that could turn to more serious forms of crime or expand their violent activities beyond animals and towards humans (Ascione 1993, Flynn 2002, Clawson 2009). Hare coursing, cock-fighting and badger-digging all involve gambling, with wagers being placed on individual animals, the outcome of a fight and other factors (including the power or strength of an animal). For some, the associated gambling is as important as the exercise of power, and significant sums are waged on fights, attracting the attention of organized crime.

Evidence from the RSPCA (2006, 2007) suggests that badger-digging is a group activity and case report evidence also confirms that group relationships replicate informal criminal networks. Maguire described some loose criminal networks as

---

3   It should be noted that hare coursing is claimed to be legal in some US states and was only recently banned in the UK with the passing of the *Protection of Wild Mammals (Scotland) Act 2002* and the *Hunting Act 2004*.

being like an 'old boy network' of ex-public school pupils, individuals would be able to call upon others for collaboration, help or services when they needed them, and would be able to verify their 'bona fides' to those they did not know' (Maguire 2000: 131). There is also a 'secret society' element to these wildlife crimes and here the community can actually encourage crime. The male-bonding element identified by Hawley is significant, as is the banding together of men from the margins of society and for whom issues of belonging, male pride and achievement are important. In discussing cock-fighting in the United States, Hawley (1993) explains that 'young men are taken under the wing of an older male relative or father, and taught all aspects of chicken care and lore pertaining to the sport. Females are generally not significant players in this macho milieu' although special events for women, such as 'powder puff' derbies, are sometimes arranged (Hawley 1993: 5). Forsyth and Evans (1998) reached similar findings in researching dog-fighting in the United States, concluding that an appeal to higher loyalties and an attachment to smaller groups took precedence over attachment to society for the dogmen, with dog-fighting having great cultural significance and wider social importance for the dogmen and other masculinities offenders. Perceptions by the offender of their actions being part of their culture where toughness, masculinity and smartness (Wilson 1985) combine with a love of excitement are significant factors in their offending. Offences are seldom committed by lone individuals and, in the case of badger-baiting, badger-digging, dog-fighting and hare coursing, for example, gambling and association with other like-minded males are factors and provide a strong incentive for new members to join already established networks of offenders (Hawley 1993, Forsyth and Evans 1998). In an interview for the author's wildlife crime research one NGO representative stated: 'I can't see a criminal society allowing Joe Soap the commoner and his mates to be having badger baiting and betting on them, without wanting a cut ... Badger crime is all about money ... I think money, tradition, the figure in the flat cap and with the whippet and the terriers is still around.' There is thus some link between these offences and low level organized crime.

Offenders involved in these types of crime often rationalize based on historical precedent or tradition. Hawley (1993) observed that cock-fighters often resort to argument 'based on pseudo-psychological notions: the birds feel no pain' and employ sophisticated arguments in denial of the pain caused. The perception of their activities as being victimless (Sykes and Matza 1957) is ingrained in their activities, sometimes viewing the fighting nature of birds as 'natural', thus any wrongdoing is both internalized and minimized. They are also especially aggressive towards NGOs like PETA and other advocacy groups whom they demonize as 'effete intellectuals and kooks' who lack understanding of their activity (Hawley 1993: 5).

Similar arguments occur in the UK concerning hunting with dogs and fishing. The conflicting arguments of the pro-ban and pro-hunt lobbies have been characterized as 'town versus country'. Resistance to legislation which bans hunting with dogs employed arguments that emphasize the traditional nature of hunting and dismissed legislation to ban hunting with dogs as Whitehall interference in the countryside. Hunting supporters also deny that hunted animals feel pain and stress hunting as necessary and effective predator control. Even after the introduction of the *Hunting Act 2004* its proponents continue to challenge its legitimacy. In *R (Countryside Alliance and Others) v. Attorney-General and Another, Regina (Derwin and Others) v. Same*, 2007, the *Hunting Act 2004* was challenged on the grounds that it was incompatible with the European Convention on Human Rights. *Jackson v. Attorney General [2005] UKHL 56* represented an unsuccessful attempt to challenge the *Hunting Act 2004*'s (legal) validity on constitutional grounds. The arguments pursued by hunt supporters are similar to those employed by cock-fighters, badger-baiters and badger-diggers. While this is not to suggest that the activities are the same in any legal sense, the rationalizations given are those of denial, unwarranted intervention by legislators and a lack of understanding on the part of those that seek to ban the activity.

The public policy response   The public policy response to masculinities crimes reflects acceptance of the propensity towards violence of offenders and is similar to that employed for organized crime. Techniques employed by enforcers include infiltration of gangs, surveillance activities and undercover operations. Masculinities offenders are considered to be more dangerous than other animal offenders (with the possible exception of wildlife crime's organized gangs) and are treated accordingly.

Model D – The 'Hobby' Criminal

Offenders who are involved in technical offences for which they often deny the criminal characterization constitute the 'Hobby' criminal category. These offences attract a disproportionately high level of attention from the criminal justice agencies and NGOs, given their relatively low threat level. Model D offenders include the egg collector who gains little direct benefit from his offence and for whom the criminal nature of his offence is denied. (Although it should perhaps be noted that egg collecting seems to be a predominantly English problem.) It also includes large-scale taxidermy collectors who do not operate mainly as traders or dealers.

Model D offenders do not commit their offence as part of a business or occupation. Instead the activities can be more readily likened to a hobby or obsession; the collection or *acquisition* of items is a primary motivator. Egg collectors, for example, are rarely committed by countryside employees but instead are employed (or unemployed) elsewhere and specifically travel to the countryside to commit offences. This element of *mens rea* accounts for the seriousness with which these offences are considered by NGOs, criminal justice agencies and the public.

Hobby criminals' obsessive pursuit of their hobby can cost them thousands of pounds annually. UK-based egg collectors have been known to travel all over the world in pursuit of eggs and some individuals involved in (illegal) taxidermy have also been found in possession of species from all over the world. There are similarities with other offenders who obsessively collect banned or expensive items such as rare books, pornography and stolen paintings (Burke 2001, Taylor and Quayle 2003) and the desire not just to obtain items but also to catalogue and categorize them is a significant behavioural factor. Examination of case records and prosecution evidence indicates that egg collectors are exclusively male as no records could be found of any female egg collectors in the UK.[4] Hobby criminals would seem to be an example of specific male activity and while issues of masculinities should be considered in examining hobby crimes these crimes are not of the distinctly masculine type identified in Model C, having other primary causes.

Rationalization and determination   Hobby animal harm defies comprehensive explanation as generally no financial gain is derived from the activity. However analysis (RSPB 1999 and Wainwright 2006) identifies some explanation of the behaviour as follows:

> [Egg collecting] is purely an obsessive and selfish activity resulting in nothing more than displaying the egg in a purpose built cabinet to gaze at until the start of the next breeding season, when additions to the collection can be made. (RSPB 1999: 20)

Egg collecting has been likened to a form of kleptomania or obsessive-compulsive disorder; offenders cannot help but commit the offence as they are driven to commit their crimes and the adventure involved in doing so. Rather like a collector of stolen paintings, some of whom pay large sums of money for stolen works, egg collectors may in part be driven by the acquisition of an item that cannot be obtained legitimately. Some stolen works of art, many of which are recognizable, cannot be traded on the open market but are acquired for private collectors to appreciate. Burke (2001) suggested that the trade in ancient manuscripts and historic books in the UK was worth millions of pounds with criminal gangs turning to trafficking for private collectors and with thefts of works by Copernicus and Ptolemy being commissioned by private collectors. Although there is evidence of some stolen works being traded (Burke 2001) the drive to obtain items for personal use and which cannot be publicly exhibited is a primary factor of the obsessive collector. Taylor and Quayle explain that 'the emotional intensity that is part of collecting behaviour' (2003: 48) is a significant factor, with the collector interacting with others who share his interests and often being driven to have a bigger, better and more comprehensive collection than others. The competitive drive and the obsessive need to acquire items can turn a hobby interest in certain

---

4   Analysis of RSPB statistics, annual reports, case reports and newspaper reports on egg-collecting cases.

items into a passionate desire to collect (Belk 1995, Taylor and Quayle 2003). The obsessive nature of such offences is confirmed by offenders themselves as egg collector Derek Lee explained to the *Guardian*:

> There are quite a few who are obsessed with it. Every single spring and summer they can't wait to get out. If you put a child in a chocolate factory their eyes light up with excitement. It's like that. When spring and summer come, the eggers are on edge. They're like big kids. (Barkham 2006)

The obsessive-compulsive nature of hobby animal harm includes collectors keeping meticulous notes of their activities which are then used by investigators as evidence of criminality (Barkham 2006, Wood 2008). Evidence exists that egg collectors and other 'hobby' offenders exist within specific communities of kindred obsessives. Analysis of court cases documents for example, demonstrates that there are specific 'clusters' of egg collectors in certain parts of the UK, mostly working-class parts of England. Egg collecting is learned from others within the community with established collectors passing on their knowledge and techniques. Spouses and others within the community may, however, disprove of the activity and contact enforcement bodies to provide evidence of offending (Nurse 2011).

The 'hobby' animal offender uses techniques of avoidance, denial of criminality, displacement of blame and challenges to the legitimacy of enforcers to explain away their actions. Much like those who are caught speeding by traffic enforcement cameras challenge the cameras' legitimacy, the fines imposed or argue that cameras are simply a revenue-raising device (Fylan et al. 2006), hobby animal offenders dispute that their activities fall within the remit of the criminal law. The fact that animal legislation falls outside mainstream criminal justice allows offenders to classify their activities as minor or victimless crime that should not be the target of law enforcement activity (Wood 2008). Denial of criminality and avoidance of responsibility is an integral part of the offender's rationalization. Egg collecting was once a schoolboy hobby in Britain given scientific legitimacy as *oology*, and it is only with the introduction of the *Countryside and Rights of Way Act 2000* that offences have carried a limited option for prison sentences although the taking of wild birds' eggs has been unlawful since the 1950s under the *Protection of Birds Act 1954* (and subsequent legislation).

Evidence (Nurse 2011) shows that egg collectors use the following rationalizations to explain their activities:

1. it is not harming anybody, the eggs are not fertile so why shouldn't they be collected;
2. everybody did it when I was a boy it's ridiculous that it's considered to be criminal;
3. the NGO needs to make the problem appear to be serious to keep raising money;
4. it's not a job for the police they should be out catching real criminals;

5. we're not criminals, we're bird enthusiasts.

The techniques of denial, avoidance and attacks on the legitimacy of the enforcement agency (in the UK this means the RSPB in the US the (state) Department of Fish and Game or US Fish and Wildlife Service) are all present. In addition, claims for the legitimacy of *oology* as valuable scientific study have been made (by for example the Jourdain Society), highlighting the fact that the study of eggs and eggshell thinning in the 1950s highlighted the harm being caused to wildlife by pesticides such as DDT.

The public policy response   Hobby animal offences attract a punitive response that is arguably excessive in comparison to the nature of the offences. In the UK there have been a number of joint police/NGO operations into egg collecting and high profile convictions for egg collecting where large fines have been imposed. Similar raids have taken place in other jurisdictions for animal collectors who have compulsively amassed large private collections. Crime prevention techniques have been employed in some areas and the nests of rare birds like the osprey and golden eagle routinely watched by volunteer wardens during the breeding season. Osprey nests in Scotland, and red kite nests in Wales, have been watched by the army in the past as part of training exercises and to gain publicity for wildlife crimes; the Guild of Taxidermists also argues that the police response on technical offences involving taxidermy has been excessive, sometimes using a disproportionate number of officers to execute search warrants (Nurse 2011).

Despite all this attention it should be noted that for most species, egg collecting and taxidermy has no effect on the species' population. In the case of the rarer bird species, the RSPB has said that egg collecting has the potential to slow the species growth by about 1 percent per year. Egg collecting is, however, the main form of wildlife crime that the public identifies with in the UK, perhaps because of regular publicity for this type of crime and the ease with which egg collectors can be demonized. It is an activity clearly at odds with contemporary notions of species protection, environmentalism and conservation and involving offenders who often spend thousands of pounds in pursuing their 'hobby'. Similarly, taxidermy cases often involving dozens of dead birds or animals attract easy publicity. Egg-collecting cases are routinely prosecuted due to the relative ease of bringing charges for offences given the strict liability nature of egg possession under the *Wildlife and Countryside Act 1981* and both egg-collecting and taxidermy cases can easily be placed in news items as quirky and portraying peculiar attitudes towards animals.

Model E – The 'Stress' Criminal

Offenders who are involved in animal harm as a result of their own stress or abuse and for which they either deny their criminal characterization or are unaware of it due to their victim status constitute the final category.

Model E offenders do not commit their animal harm for any direct personal gain other than as a stress release mechanism. Thus the offences may represent a plea for help on the part of the offender and be 'symptomatic of more deep-seated psychological disturbance' (Ascione 2001). These offences may however attract a punitive response from criminal justice agencies and NGOs who see the offender as commencing on the path to serial offending and interpersonal violence rather than being a victim themselves. Model E offenders include the child who abuses a domestic animal in the home as a means of identifying with his or her abuser or as a means of externalizing their own abuse (see Chapter 4) as well as individuals forced to commit animal harm as a survival mechanism.

Model E offenders may however be prolific, especially where they are reacting to their own persistent abuse within the home or are continually in contact with domestic abuse and interpersonal violence that has negative impacts on their behaviour. The Model E offender's behaviour is partially characterized by a need to inflict harm on animals, primarily harm that would be classed as cruelty (and occasionally torture) and which may be of a repetitive nature. Ascione (2001) identified that children who commit pathological animal harm are likely to be older than those who inadvertently commit animal harm out of misplaced curiosity. In addition he identified that 'rather than indicating a lack of education about the humane treatment of animals, animal abuse by these children may be symptomatic of psychological disturbances of varying severity' (2001: 7). In a limited number of cases, women involved in abusive relationships with a dominant male partner or spouse may also exist in this category.

Rationalization and determination   Model E animal harm is primarily explained by how the actions of others influence the actions of the offender. For example Friedrich et al. (1992) studied a non-abused sample of 880 children aged 2–12 with '276 children in the same age range who had been sexually abused in the past 12 months' (Ascione 2001) and concluded that the children who had been sexually abused were significantly more likely to have been cruel to animals than children who had not been abused. While the results are not by themselves conclusive, other studies such as McLennan et al.'s study (1995) of seriously mentally ill 5–18-year-olds also found animal cruelty to be more common among those who had been sexually abused.

Stress offending may therefore be a consequence of abuse inflicted on the offender or their response to a toxic environment. Thus offenders cannot help but commit their offence even though they may appreciate that causing harm to another family member in the form of a companion animal is wrong. In addition, where children are the offenders, the need to escape from the confines of the family home may result in covert offending behaviour such that the adults in the home or any social care agencies that may be involved in resolving any domestic conflicts may be unaware that the child is causing the harm. Feelings of shame or guilt may also force the child to commit their offending away from the home where stray or feral animals may become targets and their deaths or torture go undetected for longer periods of time.

In some cases an abuser will force a child to sexually abuse, hurt or kill a companion animal (US Department of Health 2001) as a means through which the child can be controlled. The dual fear of exposure of the animal abuse and the constant reminder of the power that the abuser has over the child can be a potent threat to keep them under control. By making the child or partner complicit in the injury or death of the companion animal the abuser teaches submission and further isolates their victim.

The stress offender is thus likely to use techniques of avoidance, denial of criminality, displacement of blame and denial of responsibility for their actions. In some respects stress offenders have limited culpability for actions that they are forced to commit but bear some blame when the harm they cause is a choice. However denial of criminality and avoidance of responsibility is a legitimate and integral part of the offender's rationalization where the offender is powerless against a more powerful abuser and has been isolated from the necessary sources of support. Thus a stress offender may engage with the following rationalizations to explain their activities:

1. I had no choice, he [the abuser] made me do it;
2. it's only an animal it's not as if I harmed a person;
3. I just did what he [the abuser] has been doing;
4. it's not a job for the police they should be out catching real criminals;
5. rather than harassing me the police/social services should be dealing with [the person abusing me, other forms of abuse within the home or 'real' real animal abuse].

The techniques of denial, avoidance and attacks on the legitimacy of the enforcement agency are present and indicate the blamelessness of the offender. Ascione and Arkow (1999) identified that witnessing abuse towards parents or companion animals may compromise a child's psychological adjustment, increase his propensity for interpersonal violence, and make children's cruelty to animals more likely to emerge as a symptom of distress. A child may not entirely understand that this is what has happened to them and be in denial about the reality of their own abuse. Thus neutralizing their own abuse and its consequences may become a survival necessity.

The public policy response   Model E offenders attract a punitive response that does not accurately reflect the whole circumstances of their crimes. Ascione (2001) identifies the difficulty of distinguishing between animal harm committed by delinquent children and animal harm committed by children who are victims of abuse. Thus the criminal justice and policy response may simply see a child who commits animal abuse. In the context of current policy debates on animal abuse as an indicator of future criminality and interpersonal violence, such abuse may draw a criminal justice response that fails to adequately address the underlying victimization. The response is further compounded by the unreliability of adult reporting of children's animal abuse where the adults are the child's abusers. Children's denial of abuse or explanation of its causes may be contradicted by the abusing adult or the parent who is unaware of the existence of child abuse and who is unwilling to believe that their spouse could be an abuser.

Preliminary Conclusions on Dealing with Offenders

An examination of the primary motivations and offending behaviour in animal harm crime shows that rather than there being one 'rational' wildlife offender committing crime for profit there are several offender types.

While the nature of the offences may be different, there is inevitably some overlap in the behaviours of offenders, although the weight attached to various determining factors varies. Egg collectors, badger-diggers and gamekeepers are all, for example, keeping a traditional activity alive but in different ways and for different reasons. The egg collector is pursuing his 'traditional' hobby, whereas the gamekeeper is perpetuating a learned traditional behaviour in the form of a type of predator control that has been handed down from gamekeeper to gamekeeper irrespective of changes in the law. The masculinities criminal may derive some financial gain from gambling but it is not a *primary* motivating factor whereas money is for the traditional criminal. What all offender types share in common is the likely knowledge that their activities may be illegal (although there may be denial as to whether this should be the case) and that the likelihood of detection, apprehension and prosecution remains low.

Current policy generally treats all animal offenders as traditional (i.e. rational financially motivated) criminals. In effect the public policy response for the traditional criminal is employed for all offenders, despite the different motivations and rationalizations shown by other groups. However, the different primary motivating factors indicate that different elements drive offenders and so there is little point in treating all offenders as if they were the same. One conclusion of this book is that a blanket approach to dealing with animal harm and offenders is unlikely to be successful. The enforcement regimes therefore need to be adapted to provide for action appropriate to the circumstances of the offender and specific nature of the offence. For traditional criminals financial penalties may work as a means of negating any benefit they derive from their activity but the same approach is unlikely to work with economic criminals. An argument can also be made that increased sentencing and use of prison has been unsuccessful in mainstream criminal justice (Wilson 1985) and so the evidence that it will be effective in reducing or prevent animal harm is lacking. For traditional criminals, greater efforts should be made to attempt situational crime prevention, making the physical cost of committing the crime prohibitive as well as the actual cost

(Clarke 1992) and removing the perception that animal harm (and particularly transnational wildlife crime) may be seen as a soft option.

For economic criminals, their employment provides the source of their offending behaviour and so any policy approach must include pressure on and penalties for the employer as well as actions which dictate that the risk of losing employment as a direct consequence of committing animal harm is a real possibility. The current legislative regime in many jurisdictions does not provide for culpability of landowners/employers for the actions of their staff, nor do countryside and game industry employees suffer the stigma of conviction. As a practical means of dealing with these offenders this position should be altered so that conviction of a wildlife crime carries with it the threat of losing employment in the countryside and in the game-rearing or fieldsports industries, as well as significant penalties for the employer. In construction and other industries, appropriate sanctions should be applied to companies that ignore animal law (mostly wildlife) regulations which should include measures to make employers culpable for the actions of their employees. These measures should be replicated across all jurisdictions.

For the masculinities offender, the effectiveness of prison or high fines is also questionable. Much like gang members in the inner-city United States and UK, those involved in organized crime, or youths who see ASBOs as a badge of honour (Youth Justice Board 2006), masculinities offenders may come to see prison as simply an occupational hazard as well as reinforcing their male identity and confirmation of society's lack of understanding of their needs and culture. For these types of offender, situational crime prevention should be attempted and a real effort at rehabilitation made alongside the traditional law enforcement approach of detection and prosecution. Consideration may also need to be given to the circumstances in which groups of young men turn to crime with a violent element and whether the type of social work intervention combined with law enforcement activity that now takes place in parts of the United States with animal abusers (Brantley 2009, Clawson 2009) could be applied in the UK.

Hobby offenders present a distinct policy and enforcement challenge as the drive to collect and the obsessive behaviour of such offenders cannot easily be overcome; fines and prison sentences could even strengthen the desire to offend by the drive to replace lost items such as a confiscated egg collection. While prevention and detection of crimes should continue to be employed for these offenders, treatment to address the issues of collecting as well as education in the effects of animal harm should be considered. Again, a strong situational crime prevention element could be attempted and in the case of hobby offenders this could be linked to sentencing to ensure that any sentencing provisions contain measures to prevent future offending as well as measures that attempt to address the causes of these crimes.

Stress offenders require an enforcement regime that recognizes their dual status as offender and victim. Ascione (2001: 10) suggests that 'teaching young people to train, care for, and interact in a nurturing manner with animals will reduce any propensity they may have for aggression and violence'. Thus any public policy response needs to positively encourage the kind of empathetic response to animals that will make further violence less likely. However, the victimized Model E offender, whether child or adult, also requires a therapeutic intervention that addresses the underlying causes of their stress and eliminates the impulse to commit further animal harm.

These offender classifications provide the preliminary outline explanation of animal harm and its associated criminality. Further more detailed aspects of animal harm drawing on these models are discussed in the following chapters in respect of specific aspects of animal harm.

References

Arkow, P. (1996). The Relationship between Animal Abuse and Other Forms of Family Violence. *Family Violence & Sexual Assault Bulletin*, 12(1–2), 29–34.

Ascione, F.R. (1993). Children Who are Cruel to Animals: A Review of Research and Implications for Developmental Psychopathology. *Anthrozoos*, 4, 226–7.

Ascione, F.R. and Arkow, P. (eds) (1999). *Child Abuse, Domestic Violence, and Animal Abuse: Linking the Circles of Compassion for Prevention and Intervention.* West Lafayette, IN: Purdue University Press.

Ascione, F.R. (ed.) (2001). Animal Abuse and Youth Violence. *Juvenile Justice Bulletin September 2001*, Washington, DC: U.S. Department of Justice.

Barkham, P. (2006). The Egg Snatchers, London: *The Guardian*, 11 December 2006. Available at http://www.guardian.co.uk/environment/2006/dec/11/g2.ruralaffairs [accessed 20 December 2010].

Becker, H. (1963). *Outsiders: Studies in Sociology of Deviance*, New York: Free Press of Glencoe.

Beetz, A. (2009). Empathy as an Indicator of Emotional Development, in A. Linzey (ed.), *The Link Between Animal Abuse and Human Violence*, Eastbourne: Sussex Academic Press, 63–74.

Belk, R.W. (1995). *Collecting in a Consumer Society*, London: Routledge.

Brantley, A. (2009). An FBI Perspective on Animal Cruelty, in A. Linzey (ed.), *The Link Between Animal Abuse and Human Violence*, Eastbourne: Sussex Academic Press, 223–7.

Browne, A. (1993). Violence against Women by Male Partners: Prevalence, Outcomes, and Policy Implications. *American Psychologist*, 48, 1077–87.

Burke, J. (2001), Britain Leads Illicit Trade in Rare Books, *The Observer*, Sunday 10 June 2001.

Burns, L., Edwards, V., Marsh, J., Soulsby, L. and Winter, M. (2000) *Committee of Inquiry into Hunting With Dogs in England and Wales*, London: HMSO.

Campbell, A. (1993). *Men, Women and Aggression*, New York: Basic Books.

Carrabine, M.L., Cox, P., South, N. and Plummer, K. (2009). *Criminology: A Sociological Introduction*, Abingdon: Routledge.

Childs, J. (2003). *Bat Crime: Is the Legislation Protecting Bats?* Sandy: BCT/ RSPB.

Clarke, Ronald V. (1992). *Situational Crime Prevention,* New York: Harrow and Heston.

Clawson, E. (2009). Canaries in the Mine: The Priority of Human Welfare in Animal Abuse Prosecution, in A. Linzey (ed.), *The Link Between Animal Abuse and Human Violence,* Eastbourne: Sussex Academic Press, 190–200.

Conboy-Hill, S. (2000). *Animal Abuse and Interpersonal Violence,* Lincoln: The Companion Animal Behaviour Therapy Study Group.

Connell, R.W. (1995). *Masculinities,* Oxford: Blackwell Publishers.

Damania, R., Seidensticker, J., Whitten, A., Sethi, G., Mackinnon, K., Kiss, A. and Kushlin, A. (2008). *A Future for Wild Tigers,* Washington, DC: The International Bank for Reconstruction and Development / The World Bank and Smithsonian's National Zoological Park.

Denzin, N. (2001). *Interpretive Interactionism (Applied Social Research Methods),* London: Sage.

Eliason, S.L. (2003). Illegal Hunting and Angling: The Neutralization of Wildlife Law Violations. *Society & Animals,* 11(3), 225–43.

Felthous, A. and Kellert, S. (1987). Childhood Cruelty to Animals and Later Aggression Against People: A Review. *American Journal of Psychiatry,* 144, 710–17.

Flood-Page, C. and Mackie, A. (1998). *Sentencing Practice: An Examination of Decisions in Magistrates' Courts and the Crown Court in the Mid-1990s,* London: Home Office.

Flynn, C.P. (2002). Hunting and Illegal Violence Against Humans and Other Animals: Exploring the Relationship. *Society & Animals,* 10(2), 137–54.

Flynn, C.P. (2009). Women-battering, Pet Abuse, and Human-Animal Relationships, in A. Linzey (ed.), *The Link Between Animal Abuse and Human Violence,* Eastbourne: Sussex Academic Press, 116–25.

Forsyth, C.J. and Evans, R.D. (1998). Dogmen: The Rationalisation of Deviance. *Society & Animals,* 6(3), 203–18.

Fox, N. (2002). Developments in Conservation of the Saker Falcon. *Wingspan,* 11(2), 9.

Friedrich, W.N., Grambsch, P., Damon, L., Hewitt, S.K., Koverola, C., Lang, R.A., Wolfe, V. and Broughton, D. (1992). Child Sexual Behavior Inventory: Normative and Cinical Comparisons. *Psychological Assessment,* 4, 303–11.

Fylan, F., Hempel, S., Grunfeld, E.A., Connor, M. and Lawton, R. (2006). Evidence-based Behavioural Change for Speeding Drivers. *Behavioural Research in Road Safety.* London: Department for Transport. Available at http://www.dft.gov.uk/pgr/roadsafety/research/behavioural/sixteenthseminar/ pdf [accessed 10 February 2012].

Goodey, J. (1997). Masculinities, Fear of Crime and Fearlessness. *The British Journal of Sociology,* 37(3), 401–18.

Green, A. (1999). *Animal Underground,* New York: Public Affairs/Perseus Books.

Groombridge, N. (1998). Masculinities and Crimes against the Environment. *Theoretical Criminology*, 2(2), London: Sage, 249–67.

Harland, K., Beattie, K. and McCready, S. (2005). *Young Men and the Squeeze of Masculinity: The Inaugural Paper for the Centre for Young Men's Studies*, Ulster: Centre for Young Men's Studies.

Hawley, F. (1993). The Moral and Conceptual Universe of Cockfighters: Symbolism and Rationalization. *Society and Animals*, 1(2), 159–68.

Henry, B.C. (2004). The Relationship between Animal Cruelty, Delinquency, and Attitudes toward the Treatment of Animals. *Society & Animals*, 12(3).

House of Commons (2004), *Environmental Crime: Wildlife Crime – Select Committee on Environmental Audit: Twelfth Report*, London: House of Commons.

Interpol (2010). *Environmental Crime, It's Global Theft*, Lyon: Interpol.

John, G., Robinson, J. and Redford, K. (1985). Hunting by Indigenous Peoples and Conservation of Game Species. *Parks and People*, 9(1). Available at http://www.culturalsurvival.org/ourpublications/csq/article/hunting-by-indigenous-peoples-and-conservation-game-species [accessed 28 January 2012].

Kimmell, M., Hearn, J. and Connell, R.W. (2005). *Handbook of Studies on Men & Masculinities*, London: Sage.

Lea, J. and Young, J. (1993 revised edn). *What Is To Be Done About Law & Order?* London: Pluto Press.

League Against Cruel Sports (1997). *Wildlife Guardian, Issue 36, Spring 1997*, London: LACS.

Linzey, A. (ed.) (2009). *The Link Between Animal Abuse and Human Violence*, Eastbourne: Sussex Academic Press.

Lombroso, C. and Ferrero, W. (1895). *The Female Offender*, London: Fisher Unwin.

McClellan, J., Adams, J., Douglas, D., McCurry, C. and Storck, M. (1995). Clinical Characteristics Related to Severity of Sexual Abuse: A Study of Seriously Mentally Ill Youth. *Child Abuse and Neglect*, 19, 1245–54.

Maguire, M. (2000). Researching 'Street Criminals': A Neglected Art, in R.D. King and E. Wincup (eds), *Doing Research on Crime and Justice*, Oxford: Oxford University Press.

Maguire, M., Morgan, R. and Reiner, R. (eds) (1994). *The Oxford Handbook of Criminology*, Oxford: Oxford University Press.

Merton, R.K. (1968). *Social Structure and Social Theory*, New York: Free Press.

Nelken, D. (1994). White Collar Crime, in M. Maguire, R. Morgan and R. Reiner (eds), *The Oxford Handbook of Criminology*, Oxford: Oxford University Press, 355–92.

Norland, S., Wessell, R.C. and Shover, N. (1981). Masculinity and Delinquency. *Criminology*, 19(3), 421–33.

Nurse, A. (2009). Dealing with Animal Offenders, in A. Linzey (ed.), *The Link Between Animal Abuse and Human Violence*, Eastbourne: Sussex Academic Press, 238–49.

Nurse, A. (2011). Policing Wildlife: Perspectives on Criminality in Wildlife Crime, *Papers from the British Society of Criminology Conference*, 11, London: British Society of Criminology, 38–53.

Roberts, M., Cook, D., Jones, P. and Lowther, D. (2001). *Wildlife Crime in the UK: Towards a National Crime Unit*, Wolverhampton: Department for the Environment, Food & Rural Affairs/Centre for Applied Social Research (University of Wolverhampton).

Robinson, P. (1991). *Falconry in Britain*, London: League Against Cruel Sports.

Royal Society for the Protection of Birds (RSPB) (1999). *Birdcrime '98: Offences against Wild Bird Legislation 1998*, Sandy: RSPB.

Royal Society for the Prevention of Cruelty to Animals (2006). *Annual Review 2005: Royal Society for the Prevention of Cruelty of Animals*, Horsham: RSPCA.

Royal Society for the Prevention of Cruelty to Animals (2007). *Annual Review 2006: Royal Society for the Prevention of Cruelty of Animals*, Horsham: RSPCA.

Scottish Institute for Policing Research (2007). *Forensic Investigation of Wildlife Crime*, Dundee: University of Dundee.

Shapland, J., Atkinson, A., Atkinson, H., Chapman, B., Dignan, J., Howes, M., Johnstone, J., Robinson, G. and Sorsby, A. (2007). *Restorative Justice: The Views of Victims and Offenders: The Third Report from the Evaluation of Three Schemes*, London: Ministry of Justice.

Sherman, L.W. and Strang, H. (2007). *Restorative Justice: The Evidence*, London: The Smith Institute.

Siegal, L.J. (2002). *Criminology*, Florence: Thompson/Wadsworth.

Situ, Y. and Emmons, D. (2000). *Environmental Crime: The Criminal Justice System's Role in Protecting the Environment*, Thousand Oaks: Sage.

Sutherland, E.H. (1973). *On Analysing Crime*, edited by K. Schuessler, Chicago: University of Chicago Press (original work published 1942).

Sykes, G.M. and Matza, D. (1957). Techniques of Neutralization: A Theory of Delinquency. *American Sociological Review*, 22, 664–73.

Taylor, M. and Quayle, E. (2003). *Child Pornography: An Internet Crime*, London: Brunner-Routledge.

U.S. Department of Health & Human Services, Administration for Children and Families (2001). *10 Years of Reporting: Child Maltreatment 1999*. Washington, DC: U.S. Government Printing Office.

Wainwright, M. (2006). The Day Britain's Most Notorious Egg Collector Climbed His Last Tree: Birder Falls to His Death from Larch Tree while Checking Out Unusual Nest, *The Guardian*, 27 May 2006. Available at http://www.guardian.co.uk/uk/2006/may/27/topstories3.mainsection [accessed 18 May 2008].

Wilson, J.Q. (1985). *Thinking about Crime*, 2nd edn, New York: Vintage Books.

Wise, S.M. (2000). *Rattling the Cage: Towards Legal Rights for Animals*, London: Profile.

Wood, A. (2008). 'Evil' Thief is Jailed over Haul of 7,000 Bird Eggs, *Yorkshire Post* [accessed 4 June 2008].

Worrall, A. (2001). Girls at Risk? Reflections on Changing Attitudes to Young Women's Offending. *Probation Journal*, 48(2), 86–92.

Youth Justice Board (2006). *Anti-Social Behaviour Orders*, London: Youth Justice Board for England and Wales.

Chapter 4
Animal Harm and Domestic Animals

This chapter looks specifically at the causes of animal cruelty and animal welfare offences involving domestic animals, particularly animal harm such as neglect, cruelty, the deliberate inflicting of harm and causing unnecessary suffering to animals whether by act or omission. It discusses the link between animal abuse and masculinities arguing that much domestic animal abuse involving companion animals is caused by and a product of masculinities and power relationships within domestic relationships.

Chapter 3 identified different types of animal offender, confirming that while masculinities are a common cause of animal harm, there is a specific type of masculinities animal harm offender. For this offender, masculinities constitute both a primary cause of their offending behaviour and a justification for the animal harm that they cause. In domestic settings, animal harm is a means through which men sometimes express and reassert their masculinity in challenging social situations, or at least those situations where a perceived loss of power or challenge to their authority needs to be addressed.

This chapter discusses animal abuse, domestic violence and control within the home, examining how some animal abuse is a means to control other family members. Children or spouses can be manipulated into remaining with an abuser by means of the control exercised over companion animals (Browne 1993, Arkow 1996) while older family members can be intimidated into remaining silent about any abuse. In this respect, domestic animal harm is less a species justice issue relating to the specific issue of animal rights (Rollin 2006, White 2008) than it is one relating to how the animal harm imposed is a means to an end, determined in part by the vulnerability of animals as powerless family members rather than their lack of any protective rights regime. The chapter also examines how the abuse of domestic animals can be an indicator of other antisocial behaviour and a possible predictor of future offending. This discussion is a precursor to Chapter 9's consideration of the links between animal abuse and violent crimes towards humans.

Domestic Animal Harm

Chapter 1 provides an overview of the legal protection afforded to animals while Chapter 2 specifies the varied nature of animal harm and the specific offences involved. As Chapter 1 notes, several countries have laws protecting domestic animals primarily through anti-cruelty laws that make it an offence to inflict pain or suffering on companion animals. In some jurisdictions this is phrased as causing 'unnecessary suffering' reflecting the fact that within domestic settings humans cannot always entirely avoid causing harm to animals. Indeed some forms of accidental harm or harm that constitutes a 'necessary' part of human–companion animal relationships (such as neutering, spaying or castrating) may constitute lawful suffering. In effect, some laws argue that by reducing animals into captivity and through the process of domesticating certain species over a period of time we have an obligation to ensure that they do not suffer harm while they are dependent on humans for food and shelter and unable to live independent lives, or at least that any suffering should be tightly controlled.

The mistreatment of domestic animals can occur for many reasons and can be either active or passive. *Passive* mistreatment can include neglect caused by 'failure to act' such that companion animals are not properly cared for and harm is caused either as a result of misunderstanding an animal's needs or through deliberate neglect. Frasch (2000) identifies that beliefs play an important part in the treatment of animals and understanding of their needs and neglect of animals can be an indicator of other problems within the family. But it is important to distinguish between *accidental* and *deliberate* neglect. Academic and policy discussions of animal abuse tend to concentrate either on *active* mistreatment or deliberate neglect where intent to cause animal harm is a significant factor and an indicator of either antisocial personality disorder, mental illness or some form of abuse within the family. However, accidental neglect, although receiving less attention in studies, can also be a potent indicator of domestic problems. First it is worth pointing out that although some accidental neglect may still be serious for the companion animal, it occurs naturally through misunderstanding of appropriate care needs or the simple process of companion animals being bought for children who are either unable to care for them adequately or who simply grow out of the relationship with a companion animal and move on to other things.

Nathanson (2009: 307) and other researchers have also examined the phenomenon of animal hoarding, 'a deviant behaviour associated with extremely deleterious conditions of comorbid animal and self-neglect', where individuals attempt to take care of more animals than is practical and neglect is the result. However hoarding also represents a dysfunctional human–animal relationship where individuals may actively 'collect' animals as companions. Patronek and Nathanson (2009: 274) explained that animal hoarding is maladaptive, destructive behaviour where 'compulsive caregiving of animals can become the primary means of maintaining or building a sense of "self"'. This may be especially true for those individuals who have suffered dysfunctional primary attachment experiences in childhood and for whom a relationship with animals can take on increased importance in their life. The RSPCA, SSPCA and environmental health agencies in the UK (and their respective organizations in other countries) frequently deal with cases where individuals have sought to care for increasing numbers of cats and dogs, seemingly unable to turn any animal away but resulting in their being unable to care properly for these animals thus causing unlawful neglect.

The American Society for the Prevention of Cruelty to Animals (ASPCA) estimates 900 to 2,000 new cases of animal hoarding every year in the United States while statistics released by the RSPCA in the UK annually show a persistent problem of animal hoarding cases. One difficulty in precisely defining this type of animal harm is the varied definitions in use. The RSPCA defines a hoarder as somebody who has accumulated a large number of animals that 'have overwhelmed that person's ability to provide even minimal standards of nutrition, sanitation and veterinary care' (2010: 10). However a narrower definition of hoarding that primarily incorporates the accumulation of animals even though 'minimal' standards of care might be present could be adopted by environmental health officers, for example in noise nuisance cases where noise is caused by excessive animal occupation or overcrowding of a property. The RSPCA definition also notes that hoarders fail to recognize the deteriorating condition of the animals in their care, examples of extreme cases include a collar growing into an animal's skin, an untreated infection of parasites, starvation, dehydration or even death as a result of inadequate care. Hoarders also often fail to recognize the negative effects of a large collection of animals on their own health and that of other members of the family. Thus their form of animal harm also inadvertently results in human harm.

While hoarding is an extreme form of passive animal harm and may initially be the result of good intentions gone awry, it indicates the serious consequences of neglect as an illegal activity unwittingly carried out by some individuals. Hoarders are, in effect, stress offenders (see Chapter 3), compulsively associating with companion animals in order to either fulfil their own need for care or as a result of some unresolved harm or stress within their lives. However inadequate food or shelter or failing to consider care or grooming needs such that an animal suffers constitutes passive animal harm.

Active animal harm consists of deliberate and intentional harm caused to animals (Daugherty 2005). Active cruelty thus indicates some malicious intent on the part of the offender which may be an indicator of psychological factors such as a predisposition towards cruelty (Ascione 1993, Boat 1995) and may also indicate that an abuser commits other forms of abuse within the home such as spousal or child abuse (Schleuter 1999, Turner 2000). The link between animal cruelty and violent antisocial behaviour is now largely accepted by the scientific and law enforcement communities and is becoming accepted within criminology (Agnew 1998, Arluke 2006, Levin and Arluke 2009). As an aspect of animal harm, however, the strength of the link should be considered with caution and acknowledgement that domestic animal abuse does not automatically escalate into violent behaviour towards humans. MacDonald (1963) identified three specific behavioural characteristics associated with sociopathic behaviour: animal cruelty, obsession with fire starting and bedwetting (past age five). The MacDonald triad was instrumental in linking these behaviours to violent behaviours, particularly homicide and identifying cruelty to animals as a possible indicator of future violent behaviour. Subsequent studies (Petersen and Farrington 2009) have confirmed that cruelty to animals is a common behaviour in children and adolescents who grow up to become violent criminals. However, in the case of adults who abuse animals it can indicate a violent or abusive family dynamic, one in which patriarchal power is enforced through inflicting harm on weaker or more vulnerable members of a family who may be unable to defend themselves. In some circumstances acts of animal abuse are used to intimidate, control or coerce women and children within an abusive relationship either to accede to a perpetrator's demands or desires or to keep silent about the abuse they are suffering. However, animal abuse may also be an outlet for aggression for male offenders or child victims within a domestic setting such that animals bear the brunt of, or are at risk of, suffering from violence from a number of sources within a family. Companion animals are often part of the family and may be attuned to the levels of tension within a family. Evidence shows that some animals experience, or at least respond to, the distress of their owners (Schleuter 1999, Wiegand et al. 1999). Thus, in addition to physical abuse and neglect, animals may also suffer from psychological abuse and be subject to the same emotional stress of living in fear from domestic abuse or other forms of violence within the home as other family members such as a spouse or children.

Animal Harm as Control

Animal harm is sometimes associated with power, especially patriarchal power. Weber (1964) identified the hierarchical nature of power within the family and its association with distinct family roles, primarily based around the father as the central power conduit with power circulating down to lesser family members. While Weber's theory was based around less varied forms of the family than exist today, male power and masculinities remain significant factors in domestic violence and animal abuse. Feminist perspectives argue that patriarchy is a means through which dominant males use violence as an expression of power to control less powerful individuals within their immediate sphere of influence. Companion animals have the least power within a family dynamic, partly through being unable to speak and exercise their 'rights' but also by virtue of their status as 'property' (Francione 2007, Shaffner 2011). Adams argues that abuse of animals is part of the wider dominance and exploitation of less powerful individuals by males (1994) through which a dominant male is able to control his immediate environment and increase both acceptance of his will and reliance on his authority.

A number of studies have identified a causal link between animal abuse and domestic abuse concluding that in homes where domestic abuse takes place, animal abuse is often present (Ascione 1993, Ascione and Weber 1995, Lewchanin and Zimmerman 2000). The relationship is a complex one; while not as straightforward as saying that an individual who abuses a spouse is also likely to be abusing animals in the home it can however be said that where an individual in a position of power within the family (i.e. the dominant male) is abusing animals, other forms of abuse such as spousal or child abuse are also *likely* to be occurring. Active or passive animal harm in the form of animal cruelty can be part of a cycle of abuse within the family, or even a consequence of domestic abuse. Definitions of domestic abuse are themselves not straightforward. The term 'domestic violence' is frequently used as shorthand to describe the most prevalent form of domestic abuse dealt with by criminal justice agencies, usually that of violence towards women by a male spouse or partner (Morley and Mullender 1994). However several criminologists and psychologists have examined domestic abuse in detail, concluding that domestic abuse is not confined to physical abuse that occurs solely within a domestic setting but can include a range of abusive behaviours that occur either within the home or within the wider domestic environment and family (including extended family) relationships (Ascione 2000, Petersen and Farrington 2009). Domestic abuse can thus incorporate physical, psychological or sexual abuse, and while policy and law enforcement attention is often concentrated on physical or sexual abuse directed either at female partners or children, psychological abuse is equally important (O'Leary 1999) and particularly relevant where animal abuse is concerned. Threats made against a companion animal can cause extreme emotional distress in both children and adult partners and can be an effective tool for an offender to both control other family members and those dependent on them or to influence control over a family dynamic. This control is particularly damaging for those vulnerable family members who have intense emotional attachments to companion animals. Morley and Mullender identified that 'domestic violence is almost always a multiple victimisation crime' (1994: 5) as attacks (whether verbal or physical) by the same perpetrator are almost always repeated, although the frequency with which this occurs is dependent on the motivation of the offender (Farrell et al. 2005). Animal harm aimed at companion animals can thus be part of an overall pattern not just of persistent animal harm but of other antisocial behaviour and violence within the home. As a result, animal harm directed at companion animals is significant in terms of influencing subsequent animal harm caused by children and adolescents, and the escalation of animal harm either as control or punishment carried out during a deteriorating (or escalating) cycle of partner abuse.

Animal Harm, Child Abuse and Youth Offending

Animal harm can have varied effects on children who can themselves be victims of abuse within the family but can also witness abuse perpetrated against other members of the family including companion animals. Moffit and Caspi (2003) identified that young children and partner violence are concentrated in the same segment of the population, the result of this is that many children witness partner violence within the home. Exposure to animal abuse may also be a common childhood experience, especially (but not only) in homes where partner abuse is present. Baldry's survey of 1,356 9–17-year-olds in Rome found exposure to animal abuse by peers reported by 63.7 percent of respondents and an exposure rate of 60.9 percent to non-parental animal abuse (2003). Pagani et al. (2007) found that 65 percent of respondents in their study of 800 Roman children had witnessed some form of animal abuse, and Thompson and Gullone (2006) in their study of a sample of 281 adolescents (aged between 12 and 18) in Australia found that 77.5 percent of the sample had witnessed animal abuse at least once. While the research studies consisted of different samples, methodologies and assessment criteria, these and other research studies have consistently found significant levels of exposure to domestic animal abuse among children and adolescents. That such exposure may impact on a young person's attitudes towards violence is increasingly accepted by mental health and law enforcement practitioners.

Researchers have discovered that companion animals can physically and psychologically benefit their owners, and some argue that one's attachment to a companion animal influences those benefits (Crawford et al. 2006, Antonacopoulos et al. 2010). Within the home children can become particularly attached to companion animals and Beetz (2009) evaluated empathy towards animals as an indicator of emotional development, concluding that emotional attachment towards animals in childhood promotes positive emotional abilities and a heightened capacity for empathy that encourages good mental health. However a lack of empathy is sometimes closely linked to animal abuse and interpersonal violence (Beetz 2009: 63). As a result, children who view their companion animals being harmed are themselves victims of child abuse arising from that animal harm. While a commonly accepted definition of child abuse may be difficult to arrive at in respect of exposure to animal harm, in a broader sense child abuse incorporates a range of activities including:

- physical harm – such as hitting or shaking, torture and (in extreme cases) drowning or actual death;
- emotional abuse – which can include persistent ill-treatment that makes a child feel inadequate, worthless or unloved;
- sexual abuse – which involves forcing or encouraging a child to take part in sexual activities, exposing them to sexually explicit material, or encouraging inappropriate sexualized behaviour by a child; or
- neglect– which includes failure to provide for a child's needs, adequate food, shelter or clothing. Neglect can be physical or psychological and can also include persistent failure to provide adequate supervision of a child where this is required.

The UK government (within its Department of Health [DOH], Home Office and Department for Education and Employment [DfEE]) identified that a range of factors may impact on parents' ability to care for their children or respond to a child's needs. The DOH identified poverty, domestic violence, mental illness and drug and alcohol misuse as stress factors that impact on effective parenting to the extent that parents may cause harm to a child or young person under 18 (2010).

Jouriles et al. (1996) studied the effect of domestic violence on children concluding that physical violence and other forms of marital aggression were sometimes 'associated with externalizing (acting out) problems in the 5–12 year old children' of the families studied (Ascione et al. 1997: 3). As children develop their values, sense of morality and are socialized to understand appropriate behaviours from within their family dynamic, therefore witnessing family violence can have severe consequences for children (Osofsky 1995). Acting out and externalizing the violence they have witnessed can be mechanisms through which children deal with the stress of having witnessed marital violence, make sense of what they have witnessed or seek the attention of the adults engaged in marital violence. However, as children learn appropriate behaviours both from observing adults and through encouragement from adults, witnessing parent and pet abuse may compromise children's psychological (and moral) development and increase their propensity for interpersonal violence and cruelty to animals (Ascione et al. 1997, Duffield et al. 1998). Animal abuse perpetrated by children may thus emerge as a symptom of their distress within a family where marital aggression occurs. Children may turn to animal abuse as an outlet for aggression or the pain linked to abuse within the family and become stress offenders (see Chapter 3) inflicting pain either on companion animals within the home or vulnerable animals outside of the home. Committing animal harm may also be a means through which children identify with their abuser, especially within a confined family dynamic where the support of other adults may not be available or there is a need to deflect the abuser's attention from them and onto another. Evidence exists that childhood animal abuse is a potential indicator of later interpersonal violence (Felthous and Kellert 1987, Ascione 1993), although the reasons for childhood animal abuse are varied and in addition to being an outlet or coping mechanism, childhood animal abuse may also indicate antisocial personality issues within a child.

Conboy-Hill (2000) identified that animal harm may be a 'rehearsal' for later behaviour rather than being a stage that individuals pass through. A child (or adolescent) may, therefore, use animal abuse as a way of both practising their techniques for killing or inflicting harm and of developing their interest (and perhaps taste) in inflicting violence. An initial fascination with the effects of torture on animals or curiosity about what may happen when certain acts are carried out on smaller creatures can frequently develop into a routine from which a child gains pleasure in harming animals (Ascione 1993). Consistency of action has the effect of desensitizing children to the violent nature of their acts with the potential consequence that an escalation from violence against insects and smaller animals develops into violence against larger animals or even violence towards humans (discussed further in Chapter 9). Of course this is not to suggest that all children who are involved in early acts of violence against animals will automatically escalate to human violence. While evidence exists that a significant number of violent offenders and the majority of American serial killers have a history of animal abuse (Lockwood and Church 1996, Lockwood and Ascione 1998, Schiff et al. 1999), childhood animal harm can itself take many forms and may be an indicator of different types of antisocial personality disorder or emotional response to circumstances within the home. Several perspectives can be used to explain such action in children and the development of subsequent criminal careers.

Strain theory (Merton 1968) indicates that children who have witnessed abuse perpetrated against their mother, another sibling, or a family pet may themselves begin to abuse animals as a result. However in some cases children learn to abuse animals as a result of being socialized towards doing so by a parent or other significant male figure in the home. Sutherland's (1939/1973) differential association theory and social learning theory help clarify how animal harm committed by children may be learned behaviour in the context of a close family dynamic, even a dysfunctional one based on interpersonal violence. Symbolic interactionism theory (Blumer 1969) suggests that interactions with others gives meaning to experiences and allows individuals to construct reality. Thus a child whose reality is one of violence and fear may come to understand that abusing the more vulnerable members of the family is both socially acceptable (within the confines of the family) and a necessary part of survival. In such circumstances animal abuse committed by children may be consistent with norms within the family and become part of their socialization. From this initial starting point, the graduation hypothesis suggests that children who begin with violence towards animals will graduate towards human violence unless there is some form of intervention that prevents this escalation. For some children their animal harm activities are a reaction to a toxic abusive environment, although Lockwood and Church (1996) argue that those with a rich history of animal abuse are likely to have independently commenced their activities.

There are several possible reasons for children to independently start their animal abuse activities. Cruelty to animals has now been included among the symptoms of conduct disorder in children and adolescents accepted by several major psychiatric diagnostic techniques (Gleyzer et al. 2002) thus animal abuse can be part of a spectrum of behavioural problems. Conduct Disorder is a repetitive pattern of antisocial behaviour that can persist into adulthood and which consists of violating the basic rights of others or age-appropriate behaviours. Animal cruelty represents a symptom due to its deviation from the normal child–companion animal relationship and the violation of the companion animal's rights. While child and adolescent motivations for animal abuse have not received the same attention as other forms of animal abuse, Ascione, Thompson and Black (1997) suggested a number of motivations for such action.

- Curiosity or exploration – particularly where the animal has been injured or killed during examination by a curious child. This is particularly notable when happening in the case of a young child or child showing signs of arrested development.
- Peer pressure – where animal abuse may form part of an adolescent initiation rite or may be aggressively encouraged through peer pressure.

- Boredom or mood enhancement – cases where animal harm results from boredom or depression and attempts by the child or adolescent to resolve or banish these feelings.
- Sexual gratification – which may itself be a symptom of abuse but where a child or adolescent seeks to achieve sexual gratification and involves an animal in their attempts (commonly referred to as bestiality).
- Forced abuse – where the child is coerced into committing animal harm by others, usually the dominant person within their environment (a parent, step-parent or guardian, but sometimes an older sibling).
- Attachment abuse – in this case a child may kill or torture a companion or other animal to prevent its torture by a third party. The child may see this act as providing mercy for the animal by ensuring that their suffering is cut short.
- Phobic animal harm – where animal harm may take place as a pre-emptive attack on an animal as a form of defence where fear of an animal is a factor.
- Identification – animal harm may be committed by a victimized child as a means of regaining power from within their vulnerable situation.
- Post-traumatic play – where a child re-enacts violent episodes with an animal possibly in a sense to achieve understanding of what has happened.
- Imitation – where a child copies an adult's abusive disciplining of an animal. In such cases the child may not necessarily fully understand either what has happened or that they are now themselves inflicting animal harm.
- Self-injury – where a child uses an animal to inflict injuries on themselves.
- Rehearsal – where a child or adolescent practices violence on stray or companion animals before engaging in other forms of interpersonal violence.
- Vehicle offending – where injury is caused to a sibling's pet as a means of frightening or controlling the sibling.

This extensive list indicates the range of variation possible in childhood and adolescent animal harm. Thus while healthy relationships with animals can have numerous positive benefits for children and adolescents and contribute greatly to their emotional and social stability, animal abuse by children can be indicative of a range of stresses and abuse factors within the home and wider environment. Children's animal abuse is thus more complex than simply being an expression of, or indicator of, cruelty and requires careful assessment before its meaning may be properly understood.

Animal Harm and Spousal Abuse

Ascione et al. (1997) identified that much information that exists about animal abuse and partner battering comes from anecdotal evidence and only a small number of studies have examined the relationship between animal abuse and women battering in any great detail. However the available evidence shows a clear link between domestic abuse directed at women and animal abuse. Criminology's analysis of domestic abuse towards women combined with green criminology's assessment of animal abuse and the author's own investigation into the causes of animal abuse and wildlife criminality (Nurse 2011) provide for effective assessment of the relationship between animal harm and spousal abuse.

Ascione et al. (1997) sampled around 50 battered women's shelters, one from each US state (excluding Utah) and the District of Columbia which met their selection criteria of providing overnight (residential) accommodation, that had children's counselling or programmes available, and which was the largest shelter in the state based on 'shelter capacity' (i.e. the number of people the shelter could hold). Ascione's team found that 84 percent of the shelters confirmed that women who came to the shelters talked about incidents of pet abuse, 63 percent confirmed that children who came to the shelters talked about pet abuse and 83 percent of the shelters confirmed the co-existence of domestic abuse and pet abuse (1997). While it should be noted that the survey was selective and many shelter programmes would not fall within its sampling methodology, interest in animal abuse as an indicator of partner-battering has developed since Ascione and his colleagues conducted their survey and a greater body of knowledge currently exists about animal harm as a form of psychological abuse specifically directed at partners and as a factor in the control or dominance exerted over a partner. Flynn (2009: 117) sums up the evidence by explaining that 'among battered women with pets, between approximately one-half and three-fourths report that their companion animals have been threatened or actually harmed by their intimate partners'.

Women's close relationships with companion animals are a significant factor in domestic abuse for a variety of reasons. The close relationship makes companion animals the target of abuse and concern for a companion can significantly influence women's response to the abuse they receive, including their willingness to remain in the home or interact with the authorities. Pets are important sources of emotional support for women who are involved in abusive relationships. Women who suffer from domestic violence are frequently isolated and suffer from low self-esteem (Gayford 1975, Pizzey and Shapiro 1982). For some women in such relationships, a companion animal represents the only source of unconditional love within the domestic setting, especially where children may be seen to side with or respond to the abuser. For women without children, a companion animal can be a source of love, emotional support and even a confidante within a domestic setting where an abuser restricts access to other sources of support. This close relationship means that male abusers may deliberately target companion animals as the threat of abuse against the one remaining 'ally' that a vulnerable woman has in the family can be especially powerful. In addition, evidence suggests that some victims of domestic abuse eventually come to accept the 'norm' of the abuse that they experience but remain distressed at witnessing the abuse of others within the family, especially a loved pet (Browne 1993, Ascione and Weber 1995). The abuser thus comes to understand that targeting their abuse at a companion animal is an effective means of control and punishment and in extreme cases will go even further and force the battered spouse's involvement in the animal abuse.

Evidence shows that women who are in abusive relationships have usually endured the abuse for a considerable period of time before they finally leave the abuser (Morley and Mullender 1994), thus repeat victimization is a factor in both the spousal abuse and the associated animal harm. Victims of domestic abuse may be fearful not just for their own welfare but for those of dependents such as children and animals. Thus in order for victims of violence to escape an abusive home and relationship, they need to find shelter not just for themselves and children but also for any pets. However, a survey of battered women shelters in the United States found that many do not house pets (Ascione et al. 1997), which, assuming this policy is replicated widely and across jurisdictions, leaves the victim with the choice of staying within the abusive relationship or leaving their companions behind. This can be a significant factor in the cycle of abuse, allowing abusive partners not only to make threats against the companion animal which force a battered partner to remain in the home, but also to inflict harm on an animal as a way of controlling their partner. Concern over a companion animal left behind, whether in the care of a friend (who may then become the target of attention from the abuser) or which remains in the home, can be a considerable source of anxiety where the abuse which took place may even be sufficient to force a return to the family home out of concern for the non-human family member. Vulnerable women, even those fearful for their own safety, may be unable to further endure the idea that their absence from the home will allow the abuse of others to continue.

The Role of Veterinarians and Animal Health Visitors

Companion animal abuse is most likely to be detected by animal welfare professionals such as veterinarians. While much abuse in the home is likely to remain a secret, the care and treatment of companion animals is sometimes a necessity as suspicion may be aroused if routine appointments are not kept or if neighbours and other observers see an animal in distress. As a result, veterinarians will often obtain evidence of domestic animal harm before anybody else and be in a position to assess the nature of that harm and its possible links to other forms of abuse. As a result, there is a case for veterinarians to be actively involved in reporting animal abuse in addition to fulfilling their obligation to treat injured animals, and Robertson (2009) notes that some American states have already made it mandatory for veterinarians to report animal abuse to a dedicated agency.[1]

The Royal College of Veterinary Surgeons (RCVS),[2] for example, has noted that veterinary surgeons are among a number of professionals who may see and hear things during the course of their professional activity which arouse suspicion of animal abuse and/or domestic violence and child abuse. The RCVS's professional conduct guidance notes that 'given the links between animal and child abuse and domestic violence, a veterinary surgeon reporting suspected animal abuse to the relevant authority should consider whether a child might be at risk'. Thus an ethical duty exists for veterinarians in the UK who are members of the RCVS to report suspected animal abuse and while this guidance does not yet have statutory force, there are liability and professional issues for veterinary surgeons who do not report such abuse. There is a question over whether the ethical and professional duty amounts to a legal duty in the UK in the same way that the legal duty exists in some US states but this is an important step forward in linking animal welfare to other forms of offending within the UK and ensuring that professionals are both alert to the signs and implications of animal abuse and take action to address them.

Linzey suggests that 'only a mandatory legal duty to report removes the moral dilemma' that many veterinarians experience (2009: 261). Client confidentiality is a professional obligation for most veterinarians. Robertson suggests that veterinarians identifying injuries to a companion animal that either are clear signs of abuse or which do not tally with the client's explanation such that non-accidental injury is the only logical conclusion may face anxieties about personal safety and loss of business should they report a case as abuse (2009: 269). Yet the RCVS professional guidance is that the overriding duty of veterinarians is the public interest in protecting the animal and there are risks to a veterinarian who ignores abuse in favour of client confidentiality, especially where animal abuse may later turn out to be linked to other abuse. As a result, the mandatory legal duty that exists in some US states for veterinarians provides a means through which injuries to companion animals can be assessed as evidence not only of animal harm but also of the potential for other harm. Montoya and Miller (2009) note that in addition to the obligation for veterinarians to report animal abuse, California, Colorado, Ohio and Maine also require animal welfare workers to report suspected child abuse. Thus the role for animal welfare workers and veterinarians is to consider the context of any animal harm that they witness and to provide evidence of the nature of the violence. Montoya and Miller suggest that this is vital 'to end the cycle of animal abuse, child abuse, and interpersonal

---

1   Arizona, California, Illinois, Kansas, Minnesota, Oregon, West Virginia and Wisconsin have mandatory reporting requirements while a further 21 states have protective laws that protect veterinarians from civil or criminal liability arising from reporting suspected animal abuse.

2   The RCVS is the professional body and regulator of veterinary surgeons in the UK.

abuse that may otherwise continue to affect all those involved, human and animal' (2009: 279).

Case Study: Animal Abuse and Domestic Abuse

Hawksworth and Balen (2009) recount the story of Family A, a case example drawn from their experiences as part of a health visiting practice in the UK. The family 'consisted of two school-age children, one child under five years, a mother, father, and uncle' (2009: 283). Concerns about the school-age children had been raised by educational staff because of their dirty appearance, the persistent presence of head lice and because they were becoming withdrawn. Health visitors, together with the school nurse, visited the property following unsuccessful attempts by school staff to gain entry. School staff had, however, noticed a pit bull terrier tied up outside the home in a small garden 'littered with animal faeces' (2009: 283). The health visitors and school nurse observed the same scene, noting that the dog had no shelter or access to food and water and its faeces were evident. This indicated the possibility of neglect within the family and the interior of the property which contained a malnourished and frightened cat, the presence of animal faeces within the home, discarded used nappies and rotting food confirmed this. In addition the home lacked hygiene with the children sharing a dirty bed and using a broken toilet and also lacking access to proper nutritional food with takeaway junk food forming a substantial part of their diet. The health visitors identified the father's 'abusive and controlling behaviour' as indicative of family violence and animal cruelty and the dog outside the family home mirrored the treatment of the children and the mother who, while showing remorse and embarrassment, was unable to address either the child abuse or the animal abuse and was likely herself suffering from some abuse and intimidation either direct or indirect (2009: 283–4). In this case, multi-agency referrals resulted in the children being placed on the child protection register, the cat being re-homed and the dog being monitored by animal welfare officers. The child protection plan also included instructions to health and social care professionals to check animal access to food and water as an indicator of the state of relationships within the family.

This case study highlights animal harm's importance as an indictor of other harms although it is not always the case that animal abuse either leads to or is indicative of other harms just that it is *likely* that where animal abuse exists so do other forms of abuse. However in some circumstances animal abuse should be examined as an indicator of future interpersonal violence which the following section discusses.

Animal Harm and Future Violent Offending

Domestic abuse involving companion animals is multidimensional. Bell (2001) identified that an increasing number of studies show that where adults are abusing animals they are also likely to be abusing their children. But, in addition, children who are abusing animals are more likely also to be victims of abuse themselves and where children show aggression or exhibit sexualized behaviour towards animals this may also be an indicator of later abuse of other children or an escalation into violence against humans (DeViney et al. 1983, Duffield et al. 1998, Linzey 2009).

Within families, domestic animal harm, particularly abuse that involves inflicting physical harm on animals, is an indicator not only of domestic abuse perpetrated on partners and children typically by the adult male in the family, but also of psychological disorders that may show a propensity towards other forms of violence and antisocial behaviour. Animal harm thus needs to be recognized not just as a factor in domestic abuse but as a form of abuse in its own right and as an indicator of antisocial behaviour or violent tendencies in both adults and children that may be associated with other forms of offending. If recognized early in children, assessing the precise nature of childhood animal abuse may be an important factor in diverting children away from future offending (Hutton 1998) or determining the correct approach to deal with abusive relationships within the family.

References

Adams, C.J. (1994). Bringing Peace Home: A Feminist Philosophical Perspective on the Abuse of Women, Children, and Pet Animals. *Hypatia*, 9, 62–84.

Agnew, R. (1998). The Causes of Animal Abuse: A Social Psychological Analysis. *Theoretical Criminology*, 2, 177–209.

Antonacopoulos, D., Nikolina, M. and Pychyl, T.A. (2010). An Examination of the Potential Role of Pet Ownership ... in the Psychological Health of Individuals Living Alone. *Anthrozoos*, 23(1), 37–54.

Arkow, P. (1996). The Relationship between Animal Abuse and Other Forms of Family Violence. *Family Violence & Sexual Assault Bulletin*, 12(1–2), 29–34.

Arluke, A. (2006). *Just a Dog: Understanding Animal Cruelty and Ourselves*, Philadelphia: Temple University Press.

Ascione, F.R. (1993). Children Who are Cruel to Animals: A Review of Research and Implications for Developmental Psychopathology. *Anthrozoos*, 4, 226–7.

Ascione, F.R. (2000). What Veterinarians Need to Know about the Link between Animal Abuse and Interpersonal Violence: Proceedings of the 137th Annual Meeting of the American Veterinary Medical Association, Salt Lake City, 25 July 2000.

Ascione, F.R. and Weber, C. (1995). *Battered Partner Shelter Survey (BPSS)*, Logan: Utah State University.

Ascione, F.R., Weber, C.V. and Wood, D.S. (1997). The Abuse of Animals and Domestic Violence: A National Survey of Shelters for Women Who Are Battered. *Society and Animals*, 5(3), 205–18.

Ascione, F.R., Thompson, T.M., and Black, T. (1997). Childhood Cruelty to Animals: Assessing Cruelty Dimensions and Motivations. *Anthrozoos*, 10, 170–77.

Baldry, A.C. (2003). Animal Abuse and Exposure to Interparental Violence in Italian Youth. *Journal of Interpersonal Violence*, 18(3), 258–81.

Beetz, A.M. (2009). Empathy as an Indicator of Emotional Development, in A. Linzey (ed.), *The Link between Animal Abuse and Human Violence*, Eastbourne: Sussex Academic Press, 63–74.

Bell, L. (2001). Abusing Children – Abusing Animals. *Journal of Social Work*, 1(2), 223–34.

Blumer, H. (1969). *Symbolic Interactionism: Perspective and Method*, Englewood Cliffs, NJ: Prentice-Hall.

Boat, B. (1995). The Relationship between Violence to Children and Violence to Animals: An Ignored Link? *Journal of Interpersonal Violence*, 10(4), 229–35.

Browne, A. (1993). Violence against Women by Male Partners: Prevalence, Outcomes, and Policy Implications. *American Psychologist*, 48, 1077–87.

Conboy-Hill, S. (2000). *Animal Abuse and Interpersonal Violence*, Lincoln: The Companion Animal Behaviour Therapy Study Group.

Crawford, E.K., Worsham, N.L. and Swinehart, E.R. (2006). Benefits Derived from Companion Animals, and the Use of the Term 'Attachment'. *Anthrozoos*, 19(2), 98–112.

Daugherty, P. (2005). *Animal Abusers May be Warming up for More*, Los Angeles Community Policing. Available at http://www.lacp.org/2005-Articles-Main/LAPDsDedicatedAnimalCrueltyUnit.html [accessed 20 January 2012].

Department of Health, Home Office, Department for Education and Employment (2010). *Working Together to Safeguard Children: A Guide to Inter-Agency Working to Safeguard and Promote Welfare of Children*, London: The Stationery Office.

DeViney, E., Dickert, J. and Lockwood, R. (1983). The Care of Pets within Child Abusing Families. *International Journal for the Study of Animal Problems*, 4, 321–9.

Duffield, G., Hassiotis, A. and Vizard, E. (1998). Zoophilia in Young Sexual Abusers. *Journal of Forensic Psychiatry*, 9(2), 294–304.

Farrell, G., Clark, K., Ellingworth, D. and Pease, K. (2005). Of Targets and Supertargets: A Routine Activity Theory of High Crime Rates. *Internet Journal of Criminology* (2005), 1–25. Available at http://www.internetjournalofcriminology.com/Farrell,%20Clark,%20Ellingworth%20&%20Pease%20-%20Supertargets.pdf [accessed 10 January 2012].

Felthous, A. and Kellert, S. (1987). Childhood Cruelty to Animals and Later Aggression Against People: A Review. *American Journal of Psychiatry*, 144, 710–17.

Flynn, C.P. (2009). Women Battering, Pet Abuse, and Human-Animal Relationships, in A. Linzey (ed.), *The Link between Animal Abuse and Human Violence*, Eastbourne: Sussex Academic Press, 116–25.

Francione, G.L. (2007). Reflections on Animals, Property, and the Law and Rain without Thunder. *Law and Contemporary Problems*, 70(1) (Winter 2007), 9–58.

Frasch, P.D. (2000). Addressing Animal Abuse: The Complementary Roles of Religion, Secular Ethics, and the Law. *Society & Animals*, 8(3), 332–49.

Gayford, J.J. (1975). Wife Battering: A Preliminary Survey of 100 Cases. *British Medical Journal*, January, 194–7.

Gleyzer, R., Felthous, A.R. and Holzer III, C.E. (2002). Animal Cruelty and Psychiatric Disorders. *Journal of the American Academy of Psychiatry and the Law*, 30, 257–65.

Hawksworth, D. and Balen, R. (2009). Animal Cruelty and Child Welfare: The Health Visitor's Perspective, in A. Linzey (ed.), *The Link Between Animal Abuse and Human Violence*, Eastbourne: Sussex Academic Press, 281–94.

Hutton, J.S. (1998). Animal Abuse as a Diagnostic Approach in Social Work: A Pilot Study, in R. Lockwood and F.R. Ascione (eds), *Cruelty to Animals and Interpersonal Violence: Readings in Research and Application*, Indiana: Purdue University Press, 415–20.

Jouriles, E.N., Norwood, W.D., McDonald, R., Vincent, J.P. and Mahoney, A. (1996). Physical Violence and Other Forms of Marital Aggression: Links with Children's Behavior Problems. *Journal of Family Psychology*, 10(2), 223–34.

Levin, J. and Arluke, A. (2009). Reducing the Link's False Positive Problem. in A. Linzey (ed.), *The Link Between Animal Abuse and Human Violence*, Eastbourne: Sussex Academic Press, 163–72.

Lewchanin, S. and Zimmerman, E. (2000). *Clinical Assessment of Juvenile Animal Cruelty*, Brunswick, ME: Biddle Publishing Company and Audenreed Press.

Linzey, A. (ed.), (2009). *The Link Between Animal Abuse and Human Violence*, Eastbourne: Sussex Academic Press.

Lockwood, R. and Ascione, F.R. (1998). *Cruelty to Animals and Interpersonal Violence: Readings in Research and Application*, West Lafayette, IN: Purdue University Press.

Lockwood, R. and Church, A. (1996). Deadly Serious. An FBI Commentary on Animal Cruelty. *Humane Society News*, Fall, 1–4.

MacDonald, J.M. (1963). The Threat to Kill. *American Journal of Psychiatry*, 120, 125–30.

Merton, R.K. (1968). *Social Structure and Social Theory*, New York: Free Press.

Moffitt, T.E. and Caspi, A. (2003). Preventing the Inter-generational Continuity of Antisocial Behavior: Implications from Partner Violence Research. In D. Farrington and J. Coid (eds), *Primary Prevention of Antisocial Behavior*. NY: Cambridge University Press, 109–29.

Montoya, C.C. and Miller, C.A. (2009). The Role of Veterinarians and Other Animal Welfare Workers in the Reporting of Suspected Child Abuse, in A. Linzey (ed.), *The Link Between Animal Abuse and Human Violence*, Eastbourne: Sussex Academic Press, 273–80.

Morley, R. and Mullender, A. (1994). *Preventing Domestic Violence: To Women, Police Research Group Crime Prevention Unit Series: Paper 48*, London: Home Office.

Nathanson, N.J. (2009). Animal Hoarding: Slipping into the Darkness of Comorbid Animal and Self-neglect. *Journal of Elder Abuse and Neglect*, 21(4), 307–24.

Patronek, G.J. and Nathanson, J.N. (2009). A Theoretical Perspective to Inform Assessment and Treatment Strategies for Animal Hoarders. *Clinical Psychology Review*, 29, 274–81.

O'Leary, K.D. (1999). Psychological Abuse: A Variable Deserving Critical Attention in Domestic Violence. *Violence and Victims*, 14(1), 3–23.

Osofsky, J.D. (1995). Children Who Witness Domestic Violence: The Invisible Victims. *Social Policy Report: Society for Research in Child Development*, 9(3), 1–16.

Pagani, C., Robustelli, F. and Ascione, F.R. (2007). Italian Youths' Attitudes Toward and Concern for Animals. *Anthrozoos*, 20(3), 275–93.

Petersen, M.L. and Farrington, D.P. (2009). Types of Cruelty: Animals and Childhood Cruelty, Domestic Violence, Child and Elder Abuse, in A. Linzey (ed.), *The Link Between Animal Abuse and Human Violence*, Eastbourne: Sussex Academic Press, 24–37.

Pizzey, E. and Shapiro, J. (1982). *Prone to Violence*, London: Hamlyn.

Robertson, I. (2009). A Legal Duty to Report Suspected Animal Abuse: Are Veterinarians Ready? in A. Linzey (ed.), *The Link Between Animal Abuse and Human Violence*, Eastbourne: Sussex Academic Press, 263–72.

Rollin, B.E. (2006). *Animal Rights and Human Morality*, New York: Prometheus.

RSPCA (2010). *Prosecutions Department Annual Report 2009*, Horsham: RSPCA.

Schaffner, J. (2011). *An Introduction to Animals and the Law*, New York: Palgrave Macmillan.

Schiff, K., Louw, D. and Ascione, F.R. (1999). Animal Relations in Childhood and Later Violent Behaviour against Humans. *ActaCriminologica*, 12, 77–86.

Schleuter, S. (1999). Animal Abuse and Law Enforcement, in F.R. Ascione and P. Arkow (eds), *Child Abuse, Domestic Violence, and Animal Abuse: Linking the Circles of Compassion for Prevention and Intervention*, West Lafayette, IN: Purdue University Press, 316–27.

Sutherland, E.H. (1973). *On Analysing Crime* (K. Schuessler, ed.), Chicago: University of Chicago Press (Original work published 1942).

Thompson, K.L. and Gullone, E. (2006). An Investigation into the Association between the Witnessing of Animal Abuse and Adolescents' Behaviour towards Animals. *Society and Animals*, 14, 221–43.

Turner, N. (2000). Animal Abuse and the Link to Domestic Violence. *The Police Chief*, 67, 28–30.

Weber, M. (1964). *The Theory of Social and Economic Organization*, edited by Talcott Parsons, New York: The Free Press.

White, R. (2008). *Crimes Against Nature: Environmental Criminology and Ecological Justice*, Devon: Willan.

Wiegand, P., Schmidt, V. and Kleiber, M. (1999). German Shepherd Dog is Suspected of Sexually Abusing a Child. *International Journal of Legal Medicine*, 112, 324–5.

Chapter 5
Animal Harm and Traditional Fieldsports

This chapter discusses animal harm in relation to traditional 'fieldsports' as a distinct type of wildlife crime falling within the remit of animal harm. It distinguishes between the traditional fieldsports of hunting, shooting and fishing as one class or activity, and the more commercial sport and trophy hunting activities which are the subject of Chapter 7. Kean (1998) suggests that ongoing opposition to traditional fieldsports represents a shift in the historical focus of animal welfare concerns from the towns to the countryside. Thus, contemporary species justice and animal rights concerns highlight a difference between the views of rural and countryside dwellers who have historically engaged in traditional forms of sport or recreation where killing of animals is acceptable and specific 'rural' notions of crime may exist (Meagher 1985, Marshall and Johnson 2005), and the environmental radicalism of town-dwellers that increasingly engages with the countryside yet finds many of its practices problematic. These concerns differ from concerns about sport and trophy hunting which are primarily based around concerns over the exploitation of and threats to extinction of the more endangered or exotic species that tend to be involved in sport and trophy hunting. Whereas in the case of traditional fieldsports, the concerns of animal activists are primarily based around the perceived cruelty inherent in sporting practices which revolve around the pursuit of animals, and the perceived excessively violent nature of traditional hunting which uses trapping and killing methods considered to be inherently cruel and indiscriminate.

Traditional fieldsports are primarily focused on native wildlife where the original hunting activity was for subsistence needs but which has now been appropriated for a social (sporting) countryside purpose whether lawfully or unlawfully. The animal harm involved is frequently either some form of animal cruelty in the handling or despatch of animals, or harm caused through failure to comply with regulations and industry practices that results in a failure to prevent animal harm.

Traditional fieldsports (hunting, shooting, and fishing) are predominantly lawful although over the years a number of activities, such as hunting with dogs or animal baiting, have been criminalized yet continue as underground 'sports' despite the illegality of doing so. In addition, some traditional hunting activity exists in areas where hunting and its associated activities are carried out for subsistence purposes. In some cases such activities also have a traditional social meaning where groups of rural dwellers participate in the activity as a social gathering. Where this is done unlawfully (i.e. in contravention of regulations) it amounts to poaching, the illegal taking of wildlife or game animals for food, and this is covered by this chapter. However the legality of some fieldsports-related activity does not negate the illegality inherent in or associated with some activities which this chapter discusses.

A significant cause of animal harm in fieldsports is masculinities (Groombridge 1996, Nurse 2011), allied to the development of a fieldsports subculture where issues of power, dominance and control predominate and drive much animal harm. This chapter also discusses the extent to which illegal fieldsports (e.g. dog-fighting and cock-fighting) are also dominated by gambling and distinctly masculine subcultures through which a hierarchy of offending is established and developed. This includes discussion of dog-fighting 'dogmen' and the cultural imperative of animal harm. The chapter also considers traditional countryside activities such as hunting with dogs in the UK and explains the cultural relevance of fox-hunting, mink-hunting, cub-hunting and stag-hunting and how illegal activity related to these activities is frequently an assertion of a particular form of social identity. As a result, despite legislation to control fieldsports in different parts of the world there remains resistance to law enforcement efforts which are rooted in cultural and traditional explanations for these activities that attempt to retain such activities in the face of perceived outsider threats. Sometimes this is presented as the 'town versus country' and attempts to negate the legitimacy of any legal interference, or is exhibited in arguments about the thrill of the chase and the concept of a 'fair chase' which is enjoyed by hunter and hunted alike. But it also reveals a 'gang' culture and group mentality which the chapter explores by comparing illegal fieldsports (i.e. those bloodsports that rely on animal harm) to inner-city gang culture with its initiation rites, denial of authority and challenges to law enforcement. Cohn and Linzey define hunting as 'socially condoned cruelty', arguing that the classification of some species as game is 'arbitrary and thus morally arbitrary' (2009: 317). While the focus of their analysis is official classifications of game, the unofficial classification adopted by those involved in illegal activity also requires consideration. Fieldsports adherents distinguish between the suffering of animals for no purpose and the bravery and combative nature of a sport that has value to all participants (Hawley 1982, Matz 1984, Huggs 1993). Cohn and Linzey suggest that the official classification of species as game refers to 'specific species that somehow are incapable of suffering' or that any suffering involved was 'necessary' (2009: 317–18). But in the illegal fieldsports world it is precisely the ability of certain animals to withstand suffering and continue fighting (e.g. fighting cocks or dogs and badgers) that identifies them as game or worthy participants in the sport. Thus the notion that legal animal rights would make any difference (except perhaps for providing additional enforcement options) is partially flawed as a policy perspective, although it is of course entirely appropriate to consider providing legal animal rights as an additional legislative measure to address or attempt to address such harm or to provide a wider range of enforcement options. However before discussing such aspects a definition of fieldsports is necessary.

Defining Fieldsports

Chapter 7 discusses sport and trophy hunting as a separate subject primarily motivated by dominion over rare species and also linked to the illegal trade in animal derivatives such as ivory. Fieldsports as defined by this chapter includes 'traditional' hunting, shooting and fishing practices carried out by countryside or rural community dwellers rather than the subsistence hunting of indigenous peoples carried out specifically as an integral part of their cultural identity (Preece 1999) which is discussed in more detail in Chapter 6. However, in addition to the (mainly British) definition of fieldsports as being country sports or blood sports, this definition also includes traditional hunting carried out by rural communities and which has a social connotation. Thus the definition of traditional fieldsports in this chapter includes game shooting in rural areas of the UK, the United States and across Europe and both commercial and traditional (rather than recreational) fishing. Eliason (2003) defined hunting as performing a traditional role, where the game taken is used and wastage is 'negatively sanctioned' (2003: 4). This definition identifies a fieldsport as being primarily based around the 'pursuit' of live quarry and representing a way of life where individuals kill animals primarily for the purpose of using them for food or fur (Brymer 1991). Thus hunters trap and kill animals in order to harvest their meat as food, or to use their fur for clothing and shelter, anglers catch fish primarily for food, and farmers and others (including animal breeders) may kill animals in order to protect livestock.

However the traditional individualistic fieldsports pursuit has developed in the United States, UK and several other countries into a fieldsports industry where significant sums of money are paid to engage in traditional fieldsports. Shooting has thus become a commercialized activity with considerable economic benefits to rural economies which are otherwise in decline due to overall losses in agricultural employment and the resultant decline in the number and size of rural settlements (McManus et al. 2012). As a result, the income derived from fieldsports, despite declines in public acceptance of shooting live quarry as a recreational activity in western countries, can be significant to rural economies. Consultants PACEC, for example, concluded in 2006 that sport shooting contributed fewer than 70,000 full-time equivalent jobs and an estimated £1.6 billion (gross added value) to the UK economy. In the developing world, hunting can be a vital source of revenue for village communities who own hunting rights and are able to either exploit these rights or their own hunting expertise in order to raise much-needed income where other forms of employment are not available.

Within fieldsports a range of activities are incorporated into the broad headings of hunting, shooting and fishing. In the United Kingdom, United States and other western countries, for example, shooting can include:

- coastal wildfowling – which involves the shooting of ducks, geese and waders on coastal land;
- deer stalking – the shooting of deer for game management purposes (i.e. to keep numbers manageable) or for crop protection;
- driven game – where lowland gamebirds are flushed over the standing guns;
- walked up game: where a shooter flushes lowland game as he/she walks over the shooting ground;
- grouse shooting – (both walked up and driven);
- inland wildfowling – shooting ducks, geese and waders on inland sites;
- pest control: shooting of legitimate 'pest species' (usually specified in legislation) as part of sporting shooting activities. Typical pests are those species recognized as doing damage to crops including pigeons, rabbits, crows (and other corvidae);
- released birds (game birds) – shooting of birds specially bred for shooting or brought in from a game farm and released into the wild for shooting; and
- reared birds – game birds bred by the shoot provider specifically for sporting shooting and released into the wild.

(PACEC 2006: 6–29)

In African countries these definitions can also be extended to include other small to medium sized game before such shooting becomes big game hunting, as a wider range of wildlife classed as legitimate game (subject to local shooting policies and regulations) is available, and the controls on hunting as a recreational or subsistence necessity may be lower.

Hunting activities such as fox-, stag- and mink-hunting (which were all until recently lawful in the UK) have also developed from their perceived 'pest' control origins into leisure pursuits, as much about the sporting connotations of chasing live quarry with hounds as they are about population control of perceived pests. It is undoubtedly true that commercial fishing and game shooting industries are also allied to food consumption, and may make claims to providing healthy and nutritious alternatives to factory farmed and processed foods (British Association for Shooting and Conservation 2011). However sporting elements are also a significant factor in non-commercial hunting and fishing activities where the challenge of pitting an individual's skills against those of live quarry which can escape are considered to be significant attractions of the sport as they are with trophy hunting (Lindsey et al. 2012).

Separate from these traditional (and legal) activities, a set of combative fieldsports have also emerged where the emphasis is less on fieldsports as a pathway to food consumption, and more on the use of animals for sport. In particular, animal-baiting activities such as badger-digging and badger-baiting are prevalent in the UK. Common factors in such activities are the pursuit of live quarry and the exploitation of animals by pitting one species against another as the following case study illustrates.

Case Study One: Badger Persecution in the UK

This case study highlights the difficulties of enforcing an area of animal harm where the nature of the offending behaviour is likely to be unaffected by a more punitive regime or the introduction of legal animal rights or legal personhood. It involves deliberate acts already prohibited by UK law.

Badger Persecution

Although badgers have been protected by a variety of different pieces of legislation some going back as far as 1835, persecution of badgers is still known to be widespread in the UK. In its 2005 fact sheet *Badgers and the Law*, the National Federation of Badger Groups (now called the Badger Trust) comments that 'it is a sad fact that many thousands of badgers are still killed each year, and the incidents appear to be increasing. Also due to the nature of the crimes, there are relatively few successful prosecutions' (2005). While exact figures are difficult to produce, estimates of 9,000–10,000 badgers killed annually are regularly produced by UK NGOs involved in badger protection.

The badger persecution problem Evidence from investigations suggests that badger-baiting takes place throughout the UK, wherever badgers are present. Although the *Protection of Badgers Act 1992* offers protection for the badger, persecution of badgers through digging and baiting is widespread. Badger-digging and badger-baiting often result in the death of badgers. Indeed, arguably this is the intent of the 'sports'. Badger-baiting often follows on from badger-digging and the nature of these forms of persecution is that badger setts are first located and then badgers are removed from their setts and ultimately killed.

By their very nature, badger-baiting and badger-digging are offences that take place in remote areas and are difficult to detect and prosecute. Naturewatch explains that the detection and investigation of badger persecution:

> is a notoriously difficult and very time-consuming operation, often without success for numerous reasons. Equally difficult is achieving a successful prosecution. Police presence is needed to make an arrest, so good-co-ordination is vital. Badger diggers are professional and in contrast the Badger Groups have an inherent weakness; they are unable to follow the case right through without the close co-operation of the police and RSPCA. Unfortunately many police forces do not view badger cruelty as important which means a lack of co-operation exists in many areas. (Naturewatch 2007)

Naturewatch highlights the fact that badger-baiters and badger-diggers are highly organized, professional and often work in groups or organized gangs. Badger-digging and badger-baiting are seen as 'sports' which are pursued enthusiastically by their followers. The unlawful nature of the activity means that precautions are taken against detection and while badger groups monitor badger activity at badger setts, it still remains the case that many incidents will go undetected.

The law   The main legislation protecting badgers in England and Wales is the *Protection of Badgers Act 1992*. This Act consolidates all previous legislation including the *Badgers Act 1973* (as amended) and the *Badgers (Further Protection) Act 1991*. The *Protection of Badgers Act 1992* protects badgers in the wild and makes it an offence to wilfully kill, injure, take or attempt to kill, injure or take a badger, possess a dead badger or any part of a badger or cruelly ill-treat a badger. The Act also contains prohibited methods of taking a badger and makes it an offence to use badger tongs in the course of killing, taking or attempting to kill a badger or to dig for a badger. It is also an offence to sell or offer for sale or control any live badger; mark, tag or ring a badger; or interfere with a badger sett by damaging a sett, destroying a sett, obstructing access to a sett, causing a dog to enter a sett or disturb a badger while occupying a sett.

The potential maximum fine for each badger offence is £5,000 per offence (i.e. the amount of the fine may be multiplied by the number of badgers) and/or six months' imprisonment. Under the *Protection of Badgers Act 1992* the courts may also order forfeiture of any badger or skin relating to the offence or of any weapon or article used; order destruction or disposal of dogs; or disqualify an offender from having custody of a dog.

Badgers are also protected in Scotland by the *Protection of Badgers Act 1992* as amended by the *Nature Conservation (Scotland) Act 2004*. Schedule 6 of the *Wildlife and Countryside Act 1981* also specifically prohibits specified methods of taking or killing wild animals and applies to badgers, meaning that the use of illuminating devices and some snares to take or attempt to take a badger would itself be an offence. Some animal welfare legislative provisions also apply to badgers making it an offence to cause unnecessary suffering, abandon an animal in circumstances likely to result in unnecessary suffering, or carry out fighting or baiting involving badgers which would result in unnecessary suffering.

The effect of the various pieces of legislation is to give protection to badgers and their setts in the wild and make it an offence to kill or interfere with wild badgers or their setts. Where badgers are reduced into a captive state they are also protected from cruelty by animal welfare legislation.

Badger Persecution Offences

Despite this legal protection, badgers continue to suffer from illegal persecution. Although badger-baiting and badger-digging are often talked of together they are two distinctly different offences. Badger-digging is the process of digging a badger out of its sett. Naturewatch provides the following description:

Small terriers are sent down into a badger sett to locate a badger and hold it at bay. The men then dig their way down to their quarry and drag the badger out of the sett. Many diggers attach a radio transmitter to the dog's collar before sending it below ground so that they can use a radio receiver/locater to determine the exact location of the dog.

If it's lucky the badger will be shot but usually the men will set their terriers on the badger and watch it suffer a long and agonising death, stabbing it with shovels for good measure. At times, the dogs and the badgers may die when the sett collapses and suffocates them. (Naturewatch 2007)

Badger-baiting is a separate activity; the process of digging a badger out of its sett and then later setting dogs on it in a barn, shed or cellar where the sport can take place undetected. The practice was, in fact, a form of public entertainment in the early nineteenth century but dates back to medieval times. Naturewatch explains that the badger is:

placed into a makeshift arena, a ring or pit from which it cannot escape. Dogs are then set upon it. The badger is often 'nobbled' by having its jaw broken, back legs tied together or even broken to allow the dog a better chance of survival. (Naturewatch 2007)

Even if the badger is lucky enough to get the better of one dog, the owner may hit or otherwise injure the badger in order to 'protect his pet'. The reality of badger-baiting is that the outcome for the badger is never in doubt and, ultimately, no matter how well it tries to defend itself, the badger, through injury and exhaustion, will reach a state when it will not be able to fight any longer. The baiters will then kill the badger, usually by clubbing or shooting it. NGOs and the police are in agreement that money regularly changes hands in badger-baiting incidents, often in large sums. The Metropolitan Police explain that badger-baiting 'has become more common in the last 20 years' and that 'large sums of money are often involved and it is usually the case that those involved in badger crime are also involved in other series crime' (Metropolitan Police Website 2012). Baiting is a highly organized contest, usually held away from the sett, and at baiting events spectators bet on the performance of the dogs against the badger and similar to the money and association with dogs in dog-fighting, masculinities and identification with the more powerful dogs are significant factors.

Enforcement activity In relation to badger-digging and badger-baiting, enforcement activity is carried out in two ways; prevention and detection of problems at setts by volunteer badger group members[1] and apprehension of

---

1   The UK has a network of volunteer badger groups who monitor activity at badger setts. The local confederation of groups collectively forms the Badger Trust network.

offenders and prosecution by the statutory agencies. While the focus of UK wildlife law enforcement is mainly the detection and apprehension of offenders rather than the prevention of wildlife crime, badger-baiting is one area where some dedicated crime prevention takes place, although this is carried out by NGOs. Volunteers from badger groups carry out monitoring activity on badger setts and this volunteer activity can reveal criminal activity. Badger groups actively report incidents to the police for investigation but there is no co-ordinated police action aimed at detecting and preventing badger crime.

Practical enforcement problems   By its very nature, much badger persecution takes place in remote areas where it would not be encountered either by police officers involved in their normal duties or by members of the public. Badgers are mainly nocturnal animals with a widespread distribution in the UK and so the likelihood of members of the public viewing persecution incidents taking place is slight. NGO Scottish Badgers explain that:

> Contraventions of the *Protection of Badgers Act 1992*, like so many other wildlife offences, are difficult to prosecute. The very nature of the locus, often in remote areas, means that there are rarely any witnesses. Often the crime is not noticed until some time after it is committed by which time any evidence left at the scene by the perpetrator has been destroyed by the elements. It is an onerous task for the Police Wildlife Liaison Officer to investigate an offence and to gather sufficient evidence for a prosecution to proceed. It is the duty of the police and not private individuals or badger groups to investigate offences. (Hutchison 2000: 1)

It remains the case, however, that the detection of badger persecution relies heavily on the work of volunteer monitors (the badger groups) to identify offences. Badger-diggers and badger-baiters operate in gangs and while the RSPCA has had some success in undercover operations aimed at gaining intelligence on these gangs or on infiltrating gangs (see Saunders 2001) the part-time nature of much wildlife policing and the lack of resources to investigate badger crime in any co-ordinated way means that many cases are not being proceeded with and are not being taken. Where cases are being taken they are relatively few in number and mainly rely on the work of the RSPCA in England and Wales.

One case highlights the difficulties involved in bringing cases to court. In February 2002, six men were acquitted of charges relating to digging for badgers and causing cruelty to a dog at Dolgellau Magistrates Court, North Wales.

The six defendants, four from Wales and two from Lancashire, were charged with interfering with a badger sett by causing a dog to enter a sett, damaging a part of a badger sett and disturbing a badger while occupying a sett. The events took place at a badger sett in Llanfrothen, Gwynedd, North Wales on 22 July 2001. One defendant was additionally charged with causing unnecessary suffering to an animal by allowing a dog to go to ground and receive injuries.

The men were found allegedly digging a badgers' sett in a wood near Llanfrothen, they were accompanied by a dozen dogs and the court heard that two dogs were seen trying to get into a tunnel at the bottom of the hole and a squealing noise could be heard. When one of the dogs, a terrier called Wilf, was pulled out of the tunnel it was heavily bloodstained and had badger hairs in its mouth. The activities of the men were typical of badger-digging yet the men told police that they were digging for a fox which had gone to ground, a lawful activity at the time of the offences.

All six men told the court that they were hunting for foxes and denied that they had visited the site to dig for badgers. The prosecution argued that this was not the case, that there was evidence of badger-digging and that the men would have been aware that the site was a badger sett. The prosecution also alleged that the injuries to the dog were consistent with badger-digging activities. However, a witness for the defence, veterinary surgeon Madalene Forsyth of Helmsley, York, disagreed and said that Wilf's injuries were 'absolutely typical' of a fox bite (*Liverpool Daily Post*, 27 February 2002).

The six men were acquitted after deliberations by magistrates. The Chairman of the Bench said that the prosecution had failed to prove that the site was an active badger sett and magistrates agreed that the defendants were fox-hunting on the day. The lack of resources to clearly establish the presence of badgers hampered the prosecution's attempt to establish the exact nature of the alleged offenders' activities and to prove that a badger crime was being attempted.

Such case studies illustrate the persistent, deliberate nature of certain aspects of animal harm and the criminality involved. This criminality is frequently linked to notions of tradition and an allegiance to a higher power (Sykes and Matza 1957) such that offenders committed to their chosen form of animal harm find themselves both unwilling and unable to depart from their offences.

Fieldsports and Tradition

Moral culpability policies are employed by NGOs according to the social legal perspective on animal harm where NGOs consider that an activity is morally wrong and should not be allowed to continue. There is some overlap here with green criminology's and utilitarianism's animal rights perspective in which the issue of human action in relation to other sentient beings is questioned. In particular, there are questions concerning whether it is morally right for humans to inflict pain and suffering on animals or to kill or take them for the purpose of sport. For example, LACS's long-running campaign to ban hunting with dogs in the UK (which ran for almost 80 years) was primarily based on discussions concerning whether it was right to chase and terrify animals if the intention of activities such as fox-hunting was predator control. LACS argued that the purpose of such activities was primarily sport and thus this represented a form of animal harm that should be prohibited by legislation. Hunt supporters argued both that hunting with hounds was, in the case of foxes at least, not only a form of predator control but also a traditional countryside recreational activity enjoyed by a range of individuals.

In its evidence to the Committee of Inquiry on Hunting with Dogs (the Burns Inquiry) which made recommendations to the UK government on legislation to ban this form of hunting, the Animal Welfare Information Service (AWIS) observed that 'foxhunting is a game that should not be confused with fox control' (Burns et al. 2000). Having carried out observations on a number of hunts, Mike Huskisson of AWIS concluded that 'where farmers perceive a need to control foxes they do so using a variety of means other than hunting with dogs. The majority of these methods involve considerably less cruelty' (Burns et al. 2000). A central feature of the campaign to end fox-hunting and other forms of hunting with dogs was, therefore, a moral objection to a form of animal control that was considered unnecessary and which could not be justified in terms of its apparent objective. (Although some doubt was cast on whether the alleged aim of 'animal control' was genuine or solely a justification put forward to provide legitimacy for hunting.) Indeed in some submissions on the draft Bill, which eventually banned hunting of live animals with dogs, advocates for a ban accepted that if foxes, mink or deer needed to be controlled this should be done. But it should be done via a humane method of control and not by first chasing the animal. However underlying resistance to the proposed legislation was a need both to protect a particular countryside way of life and a perception that traditions intrinsic to the notion of countryside and rural dwelling were under threat from those wishing to alter the traditional conception of the countryside. While the UK's tradition of country sports as being the preserve of the middle and upper classes may differ from the traditions and cultural perspectives of other countries, the importance of traditional hunting and shooting activities as a shared cultural activity in rural areas is common to a number of countries in both the developed and developing worlds.

Animal Harm and Cultural Imperatives

Complex attitudes to crime and what is perceived as crime exist within rural communities where resistance to legislation to control or criminalize traditional fieldsports continues. While NGOs sometimes continue to pursue an abolitionist agenda on moral grounds, seeking to criminalize or regulate rural activities such as shooting and fishing which are perceived as animal harm, rural dwellers may view such activities differently and deem them acceptable even where legislation dictates otherwise. As indicated earlier, the UK campaign against the *Hunting Act 2004* was often characterized as 'town versus country' (Burns et al. 2000) and discussions of traditional fieldsports and hunting activities that become subject to legislation often contain debates concerning perceptions that affluent sections of society seek to impose their will on poorer rural communities. Such ideas can represent an idealized notion of rurality where those with historical ties to rural areas or a notion of the countryside as embodying a particular notion of the natural environment consider traditional sports to be an integral part of the countryside that should be retained. By contrast town-dwelling opponents of fieldsports may show exaggerated signs of distress when confronted with images or ideas of countryside violence and animal harm as it destroys their perception of the countryside as a safe, calm place (Mingay 1989). In the case of western societies imposing conservation and animal protectionist ideals on African and Asian countries, this can appear to constitute 'colonialism' and a lack of understanding of the need for animals to be used as a resource. Continued involvement in animal harm activities by participation in fieldsports thus provides a means of reasserting identity in the face of opposition from others.

Fieldsports are inextricably linked to a rural identity and thus problems occur in the classification of rural crime in law enforcement policy, in part because rural crime has been neglected as an area of criminological study (Donnermeyer et al. 2006) but also because practitioners and policymakers with different operational parameters adopt different classifications, thus no consistent definition of rural crime exists across the criminological or policy literature. As a result, identifying rural criminality becomes problematic beyond the strictly legalistic definition, although a perspective on rurality is central to traditional fieldsports offences. Cooper (2009) explains that (in the UK at least) traditionally 'hunting has been associated with the ruling or elite classes, as a means of exerting primacy and influence' (2009: 303). The UK's feudal system meant that land was traditionally in the hands of the nobility who employed the lower classes to work the land for them while retaining property rights over both land and animals such that only the nobility were allowed to hunt and it was an offence for others to do so. Hunting was, thus, a means of asserting dominance, social superiority and even masculinity and allowed a distinct aspect of cultural identity to emerge; one of control. While this is not necessarily the case in other countries where use of the land and animals may be associated with the working classes, agricultural and livestock production and pure subsistence, traditional fieldsports are still integral to rural identities. Thus the acceptability of hunting and other fieldsports and rural dwellers' and policymakers perspectives on their continued legality (legislation notwithstanding) are determined according to a range of demographical, economical, social or cultural factors according to the ideological perspectives of different bodies involved in rural crime enforcement or policy and the social construction of rurality and land or animal use. Police perspectives generally view rural crime as less serious than urban, and particularly inner-city, crime predicated on perceptions that rural areas require less intensive policing (Muhammad 2002) and a more informal, community-oriented approach to policing. Research consistently shows that the core areas of policing (violent and serious crime) tend to be less prevalent in rural areas. For example, Sorokin et al. (1931) concluded that crime in the rural context of the United States and numerous European countries was much lower than urban crime rates, while more recent research indicates that although rural crime has risen in some areas it still remains at lower levels than urban crime.

In part this reflects the diverse nature of rural areas with wider, less densely populated areas, offering less opportunity for traditionally numerous crimes of burglary and other property crimes, as well as a more sparse population less prone to interpersonal violence. But it also reflects the fact that rural areas may define and record crime differently and are generally served by fewer criminal justice agencies (Weisheit et al. 2006) and a more multi-disciplinary approach to policing with sometimes greater emphasis on community policing than intelligence-led techniques. As a result, those involved in traditional fieldsports may begin to see themselves as being outside of the scope of mainstream policing, subject to a rural policing regime which views their activities somewhat differently and to see themselves as inherently less criminal than their city counterparts even in areas such as animal harm. Muhammad (2002) identified that rural officers generally work with fewer resources and lower budgets than their urban counterparts with rural policing often considered a 'soft' option by police managers, a view reinforced by media representations of rural policing as genteel community support unencumbered by the violent crime images of city policing (Young 2010). Jobes et al. (2004) identified that crime generally decreased across an urban–rural continuum and more cohesive and integrated community structures had less crime, while highly disorganized communities generally had higher crime levels. Sparsely populated areas may thus lack informal controls that keep crime in check, and in some areas crimes involving exploitation of wildlife or natural resources may even be tolerated where the community benefits from doing so.

Hawley's (1993) research on cock-fighters, Forsythe and Evans' (1998) research and observation of the 'dogmen', Saunders' (2001) infiltration of badger-digging groups, and the submissions of those who hunt with dogs to the UK's 2000 Burns Inquiry into Hunting with Dogs reveal much about the attitudes of those who are engaged in different aspects of wildlife crime within the hunting, shooting and fishing industries and their rationalizations and justifications for doing so.

Cohn and Linzey (2009) raise the question of whether involvement in hunting harms the hunters themselves. They point to the link between violence towards animals and violence towards humans and the common link between murderers and hunters, especially murderers who despatch their victims by shooting. While there is no clearly established, statistically significant link between hunting and either human violence or murder their argument makes sense in respect of the possible escalation from one form of killing to another. It might also be explained in terms of the desensitizing effects of killing animals and the sense in which individuals may become used to the presence of death in their lives, especially where they have caused it. It must be stressed, however, that there is no hard evidence to substantiate such a link.

Fieldsports and Associated Illegality

Gavitt (1989), Hall (1992), Wilson et al. (2007) and Nurse (2009, 2011) have all identified that wildlife law violations remain significant problems within the hunting, shooting and fishing industries. They are also a problem in areas where hunting rights are allowed to local people or as part of wildlife conservation or management regimes. Where there is a perceived need to control animal numbers, hunting provides a means through which animals can be lawfully killed while also raising revenue, particularly in poorer countries where animals are considered to be a resource (see Chapter 7 on sport and trophy hunting). This is the case in African countries where wildlife has multiple benefits to the local population and the economy. Thus wildlife may be an important source of tourism revenue, sporting revenue from trophy hunting, and also an important source of food for local populations where conservation management and hunting interests may be in conflict. However, regulating such hunting activities and ensuring that illegal activities do not proliferate alongside the legal ones is problematic as the following discussion of African hunting problems illustrates.

Illegal and commercial hunting of wildlife for bushmeat is now recognized as a significant wildlife crisis in Africa, leading to local extinction of some species. Lyndsey et al. report that 'illegal bushmeat hunting has emerged as a serious conservation threat in Zimbabwe' (2011: 1). They identify political instability and economic decline as primary factors, pointing out that in several areas that are still being managed as game ranches, 'illegal hunting is causing further declines of wildlife populations' (2011). Fa et al. (2002) also identify the bushmeat trade as representing a significant threat to wildlife populations, while the US-based Bushmeat Crisis Task Force (BCTF) identifies killing of animals for food as being the primary problem, while identifying that there are a variety of reasons why this might be the case.

Much of the hunting takes place throughout the Congo basin area where illegal bushmeat hunting is most prevalent (BCTF 2009, Mfunda and Roskaft 2010) and is primarily carried out to meet local people's subsistence needs by supplying a cheap and easily obtained meat source. Thus 'traditional hunting methods such as bows and arrows, snares and pitfalls' might be used (Mfunda and Roskaft 2010: 1) in order that familiarity, culture and tradition are satisfied and hunting is kept within the local community as a means of meeting local dietary requirements (Holmern et al. 2002, 2006). Bushmeat is an important source of protein to local people and compares favourably with other sources of meat which are often in short supply. However the BCTF concludes that 'forest antelope (duikers), pigs, and primates are most often eaten, and as much as 1 million metric tons of wildlife is killed for food in Central Africa each year' (2009: 1). Despite its illegality, bushmeat hunting is justified on grounds of necessity (Sykes and Matza 1957) given the lack of alternatives. Naughton-Treves (1998) and Neilson (2006) identified that bushmeat hunting is influenced by growth in human populations such that existing food supplies are inadequate to serve the population.

However, in addition poverty, weak governance and inadequate law enforcement are also considered to be factors. The BCTF commented that, in reality, 'policies and laws that are intended to regulate the hunting of wildlife are seldom perceived by local communities as legitimate, desirable, or enforceable' (2009: 4). As a result, the laws are widely ignored and enforcement action is largely ineffectual.

For local people, there is also an economic incentive to apply their traditional hunting practices to the illegal trade in bushmeat. The BCTF identifies that 'when wildlife are abundant hunters can make between $400 and $1,100 per year from bushmeat alone, which exceeds the average income for households across the region' (2009: 2). In addition, the money that hunters can earn from bushmeat hunting compares favourably with and sometimes exceeds the salaries paid to guards employed to protect wildlife (Wilkie and Carpenter 1999). Thus the potential income from hunting can be more profitable than conservation activities and hunting's economic power can lead to corruption among conservation staff and incentives for local people (and commercial hunters) to ignore legislation.

Another common cause of animal harm from hunting is the killing of protected species in order to protect other species. Fowler-Reeves (2007) identified that wild birds and animals are killed by the million in the UK because they pose a threat to industries and sports 'which have as their primary objective the killing of other animals or birds' (2007: 1). Thus gamekeepers and fisheries workers have been known to kill protected wildlife perceived as predators and a threat to their livelihood even though they will be aware of the illegality of their actions (Wilson et al. 2007). In addition, combative animal sports are closely associated with illegal (i.e. unregulated) forms of gambling and criminal gangs involved in dog-fighting, cock-fighting and bear-baiting are known to use cruelty in their training methods and, given the money involved in gambling, to also be associated with violence and intimidation which is used both to keep their activities secret and to maintain discipline within their networks. As a result, the police and NGO response to combative animal harm employs many of the techniques used in the investigation of organized crime such as surveillance and infiltration of the gangs (Saunders 2001).

Smith (2010) argues that 'we only have a fuzzy notion of the stereotypical rural criminal and find it difficult to acknowledge the existence of a rural criminal underclass'. Yet the opportunities for criminality provided to rural criminals make it likely that specific types of offending endemic to rural areas and the fieldsports industry exist, multiple classifications of and perspectives on rural crime notwithstanding. The author's research on wildlife crime, for example, identified distinct types of offender involved in those rural crimes containing a wildlife element, concluding that in addition to the 'traditional' criminal who commits offences for financial gain, other specific offender types exist (Nurse 2011 and developed further in Chapter 3). The dictates of countryside employment, particularly in the game-rearing industry, create economic criminals who commit wildlife crimes as a direct result of particular economic pressures (e.g. direct employer-pressure or profit-driven crime within their chosen profession).

In some cases their offences are determined by the demands of competing within a rural economy that is under both economic and political threat. However, the opportunities created by the countryside and engagement in traditional fieldsports may also be a factor in the emergence of new masculinities offenders in rural areas where advantage of the crime opportunities can be taken and where a close-knit community may encourage new offenders. Masculinities criminals – those who commit offences involving harm to animals as a representation of their male power and identity – are drawn to the countryside where their quarry (e.g. game or wild birds, badgers, hares) can be found and where their criminal behaviour exhibits a stereotypical masculine nature (Groombridge 1996, Kimmel et al. 2005) both in terms of their exercise of power over animals and the links to sport and gambling involved in such activities as hare coursing, badger-baiting and badger-digging. Thus traditional fieldsports influence a particular type of animal harm offending linked to the fieldsports activity and issues of rural identity.

Perspectives on Criminality

Offenders involved in the exploitation of wildlife, farm animals or the rural environment within traditional fieldsports, as defined by this chapter, can commit their crimes for the following general reasons:

1. profit or commercial gain;
2. thrill or sport;
3. necessity of obtaining food;
4. antipathy towards governmental and law enforcement bodies;
5. tradition and cultural reasons.

While these are the primary motivations and others may be involved, certain specific types of offending can only take place in rural areas as they are inherently reliant on countryside and wild species (e.g. hare coursing, badger-baiting, illegal fox-hunting and bushmeat hunting). Criminality has thus either emerged in a rural setting or adapted to it so that some offenders specifically travel to rural areas to commit their offences. Birds of prey, for example, suffer from illegal persecution in many areas of their range in the UK. The hen harrier, for example, a protected bird of prey, has an average of only 10 pairs breeding successfully in England and survey work has shown that many nests and birds are destroyed each year throughout the UK, leaving the birds with an uncertain future on the UK's moorlands. Illegal bushmeat hunting is now known to be endemic in many rural areas of Africa and threatens a number of wildlife populations.

Control theory dictates that crime is almost inevitable in any area where social controls are weak or ineffective (Hirschi 1969) which is a particular problem in sparsely populated countryside areas and the African bush. However, research consistently shows that rural areas generally have a greater level of informal control which in some areas results in lower levels of crime (Smith 1980). The closer social bonds of rural communities, where many residents know both each other and their local police, facilitates informal control in some communities, aided by the relative stability of the population (Wilson 1991). However, rurality impacts on communities differently dependent on population size, geography and social mix. Thus while it might generally be argued that more cohesive communities have less crime (Jobes et al. 2004) the precise make-up of a community will influence its cohesiveness and determine the extent to which this is true.

Game-rearing areas in Scotland experience a disproportionate amount of the known illegal killing of birds of prey in the UK. Studies have shown a strong link between the killing of birds of prey and management of land for game bird shooting, especially in the uplands. In 2005, LACS published the report *The Killing Game* describing the extent to which predator control can be linked to the unlawful killing of wildlife.

The LACS report highlights that persecution can take many forms, from birds (and their nests or eggs) being deliberately destroyed, through to birds being taken from the wild in order to stop them from breeding. The RSPB also produces annual reports showing that bird-of-prey persecution continues, often linking it to grouse- and pheasant-rearing areas where the birds are considered to be competitors for game birds. It is estimated that tens of millions of game birds are released onto shooting estates each year, some of which are intensively reared to ensure a plentiful supply of birds for shooting days. Birds of prey compete with game birds for some food sources but are also considered to be a threat to young grouse and pheasant chicks. Birds of prey are also perceived to be a threat in sheep-rearing areas, so much so that in the early 1990s the Welsh Agricultural Office produced a leaflet entitled *What Killed my Lamb?* as a means of educating sheep farmers that red kites, frequent victims in illegal persecution incidents, were not the obvious culprits in cases of lamb mortality. The perception of NGOs and conservationists is that a considerable number of those involved in legitimate game-rearing activities are also involved in the illegal killing of birds of prey, and some evidence exists to support this view.

Analysis of RSPB data on wildlife prosecutions shows that between 1985 and 2003, of all the prosecutions for bird of prey related offences in England, Wales and Scotland, 85 percent were committed by people 'with game rearing interests' (LACS 2005: 21). This suggests that illegal persecution by shooting estate employees is widespread and continues despite legal protection for birds of prey and enforcement activities aimed at this type of crime. Those involved in game rearing are likely to have knowledge of countryside law and be aware that the killing of birds of prey is illegal. It is difficult to believe, for example, that countryside professionals living and working in the countryside on a daily basis are unaware that such rare birds as the golden eagle and osprey are protected by law.

While it is difficult to fully evaluate the extent of illegal bird-of-prey persecution, LACS has alleged that there are:

Millions of mammals and birds slaughtered on shooting estates in order to minimise predation on gamebirds and maximise profits for the live shooting industry. According to extrapolations from the Game Conservancy Trust's own figures, every year 4.5 million animals (and possibly twice as many) are killed by employees of shooting estates. That's a minimum average of 12,300 mammals and birds shot, poisoned, snared, trapped or clubbed to death every day. This largely reported and out of control predator control regime is an animal welfare scandal of staggering proportions. (LACS 2005: 3)

In the late 1980s/early 1990s, a Scottish gamekeeper alleged that more than 400 shooting estates in Scotland were actively involved in the illegal killing of birds of prey. While these allegations remain unsubstantiated, practical casework in the UK each year demonstrates that illegal killing of birds of prey remains a persistent problem on game-rearing estates.

Illegal persecution of birds of prey takes many forms. The RSPB (2005) explains that bird-of-prey persecution falls into two broad categories; use of poisons and direct persecution through shooting and trapping of birds. Poisoning involves the actual poisoning of birds of prey and the laying of poisoned baits. Birds of prey are carrion eaters and so one method of killing the birds is to place poison on a carcass and leave it out in the open where birds may be attracted to it as a food source. The bird eats the poisoned bait and dies, although not always immediately. Any poisoned bait used in the open within habitat used by birds of prey has the potential to kill the birds (RSPB 2005: 4). The RSPB explains that:

Poisoning may be considered the greatest actual or potential threat of all forms of persecution. In contrast to shooting and much trapping activity, which require a sustained effort by the criminal concerned to produce a limited return, poisoning can produce a substantial effect with only minimal effort. Poison baits continue to be lethal over a matter of days or weeks and can kill multiple victims without further effort by the poisoner. (RSPB 2005a: 4)

Some birds of prey are particularly susceptible to poisoning. For example, LACS reported that 'of the Scottish red kites found dead for which a cause of death can be identified, 70% were deliberately poisoned' (LACS 2005: 22). Buzzards also suffer significantly from poisoning. LACS explains that:

The Scottish Agricultural Science Agency reports that, of the 40 incidents of buzzard persecution in 2003, it was possible to confirm the cause of death in 25 cases. Half of these were carbofuran or alphachloralose poisonings. These two poisons were also identified as the cause of a third of the eagle deaths, two thirds of the peregrine falcon deaths and both of the recorded sparrow hawk deaths. A single incident of alphachloralose abuse killed three kites and two buzzards. (LACS 2005: 23)

Carbofuran and alphachloralose are the poisons most widely used in bird-of-prey poisoning incidents. Carbofuran was banned by the EU at the end of 2001 and alphachloralose was banned in Scotland in March 2005. Seventy-six percent of the confirmed cases of bird-of-prey poisoning in 2003 involved alphachloralose or carbofuran and the two poisons continued to dominate in 2004 (RSPB 2005). It is hoped that the withdrawal of approval for these poisons will eventually see a reduction in the availability of the poisons for illegal use. However, relatively small quantities are needed to prepare poison baits and so the 'remaining illegal stocks may be sufficient for widespread abuse for several years' (RSPB 2005: 4).

The reality is that within the shooting and livestock industries illegal predator controls are considered to be widespread. In the United States Defenders of Wildlife have expressed concerns about possible reductions in the legal protection afforded to wolves while highlighting incidents where wolves have been killed unlawfully to protect livestock. Gamekeepers, farmers and other fieldsports staff with access to land that is not always in the public eye are at liberty to shoot protected birds of prey or animals out of sight of the public and in areas where their victims may never be found. There are also reported incidents of protected birds of prey being shot during legitimate game-bird shoots if they are unfortunate enough to be in the vicinity of guns.

Fieldsports and Resistance

The continuation of fieldsports in contemporary western societies which generally consider sporting activities that harm animals to be unacceptable is of interest both culturally and socially. While, in the UK at least, the majority do not hunt or carry out animal harming recreational activities, those that do represent a vocal minority. Protests against the introduction of the UK's *Hunting Act 2004* were widespread with the major protest attracting around 400,000 people, many of whom initially vowed to carry on the activity after the law made hunting with dogs unlawful. Cooper (2009) suggests that 'the obvious inference is that those individuals were prepared to become offenders' (2009: 302). The numbers also indicate that the hunting/shooting community is sufficiently large to be classed as a distinct social group or subculture, albeit not one that might be legally recognized as such (see Case Study Two later in this chapter).

While the evidence that there has been widespread unlawful hunting activity in the UK since the ban is lacking, there has been a steady trickle of minor incidents suggesting that some hunts or individual huntspersons are continuing to act outside the law. Of more significance is the fact that in the almost seven years since the *Hunting Act 2004* was introduced, the hunt lobby's opposition to the Act remains undiminished and indeed has arguably grown in intensity and sophistication and coalesced into a concerted campaign for repeal of the Act. The May 2010 change in government in the UK, which brought a Conservative/Liberal Democrat coalition to power, has perhaps facilitated renewed optimism in the 'opposition' camp that the Act could be repealed. However, comparable campaigns in the United States for legal protection to be removed from animals so that they might be killed, or at least an opposition to high levels of protection for predatory animals such as wolves have been observed. This suggests a shared resistance to legislation and public policy detrimental to their 'sport' among hunters and those engaged in animal harm linked to traditional fieldsports. It should be noted that there are stark differences in the US and UK legal systems given that the US written constitution provides for a right to bear arms in the way that the UK's unwritten constitution does not. The physical composition of the two countries is also different with the US's wider expanse of open spaces and more deeply ingrained notion of hunting as subsistence perhaps contrasting with the UK's smaller land mass, greatly reduced rural areas (and considerably lower urban population) and predominantly agricultural land use. The UK perspective is also one of hunting as a recreational activity linked to social class. However both the US and UK resistance to animal protection and control over hunting activities represent a form of cultural resistance that persists against what is sometimes perceived as anti-countryside legislation. The continued illegal activities of African hunters also represents a form of resistance against what may be seen as oppressive and misguided laws that lack legitimacy in the face of community and cultural needs (BCTF 2009).

In the UK use of the land has been traditionally associated with the ruling class or the elite, while in the United States, ranchers, farmers and those traditionally enjoying hunting and trapping are predominantly working class. Thus while shooting and hunting are middle- and upper-class pursuits in the UK, shooting is within the reach of the common man in the United States. However, both groups are dominated by masculinities in their exercise of power over animals but also in exerting their rights of dominance over the land. Thus legislation which seeks to determine how the land can and will be used will be resisted, as will legislation which seeks to restrict the exercise of masculine power which might be perceived as natural. There are differences in the manner in which the resistance is framed with African countries resisting by virtue of practical action and continued law-breaking while western resistance is legitimized through the use of lobby groups and political campaigns. The following case study illustrates a western perspective.

Case Study Two: The UK's *Hunting Act 2004*

The United Kingdom, through its *Hunting Act 2004*, sought to ban the traditional practice of hunting with dogs, while separate legislation (the *Protection of Wild Mammals [Scotland] Act 2002*) banned the practice in Scotland. In the UK, hunting with dogs and specifically fox-hunting was a long-standing countryside practice associated with debates around class and, in particular, the right of the middle and upper classes to hunt with dogs – a practice that had particular social connotations and was inextricably linked with the British concept of a right to enjoy and use the countryside and to exercise freedom to enjoy particular pursuits.

Legislation aimed at banning the practice thus raised controversial social issues relating to the treatment of animals, the imposition of legislation by one group on another and the specific legal and moral issue of whether there is a 'right' for humans to hunt non-human animals, whether this right should be protected by law or whether parliament could legitimately interfere with such a right in the public interest (widely construed). The proponents of (mainly) fox-hunting sought to clarify this issue through a serious of legal challenges which invoked the *European Convention on Human Rights*, in particular the notions that hunting fell within Article 8, the right to a private life, Article 11 the right of freedom of association and assembly, and Article 14 freedom of discrimination.

An initial challenge to the Act on the grounds that it was invalid because it had been passed by the House of Commons using the *Parliament Acts 1911 and 1949* to force the legislation through despite the disagreement of the House of Lords failed. This argument rested on a technical point in UK constitutional law which generally requires both Houses to agree on legislation, rather than on the specific merits of state interference with hunting. But the failure of the 'legal validity' challenge was followed by attempts to challenge the Act on human rights grounds as an interference in the 'right' to hunt which hunt proponents argued existed under the grounds outlined above. In *R (Countryside Alliance and others) v. Attorney General* [2007] UKHL 52, the House of Lords was asked to consider the compatibility of the ban on hunting with hounds with the alleged right of hunters to continue with the activity. Most human rights guaranteed under the European Convention can be interfered with where the interference is considered necessary, serves a legitimate purpose, and is proscribed by law. The *Hunting Act 2004* raised the question of whether public opinion or prevailing morality were considered sufficient grounds to restrict an activity and, in effect, whether public opposition to hunting justified the UK parliament in passing a law which prevented a group of individuals from carrying out a particular activity that had previously been lawful, especially where for some individuals (those employed professionally within the countryside with employment directly linked to or dependent on hunting) the law would have a direct effect on their livelihoods. The UK Court of Appeal had ruled that the *Hunting Act 2004* was not incompatible with the EC Treaty (Nice) or the European Convention but the appellants (hunt employees and landowners who permitted hunting on their land, and a second group of appellants who included dog breeders and providers of livery services who would be affected by the ban) claimed that the ban infringed Article 8 rights because it adversely infringed their private life, cultural lifestyle and use of their home and resulted in loss of their livelihood. An argument was also raised that the ban interfered with their Article 11 association rights, their property rights under Article 1 of the first protocol to the convention and that by virtue of the specific nature of their employment and dependence on hunting for employment, amounted to discrimination of them as a particular group.

The 'private life' issues were dismissed by the House of Lords which commented that 'fox-hunting is a very public activity, carried out in daylight with considerable colour and noise, often attracting the attention of on-lookers attracted by the spectacle'. As a result, 'no analogy' could be drawn to the 'personal and private concerns' referred to in the Article 8 cases cited by the appellants which sought to argue that hunting was part of their private life. The cultural lifestyle arguments were also dismissed by the court, which concluded that while previous cases had considered state interference in the activities of Lapps working as reindeer shepherds, fishermen and hunters living and working in the far north of Norway (*G and E v. Norway* (1983) 35 DR 30), or gypsies seeking to live in their caravans (*Chapman v. United Kingdom* (2001) 33 EHRR 399), these were 'distinctive groups, each with a traditional culture and lifestyle so fundamental as to form part of its identity', which was not the case with hunters, in part because of the 'social and occupational diversity of this fraternity, often relied on as one of its strengths'.

The issue of discrimination involved consideration of whether those who hunt are a specific group which it could be argued has a particular status. The appellants contended that hunters were a specific group and arguably were being discriminated against as such. In relation to this book's assessment of animal harm and the reasons for killing animals, it can certainly be argued that those who wish to hunt animals are likely to share certain common characteristics which inform their propensity to commit animal harm, but this is not the same as belonging to a *legally accepted* distinguishable characteristic such that action aimed at them as a group amounted to discrimination. The Strasbourg court in *Kjeldsen, Busk Madsen and Pedersen v. Denmark* (1976) 1 EHRR 711, para 56, had clarified 'discriminatory treatment having as its basis or reason a personal characteristic ("status") by which persons or groups of persons are distinguishable from each other'. The House of Lords concluded that even if those who wished to hunt were the subject of discriminatory or adverse treatment when compared with those who do not wish to hunt, as a group, hunting proponents lacked any personal characteristic or anything which could meaningfully be described as 'status' such that their adverse treatment could be classified as unlawful discrimination under Article 14.

In respect of the justifiability and proportionality of introducing a ban, the case also highlighted that a preference for carrying out a particular animal harm activity on the part of one group, even if done humanely, could be interfered with if society saw fit to do so on moral grounds. This was the case with the *Hunting Act 2004* which had been the subject of a free vote in the UK parliament. In rejecting the original challenge to the *Hunting Act 2004* the Divisional Court, in a judgement upheld by the Court of Appeal, stated that:

> the legislative aim of the *Hunting Act* is a composite one of preventing or reducing unnecessary suffering to wild mammals, overlaid by a moral viewpoint that causing suffering to animals for sport is unethical and should, so far as is practical and proportionate, be stopped.

The Scottish Court of Session, in considering a challenge to the *Protection of Wild Mammals (Scotland) Act 2002*, had previously held that:

> the making of a moral judgment is more suitable for a legislature than for a court, and the Scottish Parliament has procedures which enabled it to obtain such evidence as it thought appropriate in order to make the judgment. In that the Parliament took it upon itself to form judgments as to whether mounted foxhunting with dogs is a sport, whether it can be described as cruel, whether it can be distinguished from other methods of controlling fox numbers in terms of the efficiency, the relative suffering of the fox and so on, these all appear to [Lord Nimmo, the presiding judge] to fall within the discretionary area of judgment to which the court should defer. It follows that if and in so far as a balancing exercise requires to be carried out, the prohibition of mounted foxhunting with dogs is capable of being regarded as necessary in a democratic society for the protection of morals (Article 8(2)) and necessary in accordance with the general interest (the second paragraph of Article 1 of the First Protocol).

The House of Lords also concluded that the interference in hunting was in accordance with the law and could be considered to be necessary in a democratic society for the 'protection of morals'. The Lords accepted that while many people would not consider a ban on hunting to be of pressing social need, a majority of the country's democratically elected representatives did (i.e. Members of Parliament) and were entitled to conclude that it could be legislated against.

Following the decisions of the House of Lords, complaints were raised with the European Court of Human Rights (*Friend v. the United Kingdom* application no. 16072/06 and *Countryside Alliance and Others v. the United Kingdom* application no. 27809/08). In relation to the Article 8 claim, the European Court rejected the claim that the ban negatively affected the right to private and family life. In particular, the Court held that 'not every activity a person might seek to engage in together with others was protected under that Article'. It reinforced the view of the House of Lords that hunting was essentially a public activity, concluding that the right to private life did not extend to public activities and that being a member of the hunting community 'could not be regarded as ethnic or national minority, nor did it represent a particular lifestyle which was indispensable for a person's identity'.

In relation to the Article 11 claim, the European Court noted that the hunting bans in Scotland, England and Wales did not prevent or restrict the right to assemble with other huntsmen as hunters 'remained free to engage in many alternatives to hunting such as drag or trail hunting, which did not involve live quarry'. The Court also observed that the bans 'had been designed to eliminate the hunting and killing of animals for sport in a manner causing suffering and being morally objectionable. The bans had been introduced after extensive debate by the democratically elected representatives of the State on the social and ethical issues raised by that type of hunting'. As a result the Court indicated that it was for the national parliament to decide what activities could be prohibited in order to protect public morals and, in also rejecting the complaint that the ban on hunting would adversely affect the lifestyles of hunters, the Court commented that:

> It did not find arbitrary or unreasonable the absence of compensation for the adverse financial impact of the bans on those whose businesses depended on hunting, given in particular that people had continued to gather for hunts, albeit without live quarry, even after the passage of the Act.

These cases illustrate that while hunting may be indicative of certain characteristics and behaviours that individuals may wish to claim as being a necessary part of their private and cultural lives, the law (or at least European law) does not generally recognize a right to hunt except in the particular case of indigenous peoples or others constituting a distinct ethnic minority. Crucially it also endorses the view that state authorities can intervene in animal harm activities on moral grounds based on the judgement of the elected representatives and legislative authorities that such activities should be restricted to protect public morals. The moral imperative of outlawing animal harm, while being a matter of judgement that might be disputed by some, clearly is one that public authorities are entitled to take into account as forming a valid basis for legislation.

Conclusions

Despite legislation in various parts of the world that makes much traditional fieldsports activity either unlawful or places strict controls on what may be carried out, illegal fieldsports activity continues in a number of countries. In the UK in particular (and to a certain extent also in the United States) animal harm linked to the activities of economic offenders continues where protected animals are killed in support of traditional fieldsports activities which have now become commercialized. In these cases the perceived economic benefits of animal killing in terms of increased animal stocks for commercial exploitation outweigh the available legal sanctions such that offenders have a strong motivation to commit their animal harm. Masculinities offenders are also a factor in the context of those combative animal harm activities where harm to animals is an integral factor and offenders have an allegiance to a higher authority in the form of the social group in which they commit their offences. As Chapter 3 and this chapter indicate, such groups represent a subculture where offenders join together on the basis of shared interest in animal harm and its associated male behaviours such as gambling, and new offenders learn from existing ones in order to perpetuate their sport and culture. While such offenders are frequently the target of law enforcement activity and there are regular undercover raids and operations on dog-fighting, badger-baiting, badger-digging and cock-fighting gangs, such activities continue.

The claim of necessity and denial of the legitimacy of law enforcement activity is also employed by those traditional offenders who take part in fieldsports activities for personal gain. In the case of illegal bushmeat hunters, their need for food provides a direct personal gain by virtue of necessity but a commercial (i.e. profit-driven) motive also exists in the form of the income possible from illegal bushmeat hunting.

In part, the continued illegality associated with traditional fieldsports activities represents a form of resistance to attempts to regulate rural and countryside activities and to limit hunting activities. Hunting in the UK is very much class driven while this is not the case in the United States where legal hunting enjoys wider support than the proportion of the population who actually hunt might typically suggest. The merits or otherwise of traditional hunting are not the concern of this chapter; however the link between legal hunting and illegal hunting is and in almost every area of hunting examined, whether ostensibly legal or clearly illegal, some form of illegal animal harm occurs from the technical breach of killing higher numbers of animals than the law allows, through to the persistent killing of protected species and deliberate inflicting of suffering on animals in the name of sport.

References

British Association for Shooting and Conservation (2011). *The Taste of Game: Game Recipes*, Wrexham: BASC.

Brymer, R.A. (1991). The Emergence and Maintenance of a Deviant Sub-culture: The Case of Hunting/Poaching Subculture. *Anthropologica*, 33, 177–94.

Burns, L., Edwards, V., Marsh, J., Soulsby, L. and Winter, M. (2000). *Committee of Inquiry into Hunting With Dogs in England and Wales*, London: HMSO.

Bushmeat Crisis Task Force (BCTF) (2009). *Bushmeat: A Wildlife Crisis in West and Central Africa and around the World*, Washington: BCTF.

Cohn, P. and Linzey, A. (2009). Hunting as a Morally Suspect Activity, in A. Linzey (ed.), *The Link between Animal Abuse and Human Violence*, Eastbourne: Sussex Academic Press, 317–28.

Cooper, J. (2009). Hunting as an Abusive Subculture, in A. Linzey (ed.), *The Link between Animal Abuse and Human Violence*, Eastbourne: Sussex Academic Press, 302–16.

Donnermeyer, J.F., Jobes, P. and Barclay, E. (2006). Rural Crime, Poverty, and Community, in W.S. DeKeseredy and B. Perry (eds), *Advancing Critical Criminology*, Lanham: Lexington Books, 199–218.

Eliason, S.L. (2003). Illegal Hunting and Angling: The Neutralization of Wildlife Law Violations. *Society and Animals*, 11(3), 225–43.

Fa, J., Peres, C. and Meetuwig, G.J. (2002). Wild Meat Exploitation in Tropical Forests: An Intercontinental Comparison. *Conservation Biology*, 16, 232–7.

Forsyth, C.J. and Evans, R.D. (1998), Dogmen: The Rationalisation of Deviance. *Society & Animals*, 6(3), 203–18, Washington: Society & Animals Forum Inc.

Fowler-Reeves, K. (2007). *With Extreme Prejudice: The Culling of British Wildlife*, Tonbridge: Animal Aid.

Gavitt, J.D. (1989). Unlawful Commercialization of Wildlife Parts. *Transactions of the North American Wildlife & Natural Resources Conference*, 54, 314–23.

Groombridge, N. (1996). Masculinities and Crimes against the Environment. *Theoretical Criminology*, 2(2), London: Sage, 249–67.

Hall, D.L. (1992). Compliance: The Mission of Wildlife Law Enforcement. *Proceedings of the Annual Conference of the Southeastern Association of Fish and Wildlife Agencies*, 46, 532–42.

Hawley, F. (1982). Organised Cockfighting: A Deviant Recreational Subculture, unpublished doctoral dissertation, Tallahassee, FL: Florida State University.

Hawley, F. (1993). The Moral and Conceptual Universe of Cockfighters: Symbolism and Rationalization. *Society and Animals*, 1(2).

Hirschi, T. (1969). *Causes of Delinquency*, Berkeley: University of California Press.

Holmern, T., Røskaft, E., Mbaruka, J., Mkama, S.Y. and Muya, D.J. (2002). Uneconomical Game Cropping in a Community-based Conservation Project Outside the Serengeti National Park, Tanzania. *Oryx*, 36, 364–72.

Holmern, T., Mkama, S.Y., Muya, J. and Røskaft, E. (2006). Intraspecific Prey Choice of Bushmeat Hunters Outside the Serengeti National Park, Tanzania: A Preliminary Analysis. *African Zoology*, 41, 81–7.

Huggs, K.C. (1993). Blood Sport: A Look at the Underground World of Illegal Dogfighting. *Times of Acadiana*, 14, 20–27.

Hutchison, I. (2000). *The Protection of Badgers Act 1992 Recent Contraventions and Recommendations*, Forfar: Scottish Badgers.

Jobes, P.C., Barclay, E., Weinand, H. and Donnermeyer, J.F. (2004). A Structural Analysis of Social Disorganisation and Crime in Rural Communities in Australia, *Australian and New Zealand Journal of Criminology*, 37(1), 114–40.

Kean, H. (1998). *Animal Rights*. London: Reaktion Books Ltd.

Kimmel, M., Hearn, J. and Connell, R.W. (2005). *Handbook of Studies on Men & Masculinities*, London: Sage.

League Against Cruel Sports (2005). *The Killing Game*, London: LACS.

Lindsey, P.A., Romanach, S.S., Tambling, C.J., Chartier, K. and Groom, R. (2011). Ecological and Financial Impacts of Illegal Bushmeat Trade in Zimbabwe. *Oryx*, 45(1), 96–111.

Lindsey, P.A., Balme, G.A., Booth, V.R. and Midlane, N. (2012). The Significance of African Lions for the Financial Viability of Trophy Hunting and the Maintenance of Wild Land. *PLoS ONE*, 7(1), e29332. doi:10.1371/journal.pone.0029332.

McManus, P., Walmsley, J., Argent, N., Baum, S., Bourke, L., Martin, J., Pritchard, B. and Sorensen, T. (2012). Rural Community and Rural Resilience: What is Important to Farmers in Keeping their Country Towns Alive? *Journal of Rural Studies*, 28, 20–29.

Marshall, B. and Johnson, S. (2005). *Crime in Rural Areas: A Review of the Literature for the Rural Evidence Research Centre*, London: Jill Dando Institute of Crime Science, University College London.

Matz, K.S. (1984). *The Pit Bull Fact and Fable*, Sacramento: De Mortmain Publishing.

Meagher, M.S. (1985). Police Patrol Styles: How Pervasive is Community Variation? *Journal of Police Science and Administration*, 13(1), 36–45.

Metropolitan Police (2012). Badgers, London: Metropolitan Police. Available at http://content.met.police.uk/Article/Badgers/1400005893339/1400005893339 [accessed 23 January 2012].

Mfunda, I.M. and Roskaft, E. (2010). Bushmeat Hunting in Serengeti, Tanzania: An Important Economic Activity to Local People. *International Journal of Biodiversity and Conservation*, 2(9), 263–72.

Mingay, G.E. (1989). *The Rural Idyll*, London: Routledge.

Muhammad, B. (2002). *Rural Crime and Rural Policing Practices (Multicultural Law Enforcement)*, Detroit: Detroit Police Department.

Naturewatch (2007). *Fact Sheet on Cruelty to Badgers*, Cheltenham: Naturewatch.

Naughton-Treves, L. (1998). Predicting Patterns of Crop Damage by Wildlife around Kibale National Park, Uganda. *Conservation Biology*, 12, 156–88.

Neilson, M.R. (2006). Importance, Cause and Effect of Bushmeat Hunting in the Udzunga Mountains Tanzania: The Importance of Migratory Herbivores. *Biological Conservation*, 128, 509–16.

Nurse, A. (2009). Dealing with Animal Offenders, in A. Linzey (ed.), *The Link Between Animal Abuse and Human Violence*, Eastbourne: Sussex Academic Press, 238–49.

Nurse, A. (2011). Policing Wildlife: Perspectives on Criminality in Wildlife Crime. *Papers from the British Criminology Conference*, 11, 38–53.

PACEC (2006). *The Economic and Environmental Impact of Sporting Shooting*, Cambridge and London: PACEC.

Preece, R. (1999). *Animals and Nature: Culture Myths, Cultural Realities*, Vancouver: University of British Columbia.

Royal Society for the Protection of Birds (2005). *Birdcrime 2004: Offences against Wild Bird Legislation in 2004*, Sandy: RSPB.

Royal Society for the Protection of Birds (2005a), *Persecution: A Review of Bird of Prey Persecution in Scotland in 2004*, Edinburgh: RSPB.

Saunders, T. (2001). *Baiting the Trap: One Man's Secret Battle to Save Our Wildlife*, London: Simon & Schuster.

Smith, B.L. (1980). Criminal Victimization in Rural Areas, in B.R. Price and P.J. Baunach (eds), *Criminal Justice Research: New Models and Findings*, Beverly Hills: Sage, 36–54.

Smith, R. (2010). Policing the Changing Landscape of Rural Crime: A Case Study from Scotland. *International Journal of Police Science and Management*, 12(3), 373–87.

Sorokin, P., Zimmerman, C.C. and Galpin, C.J. (1931). *A Systematic Sourcebook in Rural Sociology* (2 vols). Minneapolis: University of Minnesota Press.

Sykes, G.M. and Matza, D. (1957). Techniques of Neutralization: A Theory of Delinquency. *American Sociological Review*, 22, 664–73.

Weisheit, R.A., Falcone, D.N. and Wells, L.E. (2006). *Crime and Policing in Rural and Small-Town America.* 3rd edn. Prospect Heights, Illinois: Waveland Press.

Wilkie, D.S. and Carpenter, J.F. (1999). Bushmeat Hunting in the Congo Basin: An Assessment of Impacts and Options for Mitigation, *Biodiversity Conservation*, 927–55.

Wilson, T.C. (1991). Urbanism, Migration, and Tolerance: A Reassessment. *American Sociological Review*, 56(1), 117–23.

Wilson, S., Anderson, L. and Knight, A. (2007). *The Conservation of Seals Act 1970: The Case for Review*, Scotland: Seal Forum.

Young, A. (2010). *The Scene of Violence*, Abingdon and New York: Routledge.

Chapter 6

Animal Harm, Culture and Self-Expression

Separate from traditional, in the sense of socially accepted, animal harm practices, some forms of animal harm are an integral part of cultural and ethnic identity. Rollin suggests that the closest we have come to an ethical position on the treatment of animals is to not be cruel 'which essentially enjoins us not to maliciously, wilfully or sadistically hurt animals for no purpose' (2006: 36). However the question of what constitutes a legitimate purpose presents difficulties for legislators and policymakers and is socially constructed allowing for different interpretations in different jurisdictions and cultures. While contrary to western notions of animal welfare and animal protectionism, some cultures embrace animal harm as integral to their cultural identity, adopting attitudes towards animals that incorporate different perspectives on animal use. A variety of practices ranging from subsistence fishing to full-scale harvesting of wild animals and their derivatives (skin, tusks and internal organs) are deeply ingrained in some traditional practices which can have cultural, religious and social significance, especially to indigenous people. This chapter deals with such practices and the issue of animal harm as a distinct issue of self-expression.

Separate from Chapter 5's discussion of traditional fieldsports activities, this chapter considers animal use or exploitation including killing which when carried out in accordance with the law may be recognized as a fundamental human right of indigenous peoples and ethnic minorities. But where the law is not followed it may criminalize activities which are claimed as distinct characteristics of ethnic identity setting up a conflict between the practices of indigenous cultures and the animal protectionism of contemporary legislation which would define some cultural practices as unlawful animal harm.

The chapter examines a range of examples of cultural endorsed animal harm including whaling and the reindeer husbandry practices of ethnic minorities and indigenous peoples as well as the traditional animal killing practices employed in the Mediterranean. Its focus is the cultural importance of certain animal killing practices to a specific notion of ethnic or cultural identity, such that animal killing activities continue in spite of legislative or political efforts to eliminate them. For many indigenous peoples a historically and culturally important spiritual relationship with animals persists despite the rise in animal rights and environmentalism that views such cultural practices as unlawful and socially unacceptable. Thus, animal harm, socially constructed to have different meanings according to the society in which it occurs, can allow the same act (for example the killing of a whale) to have multiple meanings; illegal wildlife crime in the view of animal activists and legislators, legitimate cultural practice in the eyes of the indigenous person committing the act. As Linzey (2009) identifies; 'willed ignorance' or looking the other way sometimes allows animal 'abuse' to continue. Thus the simple justification of animal harm as culturally important does not excuse it when animal law is violated. But it is also true that animal harvesting essential to indigenous cultural identity is not treated the same as other types of animal killing and is generally subject to legislative regimes that permits it (subject to certain conditions). However cultural animal harvesting that takes places in defiance of animal legislation *is* animal harm as defined throughout this book – an illegal act that has its distinct criminal characteristics – albeit they exist within the broader context of animal harm that this book discusses.

Animal Harm and Cultural Identity

In some cultures, animal harm through the hunting, trapping and killing of animals was historically a necessity for subsistence. Though for many native peoples animals and humans shared a kinship, people hunted, fished and harvested animals purely as a means of survival (Schmidt 1988). Particularly in remote areas of the world, where the availability of other food sources was limited even as society began to develop the means of mass production and distribution of food, animals remained critical to the subsistence needs of native peoples living outside of conventional society. In addition, animals were sometimes spiritually important to indigenous peoples whose philosophy was one of living in harmony with the land such that animals might be seen as kin (McLuhan 1971), part of an extended family (Matthews 1995), or thought to possess a spiritual power or consciousness equal or even superior to that of humans (Gill 1983, Harrod 1987). As a result, the killing of animals for sustenance was of spiritual and cultural significance to indigenous people such that for many indigenous peoples hunting, fishing and the killing of wildlife achieved special significance, becoming subject to rituals and, for some peoples, became a sacred responsibility entrusted only to particular members of a tribe.

Brown (1991) identified that in some cultures hunting, fishing and trapping were considered to be spiritual acts carried out only with the consent of those animals killed. As a result, a spiritual ethos grew up around the killing of wildlife with rituals and specific practices being developed to ensure that those who hunted were able to demonstrate that hunting was carried out in as sustainable a manner as possible. But such practices were also designed to show that hunters, by observing specific religious practices, were considered deserving and would obtain the permission of those animals they killed (Preece 1999). In consequence, certain indigenous peoples identified themselves closely with their traditions as hunters and people who lived off the land. As people who hunted through necessity in order to survive they adopted a belief structure based around their critical subsistence needs as well as cultural practices that reflected these needs. As a result, even for contemporary descendants of indigenous peoples, underlying spiritual beliefs may inform attitudes towards animals such that any animal killing that now takes place represents a loyalty both to tradition and established cultural practices, but also to a higher power (Sykes and Matza 1957).

Fisher (2008: 17) identifies that indigenous people comprise around 4 percent of the world's population and that pockets of indigenous peoples still carry out 'sacred ways handed down from their remote ancestors and adapted to contemporary circumstances'. As a result, forms of animal killing such as fishing, reindeer herding, whaling and even big game hunting have cultural significance to indigenous peoples and are integral to their ethnic identity persisting even where such practices might otherwise be classed as unlawful. While many legal systems prohibit animal killing (except in respect of so-called 'pest' species and certain species classed as legitimate fieldsports quarry) exceptions are sometimes made in respect of indigenous peoples and certain animal killing practices recognized as culturally significant. However as Chapter 3 outlines, some animal killing is justified when individuals either do not recognize the legitimacy of the law or consider its restrictions to be unnecessarily harsh. John et al. (1985) identified that the goals of animal conservation and those of indigenous peoples wishing to hunt are not always compatible. They suggest that where legislative restrictions are in conflict with animal harm seen as integral to cultural identity this may provide a powerful motive for animal harm to take place, reflecting White's view that human interests become privileged in determining the relationship between nature and society (2008). While legislation may in some respects preserve species justice as a conservation priority, cultural expression rights may dictate that animal harm should continue.

Animal Harm and Cultural Self-Expression

In certain cultures, animal harm represents a form of self-expression at odds with accepted notions of animal abuse as inherently criminal or evil, reflecting different cultural notions concerning the acceptability of animal killing (Preece 1999). However, human rights law explicitly recognizes this difference via its incorporation and classification of the rights of indigenous peoples into a framework of exemptions from certain legislative provisions. Specifically, human rights law provides land rights and rights of cultural preservation that sometimes recognizes that indigenous peoples should be exempt from the confines of national animal law where it is considered necessary to do so in order to give effect to cultural self-preservation and expression.

Indigenous peoples are broadly recognized as distinct ethnic groups by international and regional regulatory bodies. They are given a legal status in international law that acknowledges both historic and present threats and the assimilation and alienation of their traditional way of life. The International Labour Organisation's (ILO) 1953 guidelines (still in force today) describe indigenous peoples as:

descendants of the original aboriginal population living in a given country at the time of settlement or conquest (or successive waves of conquest) by some of the ancestors of the non-indigenous groups in whose hand political and economic power at present lies. In general these descendants tend to live more in conformity with the social, economic and cultural institutions which existed before colonisation or conquest ... than with the culture of the nation to which they belong; they do not fully share in the national economy and culture owing to barriers of language, customs, creed, prejudice, and often out-of-date and unjust systems of worker-employer relationship and other social and political factors. (ILO 1953: para 25–6)

The International Covenant on Civil and Political Rights of 1966 also states that:

In those States in which ethnic, religious or linguistic minorities exist, persons belonging to such minorities shall not be denied the right, in community with the other members of their group, to enjoy their own culture, to protect and practice their own religion or to use their own language. (Article 27)

In addition to the general provisions in international law such as the International Covenant on Civil and Political Rights which puts states under an obligation to positively protect minority rights, specific provisions exist in national laws to provide aboriginal subsistence rights. Such rights are the main route through which aboriginal people may achieve food security and thus the animal killing which takes place in exercising those rights constitute legal activities that would otherwise be unlawful. However, such activities are usually strictly controlled mainly through the use of quotas which determine the number of animals that can be killed and permits which specify who is authorized to carry out this form of animal harm. Where either quotas are exceeded or animal hunting trapping or killing is carried out in contravention of the regulations, unlawful animal harm occurs. However such animal harm may still be argued as a form of cultural self-expression, raising questions about both the mechanisms through which cultural identity is controlled and the cultural necessity of such animal harm. In common with other forms of legitimized animal harm (such as the trade in wildlife discussed in Chapter 8) legal animal harm may exist alongside illegal animal harm in subsistence and 'cultural' killing, and understanding both the purpose of the legislation and the extent to which it is (or is not) complied with aids understanding of animal killing as cultural self-expression.

As a result 'whale hunting, reindeer husbandry and a variety of other usufructory rights' can be granted to indigenous peoples to the exclusion of others (Smith 2010: 583). This allows indigenous peoples to kill, hunt and harvest otherwise protected animals where considered necessary to their cultural expression and to preserve a minority way of life; making the animal harm involved of a type justified by the neutralization of necessity (Sykes and Matza 1957) and in some cases of providing a means of survival integral to a specific way of life that is otherwise under threat.

In theory at least, this distinguishes this form of animal harm from sport and trophy hunting (discussed in Chapter 7) or the commercial killing and trade in wildlife (discussed in Chapter 8) in that it represents an integral part of a particular 'ethnic' lifestyle. However in practice there are questions over the extent to which animal harm of this type remains a cultural necessity despite its acceptance by courts in numerous countries that it should be allowed to continue. Under Article 27 of the International Covenant on Civil and Political Rights, minority cultural rights can only be secured by persons belonging to the specified minority group and the right of self-determination provided under Article 1 of the Covenant is a group rather than individual right. As a result, indigenous people wishing to carry out animal husbandry activities may need to demonstrate compliance with certain criteria determining their participation in the cultural life of an ethnic minority, rather than individually claiming a right to be exempt from laws that prohibit animal killing. This potentially raises the question of how to determine which animal killing is (legally) acceptable as part of the expression of cultural identity and which animal killing may be carried out by individuals under the cloak of self-expression. As with other forms of animal harm discussed throughout this book there is scope for illegal animal harm to exist alongside or under the guise of legal animal use activities. The examples of fishing, whaling and reindeer herding by indigenous people help clarify the social construction of this form of animal harm.

Fishing and Whaling by Indigenous Peoples

Despite the general ban on whaling introduced in 1986, aboriginal groups are allowed to harvest otherwise protected species by way of fishing and hunting whales in order to meet 'cultural and subsistence' needs, recognizing centuries-long traditions of killing whales by indigenous (native) peoples. Indigenous whale-hunting traditions are recognized by the International Whaling Commission (IWC) as being distinct from commercial whaling. The IWC regulations thus permit aboriginal subsistence whaling and the IWC sets limits for aboriginal subsistence hunts that cover a five-year period and are reviewed on this basis. Under IWC regulations, aboriginal subsistence whaling is permitted for Inuit and Bequian people (IWC 2011) allowing hunting of whales in Denmark (Greenland, fin and minke whales), the Russian Federation (Siberia, grey and bowhead whales), St Vincent and The Grenadines (Bequia, humpback whales) and the United States (Alaska, bowhead and grey whales). Whaling carried out in accordance with IWC regulations and subject to IWC monitoring is therefore lawful although strict adherence to regulations is required and a number of examples exist where animal harm incidents by indigenous people have occurred when IWC regulations have been challenged.

The IWC requires whaling to be carried out as humanely as possible but recognizes this form of animal harm as legitimate for cultural reasons. The Makah people of North America contend that whaling is central to their culture and social organization and 'the conduct of a whale hunt requires rituals and ceremonies which are deeply spiritual' (Makah Tribal Council and Makah Whaling Commission 2005: 5). Whaling, which has been carried out by the tribe for over 1,500 years, is a right guaranteed to them under US law, specifically the Makah Treaty of Neah Bay 1855, Article 4 of which provides the rights of taking fish, whaling and sealing 'at usual and accustomed grounds'. While the *Marine Mammal Protection Act of 1972* (16 U.S.C. 1361-1407, P.L. 92-522, October 21, 1972, 86 Stat. 1027) established a moratorium on the taking and importation of marine mammals as well as products derived from them, amendments to the *Act* in 1994 expressly preserved aboriginal fishing and whaling rights. Section 14 of the Act states that 'nothing in this Act including any amendments to the *Marine Mammal Protection Act of 1972* made by this Act alters or is intended to alter any treaty between the United States and one or more Indian Tribes'. Thus provisions exist in US law (and which are replicated in the laws of certain other jurisdictions) specifically acknowledging the cultural difference between indigenous people and mainstream society. Thus this form of animal use, socially constructed through traditional practices, is allowed to continue although the Makah had, in fact discontinued whaling in the 1920s after the grey whale population in the Eastern North Pacific declined dramatically due to commercial whaling. However when whale populations recovered in the 1980s and 1990s the Makah entered into an agreement with the US federal government (in 1996) which would allow the tribe to begin harvesting whales again based on quotas approved by the IWC, after the grey whale was taken off the federal endangered species list. Arguably this makes this form of animal harm one that while culturally significant to the Makah people is not an integral part of their cultural identity such that it *must* be carried out. Instead it is an activity that *certain* members of the tribe who identify with a specific cultural notion of what it means to be Makah, wish to carry out where it is sustainable to do so. However, as society changes and the numbers of indigenous peoples sustaining traditional ways of life dwindle, complex arguments may exist about the need to pursue or sustain historical practices involving animal harm (Otis and Melkevik 1996), especially given contemporary developments in food distribution and supply which arguably make subsistence hunting less of a necessity. In 1997 the IWC set a catch limit of 620 Eastern North Pacific grey whales for the five-year period 1998 through to 2002, alllowing the Chukotkan people of the Russian Federation to catch up to 600 whales and the Makah to catch up to 20. In September 1998 the US District Court for the Western District of Washington passed a judgment which allowed the Makah to resume whaling and in May 1999 the Makah successfully hunted and landed a grey whale. However, a number of animal advocacy groups including the Humane Society of the United States (HSUS) challenged the federal government's acceptance of whaling by the Makah claiming this violated both the *National Environmental Policy Act of 1969*, 42 U.S.C. §§ 4321–70 and the *Marine Mammal Protection Act of 1972*, 16 U.S.C. §§ 1361–421. Initially in *Metcalf v. Daley*, 214 F.3d 1135 the Ninth Circuit Court of Appeals reversed the District Court's September 1998 opinion, concluding that the environmental impact of the Makah's proposed whaling had not been sufficiently considered.

Subsequently in *Anderson v. Evans*, 371 F.3d 475 (9th Cir. 2004) the Ninth Circuit Court halted the whale hunt when it concluded that the Makah were required to obtain a permit or exemption under the *Marine Mammal Protection Act of 1972*. However, in doing so, the court also concluded that the *Marine Mammal Protection Act of 1972* does not nullify treaties which allow indigenous peoples to carry out whaling. Such legal challenges are indicative of the conflicts inherent in socially constructed notions of human–animal relations. They also indicate the power of animal lobby groups exercising the social-legal (and moralistic) view of animal harm that defines some legal animal use activities as illegal, on moral grounds (Situ and Emmons 2000, Lynch and Stretesky 2003) and seeks to extend the legal definition of animal harm by further criminalizing some activities.

Whale hunting is a particularly emotive form of animal killing given the social nature of the animals and the threat of extinction faced by some whale populations. However it also represents a challenge for one of the few international animal law measures with the potential to combine trade and conservation efforts. A 10-year moratorium on commercial whaling was implemented in 1986 although three whaling nations, Norway, Japan and Iceland, had either opted out of the international whaling treaty or claimed to be taking animals solely for scientific study despite suspicions that whale meat was being sold to supply an illegal black market (Steinhauer 2010). Clapham and Baker suggest that since its inception 'the IWC was hampered by the unwillingness of the whaling nations to pay attention to the mounting evidence of decline in whale populations, and by the complete lack of any enforcement or independent inspection measures' (2002: 4). Thus the killing of whales by indigenous peoples may need to be seen in the wider species justice context of social opposition to the use and harvesting of whales for any purpose and the general failure of international law efforts and the regulatory regime to effectively regulate whaling whether commercial or indigenous. This application of species justice principles to a regulated trade has brought pressure on the IWC to limit whaling and seek to justify its continuance as a sustainable activity. Yet in neither the commercial sense where the convention is technically being complied with nor the indigenous setting where the IWC seeks to balance the needs and rights of indigenous people with its conservation principles is animal harm being effectively managed. Cultural notions relating to whaling, whether at the country level with Japan, Norway and Iceland, or at a 'local' level with indigenous peoples, frequently result in continued animal harm as the case study later in this chapter illustrates.

Reindeer Husbandry

Indigenous peoples are also allowed to carry out reindeer husbandry where Arctic and subarctic nomadic tribes are permitted rights to herd reindeer for meat, hides and antlers. Reindeer husbandry is of both economic and cultural significance to indigenous peoples who live in extreme conditions and who may be denied other socio-economic opportunities for reasons of location and education. For example, Greenland's Inuit tribes rely on hunting both culturally and for food and Klokov (2007) concluded that reindeer husbandry is 'the basis of the cultures of many northern indigenous peoples, who have varied traditions and wide experiences of reindeer herding in a diversity of landscapes' (726). Melkevik (2002) argues that for the Sami people of the Sápmi region of Norway, Sweden and Finland, reindeer herding became their main source of cultural self-identification to the extent that they became known as 'the reindeer people', even though only a small minority of the population practice the activity. While reindeer herding for the Sami people is a relatively recent activity by virtue of only being practised from the sixteenth and seventeenth centuries onward, it is linked to the extensive practice of hunting by the Sami people. UN Special Rapporteur on the Rights of Indigenous Peoples James Anaya observed that:

> The Sami people have traditionally relied on hunting, fishing, gathering, and trapping and have a deep knowledge of the far north region that has been handed down for many generations. Reindeer herding, in particular, is of central importance to the Sami people. Many Sami communities historically practiced a semi-nomadic lifestyle, moving reindeer between the mountain areas and coastal areas according to the season. Other groups practiced reindeer herding in forested areas. (Anaya 2011: 4)

As with other indigenous animal killing, reindeer husbandry is controlled through legislation. Norway's *Reindeer Herding Act of 1978* (as amended in 2007) regulates the permits for Sami reindeer husbandry, requiring applicants to be of Sami ancestry meaning they must have either a parent or grandparent whose main occupation was reindeer herding. In addition reindeer herding applicants are required to either own or be associated with an operational hunting unit. The aim of the law is to restrict a form of animal hunting and killing that would otherwise be considered unlawful to those with a specific cultural need to carry it out and to prevent casual or recreational hunting which is not linked to indigenous cultures. However, the right to reindeer husbandry is 'a usufruct right that applies over certain land areas regardless of the ownership of those lands' (Anaya 2011: 7) so that Norwegian law gives priority to positively exercising indigenous rights. Swedish law states that membership of a Sami village (for the purpose of holding and exercising reindeer breeding rights) is lost by any person who engages in another profession for more than three years. While the purpose of this law is to protect those who practise reindeer husbandry as their main source of income it had the unfortunate effect of effectively stripping individuals of one aspect of their cultural identity if they chose to carry out another profession. Finland's *Reindeer Husbandry Act of 1990* does not grant any specific rights to the Sami people or any other recognized ethnic minority and allows reindeer husbandry to be carried out by any EU citizen. As a result, reindeer husbandry may be carried out as a commercialized activity in Finland subject to compliance with the regulations. The main issue relating to reindeer husbandry as a form of animal harm is the lack of efficient monitoring of reindeer use. While legislation relating to indigenous peoples generally aims to reflect the cultural necessity of reindeer herding, a more commercialized form of reindeer herding is now possible (especially in Finland) which allows for less well regulated animal use and illegal killing. The problem highlighted by the Finnish law is replicated in the controversy over the annual Canadian seal hunt where questions over its cultural importance threaten to undermine acceptance of its legality as subsistence hunting.

The Canadian Seal Cull

While the annual Canadian seal cull is widely perceived by NGOs as a purely commercial seal hunt, its 'official' basis is one of subsistence hunting relied on by coastal communities that are also attempting to preserve a specific way of life. Linzey (2006: 87) identifies the annual Canadian seal hunt as being 'the largest marine mammal hunt in the world', estimating that between 2003 and 2006 almost a million harp seals were killed. For 2012 the Canadian Ministry of Fisheries has set a harp seal quota of 400,000 as the total allowable catch. IFAW (2009) describes the seal hunt as competitive arguing that haste takes priority. The NGO (and others) dispute the Canadian government's assertion that seal harvesting is a form of subsistence fishing but instead consider it to be a hunt without the element of a 'fair chase' that is considered integral to traditional hunting (see Chapter 5).

The government's argument is that sealing is economically important to rural communities and thus is culturally important to retaining a specific way of life. The Canadian Department of Fisheries and Oceans (DFO) states that its estimate is that 'between 5,000 and 6,000 individuals derive some income from sealing. This is approximately 1 per cent of the total provincial population, and 2 per cent of the labour force. This is a substantial number of individuals in the context of small rural communities' (2012). Thus the Canadian government argues that the seal hunt is subsistence hunting and an integral part of a rural way of life as well as traditional activity and should be allowed under the control of the DFO. This is, however, disputed by NGOs who contend that the annual seal cull is a commercial hunt.

Lavigne et al. define subsistence hunting as 'using wildlife locally for food, clothing, and shelter, and for making tools, rather than putting wildlife products into trade' (1999: 37). The annual seal hunt is considered to meet this definition by the Canadian government by virtue of being integral to rural community survival and its origins in Inuit subsistence harvesting. Thus the exemptions allowed for indigenous peoples are also applied to the Canadian seal hunt, although Linzey argues that 'over the past decades, successive Canadian governments have strategically hidden non-aboriginal commercial wildlife slaughters behind a veil of native subsistence hunting' (2006: 107). Thus NGOs and activists argue that a seal hunt which began as an aboriginal subsistence hunt and which could conceivably be both morally and legally justified *purely on that basis*, has now developed into a commercial hunt which should properly be classified as wildlife trade but which is still officially (and erroneously) classified as subsistence hunting. Lavigne et al. (1999) suggest that in part this is allowed because of a redefinition of subsistence hunting by the Canadian government which provides for wider use of the term 'subsistence' than just its application to indigenous cultures. The Canadian government states that 'only individuals with a valid sealing licence, or Aboriginal peoples participating in a subsistence hunt in designated areas, are legally allowed to harvest seals' (Department of Fisheries and Oceans (DFO) 2012). However their own statistics also state that between 5,000 and 7,000 commercial licences were active in 2011 and 2,700 personal licences were issued which allow individuals to take up to six seals 'for personal consumption' (DFO 2012). This suggests large-scale commercial activity rather than a purely subsistence hunt.

In addition to ethical concerns over the nature of a hunt that is considered to be inherently cruel, NGOs contend that the seal hunt is poorly regulated such that animal harm is an integral part of its operation. Thus even if its continued existence could be justified as subsistence hunting (which is hotly disputed), the manner in which the hunt is carried out constitutes illegal animal harm. Observations of the hunt by NGOs as well as veterinary studies (Smith 2005) show that seals are often killed in an inhumane manner with many wounded animals left to suffer until hunters make a second attempt at killing them (Linzey 2006). IFAW (2012) claim that hunters regularly ignore the sealing regulations knowing that they are unlikely to either be charged or convicted of unlawful killing. IFAW also contends that when hunts are monitored 'few sealers are observed confirming unconsciousness or death prior to skinning a seal, and many continue to use illegal weapons (including gaffs) to strike seals, or illegal ammunition to shoot them' (2009: 6). Thus animal harm contrary to the hunt's regulations is committed when animals are skinned alive. In addition, IFAW highlights the fact that the killing and sale of blueback seal pelts which contravenes the regulations has also been a commonplace activity. It cites Mark Small, a sealer convicted of the illegal practice in 2009, as giving court testimony that confirmed that the regulations were not being effectively enforced and that the government was aware of the practice (2009: 15).

While the market for seal products has reduced somewhat with the EU's decision to ban the importation of seal products following a vote by the European Parliament in May 2009, the annual seal cull continues. The EU's decision allows trade in seal products to continue only where such trade is 'derived from hunts traditionally conducted by Inuit and other indigenous communities and which contribute to their subsistence' (European Commission 2009). In principle, this mean that products derived from the commercial licences cannot be imported into the EU. However despite this policy and international condemnation the Canadian government continues to sanction this form of animal harm.

Animal Harm and Contemporary Culture

One rational for the Canadian seal hunt is societal acceptance of the hunt as an annual activity with its roots in a perception of Canadian identity. Separate from the cultural identity of indigenous peoples, national cultural perceptions can also be a factor that permits animal harm. Thus the endorsement of seal killing by the Canadian government via its continued granting of annual seal quotas by the DFO in defiance of strong NGO and political opposition to the hunt has the effect of legitimizing the hunt and the alleged illegal practices. The failure to properly regulate the hunt also suggests prioritizing the continued existence of the hunt and its importance to the economy and cultural notions of Canada as continuing its ocean-based economy over any animal welfare concerns (Department of Fisheries and Oceans Canada 2005). White (2008: 172) suggests that profit-making in environmental crime is made possible because of the 'overlapping relationship between licit and illicit markets, and the close connection between legal and illegal practices'. While illegal markets are usually defined as those that are unregulated and untaxed, illegal markets also exist because of the structural economic and regulatory conditions which allow them to exist. Thus a market like the Canadian seal product market continues despite greatly reduced demand because it is considered to be culturally important and its illegalities are officially minimized. Its benefit is in part that its positive connotations, e.g. living off the land, maximizing natural resources, continuing a traditional practice, are an integral part of cultural identity and need to be reinforced while the negative connotations, e.g. the alleged cruelty, lack of humane killing methods, wastage, can be downplayed.

Such cultural imperatives exist in a range of cultures where animal harm activities prohibited by legislation continue without attracting official sanction. Animal harm activities which are culturally condoned emphasize the need for fundamental social change so that citizens are able to make best use of existing legal and enforcement mechanisms (White 2008: 182). However the problems identified in the Canadian seal hunt are replicated in a number of countries. A number of Mediterranean countries, for example, have strong traditions of shooting and trapping wild birds despite EU legislation (the *EU Birds Directive of 1979*) which prohibits such activities and has been enacted in a number of countries.

Lindell and Wirdheim (2001: 1) concluded that 'of about 5 billion migrating birds passing through the Mediterranean area each year, 500 million are shot or trapped. In other words: one migrating bird in ten is killed by hunters in the Mediterranean!' Raine (2007: 7) identified that 'Malta has developed a notorious reputation as one of the black spots in the Mediterranean due to uncontrolled hunting and trapping activities'. Conservation organization BirdLife International also identified that 'Malta also has an exceptionally high density of hunters and per square kilometre has the densest population of hunters in the European Union' (2010: 1).

Hunting and trapping of migrating birds are in part traditional practices in the Mediterranean area but are linked to cultural expression not only for life in the countryside but also for those countries where hunting of animals is linked to notions of masculinity and culture. While some birds are killed for commercial reasons and the trade in wildlife (discussed in Chapter 8), songbirds are a cultural delicacy, served in some restaurants despite being subject to protection under European law. Blackcaps, for example, a common warbler in Europe, are a traditional national delicacy on Cyprus, where songbird trapping operations are commonplace despite being unlawful since 1974.

To many Mediterranean men, hunting is a way of life rather than sport or recreation. Birdlife reports that the high density of hunters in Malta, 'combined with a lack of law enforcement and environmental education', makes illegal hunting a widespread and serious problem that continues all year round (2010: 2). The perception of hunters is that bird protection legislation interferes with their tradition and constitutes foreign interference. This perception is shared by trappers and shooters in Italy and other countries who consider their activities tradition or culture and actively resist any efforts to restrict their activities.

The extent to which cultural acceptance of these forms of animal harm has been achieved is demonstrated in part by the weakness of enforcement measures and resistance to legislation. BirdLife reports that 'in 36.6% of [Maltese] cases, the minimum fine was given to individuals convicted of illegal hunting or trapping offences and in a further 29.6% of the cases, fines were allocated which were actually below the minimum fine' (2010: 6). Thus the judiciary are considered to be complicit in allowing illegal hunting to continue and consider that these are not really criminal offences. In addition BirdLife Malta reports that its staff and volunteers are regularly subjected to threats, intimidation and serious attacks. As an example the BirdLife Malta Foresta 2000 ranger has been shot twice in the last few years (once in 2007 and again in 2009) 'and had his family farm burnt down in June 2008' (2010: 3).

Raine, in a survey of migratory birds, identified that 'birds from a *minimum* of 35 countries have been subsequently killed in Malta by Maltese hunters. Only a small proportion of these ring recoveries came from legally huntable species, with the vast majority being protected species' (2007: 20). He concluded that illegal hunting significantly affected birds using the central Mediterranean flyway and was an issue of pressing international concern. The issue of illegal killing, trapping and trading of birds in Mediterranean countries has been regularly on the agenda of the meetings of the Standing Committee to the Bern Convention in the recent past.

At its 30th meeting, in December 2010, the Standing Committee concluded that illegal killing of birds is still carried out, and in some Contracting Parties it is a growing phenomenon; it realized that the implementation of national legislation is often weak; that the issue also involves other transversal questions like the transit of the killed and captured birds through third countries; the difficulty to identify the illegally killed species; the capture of endangered species; the need for countries to co-operate and to work with nature conservation NGOs; the need for proper enforcement with appropriate penalties at all levels.

Case Study: The Makah Whale Hunt

According to the IWC, the Makah people's whale hunt 'invokes ancient rituals and ceremonies that are deeply spiritual to the tribe' (2006: 1). In the 1920s the tribe had suspended the exercise of their whaling rights enshrined in the 1855 Treaty of Neah Bay due to a decline in grey whale stocks, but had reasserted these rights in 1999 given that grey whale stocks had recovered sufficiently for whale hunting to be considered sustainable. Thus in 1999 the Makah, with the permission of the IWC and the US government, harvested a grey whale. However, following litigation concerning the new conservation status of grey whales which had been placed on the US Endangered Species list in 1994, hunts were again temporarily suspended. However following the decision in *Anderson v. Evans*, 371 F.3d 475 (9th Cir. 2004) and earlier litigation, the Makah people's right to hunt whales was allowed subject to regulations that required the tribe to either make an application or obtain an exemption under the *Marine Mammal Protection Act of 1972* before they could hunt grey whales.

The nature of the animal harm involved in Makah hunts was assessed by the IWC in 2006. The IWC considered the Makah's hunting techniques, which now involved 'substituting the traditional killing lance for a large caliber rifle both to eliminate a prolonged pursuit and because the use of the killing lance would be considered inhumane by modern standards' (2006: 2). Gosho (1999 cited in Makah Tribe 2007) concluded that the whale that had been harvested in 1999 had expired eight minutes after being harpooned and the IWC concluded on the basis of its evidence that the .50BMG or .577 caliber firearms proposed to be used in the grey whale hunt would be 'more than adequate to humanely dispatch' grey whales during the Makah hunt (IWC 2006).

The question of whether the revised hunt constituted traditional subsistence hunting or commercial hunting was also considered by the IWC, which concluded that:

> The Tribe's current harvest methods retain all of the ceremonial aspects of the spiritual, physical, and mental preparations required for a traditional Makah whale hunt. The substitution of a high caliber rifle over the traditional killing lance is necessary to ensure a safe and humane harvest and eliminates a prolonged pursuit. The Tribe's harvest techniques are more than sufficient to quickly and humanely dispatch gray whales. (IWC 2006: 3)

However on 8 September 2007 five members of the Makah tribe conducted a hunt and killed a grey whale in the Strait of Juan de Fuca during a hunt that had not been authorized either by the tribe or NOAA Fisheries. While there was scope for whales to be hunted lawfully in accordance with the regulations, the unauthorized hunt failed to comply with various elements of the tribe's application and the restrictions on hunting and killing grey whales and thus constituted unlawful animal harm. The permit restricted hunting of whales to specific areas of the Makah land on the north Olympic Peninsula at Neah Bay and prohibited the taking of whales within the Strait of Juan de Fuca. Permit restrictions 'also required the whale to be secured with a harpoon from a traditional canoe before being dispatched with shots from a high-powered rifle' (Mapes and Ervin 2007).

Subsequent trials took place when on 5 October 2007 the five tribal members involved in the unlawful killing of the grey whale were indicted in federal court on charges of unauthorized whaling, unauthorized taking of a marine mammal and conspiracy to engage in unlawful whaling. Civil penalties under the Act consisted of a $20,000 fine, with the options for criminal prosecution and seizure of vessels and equipment used in the illegal act. On 16 November 2007, the five tribe members were also charged in tribal court for violating the tribe's grey whale management plan, violating state and federal laws, and reckless endangerment.

In March of 2008 three out of five of the tribal members involved in the illegal whaling entered guilty pleas to unlawful taking of a marine mammal in violation of the *Marine Mammal Protection Act of 1972*. However two members declined to make guilty pleas, arguing that they had not committed any crime. Despite contravening the regulatory requirements of the *Marine Mammal Protection Act of 1972*, the two remaining members declined to accept a plea deal that would have had them accept probation rather than a jail term on the grounds that they did not accept they had done anything wrong. Clarridge (2008) reported in *The Seattle Times* that the two tribesmen believed they should be allowed to carry out their traditional hunting activities without governmental oversight. Both were convicted of federal misdemeanour charges.

Critical Perspectives on Cultural Illegal Killing

The Makah and Canadian seal case studies and other incidences of illegal subsistence hunting identify some of the difficulties inherent in this form of animal harm. Killing of animals by indigenous people is inextricably linked to their cultural identities such that legislative efforts by governments and international regulatory bodies might be resisted. Such regulation might be seen by activists within the indigenous community as a further attempt to impose a westernized view of animals and animal exploitation on indigenous peoples that is inconsistent with their beliefs on animals and animal killing. In extreme cases it can be seen as culturally motivated on a human level, similar to the views held by western colonialists who saw themselves as 'civilizing' lesser developed societies and ensuring that they adopted cultural notions appropriate to integration with western cultures (Winthrop 1968, Bolt 1971). Thus regulatory control of indigenous hunting practices could be seen as a subtle form of racism practised by predominantly Anglo-American and Anglo-Saxon governments on races of colour and incorporating continued efforts at subjugation by requiring the submitting of permit applications, making traditional practices subject to monitoring, control and modernization, and making such practices subject to the jurisdiction of municipal and federal rather than tribal courts. (Although in the Makah case it should be noted that it was the decision of the Makah tribal court that the federal courts should hear the case when there were difficulties in empanelling a tribal jury.)

Resistance to regulation exists not just in indigenous cultures but also in contemporary societies where international legislative or political pressure is seen as foreign interference that should be resisted. Where cultural acceptance of animal harm is strong and legal and regulatory regimes are weak or poorly implemented, animal harm will continue both as a means of resistance and as a means of reasserting cultural identity which may integrate animal harm and masculinities into cultural practices that result in animal deaths. The reality of animal killing that is socially constructed to be acceptable within a country or region such as the Mediterranean is that it has meaning to the people who carry out the killing but also to the society which endorses that killing.

References

Anaya, J. (2011). *Report of the Special Rapporteur on the Situation of Human Rights and Fundamental Freedoms of Indigenous People: The Situation of the Sami People in the Sápmi Region of Norway, Sweden and Finland*, New York: United Nations.

BirdLife Malta (2010). *Illegal Hunting and Trapping of Wild Birds in the Maltese Islands*, Ta' Xbiex: BirdLife Malta.

Bolt, C. (1971). *Victorian Attitudes to Race*, London: Routledge and Kegan Paul.

Brown, J.E. (1991). *The Spiritual Legacy of the American Indians*, New York: Crossroads.

Clapham, P.J. and Baker, C.S. (2002). Modern Whaling, in W.F. Perrin, B. Würsig and J.G.M. Thewissen (eds), *Encyclopedia of Marine Mammals*, New York: Academic Press, 1328–32.

Clarridge, C. (2008). 3 Makah Whale Hunters Plead Guilty, *The Seattle Times*, 27 March.

Department of Fisheries and Oceans Canada (DFO) (2005). Canada's Seal Hunt: Beyond the Rhetoric, Commentary by the Minister of Fisheries and Oceans, Canada, 17 March, 1–2.

Department of Fisheries and Oceans (DFO) Canada (2012). *Sealing in Canada – Frequently Asked Questions*, Ottawa: DGO. Available at http://www.dfo-mpo.gc.ca/fm-gp/seal-phoque/faq2012-eng.htm#p [accessed 13 March 2012].

European Commission (2009). *Commission Welcomes the Agreement Reached on Seal Product Ban* (Press Release), Brussels/Strasbourg: European Commission.

Fisher, M.P. (2008). *Living Religions: A Brief Introduction*, New Jersey: Prentice-Hall.

Gill, S.D. (1983). *Native American Traditions: Sources and Interpretations*, Belmont: Wadsworth.

Harrod, H.L. (1987). *Renewing the World: Plains Indian Religion*, Tucson: University of Arizona.

IFAW (2009). *Canada's Commercial Seal Slaughter*, Ontario: IFAW.

IFAW (2012). *Why Commercial Sealing is Cruel*, Ontario: IFAW.

International Labour Organization (ILO) (1953). *Indigenous Peoples: Living and Working Conditions of Aboriginal Populations in Independent Countries, Studies and Reports, Series 35*, International Labour Office: Geneva.

International Whaling Commission (IWC) (2006). *A Review on the Technique Employed by the Makah Tribe to Harvest Gray Whales*, Cambridge: IWC.

International Whaling Commission (IWC) (2011). *Report of the International Whaling Commission*, Cambridge: IWC.

John, G., Robinson, J. and Redford, K. (1985). Hunting By Indigenous Peoples and Conservation of Game Species. *Parks and People*, 9(1). Available at http://www.culturalsurvival.org/ourpublications/csq/article/hunting-by-indigenous-peoples-and-conservation-game-species [accessed 15 January 2012].

Klokov, K. (2007). Reindeer Husbandry in Russia. *International Journal of Entrepreneurship and Small Business*, 4(6), 726–84.

Lavigne, D.M., Scheffer, V.B. and Kellert, S.R. (1999) The Evolution of North American Attitudes toward Marine Mammals, in J.R. Twiss Jr., and R.R. Reeves (eds), *Conservation and Management of Marine Mammals*, Washington and London: Smithsonian Institution Press, 10–47.

Lindel, L. and Wirdheim, A. (2001). *Killing Fields: An Increase in Bird Hunting in Southern Europe, Var Vagelwaerld 5* (translated from Swedish).

Linzey, A. (2006). An Ethical Critique of the Canadian Seal Hunt and an Examination of the Case for Import Controls on Seal Products. *Journal of Animal Law*, 12, Michigan State University College of Law, 87–119.

Linzey, A. (ed.) (2009). *The Link Between Animal Abuse and Human Violence*, Eastbourne: Sussex Academic Press.

McLuhan, T.C. (1971). *Touch The Earth*, New York: Promontory.

Makah Tribal Council and Makah Whaling Commission (2005). *The Makah Indian Tribe and Whaling*, Neah Bay, Washington: Makah Tribal Council.

Makah Tribe (2007). *Report on Concerns raised at September 11, 2007 Meeting on Unauthorized Whale Hunt*, Neah Bay, Washington: Makah Tribal Council. Available at http://www.turtleisland.org/resources/makah07.pdf [accessed 30 January 2012].

Mapes, L. and Ervin, K. (2007). Gray Whale Shot, Killed in Rogue Tribal Hunt, *The Seattle Times*, 9 September.

Matthews, R. (1995). *World Religions*, St Paul: West.

Melkevik, B. (2002). The Law and Aboriginal Reindeer Herding in Norway, in G. Duhaime (ed.), *Sustainable Food Security in the Arctic. State of Knowledge*, Edmonton: University of Alberta, CCI Press & GÉTIC, Occasional publications series no. 52, 197–203.

Otis, G. and Melkevik, B. (1996). *Natives and International Norms. Analysis and Texts Relating to Regimes of Protection and Identity of Indigenous (Native) People*, Cowansville: Yvon Blais.

Preece, R. (1999). *Animals and Nature: Culture Myths, Cultural Realities*, Vancouver: University of British Columbia.

Raine, A.F. (2007). *The International Impact of Hunting and Trapping in the Maltese Islands*, Ta' Xbiex: Birdlife Malta.

Rollin, B.E. (2006). *Animal Rights and Human Morality*, New York: Prometheus.

Schmidt, R. (1998). *Exploring Religion*, Belmont: Wadsworth.

Situ, Y. and Emmons, D. (2000). *Environmental Crime: The Criminal Justice System's Role in Protecting the Environment*, Thousand Oaks: Sage.

Smith, B.L. (2005). *Improving Humane Practice in the Canadian Harp Seal Hunt. A Report of the Independent Veterinarians' Working Group on the Canadian Harp Seal Hunt*, BLSmith Groupwork, August, 21.

Smith, K. (2010). *Texts and Materials on International Human Rights*, New York: Routledge.

Steinhauer, J. (2010). Sushi Spot is Charged with Serving Whale Meat. *The New York Times*, 10 March 2010. Available at http://www.nytimes.com/2010/03/11/us/11sushi.html [accessed 20 December 2011].

Sykes, G.M. and Matza, D. (1957). Techniques of Neutralization: A Theory of Delinquency. *American Sociological Review*, 22, 664–73.

White, R. (2008). *Crimes Against Nature: Environmental Criminology and Ecological Justice*, Devon: Willan.

Winthrop, J. (1968). *White Over Black: American Attitudes Toward the Negro, 1550–1812*, Baltimore: Penguin.

Chapter 7
Sport and Trophy Hunting

This chapter examines sport and trophy hunting and the associated traditions of violence and dominion over animals inherent in these activities as a cause of animal harm. It examines the link between trophy hunting, masculinities and identity, and the illegality of much big game hunting (i.e. the killing of protected species or killing that takes place in contravention of regulations). It also examines how sport tourism and the commercial killing of wildlife for sport constitute a distinct type of crime and criminal behaviour.

While it is important to note that sport and trophy hunting are not inherently unlawful, research indicates that illegality and corruption are endemic in the sport and trophy hunting industries. Separate from the lawful killing of small numbers of animals carried out under permit and quota systems, a wider problem of the illegal killing of protected animals and collection or harvesting of their parts for trophies or animal products exists. Trophy hunting thus contributes to other illegal trades and has implications beyond its immediate animal harm activities.

The chapter also discusses the myth of trophy hunting as either being for conservation purposes or contributing to the conservation of rare species. It discusses how trophy and big game hunting also involve other types of criminal behaviour such as fraud and bribery where those involved are driven in pursuit of rarer, endangered species. Illegal trophy hunting can involve either making profits from dealing in animal carcasses (e.g. supplying the ivory or Asian medicine markets) or the masculinities driven trophy and memorabilia aspects of killing a protected species of big game for personal satisfaction.

Defining Sport and Trophy Hunting

Sport and trophy hunting evoke strong feelings among their supporters and opponents. Public debate about trophy hunting often centres on questions of morality concerning the 'sport' elements of such hunting and the extent to which money paid by hunters benefits game animal populations and the local economy.

Big game hunting is predominantly an African concern, closely associated with wildlife safaris in the African countries of Namibia, South Africa, Kenya, Tanzania, Zimbabwe, Botswana and the Democratic Republic of Congo. Lindsey et al. (2006) identify 23 African countries as having hunting industries with the largest in South Africa generating revenues of US$100 million a year (revenues paid to operators and taxidermists). However, big game ranches exist in other parts of the world and animals have been brought, for example, from African and

Asian countries to the United States to populate ranches and safari parks (Green 1999) and Palazy et al. identify that 'especially in Texas' some species considered to be extinct in the wild are available for hunting in US ranches (2011: 5). Lindsey et al. (2012) identify that hunting safaris are usually sold in packages based on the key 'Big 5' species; those which are the five most prized specimens for hunters; the rhino, the elephant, the leopard, the lion and the Cape buffalo. Some rarer antelope species are also prized by hunters. While many of these species are prevented from being traded due to their CITES status as endangered, they may be legally shot in certain limited circumstances in African countries where populations are considered by local authorities to be stable and well managed, and where there is economic benefit in allowing a certain level of hunting. Indeed, given the availability of hunting licences as a saleable commodity, professional hunting companies have emerged to provide commercial hunting trips to Africa, offering big game shooting experiences for consumers from anywhere in the world willing to pay for an 'authentic' wildlife safari. As a result, trophy hunting has become a legitimate form of sport tourism adding to the economy of African or sub-continent countries where the exploitation of such natural resources has become an economic (and sometimes political) necessity.[1]

This chapter distinguishes sport and trophy hunting from the traditional hunting and shooting activities discussed in Chapter 5 by defining sport hunting as a commercially driven activity where individuals pay to hunt animals in a sporting context. The traditional hunting activities discussed in Chapter 5 have their origins in subsistence hunting and the killing of animals for food and even in their commercialized form have some links to supplying meat or fish for consumption. While contemporary food production methods mean that such hunting is no longer necessary except perhaps in remote rural areas where trappers and hunters live off the land and in the case of subsistence hunting by indigenous peoples (as discussed by Chapter 6), game laws have developed from traditional forms of hunting to specify a range of animals classed as game which can be legally shot or otherwise killed primarily for food consumption purposes. Commercial shooting operations such as the grouse and pheasant shooting estates of the UK have thus adapted traditional hunting to commercialized sporting hunting where only a limited proportion of the animals killed will enter the food market.

By contrast, the basis of sport and trophy hunting is power, masculinities and recreation. Sport and trophy hunters are predominantly male and tend to target larger males for shooting (Short and Balaban 1994, Palazy et al. 2012), thus overtly exercising male power over less powerful males; those animals selected for hunting purposes. However the perception of certain animals as having equal power, in particular the 'Big 5', is also a factor where hunting males positively wish to assert their dominance over a competitor. An important aspect of recreational gun culture, masculine notions of the right to hunt and to exercise

[1] Big game hunting also exists as a recreational activity within the United States although species other than the 'Big 5' such as black bear, oryx or gazelle tend to be involved.

power over others is the extent to which the use of violence is an appropriate means of resolving conflicts (see Chapters 3 and 4). Such ideas are ingrained in some aspects of western society where masculinities and the social acceptance of male power influence the extent to which male violence and perspectives on male dominance are generally accepted as a social norm although excessive use of violence is criminalized and socially unacceptable. However within such societal constructs certain males will naturally be attracted to activities which emphasize the expression of male power and male behaviours. Big game hunting, for example, sometimes places the hunter at personal risk and incorporates a range of stereotypical male behaviours relating to aggression, dominance and the thrill of chasing after an animal in its natural environment where nominally, at least, it should have the upper hand.

Trophy Hunting and Territorial Dominance

Palazy et al. (2012) explain that in contrast to subsistence hunting where survival or providing for others are factors, 'trophy hunting consists of killing few animals, for recreational purposes, both for pleasure, that is the experience of the hunt, and in order to collect and display trophies made of horns, antlers, skulls, tusks or teeth' (2012: 4). The hunting experience is expressly sold by a number of safari or big game hunting tour operators as a means of ensuring that hunters will not only be able to participate in hunting activities but crucially will be able to relive the experience through collecting and retaining trophies. Horns, antlers, skulls, etc. serve as a permanent reminder of the hunter's victory but can also act as a memory trigger, taking the hunter back to his victory and dominance over the animal and allowing him to relive the experience. Thus, both the act of hunting and the removal and retention of a trophy are explicit acts of dominance and integral to the trophy hunting experience and its continued significance to the hunter. As a result it both appeals to and is marketed at a particular personality type who seeks more challenging and memorable game rather than the lower level recreational hunter whose interest may be more in shooting as an activity than the specific type of target and experience offered by trophy hunting. Trophy hunting's reliance on species which offer trophy opportunities represents an incursion into wild areas not entirely controlled by man and is recognized by animal rights theory as direct predation against animals of a type that goes beyond simple killing. Francione argues that humans should simply leave animals alone (2008: 13) and that a 'hands off' approach to animals combined with strict prohibitions on direct harm would provide a minimal animal rights framework. Yet man generally exercises control over animal habitats, not only through the encroachment of human developments on areas where traditionally animals have held sovereignty by being free to handle their own affairs (which can include killing each other where necessary for survival), which sometimes forces animals to relocate, but also by actively managing many areas where animals live free. Trophy hunting represents interference in the lives

of wild animals of a type that does not exist in companion animals; given the fact
that the wild animals involved in trophy hunting generally exist separate from
human developments and that one aspect of the activity is that attempts are made
to provide animals that are as 'wild' as possible. Dunayer suggests that separate
from the right not to be murdered by humans 'the most important right for free
nonhumans probably is the right to their habitats' (2004: 143). Yet the conflicting
interests of man and animal are such that, in some cases, the only way that some
natural habitats can be preserved is by attaching value to them in the form of
assigning property or other rights. Donaldson and Kymlicka (2011) argue that wild
animals form their own sovereign communities which are entitled to protection
against colonization, invasion, domination and other threats to self-determination.
However interference with animals' sovereignty is an integral part of animal
hunting and provides a means of exerting territorial dominance over the world's
last remaining wild areas. Thus while animals may generally be left to their natural
behaviours in wildlife parks and game reserves, their autonomy is limited to the
extent that it is allowed by man and may be periodically (temporarily) revoked.

In practice game reserves and other wilderness areas often fall within the remit
of the relevant government's conservation or wildlife authority and are managed
either for tourism or wildlife exploitation through the sale, lease or temporary
purchase of hunting or fishing rights. Thus while animals might be deemed by
animal rights theorists to either have natural property rights or to be entitled to
claim such rights (Hadley 2005) they lack permanent sovereign control of their
territory and hunting provides a means by which this lack of sovereignty is
reinforced through hunters' territorial dominance.

Species justice perspectives and Donaldson and Kymlicka's animal citizenship
arguments (2011) suggest that formal recognition of animal sovereignty would
limit man's interference with or exploitation of wild animals. Donaldson and
Kymlicka propose a new model of animal citizenship which suggests removing
animals from human stewardship and to instead develop a sovereignty model
for wild animals based 'on the capacity of animals to pursue their own good,
and to shape their own communities' (2011: 170). This model extends the basic
animal rights perspective by recognizing the right of wild animals to be present
as permanent residents of natural environment areas on the basis of sovereign
citizenship, and provides a check on human activity and interventions in the wild
by allocating territory and limiting human interventions in a sovereign animal
community.

Donaldson and Kymlicka's proposal represents an attempt to develop animal
rights discourse beyond discussion of direct violence towards animals and to
address the complexities of human relations with wild animals (2011: 205).
However, within these complexities attitudes towards animals and natural habitats
exist that cannot be resolved solely through a rights or citizenship framework
and which are closely associated with masculinities and perspectives on power
relationships. Thus illegal hunting takes place not solely because legislation does
not provide for effective animal protection or rights but because it provides a

means through which individuals who wish to commit violence and exert power over the vulnerable (which includes big game animals) are provided with a means to do so and can express their desires. While legal trophy hunting is theoretically controlled, one theme emerging from this book's discussion of different animal harm activities is that legal animal harm frequently facilitates illegal animal harm and encourages the development of illegal activities where profit and demand for animal harm are possible. Thus the principle that animals may be killed for sport and trophy purposes not only makes it likely that individuals will wish to do so but also makes it likely that entrepreneurs wishing to make larger profits will find a way to bypass any regulations and further develop the hunting market. But even where strict prohibitions on killing animals are in force individuals disposed towards such activities will continue to break the law where they are able to legitimize their activities through the techniques of neutralization and justification discussed in Chapter 3, or where the killing of animals serves some personal need to do so and they are sufficiently motivated to find a means to fulfil this need.

Trophy hunting in African countries also represents continued dominance by western societies over the developing world. Although African hunting is not exclusively carried out by white male hunters, this group makes up a significant proportion of hunters in part because of the socio-economic considerations that are determining factors in hunting. Kotler et al. (2008) identified that the price fixed by hunting companies is determined by market rules and that while prices need to be adjusted to meet demand, the perceived value of the trophy is a significant factor in determining price. Palazy et al. (2012) identified that human attraction to rarity is a pricing factor, thus inevitably the rarer and more challenging species are more expensive to hunt and will attract those hunters from more affluent backgrounds willing and able to pay a premium for rarer species. In contrast local residents may be unable to afford trophy hunting opportunities except where concessions or exemptions from regulations are provided for. Thus the premiums paid for big game trophy hunting will be beyond the reach of many local residents but allied to the tourism industry (discussed later in this chapter) become economically viable for visitors. In this respect trophy hunting illustrates the continued reliance of local communities and the economies of the developing world on outside investment and sources of capital. African countries, with a limited industrial base and little to offer by way of manufacturing or exports, are nevertheless abundant in wildlife and thus in times of economic crisis may need to exploit what little resources are available to them. Positive attitudes towards animal protection may thus need to give way to practical considerations that view exploitation of natural resources such as wildlife as a necessity and dictate that the killing of animals is directly in human interests. There is, however, potential conflict over how wildlife resources should be exploited and whether ecotourism that allows western visitors to view animals in their native habitat is more desirable than sport and trophy hunting which also provides a means through which conservation management objectives such as population control can also be achieved. In part the conflict is resolved according to economic assessments of the relative merits of each industry, but animal harm perspectives are also a factor, as the following section illustrates.

State-Sponsored Animal Harm:
The Myth of Sport Tourism as Conservation

Trophy hunting in African and Asian countries is allowed primarily for economic reasons although conservation is also frequently advanced as a justification. The conservation argument is primarily one of management; that hunted animals are those 'surplus' animals that would need to be culled in the absence of hunting because their populations cannot be sustainably managed within their ecosystem and sustainable use is essential where resources are scarce (Baker 1997). The sustainability arguments relate not just to the need for wildlife populations to be effectively managed according to the demands of the available food source and habitat within designated wildlife areas such as national parks and game reserves, but also to prevent crop loss from wildlife and livestock depredation should populations begin to encroach onto human areas. As a result, state conservation authorities, usually acting either within national legislation or in accordance with the CITES regulations, periodically review population density and compatibility with available resources. The outcome of such reviews is often that a certain number of animals need to be culled under a quota system to prevent one species from achieving dominance or that certain animals' population density grows beyond optimal numbers. When animal numbers exceed the available food supply a number of animals may die as a result of mass starvation, or there is increased predation and an adverse impact on other species which then have increased competition for food. Beard (2008), for example, details the crash of elephant populations in Kenya's Tsavo region in the 1970s when the Kenyan government declined to cull some elephant populations during the drought period, a measure that was considered necessary by some conservationists in order to preserve other animal populations. Proponents of hunting argue this case and the resultant death of thousands of elephants and other game animals as indicative of the need for culling whether through hunting or other means. The necessity of culling has thus generally become accepted as a conservation measure and, where possible, conservation authorities seek to combine the necessity of population control with the income generation potential of trophy hunting.

Bond et al. (2004) argue that trophy hunting can be an important factor in endangered species conservation and the rehabilitation of wildlife by providing income for conservation efforts without impacting on population growth. Lindsey et al. (2006: 1) suggest that 'offtake rates are typically only 205% of male populations', thus trophy hunting is considered sustainable because the removal of a small number of males by hunting has a minimal impact on breeding rates and overall population size. However, the reliability of quotas can be contested; Whitman et al. (2004) suggested that for some hunted species the removal of young males can have a significant impact even where conservative quotas are in place. The reality is that trophy hunting does not occur in a vacuum and the loss of even a small number of males to trophy hunting can easily be compounded by other factors (e.g. illegal poaching, habitat loss) such that the effect on populations is more serious than that envisaged by conservation management programmes. In addition Baldus and Cauldwell (2004) suggest that high profit margins in some countries create a demand for increased quotas and smaller hunting areas while other countries have required increased offtake to sustain revenues due to static pricing. Thus, the revenue from trophy hunting sometimes takes priority in determining conservation strategies such that quotas are fluid (and sometimes ignored) although the number of hunted animals theoretically remains below breeding rates so that, by itself, the number of animals hunted should only occasionally impact on populations. However such conflicts indicate that once initiated trophy hunting becomes an income-generating industry that must be sustained and while it is claimed to be a conservation tool effectively becomes an animal harm industry. Lindsey et al. identify that the 'emphasis placed on trophies by some hunters reduces the conservation role of sport hunting in some instances' (2006: 2). They explain that in South Africa and Namibia where game ranches are required to have high fences, 'the value of wildlife as trophies has inhibited the removal of fencing between neighbors, stifling the formation of conservancies and maintaining the division of ranchland into small blocks' (2006: 2). Thus South African ranches have become dominated by trophy hunting rather than conservation; other researchers have also observed that conservancies are more common where ecotourism is more prevalent (Lindsey et al. 2006) and that rather than benefiting animal populations trophy hunting is, for example, negatively impacting on some big cat populations (Packer et al. 2011).

Tom identifies potential conflict between animal welfarists and conservationists. Welfarists are primarily concerned with the well-being of animals while conservationists 'are primarily concerned with ecological collectives and not with individual sentient animals' (2002: 78). Thus the welfare of individual animals as sentient beings is not a priority in culling operations and conservation priorities are primarily around preventing destruction of ecosystems, habitats and species rather than individual animal welfare. As a result, where trophy hunting is employed as a conservation measure, animal welfare arguments might be ignored in relation to individual animals because of the overall benefits that trophy hunting as a form of culling generates. The dominant attitude in managing trophy hunting thus seems to be one of viewing animals as a commodity rather than a sustainable resource or sentient species requiring protection and management. In effect, killing individual animals, even where this results in illegal animal harm, is preferable to the greater harm of a species becoming extinct or other adverse effects on animal populations. In which case, the potential for over-exploitation of animals linked to a denial of harm becomes understandable. If animals are available for exploitation, and killing is a necessary part of that exploitation, then potentially the divide between legal and illegal hunting is simply a question of degree and how many animals it is acceptable to kill. Where this perception gains primacy authorities may fail to provide adequate resources for enforcement of hunting regulations. Thus hunting may be under-resourced when compared to ecotourism although questions might also be raised about the effectiveness of ecotourism as a conservation measure.

Damania et al. (2008) argue that ecotourism is a solution to many of the problems experienced by endangered species conservation efforts, and if successful ecotourism would significantly reduce the animal harm associated with trophy hunting. They suggest that where it is possible to implement ecotourism, it should be developed to 'provide a valuable source of revenue and an opportunity to generate and share benefits' which are directly linked to the presence of threatened wildlife species (2008: 3). Thus in addition to preserving threatened species and their habitats, ecotourism would provide a sustainable non-violent use of wildlife and would allow conservation and animal welfare concerns to co-exist. However one criticism levelled at trophy hunting is that local communities do not directly share in the benefits (Mbwaia 2004) and the same can be said of ecotourism where revenues go to tour operators and government agencies rather than directly to local communities. Livestock keeping and crop production are important activities in most townships that border game and conservation preserves. But poorly managed game animal populations can threaten the livelihoods of rural dwellers via crop damage and predation so that in some African and Asian countries rural inhabitants see game animals as a threat to their livelihoods rather than a benefit. As a result local communities may place a negative value on wildlife as a threat such that they are sympathetic to hunting operations and may derive spin-off benefits from trophy hunting in a way that they do not from ecotourism. However Lindsey et al. identified 'a significant market among U.S. clients for conservation-friendly hunting' (2006: 3) such that in their survey of prospective hunting clients, 86 percent said they would be more willing to purchase a hunt if local communities benefited.

Palazy et al. (2011) have highlighted that in some circumstances hunting is less profitable than photographic tourism. While hunting inevitably attracts high fees, the management and administrative costs of regulating hunting are high and can constitute an excessive administrative burden on under-resourced wildlife departments. In addition ecotourism is considered to be one of the fastest growing industries in the world (Damania et al. 2008: 3), providing alternative employment opportunities for employment for local people (for example as tour guides) and capitalizing on wildlife resources as a public good. If managed properly ecotourism has the capacity to contribute to species justice and animal welfare concerns not only by eliminating animal harm but also by providing education opportunities linked to conservation objectives. However, while ecotourism has developed as a sustainable business in some areas so that for example whale watching is said to generate $1.1 billion annually for the United States and Canada, Damania et al. identified that the average Indian tiger reserve 'receives 60,000 tourists per year but collects little in revenues, largely due to low entry fees' (2008: 18).

As a result, the success of ecotourism is limited by its organization and the involvement of local communities.

Dinerstein et al. (1999) examined a successful community-based tiger ecotourism project in Nepal, concluding that its success was in part due to strong local institutions that enforce conservation rules and ensure equitable distribution of benefits, together with a co-operative working relationship between local people and conservation officials. By commencing with a privately-owned ecotourism system that then allowed a community-based approach, the initial costs of developing ecotourism were absorbed while local communities were given the tools and resources to regenerate lands adjacent to the conservation area. As a result, local people developed an interest in species conservation and viewed wildlife as an asset to be preserved rather than a resource to be utilized or an inconvenience to be disposed of. Developing these attitudes is an important part of any policy aimed at reducing animal harm given the endemic illegal activity that coincides with any legal killing of animals such as that contained in sport and trophy hunting or the illegal poaching that also takes place in conservation areas. The following case study illustrates these points.

Case Study: Elephant Killing

Illegal hunting of elephants illustrates the debate over sport hunting and conservation. Trophy hunting is vital to the economies of some African states with Lindsey et al. estimating that trophy hunting results in around US$30 million a year in Namibia and US$100 million in South Africa (2007). Burke et al. (2008) suggest that African elephants hold 'special appeal' to humans because of their high tourist value by virtue of their status as one of the 'Big 5' species which tourists wish to see. But they also have value as they are social animals which develop long-lasting bonds, thus humans develop empathy with them. The 'Big 5's' charisma, size, danger and 'drama', combined with their status as threatened or endangered species, not only make them desirable attractions to tourists and wildlife photographers (Reynolds and Braithwaite 2001, Mbenga 2004 cited in Burke et al. 2008) but also to hunters wishing to test their skill against the most challenging and valuable game.

However while African elephants might legally be hunted as part of the controlled management of herds and under certain specified conditions, they are frequently illegally hunted, primarily for their tusks in order to satisfy demand for ivory products. The international trade in Asian elephant ivory was banned in 1975 when the Asian elephant was listed in Appendix I of CITES, while the African elephant was listed in CITES Appendix I in 1990. However, in 1997, Botswana's, Namibia's and Zimbabwe's populations of African elephants were transferred to CITES Appendix II for certain commercial trade purposes following the 1997 CITES Conference of the Parties (CoP10) when CITES agreed to allow a one-time 'experimental' export of 49 metric tons of ivory from Botswana, Namibia and Zimbabwe to Japan; this took place in 1999. The US Fish and Wildlife Service reports that the price of a kilogram (kg) of ivory:

> hovered at approximately $5.50 and moved up slightly to about $7.50 by 1970. However by 1978 the price had skyrocketed to almost £75 per kg and by 1989, it fetched $150 per kg in Africa and up to $400 per kg in Japan. This stimulated an enormous upsurge in organized poaching and ivory trafficking networks. (2001: 6)

Estimates from various sources suggest that during the 1980s an average 200 elephants a day were being killed for their ivory. Current estimates put the price of ivory as high as $1,500 in the Far East with the Kenya Elephant Forum reporting that 'even a small pair of 10-kg tusks would bring a poacher the equivalent of $400, more than casual workers earn in a year' (2010: 2). The HSUS (2002) also reports that the market for ivory has increased and most conservation commentators agree that, as a result, elephants are increasingly being killed illegally to supply the ivory trade. The illegal killing is sometimes associated with the legal hunting industry, as well as with illegal poaching.

While CITES requires that any killing of elephants should be strictly monitored difficulties exist in regulating the hunting industry. Lewis and Jackson (2005) identify that corruption is endemic so that government scouts are paid to ignore overshooting (which constitutes illegal killing and is thus unlawful animal harm) while politicians are paid to favour certain trophy hunting operators. In addition, Lindsey et al. identify a range of animal harm activities which have become subject to specific legal restrictions, including 'shooting from vehicles; shooting young or uncommon animals; luring animals from parks; use of bait, spotlights, and hounds; canned hunting (i.e., where captive-bred animals, typically lions [*Panthera leo*], are hunted in small enclosures)' (2006: 2).

In 2006 a series of poaching raids in the Zakouma National Park in southern Chad resulted in the killing of around 100 elephants. In early 2012, 300 elephants were confirmed killed in a poaching attack on Cameroon's Bouba Ndjida National Park although IFAW (2012) estimate that the final total could be as high as 50 percent of Bouba's 1,000 elephant population.

The HSUS explains that 'since January 1, 2000, at least 1,609 African and 79 Asian elephants were reported poached for their ivory, while 54,462 ivory pieces, 3,892 ivory tusks (equal to 1,946 dead elephants), and 11.1 metric tons of raw ivory (equal to about 1,400 dead elephants) were seized' (2002: 3). The Kenya Elephant Forum estimates that 38,000 elephants are killed annually to supply the ivory trade and that 'killing of elephants is increasing in East, Central and West Africa, as evidenced by increased poaching and increased seizures of ivory originating in Africa' (2010: 2). Lewis and Jackson (2005) identify that in several countries large citizen quotas are provided allowing for local residents to pursue hunting. They argue that not only does this reduce revenues from trophy hunting and reduce incentives for communities to conserve wildlife, but that the allocation of cheap hunting concessions to unlicensed operators also means that unregulated (and illegal) hunting takes place.

While a distinction can be made between 'technically' illegal hunting that breaches or fails to comply with regulations, and poaching which is deliberately and knowingly unlawful activity, the existence of legal hunting facilitates illegal activity from which ivory can be obtained. The HSUS explains that 'the fact that nearly all of the recent ivory seizures in China or destined for China originated from Africa are a strong indication that the illegal ivory trade route leads from poached elephants in African countries to China' (2002: 3). In effect, ivory traders will source their products from whatever means possible and both legitimate and illegitimate hunting provide a means through which ivory can be obtained. The Kenya Elephant Forum reports that confiscations of illegal ivory have increased in recent years (2010). Given the difficulties in legally obtaining sufficient ivory to meet demand, it is inevitable that illegal hunting and poaching have also increased to supply the current trade.

Preliminary Conclusions on Sport and Trophy Hunting

Sport and trophy hunting inevitably attract those individuals disposed towards direct animal harm and for whom the notion of animal rights and species justice is, at best, secondary to their own interests. The animal harm associated with sport and trophy hunting consists of deliberately exercising power over an animal by consciously taking its life. However sport hunting, aimed at smaller species, perhaps lays more claim to being a recreational activity than trophy hunting which is more closely associated with the hunting experience and dominion over animals and wild places.

The higher costs of trophy hunting, particularly safari packages in Africa and Asia, increase its exclusivity while also adding to its attractiveness. Roulet (2004) calculated that approximately 18,500 foreign hunters visit sub-Saharan Africa annually, generating US$201 million per year for beleaguered local economies. For countries in the developing world, this constitutes a considerable sum of money such that species justice concerns will become secondary and the exploitation of wildlife will be viewed favourably. In such a context, maintaining positive views of animal welfare and a political will to reduce or eliminate animal harm is problematic. Lindsey et al. (2006) suggest that resolving the problems associated with illegal hunting, such as over-killing, corruption, cruel hunting methods and lack of sustainability, requires co-ordinated efforts from the hunting industry, conservationists and governments. Yet arguably the hunting industry has no incentive to improve its practices as the negative publicity from hunting does not necessarily impact on availability of animals and permits although there have been bans on hunting in some areas (for example in Tanzania 1973 to 1978, Zambia from 2000 to 2003). However these bans resulted in the loss of wildlife due to the removal of incentives for conservation (Baker 1997, Lewis and Jackson 2005) and thus revenues from hunting, where there is no ecotourism alternative, can be so valuable that countries take only limited enforcement action against illegal hunting and provide minimal resources for effective regulation.

The argument that it is morally wrong to allow trophy hunting or animal culling because of the harm that it causes to animals has, regrettably, become redundant to conservation and regulatory authorities in trophy hunting countries. Animal welfarists have argued that the culling or hunting of animals causes distress to the remaining animals in some cases. Hoyt (1994), for example, argues that because elephants are animals with complex social relations, killing some of them causes disruption to these relations and suffering to the remaining animals. Burke et al. also found increased levels of stress in bull elephant populations following hunts, concluding that both those bulls that were present at hunts and the broader bull elephant population showed increased stress hormone levels afterwards although they concluded that these effects were 'relatively minor' (2008: 1). But within the context of legally permissible culling and trophy hunting, the goal should be to limit or eradicate unnecessary suffering, identify and reduce illegal killing and to directly address the criminality inherent in illegal trophy killing and poaching. In doing so animal harm might be reduced and future animal harm prevented and the conservation benefits of sport and trophy hunting increased by ensuring that any impact on populations is minimized and strictly controlled through proper implementation of any quota system. Yet, while in principle legal trophy hunting is regulated and monitored by law enforcement and conservation authorities, the large sums of money involved dictate that illegal activity is closely associated with trophy hunting which in reality is poorly regulated, subject to weak enforcement, lacklustre prosecutorial efforts and provides opportunities for corruption (Lindsey et al. 2006). Thus regulatory and legislative frameworks that govern the trophy hunting industry require improvement (Lindsey et al. 2006) and require dedicated resources to be in place not only aimed at the ensuring that the 'legal' trophy hunting industry is effectively monitored and its regulations complied with, but that the illegal aspects of trophy hunting are properly enforced. The seemingly minor breaches of sport and trophy hunting regulations indicated by illegal activities carried out as part of legal trophy hunting show a disregard for animals that leads to them being considered only in respect of their value as trophies and subjects of the hunt. While the illegal poaching and trophy hunting that takes places shows illegal commercial activity that firmly views animals as disposable and ignores the conservation imperatives of sport and trophy hunting and the need to preserve rare and threatened animals for future generations.

References

Baker, J. (1997). Trophy Hunting as a Sustainable Use of Wildlife Resources in Southern and Eastern Africa. *Journal of Sustainable Tourism*, 5, 306–21.

Baldus, R. and Cauldwell, A. (2004). *Tourist Hunting and its Role in Development of Wildlife Management Areas in Tanzania. Tanzanian-German Development Cooperation*, Dar es Salaam, Tanzania. Available at http://www.wildlife-programme.gtz.de/wildlife/download/hunting_wma.pdf [accessed 20 January 2012].

Beard, P. (2008). *The End of the Game: The Last Word from Paradise*, Köln: Taschen GmbH.

Bond, I., Child, B., de la Harpe, D., Jones, B., Barnes, J. and Anderson, H. (2004). Private Land Contribution to Conservation in South Africa. Pages in B. Child (ed.), *Parks in Transition*, Earthscan, London, 29–61.

Burke, T., Page, B., Van Dyk, G., Millspaugh, J. and Slotow, R. (2008). Risk and Ethical Concerns of Hunting Male Elephants: Behavioural and Physiological Assays of the Remaining Elephants. *PLoS ONE* 3(6): e2417. doi:10.1371/journal.pone.0002417.

Damania, R., Seidensticker, J., Whitten, A., Sethi, G., Mackinnon, K., Kiss, A. and Kushlin, A. (2008). *A Future for Wild Tigers*, Washington, DC: The International Bank for Reconstruction and Development / The World Bank and Smithsonian's National Zoological Park.

Dinerstein, E., Rijal, A., Bookbinder, M., Kattell, B. and Rajuria, A. (1999). Tigers as Neighbours: Efforts to Promote Local Guardianship of Endangered Species in Lowland Nepal, in J. Seidensticker, S. Christie and P. Jackson (eds), *Riding the Tiger: Tiger Conservation in Human-dominated Landscapes*, Cambridge: Cambridge University Press, 316–33.

Dunayer, J. (2004). *Speciesism*, Derwood, MD: Ryce Publishing.

Donaldson, S. and Kymlicka, W. (2011). *Zoopolis: A Political Theory of Animal Rights.* New York and Oxford: Oxford University Press.

Francione, G.L. (2008). *Animals as Persons: Essays on the Abolition of Animal Exploitation*, New York: Columbia University Press.

Green, A. (1999). *Animal Underworld: Inside America's Black Market for Rare and Exotic Species*, New York: Public Affairs.

Hadley, J. (2005). Nonhuman Animal Property: Reconciling Environmentalism and Animal Rights. *Journal of Social Philosophy*, 36(3), 305–15.

Hoyt, J. (1994). *Animals in Peril*, New York: Avery Publishing Group.

HSUS (2002). *An Investigation of Ivory Markets in the United States*. The Humane Society of the United States, Washington, DC, USA.

IFAW (2012). *Elephant Population Halved in Cameroon Killing Spree*, Yarmouth Port: IFAW. Available at http://www.ifaw.org/united-states/news/elephant-population-halved-cameroon-killing-spree-graphic-images [accessed 25 March 2012].

Kenya Elephant Forum (2010). *Elephant Poaching and the Ivory Trade*, Nairobi: Kenya Elephant Forum.

Kotler, P., Armstrong, G., Wong, V. and Saunders, J.A. (2008). *Principles of Marketing*, 5th revised edn, London: Pitman Publishing.

Lewis, D. and Jackson, J. (2005). Safari Hunting and Conservation on Communal Land in Southern Africa, in R. Woodroffe, S. Thirgood and A. Rabinowitz (eds), *People and Wildlife: Conflict or Coexistence?* Cambridge: Cambridge University Press, 239–51.

Lindsey, P.A., Balme, G.A., Booth, V.R. and Midlane, N. (2012). The Significance of African Lions for the Financial Viability of Trophy Hunting and the Maintenance of Wild Land. *PLoS ONE* 7(1), e29332. doi:10.1371/journal.pone.0029332.

Lindsey, P.A., Frank, L.G., Alexander, R., Mathieson, A. and Romanach, S.S. (2007). Trophy Hunting and Conservation in Africa: Problems and One Potential Solution. *Conservation Biology*, 21, 880–83.

Lindsey, P.A., Frank, L.G., Alexander, R., Mathieson, A. and Romanach, S.S. (2006). Trophy Hunting and Conservation in Africa: Problems and One Potential Solution. *Conservation Biology*, 20, 880–83.

Mbwaia, J. (2004). Socio-economic Benefits and Challenges of a Community-based Safari Hunting Tourism in the Okavango Delta. *Botswana. Journal of Tourism Studies*, 15, 37–50.

Packer, C., Brink, H., Kissui, B., Maliti, H. and Kushnir, H. (2011). Effects of Trophy Hunting on Lion and Leopard Populations in Tanzania. *Conservation Biology*, 25, 142–53.

Palazy, L., Bonenfant, C., Gailard, J.M. and Courchamp, F. (2011). Cat Dilemma: Too Protected To Escape Trophy Hunting? *PLoS*, 6(7), 1–6.

Palazy, L., Bonenfant, C., Gailard, J.M. and Courchamp, F. (2012). Rarity, Trophy Hunting and Ungulates. *Animal Conservation*, 15, 4–11.

Petersen, M.N. (2004). An Approach for Demonstrating the Social Legitimacy of Hunting. *Wildlife Society Bulletin*, 32, 310–21.

Reynolds, P. and Braithwaite, D. (2001). Towards a Conceptual Framework for Wildlife Tourism. *Tourism Management*, 22, 31–42.

Roulet, P. (2004). La chasse sportive en Afrique Centrale. PhD thesis, University of Orleans, Orleans, France.

Short, R.V. and Balaban, E. (1994). *The Differences between the Sexes*, Cambridge: Cambridge University Press.

Tom, P. (2002). The Debate over Elephant Culling: Is it Ever Morally Justified to Cull Elephants? *Zambezia*, XXIX(i), 76–81.

US Fish and Wildlife Service (2001). *African Elephant Conservation Act: Summary Report 1998–2000*, Washington, DC: U.S. Department of the Interior.

Whitman, K., Starfield, A., Quadling, H. and Packer, C. (2004). Sustainable Trophy-hunting of African Lions. *Nature*, 428, 175–8.

Chapter 8
Trade in Wildlife and Derivatives

The trade in wildlife and derivatives is an area of animal harm that attracts considerable attention from academics and policymakers. Perhaps because it is the area most closely allied to mainstream criminology given the involvement of identifiable criminal actors in the form of organized crime and other offenders seeking profits, and its links with other forms of crime such as human trafficking or the illegal trade in drugs, it is easy for the public, policymakers and enforcers to understand. This chapter considers the motivations and criminal behaviour of those involved in the illegal trade in wildlife and derivatives, including the illegal trade in animal parts for medicines and the illegal trade in wildlife for use in zoos, safari parks, falconry and as pets. This form of animal harm is primarily motivated by profit so that those involved are predominantly the *Model A* offenders referred to in Chapter 3, offenders for whom animal harm is a means through which profit can be derived and the use of animals is simply a form of commoditization. However, the criminality involved can be complex, involving a variety of criminal actors.

The trade in wildlife and derivatives is often commercial activity and an area where the legal and illegal trade co-exist such that legitimate businesses can sometimes use illegal means to trade unlawfully and enter the criminal arena. But it is also an area where operations entirely geared around illegal activity can exist, taking advantage of existing transnational flows and global structural conditions that facilitate trade (Edwards and Gill 2003). Wildlife trade ranges from small-scale trading in companion animals, exotic animals (or pets) or derivatives such as ornaments made out of ivory, to the large-scale smuggling of endangered wildlife for private collectors (Green 1999) or to feed the (mostly legitimate) animal education and entertainment market (circuses, falconry centres, safari parks and zoos). However in recent years the wildlife trade has attracted the attention and involvement of organized crime which increasingly sees wildlife trade as a 'soft option' when compared to the drugs trade due to the generally lower level of fines and less co-ordinated enforcement activity of wildlife crime agencies in comparison to the drugs, guns and human trafficking criminal justice regimes. The nature of organized crime consisting of criminal hierarchies organized to maximize profit (Williams 2001, Woodiwiss and Hobbs 2009) is one that continually adapts, develops and exploits criminal networks and supply routes to supply a range of products from counterfeit goods (Gail et al. 1998) to drugs and now wildlife (Nurse 2011, South and Wyatt 2011) with the expressed goal of maximum profit for minimum outlay. This chapter makes an argument for this type of criminal behaviour to be considered as mainstream crime where wildlife has been substituted for drugs or counterfeit goods (although in some cases exists alongside these trades) but where the approach of the justice agencies has not yet kept pace with the development of a global wildlife trade. In addition to its size and the overlap with other forms of criminality, particularly violence and other serious crimes, wildlife trafficking requires a criminal justice response similar to that provided for other forms of organized crime.

Scope of the Wildlife Trade

While difficult to monitor, wildlife trafficking is thought to be the second or third most valuable illicit commerce in the world after drugs and weapons (Webster 1997), and is worth an estimated $10 billion a year, according to the US Department of State (2009) while other estimates place it at between $10 and $20 billion annually (South and Wyatt 2011). Difficulties naturally exist in any attempt to identify the scale of an illegal trade, much of which takes place outside of the sphere of the legitimate monitoring bodies and which, like much animal harm, is subject to variations in the way the activity is measured. But estimates based on CITES and NGO data and extrapolated from seizures by enforcement bodies consistently reinforce the perception of a large-scale trade with a minimum value of $10 billion and which is consistently considered to be second only to the drugs trade. Birds are the most common contraband, with the US Department of State estimating that between two million and five million wild birds, from hummingbirds to parrots to harpy eagles, are traded illegally worldwide every year (2009). The trade is influenced by the ease with which wild birds can be caught, traded and sold and the difficulties that sometimes exist in distinguishing between legal specimens and those prohibited from trade by CITES. Many rare parrots, for example, are similar in appearance to less threatened species requiring expert identification to distinguish between species listed in CITES Appendix I or II and which are subject to trade controls, and those which can be freely traded and breed easily in captivity. However millions of turtles, crocodiles, snakes and other reptiles are also trafficked, as well as mammals and insects.

Wyatt proposed 'processed commodities, collector's items, traditional medicines, and food' (2011: 1) as the main four categories of wildlife trafficking, while Cook et al. (2002: 4) suggested that the illegal wildlife trade broadly consists of the following five areas of activity:

- specimen collecting;
- skins, furs and traditional Asian medicines (where parts of animals such as bones may be used);
- activities associated with drug trafficking;
- caviar trafficking; and
- illegal timber trade.

In the context of animal harm, both Wyatt's (2011) and Cook et al.'s (2002) categories, except for the illegal timber trade, are relevant classifications in assessing animal harm criminality as they will frequently involve *direct* harm to animals that are the target of the trade, whereas this is not always the case with the timber trade. However, the timber trade has an indirect effect on animals where the removal of timber from forests indirectly results in the loss of habitats. Deforestation can also result in the destruction of active wildlife habitats causing *direct* harm to animals in the process and has been cited by some NGOs as either causing the extinction of certain species or severely impacting on their populations (de Bohan et al. 1996). While the timber trade is not discussed in any great detail in this chapter, illegal logging and the timber trade are an aspect of animal harm, albeit one where the intent to kill and harvest wildlife is generally less than in other forms of animal harm associated with the wildlife trade. But timber traders negligent as to the consequences of their activities on animals are nevertheless involved in animal harm and their failure to consider the impact of their activities on animals in the pursuit of profits has the potential to cause significant animal harm given that habitat loss is a major factor in the decline of some wildlife species.

The sheer scale of the legal wildlife trade facilitates an illegal trade which often exists alongside its legal counterpart but also illustrates the profits to be made by trading in wildlife. The CITES Secretariat's most recent data indicates that the current trend of CITES transactions is generally upwards 'and averages 850,000 permits a year nowadays' (CITES 2010: 4). With many species of wildlife selling for several thousands of pounds per specimen this is a significant level of ostensibly legal trade although, as discussed later in this chapter, there are difficulties with determining the legality of much trade. This fact is readily exploited by traders wishing to disguise illegal transactions as legal ones. The level of trade indicates considerable global consumer demand for wildlife and wildlife products, thus a substantial market exists that may be difficult to sustain entirely through legal means providing opportunities for criminal actors to enter the market. In 2009 the US State Department concluded that the illegal trade in wildlife has developed to meet 'unchecked demand for exotic pets, rare foods, trophies and traditional medicines', and Cook et al. report that each category of (illegal) wildlife trade has particular 'methods, markets, routes and "tricks of the trade"', which include concealment, mis-declaration, permit fraud and the laundering of illegal wildlife products through the complexities of re-exports' (2002: 4). According to Schneider, the trade's basis is simple in that 'going beyond the simple notion that thieves steal to make money, preliminary market-level analyses reveal that thieves steal because they know there are ways for them to sell the goods they steal. In other words, the crime of handling is supported by a structure that allows thieves the opportunity to sell stolen property either to people who use the items themselves or to those who sell it on to others' (2008: 276). Thus wildlife traders seek both to obtain wildlife and sell to an end consumer, or to a dealer or other middleman who has consumers ready to purchase wildlife or wildlife products. However the complexity of the illegal trade, particularly in its transnational elements, is such that a range of criminal actors, from low-level thieves, poachers and handlers through to sophisticated sellers and large-scale commercial operators, are involved at various stages. Thus identifying wildlife traffickers is problematic as these criminal actors operate from capture through to eventual sale given that at each stage, money can be made without necessarily relying on the eventual sale of an animal (except in the sense that this is necessary for the trade to continue). This provides a simple motivation for much of the trade; profit. At the upper end of the scale, profits can be in the tens of thousands of pounds or dollars, sometimes for a relatively small operation in terms of numbers of species sold and, as the CITES data shows, the trade is now global, highly organized and employing sophisticated methods to achieve its profits.

Zimmerman argues that whereas exotic animal traders 'were once viewed as small-time criminals' who sold birds in fairs, the international community must now recognize 'the extensive, powerful involvement of organized criminal rings in the illegal wildlife trade' (2003: 1659). Consistent with the analysis of criminality outlined in Chapter 3, Wyatt also identifies that 'what is true for one product in terms of market forces and criminal elements, might not be true for another product' (2011: 4), thus the specific dimensions of animal harm involved in the wildlife trade require further examination.

As Chapter 1 observes, most endangered species are protected under CITES which contains a sophisticated transnational enforcement regime designed to prevent illegal trading in endangered wildlife but which also regulates a lawful trade in (less) endangered flora and fauna. In addition to implementing CITES, many states have their own endangered species legislation which seeks to provide an additional level of protection for nationally (or regionally) recognized 'threatened' or endangered species or which implements CITES with state specific conditions or variations. However, the very fact of the enforcement regime combined with the relative scarcity of some of the animals involved means that criminal activity has developed to keep pace with the challenges faced by increased law enforcement activity aimed at the wildlife trade and the increased premiums that collectors and practitioners will pay for increasingly rare specimens. Schneider comments that 'because of the purported size, scope, and global nature of the illicit trade in flora and fauna, the potential profits are enormous' (2008: 289) and the market is likely to endure both as long as there are species to exploit and consumer demand for wildlife and wildlife derivatives. Zimmerman (2003) suggests that CITES has generally been effective but Kosloff and Trexler (1987) argue instead that CITES has experienced difficulties almost from its inception and in some countries the resources of criminal networks involved in wildlife trade far outweigh those of the CITES enforcers who are routinely under-resourced. Fleming (1994) also observed that 'it is widely acknowledged that many, if not most, Parties to the Convention on International Trade in Endangered Species of wild Fauna and Flora (CITES) have problems in implementing and enforcing the provisions of the Convention' (1994: 3). While this does not suggest that CITES is ineffective as an enforcement tool (and there have been some notable successes in CITES enforcement), the scale of wildlife trade and its attractiveness to both small-scale traders and organized crime as a profit maker means that serious co-ordinated criminal activity is often in direct conflict with low level enforcement activity.

Aspects of the Wildlife Trade

While the involvement of organized crime in the illegal wildlife trade receives much of the academic and law enforcement attention, a range of activities including smaller scale trade is also involved. The trade in animal meat which can constitute significant trade volumes is dealt with in Chapter 7 as this is often either a by-product of or is associated with the (illegal) hunting, shooting and fishing industries. Within these industries, where the sale of products such as bushmeat for consumption is associated with the game and sport tourism industry and its exploitation of wildlife, there are indications of a growing illegal trade that exists alongside the legal one and thus represents unsustainable use of wildlife and is a factor in the decline of some wildlife populations (Robinson and Bennett 2004, Redmond et al. 2006, Mfunda and Roskaft 2010). Consumers of wildlife through illegal wildlife trade similarly risk contributing to species declines and represent a threat to wildlife populations, and it is worth noting that consumers have a variety of motives, including consuming for profit, collection and obsession. Thus the role of the wildlife trade consumer is a factor as while dealers operate as a response to consumer demand, law enforcement needs to consider the circumstances in which wildlife trade continues. Attention focused on consumers has primarily been the province of NGOs through publicity campaigns aimed at educating consumers about the dangers of wildlife trade or the legality of certain products and encouraging them to buy only legitimate wildlife products.[1] However, the focus of law enforcement on wildlife crime is primarily on offenders as rational choice offenders with the result that wildlife trade enforcement addresses only part of the criminality and criminal behaviour inherent in the illegal trade in wildlife.

The inadequacies of enforcement initiatives are a common theme in green criminology and are particularly acute within transnational environmental crime discourse. White (2008) identified that the local, regional and global dimensions of wildlife crime represent both practical problems in international collaboration by policing agencies as well as policy difficulties and a lack of clear agreement on how such offences should be dealt with. Tomkins (2005) raised the question of who is going to police international environmental crime although perhaps a more fundamental question in wildlife trafficking is how should legislation deal

---

1   See, for example, the WWF's online guide for consumers on what to look for when buying wildlife souvenirs. The guide provides an outline of CITES regulations and indicates which souvenirs are CITES compliant and which are strictly prohibited. The guide is available to download at: http://assets.wwf.org.uk/downloads/souvenirs.pdf [accessed 20 January 2012].

with illegal wildlife trade as a distinct aspect of animal harm? In May 2002 the University of Wolverhampton published a report on *Crime and Punishment in the Wildlife Trade*. The Wolverhampton researchers concluded that:

> the attitude of the UK's legal system towards the ever-increasing illegal wildlife trade is inconsistent. It does not adequately reflect the nature and impact of the crimes, and it is erratic in its response. The result is that the courts perceive wildlife crime as low priority, even though it is on the increase. (Lowther et al. 2002: 5)

Although this aspect of the Wolverhampton report was an assessment of the UK's legal system, its conclusions on the inadequacies of legislation and inconsistency in the way that legislation is enforced are echoed by NGOs who assess the wildlife trade around the world. While CITES provides the international law framework for the wildlife trade the picture of wildlife trafficking that emerges through examining the available literature, enforcement reports and assessments of criminality in different jurisdictions is that of inconsistent and inadequate legislation, subject to an equally inconsistent enforcement regime (albeit one where individual police officers or other enforcers contribute significant amounts of time and effort within their own geographical area or area of expertise). Zimmerman identifies that 'CITES does not mandate criminal sanctions or provide enforcement mechanisms' (2003: 1674). So that while Article VIII of CITES requires states to implement measures to penalize trade in endangered species where such trade is in contravention of CITES, the manner in which states do so is a matter for their own national legislation. As a result, CITES enforcement legislation in the UK differs from CITES enforcement legislation in African states which also differs from CITES enforcement legislation in Japan. Thus the extent to which CITES violations are provided for in national legislation as part of the criminal law (discussed further in Chapter 10) varies and reflects societal construction of wildlife trade as serious crime (or not). Thus inconsistency between wildlife trade legislation and subsequent enforcement across jurisdictions (for example different penalties, different police powers and different enforcement agencies existing in different jurisdictions) is inevitable and is often reflected in NGO policies as demonstrating that wildlife trade legislation is inadequate and needs wholesale reform. However, the ad-hoc development of CITES enforcement across jurisdictions reflects national perspectives and the differences in legal regimes as much as it does any lack of willingness to engage with wildlife trade as serious crime. There is thus a risk that no matter what the international legislative regime, the enforcement of wildlife trade legislation through CITES will inevitably be inconsistent, although Zimmerman argues that legislation seeking to combat wildlife trafficking should reflect two central ideas as follows:

- CITES enabling legislation should send a clear message that wildlife crime is a serious crime in the view of the state; and
- the penalties for wildlife crime should reflect the gravity of the crime. (Zimmerman 2003: 1675)

This approach provides a basic approach to dealing with wildlife trade as serious crime but requires further development to effectively deal with the range of criminality in the illegal wildlife trade. While it can be argued that wildlife trade is predominantly committed by Model A traditional offenders operating for profit (see Chapter 3), Cook et al. concluded that the illegal wildlife trade 'comprises a range of illicit activities at varying scales of operation and with differing levels of seriousness' (2002: 9), thus different aspects of trade identify different elements of criminality and varied attitudes towards animal harm. The categories of trade identified by the Wolverhampton researchers (and Wyatt's further consideration of different trade aspects) merit individual examination concerning the animal harm and offender motivations involved.

Specimen Collecting

The illegal trade in live specimens incorporates trading in larger, rare or exotic specimens and is perhaps the most global aspect of the illegal wildlife trade. Trade in live animals (particularly rarer species) is driven to supply demand from private collectors for rare species, or to supply zoos, private ranches and safari parks with specimens for exhibition or hunting as well as the commercial exotic animal trade. Zimmerman identifies that a thriving global black market in wildlife exists and that demand for wildlife and wildlife by-products comes from developed nations while developing nations tend to supply the wildlife (2003: 1669). As an example, pet shops in the west are significant retailers of wild birds. The New York Zoological Society estimates that the United States and Europe are the largest international market for birds with 14 to 20 million birds taken annually from the wild to supply the trade, although 'as many as three-fourths will die before they ever reach the pet stores' (1992: 1). Birds are taken to supply the falconry trade in both the west and the Middle East and the perception that wild birds hunt better than captive bred ones provides incentive for wild birds to be taken to supply the trade even though captive-breeding and thus legitimate trade is possible (Nurse 2003, 2011, Wyatt 2009, 2011). Revill (2002) also suggested that for many criminals, private zoos of endangered species have become status symbols and thus animals are actively sought by private collectors willing to pay a premium for specific specimens.

The specimen trade is characterized by fraud and deception. The small amount of legal trade in endangered species through CITES provides a means through which illegally captured species can be transported. Specific techniques include misidentifying the species' country of origin, the type and number of species or the precise commercial nature of the shipment. Thus animals being illegally smuggled for 'canned hunts' might be identified as zoo specimens as might animals intended for experimentation (Zimmerman 2003). Identifying wild species as captive-bred (and thus permissible trade) is a common means of facilitating trade thus many specimens 'are traded under the guise of legality with falsified documentation' (New York Zoological Society 1992: 12) placing the onus on regulatory authorities to prove the illegality of specimens. Intimidation and bribery of local CITES officials as a means of obtaining permits are also used as tactics to facilitate trade. Current enforcement systems were not established to tackle such crime, and weak governance, low capacity and inadequate resources facilitate the trade. Anderson (1997) and Zimmerman (2003) identified that certain geographical areas are well known for having weak border controls that make it easy to smuggle wildlife through customs, citing the US–Mexico border and the UK as examples of poor control. Although it should perhaps be noted that CITES enforcement represents a challenge in almost every jurisdiction.

Specimen collecting illustrates animal harm as disregarding the welfare of animals and viewing them purely as commodities. In this respect, it represents direct animal harm where the intent is exploitation of animals irrespective of the consequences for those animals. Mortality rates in the wild bird trade are high (New York Zoological Society 1992) and are likely also so within other forms of wildlife trade where animals will die from trapping and in transit as well as being unsuitable for captivity, ornamental use, or their use in canned hunts (Zimmerman 2003). Thus wildlife trade's exploitation of wildlife uses a range of criminal techniques in pursuit of animals to be traded and to fulfil consumer demand.

Skins, Furs and Traditional Asian Medicines

A substantial illegal trade in dead specimens also exists, particularly where skins, furs and other derivatives might be sold as part of either the wildlife souvenir market or the traditional Asian or Chinese medicine market (TCM) where parts of animals are used for their perceived potency (see case study later in this chapter). Currey's analysis of illegal poaching in India during the 1990s concluded that 'poaching for bones for Chinese medicine, for skins, penises, teeth and nails is responsible for the death of at least one tiger a day in India' (1996: 1) with Japan, a country with no wild tigers, identified as a major destination for tiger parts and derivatives. Bennett (2011) suggests that in 2010, South Africa lost almost 230 rhinoceroses to poaching; and that less than 3,500 tigers now roam in the wild, occupying less than 7 percent of their historic range. His analysis suggested that the primary reason behind these population declines is hunting for the illegal trade in highly valuable body parts, increasingly operated by sophisticated organized criminal syndicates supplying wealthy East Asian markets. The IUCN, TRAFFIC and WWF agreed, noting that serious poaching in Southern Africa continues unabated:

> In summary, between 2000 and 2005, 3.5 rhinoceroses were illegally killed each month in all of Africa, but currently in South Africa and Zimbabwe alone,

12.4 rhinoceroses are being poached each month or between two and three rhinoceroses every week.

> Illegal rhinoceros horn trade to destinations in Asia is driving this killing, with growing evidence of the ongoing involvement of Vietnamese, Chinese and Thai nationals in the illicit procurement and transport of rhinoceros horn out of Africa. (IUCN, TRAFFIC and WWF 2009: 3)

Wyatt (2011) confirmed that the demand for traditional medicines incorporating original animal derivatives mostly originates in Asia and particularly in China. While the World Chinese Medicine Society (WCMS) has officially declared that tiger parts are not necessary ingredients in traditional medicines (Damania et al. 2008) the trade persists in part due to reliance on claims of authenticity as a market factor. Wyatt explains that 'there are long held beliefs that wild animals and plants contain better medicinal properties for their supposed treatment uses than captive bred sources, so animals and plants taken from the wild are preferred' (2011: 2). As a result, even though species such as tigers and rhinoceroses are at critically endangered levels, there remains a persistent and growing trade in these species. Indeed the increased scarcity of the source animals means that they continue to attract a premium among dealers which could contribute further to their demise with smugglers being able to make considerable profits on the trade in such prohibited substances. While legitimate traditional medicine practitioners no longer use wild animal parts in their products there remains a persistent and growing illegal market contributing to animal harm. The criminality inherent in TCM and use of animal derivatives is based on exploitation of animals as a commodity for perceived human benefit and profit. As there is no legal trade in species used for TCM, smuggling of products is an endemic part of the trade which, together with the illegal poaching involved, represents deliberate bypassing of regulations and evasion of law enforcement in order to fulfil the trade. Thus the increasing rarity of species such as bears, tigers and rhinoceroses and their known conservation status has combined to make the trade an underground one where organized criminality has become a feature.

Despite consistent campaigning by the likes of PETA and other NGOs against the use of skins and furs as fashion accessories, a global market in these items also persists and trappers, manufacturers and importers and exporters continually develop their trapping and manufacturing mechanisms to meet demand in the trade. Currey (1996) identified China as a major market for animal derivatives while PETA currently (2011) identifies China as the source of half of the fur in the United States and has cited concerns about the illegal unnecessary suffering caused to animals on fur farms (Mason et al. 2001). Commercial animal fur breeders have incentives to maximize profits by employing high volume techniques which in many cases are either barely compliant with legislation or which exploit the fact that legislation does not directly apply to their operations. Enforcement of such activities relies on the diligence of animal welfare investigators to identify where battery farming techniques constitute abuse under animal welfare statutes. As a result, the fur industry remains poorly regulated although the UK and Netherlands have banned factory farms (European Commission 2001) and animal welfare NGOs in various countries continue their investigations work to prove the nature and scale of the animal harm endemic to the skin and fur trade.

Animal harm is an integral part of trapping of animals for the fur and skin trade where undercover investigations consistently prove that humane animal killing methods are not used as required. PETA's investigation into the trade in exotic skins (2010) identified that the slow metabolism of reptiles means that lizards and snakes killed for their skins are frequently alive when skinned. Skinners have little or no incentive to humanely kill animals and often lack the required knowledge to implement humane killing methods so that animals are sometimes simply clubbed to death (Reid 1997). In addition in some areas where animas have dual use for fur and meat, animal laws may not apply to the fur industry and thus there are no applicable standards of animal welfare for traders to follow (Littlefair 2005).

Activities Associated with Drug Trafficking

While this is discussed further in the section on organized crime later in this chapter, one element of the illegal wildlife trade is its use to facilitate the drug trade. Currey identified that the main Indian tiger trade routes followed traditional trade routes, were mostly overland 'and involve bartering other products – including wildlife, drugs and arms' (1996: 5) to facilitate the trade in tiger bone from India to China where the manufacture of medicines takes place. South and Wyatt (2011) draw parallels between criminal actors in the illegal drug trade and the wildlife trade, identifying several key actors involved in both trades as follows:

1. Trading charities – collectors and TCM practitioners involved because of an ideological attachment to TCM, and enterprises involved in drugs because of quasi-ideological commitments to drugs. Profit is a secondary motive when dealing in drugs or wildlife, the ideological attachment is the primary motivator.
2. Mutual Societies – traffickers and traders whose lifestyle revolves around their work and who effectively deal to order in wildlife. This category also includes friendship networks of user dealers who support each other and deal drugs to order and within the framework of their mutually beneficial society.
3. Business sideliners – legal entrepreneurs who view drugs or wildlife as lucrative sidelines to their main often legal business. Thus legitimate wildlife dealers may deal in illegal specimens such as exporting more wildlife than their permits or the quota system allows, or an importer whose legal business provides cover for an illegal drugs shipment.

4. Criminal diversifiers – traditional criminals who identify profitable opportunities in either drugs or wildlife trafficking and exploit these as an adjunct to their main business.
5. Opportunistic irregulars – street level operatives who take advantage of opportunities whether in the form of drugs or wildlife, whenever the opportunity arises. (South and Wyatt 2011: 552–5)

South and Wyatt's categories identify that overlap between drugs and wildlife trade sometimes occurs outside of the large-scale wildlife trafficking of organized crime and is not confined to transnational crime. While profit is a significant motive in illegal wildlife trade, it sometimes occurs as a secondary business or is the product of opportunity rather than specific intent to deal in illegal wildlife.

Caviar Trafficking

The illegal caviar trade primarily exists in the former Soviet Union. Caviar is made from sturgeon roe (or eggs) and illegal poaching of sturgeon in the Black Sea region in order to supply demand for caviar was considered to be of sufficient concern that in 2005 the US Fish and Wildlife Service implemented a ban on the importation of Beluga Caviar into the United States. In 2006 CITES introduced a ban on caviar from the Caspian and Black Sea regions and in 2007 launched a caviar trade database funded by the EU.

The aim of the CITES caviar database was to prevent 'laundering' of caviar of illegal origin that occurred when traders were able to obtain genuine CITES documents by making false statements about where the caviar had been obtained (CITES 2010). Suri (2002) noted that the high prices that could be obtained from selling caviar led to the involvement of Russian gangs who sold illegally obtained caviar to western nations. Lowther et al. note that sophisticated smuggling techniques might be used, citing the case of US Caviar & Caviar, a trader who smuggled sturgeon roe out of the Caspian Sea area, routing it through the United Arab Emirates where counterfeit labels were attached to the caviar tins in order to hide their origins and export them to the United States 'as legitimate Russian produce' (2002: 38).

The CITES database recognizes the involvement of organized crime in the lucrative caviar trade and seeks to record details of all permits and certificates for caviar so that regulatory authorities can detect fraudulent applications. CITES also aims to trace caviar shipments, verify the legality of the original export and the quantities involved. The criminality involved in the caviar trade is deliberate and its lucrative nature attracts the attention of organized crime although local people living in proximity to the trade may become involved both through necessity and opportunity where organized crime or local dealers make it possible (and lucrative) to do so. Central to the trade in caviar is high consumer demand for a food product widely acknowledged as a delicacy and whose nine-year ban has arguably increased demand with the legal catch of sturgeon falling from

22,000 tons to less than 1,000 tons by 2001 with some species at near-extinction levels (Arnold 2001, Luis 2011). The reality is that markets, restaurants and consumers play a significant role in facilitating smuggling and selling of wildlife as food either by ensuring a steady supply of consumers who will buy exotic food dishes or, in some cases, dealing direct with poachers and traders providing a point of sale for illegally obtained wildlife. Thus, evading CITES controls involves trappers prepared to illegally obtain caviar, dealers willing to ship it and employ criminal smuggling techniques to maintain the trade.

Trade Dimensions and Criminality

The illegal wildlife trade has developed to take advantage of new technologies and offenders frequently portray a level of sophistication that law enforcement struggles to match. Globalization has been a significant factor in extending the illegal trade in wildlife, opening up new markets and ways of trading. South and Wyatt comment that 'increasingly even the most localized crime group can connect to the global stage (whether dealing in commodities from elsewhere or seeking to move profits out of the country)' (2011: 539) thus the illegal trade in wildlife is no longer a local or national problem but a global one. Wildlife trafficking now mirrors that of other organized transnational crime where local smugglers are part of a larger network which can incorporate both legal and illegal actors such as 'bankers, lawyers, accountants, and others working outside the local jurisdiction who help to launder profits or disguise the provenance of stolen goods' (South and Wyatt 2011: 539–40). In addition to the general criminality inherent in wildlife trafficking, the complex nature of trafficking activities and the size of the wildlife trade also provides for distinct aspects of criminality and animal harm at various stages as follows:

> **Capture and trapping** – in the trapping and capture stages, the level and type of animal harm is determined in part by the nature of the wildlife trafficking involved. Animals trapped for the live market (i.e. for sale as live specimens) may suffer less than animals intended for the processed market (Wyatt 2009) where animals may be seen as partially disposable given that the goal is to secure products or derivatives and only part of the animal is used. Because of traders' interest in being able to obtain healthy live animals for sale in the live animal market they have a vested interest in securing animals alive and ensuring that they remain so during capture and subsequent transit to their end destination. However, given the clandestine and unregulated nature of the trade, mortality levels are likely to be high during trapping with traders accepting a certain level of wastage. The lack of incentives to use humane trapping methods may also mean that poachers and traffickers will accidentally kill a number of their targets either through use of incompetent trapping and handling methods or simply through

unintended ineffectual handling of animals. Smaller birds or animals, for example, unused to being handled by humans or placed in captivity, may simply die of shock when handled or suffer further shock during the holding phase where they are waiting to be transported. A variety of trapping methods are used for wild birds ranging from the use of mist nets or glue spread on branches, perches or roosting sites through to 'cutting down the nesting tree or hacking open the nest cavities', a method popularly used to collect wild parrots in South America (New York Zoological Society 1992: 7). An RSPB, EIA and RSPCA joint investigation into the international illegal wild bird trade concluded that mortality rates are high in the wild bird trade as trappers and traders accept that many birds will die before they reach their sale destination thus trappers need to take higher numbers of birds from the wild in order to maintain their profit margins (RSPB 1991, Bowles et al. 1992). This perception is likely replicated across wildlife trafficking so that a disregard for animals as sentient beings and a general lack of concern for their welfare is an integral part of illegal trafficking. Zimmerman (2003) notes that in addition to the involvement of more 'traditional' organized crime in wildlife trade some capture is carried out by groups of local farmers wishing to supplement their income and also that some larger traders sometimes rely on poor local residents to capture wildlife (Veash 1999). Thus capture of animals can range from amateur operations where inexpert trapping mechanisms are used by low-level trappers employed by larger operations or supplementing their income, through to larger-scale sophisticated operations that may incorporate some consideration of animal welfare in order to maximize profit. Separate from the capture and trapping activities of 'ordinary' traders a more militarized and serious crime oriented form of poaching has emerged as an aspect of wildlife trade and this form of wildlife trade incorporates the use of violence and intimidation as an integral part of its operation. Militarized poaching raids are a response to increased enforcement activity which has escalated the poachers' activities. For example in Cameroon's Bouba Ndjida National Park poaching incidents of February 2012 involved a group of 50 heavily armed poachers who crossed over from Chad and Sudan into Cameroon and who killed six guards who attempted to stop them (Reuters 2012). Cross-border crime of this type indicates that the lucrative nature of poaching is such that animal trappers go beyond the killing of animals to actively inflicting violence on humans in order to secure animals or animal derivatives (e.g. ivory). Thus in some aspects of wildlife trafficking there is clear overlap with serious crime (e.g. murder) such that the criminality involved must be considered as serious crime and policed accordingly.

Holding and transportation – the transit stage of wildlife trafficking frequently incorporates conditions which constitute further animal harm. In the larger trapping operations, birds and animals are often kept in poor conditions that cause suffering. In particular, wild birds which can be transported in large numbers are often 'subject to overcrowding, disease and a radical change in diet' that increases mortality (New York Zoological Society 1992: 7) while other animals are often kept in cages or holding pens inadequate to their needs. During the transit stages, smuggling to evade law enforcement scrutiny takes place by moving animals outside of accepted transit routes or by evading quarantine through labelling shipments as something other than animals. But in some cases animals are openly transported either with fraudulent documentation such as forged or inaccurate permits or with only rudimentary documentation in the knowledge that checks in transit may be insufficient to identify fraudulent shipments or may only detect a few of the many illegal shipments taking place. The International Air Transport Association's (IATA) Live Animal Regulations provide a standard for the humane treatment of animals in transit and ensuring that humane standards of animal care are applied, minimizing harm to animals and the spread of disease. But inconsistency in the application of IATA's Regulations across different jurisdictions (New York Zoological Society 1992) together with failures in enforcement mean that market forces often dictate that trading is worth the relatively low risk of apprehension or confiscation of illegal shipments (Beissinger 2001). Green identified that moving exotic animals across the United States takes place with only a rudimentary examination of documentation so that 'lions, tigers and wallaroos, for example, move freely across the country with only pro forma attention paid to the documents that accompany them' (1999: 71). In theory animals in transit should receive health checks to ensure that they are free from disease, and be subject to examination of their captive-bred or endangered (i.e. CITES prohibited) status. However the evidence of investigations into both international and inter-state or domestic movements of wildlife consistently reveals flaws in monitoring regimes and a failure to carry out the required checks on animals in transit. As a result, fraudulent documentation frequently goes undetected, species are regularly moved in contravention of regulatory controls and illegal trade masquerading as legal trade provides a means through which animals can be transported (Green 1999, Zimmerman 2003). Thus wildlife trafficking frequently involves explicit evasion of regulations and the use of varied techniques to bypass regulatory regimes with the larger trading operations employing considerable resources to ensure profitability from their operations. Cazaux (2007) identifies electronic tagging of animals as a potentially useful technique for wildlife law enforcement and, in particular, detecting illegal trafficking of endangered species (Buhlmann and Tuberville 1998, Anon. 2000). But although placing transponders under the skin of animals provides a means of confirming identity or origin, the measure is only useful where used and it is not yet widespread enough that all legal captive-bred specimens are tagged and can be distinguished from wild animals that have been misleadingly labelled as captive-bred. Given the profits that can be made in high volume or high value trade, the larger scale, sophisticated or dedicated illegal trading operations may replicate microchips so that in effect the 'same' animals are repeatedly traded, or they may find other ways to bypass the system. Given the relatively low number of checks made on animals in trade (Green 1999) the chance that insufficient checks will be carried out or that checks will fail to establish misidentification remains high.

Sale and final delivery – the final wildlife trafficking stages of sale and delivery contain criminological aspects which incorporate fraud, deception and evasion of regulations, as well as sometimes efforts to deliberately mislead customers. While delivery is the final stage for many wildlife traffickers, final sale which can constitute purchase to order or sale in the conventional sense of sale through a pet shop or other animal dealer, can also involve direct or indirect animal harm. Illegally taken animals are sometimes sold to consumers who are unaware that the allegedly captive bred specimen that they have bought is in fact a wild bird or animal illegally trapped for the purpose. As a result, consumers unprepared for an animal's needs may provide inadequate care which can result in the owner causing unnecessary suffering to an animal or the animal simply dying. Deception by traders can also involve misrepresenting the nature of their business such that consumers believe they are dealing with a private breeder rather than a commercial enterprise. For example, as part of their campaign against the reptile trade, UK-based NGO Animal Aid wrote to the Inland Revenue noting that 'many of those who trade animals at "one-day events" and may make significant sums of money, do not operate formal businesses but front their trading activities as an elaborate hobby' (Animal Aid 2002). Traders may use this mechanism either to sell 'surplus' items and shift high volume, low value stock, or as a means of selling animals outside of the scrutiny of animal welfare, pet licensing or wildlife trade regulations. Traders are thus more than likely aware of the illegality of their actions and such methods of sale represent a deliberate trading tactic where illegally taken wild specimens can be passed off as captive-bred or any tax or duty applied to the sale can be avoided. In some cases, such as some aspects of the falconry trade and the acquisition of specimens for ranches and private zoos (Green 1999) illegally taken animals have been obtained to order for collectors and dealers, either for their own purchase and use, or for subsequent sale to customers. Where this is the case, evasion of purchasing and sale regulations can be a factor, although, particularly in the case of wildlife souvenirs, customers may be unaware of how their purchasing may involve regulatory breaches.

As Zimmerman notes (2003), wildlife trafficking is big business and has developed to take advantage of the possibilities offered by globalized markets and transnational flows of goods and services (Ruggiero 2002, Schendal and Abraham 2005). New technologies are actively being used to facilitate wildlife trafficking and illegal trade and to take advantage of the integration of markets such that transnational trading is now relatively easy. Wall identified the Internet as not only a 'vehicle for existing patterns of harmful activity such as hate speech, bomb-talk and stalking' (1999: 17) but as also creating new opportunities for existing prohibited activities and crucially engendering 'entirely new forms of (unbounded) harmful activity … linked to the increasing commercial potential of cyberspace' (1999: 17–18). Thus CITES suggests that the Internet has facilitated the illegal wildlife trade evidenced by 'the burgeoning number of websites where wildlife goods are offered, often with clearly suspect origins' (Wu 2010: 6). Currently a wide range of species are available and openly advertised on wildlife trading websites around the world, including those derived from 'high profile' animal species, such as elephants, rhinoceroses, the tiger and marine turtles (Williamson 2004, IFAW 2005, 2008, Wu 2007). While wildlife law enforcement has made gains in policing physical markets for wildlife, the Internet presents a set of new challenges via 'virtual' markets that have yet to be properly regulated, which are inefficiently monitored and for which the veracity of any species offered for sale cannot easily be verified. In addition, the difficulties inherent in other forms of online crime such as identifying the host country for any sale, the relevant jurisdiction in which law enforcement action needs to be taken or even which law (and of which country) has been broken, are compounded in online wildlife trading given the already problematic lack of co-ordinated enforcement action for wildlife trading. Thus traders and organized crime are able to exploit the global nature of their wildlife markets while law enforcement, which is frequently conducted outside of the criminal justice mainstream, fails to keep pace. Green (1999) identified that assessing documentation for the wildlife trade is made more complex because of the lack of centralized records for some species and the failure of many animal dealers to provide clear records to the relevant recording systems. But in most cases there is a paper trail that through careful checking will reveal the origins and identity of animals and provide evidence of legality or illegality. Thus, where animals are being traded, whether through 'traditional' or online routes, there is scope to match the original description or advertisement of an animal with its identification and documentation in order to establish its identity. In order to do so a concerted effort is needed by CITES Parties, international agencies and the private sector to combat the danger that expanding online availability poses to wild populations of endangered animal and plant species.

Species are sold as live or whole, as well as products derived from them. Wu (2007, 2010) identified that many of the rhinoceros horn and tiger products (apart from tiger 'wine') offered on Chinese-language auction websites are advertised as historical artefacts, with some sellers claiming to have documentation showing their provenance. However, the veracity of such documents is difficult to confirm and this aspect of the trade is poorly monitored by enforcement agencies. Many products derived from wild species are sourced from a wide geographical area, and these are not necessarily the countries where the website domains are hosted. For example, a TRAFFIC investigation into the use of Internet auction websites involved in the illegal ivory trade in the United States found that some of the sites were actually based in China thus presenting a law enforcement difficulty (Williamson 2004). Furthermore, between July 2005 and February 2006, TRAFFIC found 4,291 unique advertisements offered by almost 2,000 sellers for CITES-listed species on the Chinese-language Internet, this included auction websites and chat rooms in the thematic websites (Wu 2007). Most of the sellers were individuals and not professional wildlife traders, which poses questions about their eligibility to sell CITES Appendix-I species within national borders. It also indicates that Internet trade in wildlife might not yet be dominated by organized criminals and that the 'business sideliners' and 'criminal diversifiers' identified by South and Wyatt (2011) may make up a significant proportion of the wildlife traders on the Internet with only a small proportion of online traders being 'mutual societies' and the more serious aspects of organized crime. It is likely, however, that organized crime (discussed further in the next section) has no need to pursue online trading given the existence and exploitation of their existing trade routes and established criminal enterprises for wildlife trafficking.

Organized Crime and the Wildlife Trade

Several researchers have identified the involvement of organized crime in the illegal wildlife trade (Lowther et al. 2002, Nurse 2003, 2011, Zimmerman 2003, Wyatt 2009, 2011, South and Wyatt 2011). However, the nature of organized crime groups is worthy of consideration in assessing the criminality and motivations involved. Interpol acknowledges that definitions of organized crime vary from country to country but makes the following useful identification:

> Organized crime is not just national and international activities, although they may form an integral part, are only one aspect of what organized crime can be. As crime situations vary from country to country so do laws, judicial procedures, personal experience and opinion, all have a bearing on how organized crime is perceived. A universally acceptable definition is therefore virtually impossible to formulate. Organized crime activity is not limited or defined by geographical areas. An organisation may exist as separate entities in different localities around the world or as a group in a certain sector of a city. Organized crime is a flexible and adaptable organism that takes advantage of all available circumstances and grows in response to consumer demand for the service and goods that are offered. Generally it can be said that organized crime consists of a continuing criminal activity committed by a group of individuals to gain profits, power or influence. (Interpol 1988)

This definition identifies that a range of organized crime operations may be involved in wildlife trafficking, attracted by the profits to be made, the global nature of the market and the lack of effective enforcement regimes making wildlife trafficking a relatively low risk operation. Zimmerman identified three categories of organized crime as being involved in wildlife trafficking as follows:

1. Low level – groups of farmers who sell species illegally in order to supplement their incomes.
2. Mid-level – mafia-style groups that purchase species from peasants to sell at a large profit.
3. High-level – major international smuggling rings who are also involved in other illegal trades and utilize the same smuggling routes and use violence and intimidation to facilitate their trade. (Zimmerman 2003: 1668)

Zimmerman's classifications are broadly compatible with South and Wyatt's (2011) typology (discussed earlier) which distinguishes between individual and low level traders such as the 'business sideliners' and 'criminal diversifiers'. While organized crime as defined by Interpol generally involves multiple persons, the practice of corruption and operations that cross national borders to supply illegal goods in order to meet consumer demand (Lee 1999, Guymon 2000), not all wildlife trafficking is carried out by major smuggling organizations. Thus the challenge for law enforcement and conservation authorities may be in determining exactly what type of operation and type of criminality is involved and thus where law enforcement attention should be directed. Ferrer (1995) identified that major organized crime's participation in wildlife trafficking occurs primarily in either the former Soviet Union (especially in the illegal caviar trade but also in the trade in wild birds) and in central drug production and distribution states which are 'often major wildlife suppliers' (Zimmerman 2003: 1669). Wolverhampton University researchers Cook et al. explicitly considered the role of organized crime in the wildlife trade in a report for WWF and TRAFFIC. They analysed the evidence of organized crime's involvement and concluded that:

There is evidence that organized crime elements are becoming increasingly involved in the most lucrative parts of the illegal trade and they are prepared to use intimidation and violence: the report gives examples of wildlife wardens and border guards killed by organized and armed gangs. Where links with the drugs trade are concerned, these may take different forms, including:

- Parallel trafficking of drugs and wildlife along shared smuggling routes, with the latter as a subsidiary trade;
- The use of ostensibly legal shipments of wildlife to conceal drugs; and
- Using wildlife products as a currency to 'barter' for drugs, and the exchange of drugs for wildlife as part of the laundering of drug traffic proceeds. (Cook et al. 2002: 4–5)

While organized crime discourse theorizes different types of organized crime incorporating mafia-styled family organizations, ethnically organized crime organizations, terrorist and professional crime organizations (Williams 2001, Wright 2006, Varese 2010) not all are involved in the illegal wildlife trade. The particular attractions of wildlife trafficking to organized crime vary according to the structure of the organization (South and Wyatt 2011) and the interaction between organized crime and legitimate authorities. Cook et al.'s analysis (2002) and their linking of wildlife trade to organized crime and the drugs trade highlights the role of professional criminal organizations rather than looser organized crime gangs as the main threat within the illegal wildlife trade, exploiting their traditional structures to facilitate this particular type of crime as an addition to or adjunct to their normal activities. But in some cases it can be a primary business, especially where other forms of crime are proving less profitable. During interview for the author's wildlife crime research the National Criminal Intelligence Service (NCIS) commented on this from a policing point of view, explaining that:

> ... an organised criminal group will deal with anything that will make a profit and there [are] profits to be made from the trade in rare and endangered wildlife ... One particular area of interest is to determine where an organised gang might have established routes for the trade in various commodities. Where this is the case, it is possible for a gang to switch from one item, such as drugs, to another like wildlife. While the commodity may change the criminal activity doesn't. (Nurse 2011: 41)

Bennett (2011) explains that organized crime syndicates using sophisticated smuggling operations have even been able to penetrate 'previously secure' wildlife populations. Some of the elaborate methods include: hidden compartments in shipping containers; rapid changing of smuggling routes; and the use of e-commerce whose locations are difficult to detect. Guymon (2000) identifies that organized crime's involvement in wildlife crime causes problems for states in other areas because organized crime is able to channel the profits from wildlife crime into other illegitimate businesses such as human trafficking and drug trafficking. In addition organized crime's increased use of violence and intimidation makes it difficult to provide for effective enforcement in wildlife trafficking cases. Organized crime's willingness to kill to pursue its trade provides a challenge for conservation and wildlife management services. These organizations, often at the forefront of wildlife policing initiatives, are ill-equipped to deal with serious crime that requires deployment of organized crime disruption and dedicated enforcement techniques which can sometimes take years of effort to achieve results (Green 1998, Hammersley 2008).

In addition organized crime's power and influence allows their involvement in wildlife trafficking to affect the proper functioning of society and the effectiveness of government by bribing officials, undermining legitimate state structures and impacting on law enforcement (Guymon 2000, Monahan 2002, Zimmerman 2003).

Lee (1999) identified that criminal funds are often channelled into corruption in central government institutions providing influence over law-enforcement and legislative measures. In Russia, for example, illegal fishing backed by the Russian Mafia has removed 'billions of dollars of fish from the Bering Sea and is a factor in the downfall of legitimate fisheries' (Zimmerman 2003: 1673). In addition to obstructing legitimate businesses and hampering the operation of the free market, organized crime's bribery of officials has allowed illegal wildlife to cross borders and stifled investment. The nature of such activities and the occasional links with terrorism and funding of terrorist causes (Guymon 2000, Zimmerman 2003) provides a compelling case for wildlife trafficking to be dealt with as serious crime and one aspect of the fight against organized crime. While Interpol has begun to consider this and has identified environmental crime and particularly wildlife trafficking as a priority it has still to be recognized as such both within mainstream criminology and mainstream (i.e. national) police and criminal justice priorities.

Wildlife Trade as Mainstream Criminality

Despite common acceptance of the scale of the illegal trade in wildlife it remains an area of law enforcement that is significantly under-resourced and remains on the fringes of criminology. White (2008) and others have highlighted the problems of transnational environmental crime and the illegal trade in wildlife is an area of global significance in respect of the harm it can do. White identifies that a central dilemma for green criminologists is 'how to sensibly move the debate beyond standard approaches to environmental crime, and how to shift policy and practice in ways that are more effective than conventional forms of environmental regulation' (2008: 46). The policy and law enforcement response to the illegal wildlife trade illustrates this dilemma perfectly. A common theme running through most analyses of the illegal wildlife trade is the claim of environmental harm, depletion of stocks of protected wildlife and the resultant damage to biodiversity and loss of some of the world's rarest animals. Yet effective enforcement of the illegal wildlife trade needs to directly address the criminality involved as part of mainstream crime rather than solely examining it as an environmental or conservation problem. In reality, however, effective enforcement is sadly lacking with little attention paid to consumers or the causes of the trade.

Case Study: Illegal Wildlife Trade: TCM

Traditional Chinese medicine using natural remedies and compounds derived from animals has been practiced for more than 3,000 years, with generations of families relying on it to maintain their health and cure illness. However there is evidence of links between the illegal trade in wildlife and the market for traditional Chinese medicines. Canadian environmental enforcers highlighted this fact when in 2006 they laid charges against a traditional Chinese medicines firm based in British Columbia following an investigation into their use of endangered species derivatives.

Traditional Chinese medicines use parts from a range of wildlife species including tigers, rhinos and musk deer. Prior to the enactment of endangered species legislation, tiger bone was a preferred treatment for joint ailments like arthritis, while rhino horn has been used to treat fever, convulsions and delirium. Bear gall bladder bile has been used to treat various ailments including inflammation and bacterial infections.

However reductions in populations mean that species such as bears, rhinos and tigers are now protected by CITES which regulates trade in specific species of wild animals and plants, as well as their respective parts and derivatives. CITES is implemented in Canada by the *Wild Animal and Plant Protection and Regulation of International and Interprovincial Trade Act 1992* (WAPPRIITA). Offences under WAPPRIITA are punishable on summary conviction by a fine not exceeding CAN$50,000 or imprisonment for a term not exceeding six months, or both. Environment Canada is Canada's regulatory body for CITES enforcement and takes CITES prosecutions under Canadian legislation. While many traditional Chinese medicine practitioners no longer use products that consist of endangered species the historical use of these products has become engrained in traditional East Asian practices and the perceived symbolic potency of strength and power from certain animals means that a distinction might be made between 'authentic' medicines and synthetic ones. As a result, practitioners will pay a premium for real ingredients and despite current legislative restrictions on the trade in endangered species parts there is a strong profit motive to source authentic materials and ignore endangered species legislation. Some CITES listed species, including tigers and rhinos, are close to extinction as a result of illegal trade and poaching, and WWF and other NGOs have made a link between the increase in popularity of traditional Chinese medicines and an increase in illegal trade and poaching. Most experts agree that the trade in tiger bone for medicinal purposes was a major factor fuelling the tiger conservation crisis of the 1980s and 1990s (Ellis 2005) and WWF has claimed that:

> Booming economies and growing wealth in parts of Asia have caused demand and prices to rise for many wildlife products. The combined pressures of commercial demand, excessive hunting and habitat destruction have depleted Asia's bear, tiger and rhino populations. (WWF 2011)

Wing Quon Enterprises of British Columbia was charged with importing CITES specimens without the required permits and of unlawfully possessing and distributing medicines containing tiger, bear, pangolin, musk deer and rhinoceros derivatives. The company was charged with three counts of importing CITES controlled plant species without a permit in contravention of Section 6(2) of the *Wild Animal and Plant Protection and Regulation of International and Interprovincial*

Trade Act 1992 (WAPPRIITA). The company was also charged with nine counts under Section 8(a) of the Act for unlawful possession of medicines containing tiger, bear, pangolin, musk deer and rhinoceros derivatives and two counts under Section 8(c) of the Act related to the distribution of medicines containing tiger and rhinoceros.

In 2009 Wing Quon Enterprises pleaded guilty to possessing tiger parts for the purposes of dealing and was fined CAN$45,000 (at the time approximately US$36,000) by a Richmond Provincial Court, close to the maximum fine of CAN$50,000 (which was then about US$40,000). The court also ordered the company to forfeit seized medicines and products made from other endangered species, including costus root, agarwood, bear, pangolin, musk deer and rhinoceros. All are listed in CITES (the *Convention on International Trade in Endangered Species of Wild Fauna and Flora 1973*), which strictly controls any international trade in them.

As part of its ruling, the court also gave approximately CAN$40,000 (about US$31,000) of the fine to TRAFFIC (the wildlife monitoring network) to help further its efforts to ensure that wildlife trade is not detrimental to the conservation of nature.

Summary

Wildlife trafficking is big business and this undoubtedly influences the motivations and behaviour of offenders involved in the illegal wildlife trade. With estimates consistently placing the annual global trade as being worth at least 10 billion US dollars, it is inevitable that organized crime, seeking to have influence or dominance in any area of transnational crime where profits can be made, will become involved.

However while criminologists have considered aspects of wildlife trafficking since at least 2002 (Lowther et al. 2002) there is still a lack of research into the specifics of wildlife trade, its quantity or quality (Schneider 2008) or the precise criminality involved (Nurse 2011). Green criminological discussions of wildlife trafficking frequently make the link between organized crime and wildlife trafficking but at a level which while identifying organized crime's involvement rarely examines the criminality in detail. However this chapter goes beyond descriptions of organized crime as being motivated by profit, exploiting the availability of wildlife, and the lower level of risk when compared to other more serious crimes such as drugs, arms dealing or people trafficking, to show that there is scope to assess the criminality involved in organized crime's involvement in the illegal wildlife trade.

Organized crime fits into the definition of traditional offending (see Chapter 3's Model A) by being primarily motivated by profit and disregarding wildlife as being anything other than a commodity. However, masculinities, a factor in much animal harm, are also a factor given that some organized and transnational wildlife trade employs techniques of coercion, domination and violence exhibiting stereotypical male behaviours both in the manner in which the illegal trade is carried out and in the masculinities based organization of the criminal network (Miller 1995, Mac an Ghaill 1996). Zimmerman (2003) identifies that a range of criminal groups are involved from low-level informal groups of farmers through to sophisticated major international smuggling rings, while South and Wyatt (2011) identify that even within these different types of groups a range of different behaviours, motivations and organizational models exist. Thus an organized crime group may have wildlife trafficking as the primary focus of its operation or may have diversified into wildlife crime as a means of securing additional profits from its existing operations. In addition, legal traders may have developed a network to take advantage of the additional opportunities for profit that can be obtained by dealing in illegal specimens on an ad-hoc basis alongside what may be an otherwise primarily lawful operation.

Assessment of criminality in wildlife trafficking thus identifies that varied criminality exists, presenting problems for a wildlife trade regime that is frequently found to be inadequate to dealing with the scale and complexity of the illegal wildlife trade. Endemic to the problems of wildlife trade enforcement are inconsistencies and failings in the practical implementation of legislation. While NGO perspectives on wildlife trade frequently suggest that legislation is inadequate (Nurse 2003) a more complex reality exists where in some cases, effective legislation is in place but its enforcement is ineffective. The World Bank and Smithsonian's National Zoological Park, in discussing the illegal tiger trade, commented that 'the penalties for poaching are often harsh, but the likelihood of apprehension remains low and that of a conviction even lower' (Damania et al. 2008: 6). Their analysis showed that even in India, where a well-developed institutional conservation structure has been developed, 'a mere ten tiger poachers have been convicted in the past five years, and not a single trader has been penalized' (2008: 6). Thus penalties are not being employed and for the most part, the activities of poachers and wildlife traffickers are not being disrupted. A significant factor in enforcement failures is the lack of resources for effective enforcement action as well as a lack of understanding of the criminality involved.

However there is a case for examining wildlife trade laws to provide a framework for a better and more consistent enforcement regime. Zimmerman identifies that the nature of CITES is such that its varied implementation in different countries creates an inconsistent wildlife trade regime, which while theoretically providing for a global enforcement regime provided by each country which is a CITES signatory, is, in practice, one where a range of legislation providing different levels of protection and criminal or administrative sanctions exists. This causes confusion both for the public and enforcers but is exploited by traffickers, especially those high-level traders with considerable resources behind their operation and who are willing to use violence and intimidation to continue their trade.

As with many other areas of animal harm, wildlife trafficking is primarily enforced reactively, with the focus on detecting and seizing illegal shipments once they are already in transit. Arguably this constitutes the CITES 'model' where tracking of shipments and permits provides for a traditional law enforcement approach while it is primarily down to NGOs to carry out educational and preventative measures on the ground. But while seizures may represent the detection of illegal shipments it should be accepted that as with drugs or people trafficking, those involved in the illegal wildlife trade build redundancies into their systems and acknowledge that some shipments will be disrupted. Yet as long as most get through (and the perception is that they do) the damage to wild populations and the criminality involved in wildlife trafficking continues. As Zimmerman notes, while no single method will eliminate organized crime's participation in, and no single method will solve every facet of, the wildlife trade problem, there is a need for effective international co-operation and effective national legislation that implements CITES and provides for *criminal* sanctions for illegal wildlife trading (2003). The diverse nature of criminality involved in the wildlife trade dictates that it should be treated as serious crime, as part of the organized crime continuum and should be enforced through the criminal law as mainstream criminality. The enforcement approach needs to recognize the existence of different criminal groups and modes of behaviour as well as different levels of involvement in the wildlife trade. This requires the political will to commit the money and manpower necessary to crack down on an area of crime which is expensive and time-consuming to address and which generally ranks low on the list of public priorities for law enforcement but has implications for other areas of crime. This is discussed further in Chapters 9 and 10.

References

Anderson, R.S. (1997). Investigation, Prosecution, and Sentencing of International Wildlife Trafficking Offenses in the U.S. Federal System. 12 *National Environmental Enforcement Journal*, 14.

Animal Aid (2002). Unlawful Exotic Animal Markets/Inland Revenue Investigation, *News Bulletin: October 2002*, Tonbridge: Animal Aid.

Anon. (2000). Microchips and Their Uses in Monitoring Movements of Sakers and Peregrines in Asia and the Middle East. *Supplement of Falco*, Newsletter of the Middle East Falcon Research Group, January.

Arnold, J. (2001). Crunch Time for Caspian Caviar, BBC News Online, 19 June. Available at http://news.bbc.co.uk/1/hi/business/1394717.stm [accessed 20 January 2012].

Beissinger, S.R. (2001). Trade of Live Wild Birds, Potentials, Principles and Practices of Sustainable Use, in J.D. Reynolds, G.M. Mace, K.H. Redford and J.G. Robinson (eds), *Conservation of Exploited Species*, Cambridge: Cambridge University Press, 182–201.

Bennett, E. (2011). Another Inconvenient Truth: The Failure of Enforcement Systems to Save Charismatic Species. *Oryx*, 45, 476–9.

Bowles, D., Currey, D., Knights, P. and Michels, A. (1992). *Flight to Extinction: The Wild-Caught Bird Trade*, Washington, DC: Environmental Investigation Agency and Animal Welfare Institute.

Buhlmann, K.A. and Tuberville, T.D. (1998). Use of Passive Integrated Transponder (PIT) Tags for Marking Small Freshwater Turtles. *Chelonian Conservation and Biology*, 3(1), 102–4.

Cazaux, G. (2007). Labelling Animals: Non-speciesist Criminology and Techniques to Identify Other Animals, in P. Beirne and N. South (eds), *Issues in Green Criminology: Confronting Harms against Environments, Humanity and Other Animals*, Devon: Willan, 87–113.

CITES (2010). *Activity Report of the CITES Secretariat: 2008–2009*, Geneva: CITES/United Nations Environment Programme.

Cook, D., Roberts, M. and Lowther, J. (2002). *The International Wildlife Trade and Organised Crime: A Review of the Evidence and the Role of the UK*, Wolverhampton: Regional Research Institute, University of Wolverhampton.

Currey, D. (1996). *The Political Wilderness: India's Tiger Crisis*, London and Washington, DC: The Environmental Investigation Agency.

Damania, R., Seidensticker, J., Whitten, A., Sethi, G., Mackinnon, K., Kiss, A. and Kushlin, A. (2008). *A Future for Wild Tigers*, Washington, DC: The International Bank for Reconstruction and Development / The World Bank and Smithsonian's National Zoological Park.

De Bohan, V., Doggart, N., Rryle, J., Trent, S. and Williams, J. (eds) (1996). *Corporate Power, Corruption and the Destruction of the World's Forests: The Case for a Global Forest Agreement*, London and Washington, DC: Environmental Investigations Agency.

Edwards, A. and Gill, P. (eds) (2003). *Transnational Organised Crime: Perspectives on Global Security*, London: Routledge.

Ellis, R. (2005). *Tiger Bone and Rhino Horn: The Destruction of Wildlife for Traditional Chinese Medicine*, Washington, DC: Island Press.

European Commission, Scientific Committee on Animal Health and Animal Welfare (2001). *The Welfare of Animals Kept for Fur Production*, European Commission, 13 December.

Ferrer, Y. (1995). *Colombia-Environment: Animal Smuggling Second Only to Drug Trade*, International Press Service, 21 July.

Fleming, E. (1994). *The Implementation and Enforcement of CITES in the European Union*, Brussels: TRAFFIC Europe.

Gail, T., Garibaldi, B., Zeng, Y. and Pilcher, J. (1998). Consumer Demand for Counterfeit Goods. *Psychology and Marketing*, 15(5), 405–21.

Green, A. (1999). *Animal Underground*, New York: Public Affairs/Perseus Books.

Green, P. (1998). *Drugs, Trafficking and Criminal Policy: The Scapegoat Strategy*, Winchester: Waterside Press.

Guymon, C.D. (2000). International Legal Mechanisms for Combating Transnational Organized Crime: The Need for a Multilateral Convention. 18 *Berkeley Journal of International Law* 53, 61–2, 64.

Hammersley, R. (2008). *Drugs and Crime*, Cambridge: Polity Press.

IFAW (International Fund for Animal Welfare) (2005). *Caught in the Web: Wildlife Trade on the Internet*, London: IFAW.

IFAW (2008). *Killing with Keystrokes: Wildlife Trade on the Internet*, London: IFAW.

IUCN, TRAFFIC and WWF (2009). Status, Conservation and Trade in African and Asian Rhinoceroses: An IUCN, TRAFFIC and WWF Briefing for the 58th Meeting of the CITES Standing Committee, Geneva, 6–10 July, Geneva: CITES.

Kosloff, L.H. and Trexler, M.C. (1987). The Convention on International Trade in Endangered Species: No Carrot, But Where's the Stick? 17 *Environmental Law Report*, 10222.

Lee, R.W. III (1999). Transnational Organized Crime: An Overview, in T. Farer (ed.), *Transnational Crime in the Americas*, New York: Routledge, 1–38.

Littlefair, P. (2005) *The Slaughter behind 200-million-yuan Revenue from Fur, RSPCA International*. Available at http://www.animal-protection.net/furtrade/more/beijing_news.pdf [accessed 20 January 2012].

Lowther, J., Cook, D. and Roberts, M. (2002). *Crime and Punishment in the Wildlife Trade*, Wolverhampton: WWF/TRAFFIC/Regional Research Institute (University of Wolverhampton).

Luis, C. (2011). Russian's Caviar in Europe, Newzy.Net. Available at http://www.newzy.net/2011/02/15/russians-caviar-in-europe/ [accessed 30 January 2012].

Mac An Ghaill, M. (1996). *Understanding Masculinities*, Buckingham: Open University Press.

Mason, G.J., Cooper, J. and Clarebrough, C. (2001). Frustrations of Fur-Farmed Mink. *Nature*, 410, 35–6.

Mfunda, I.M. and Røskaft, E. (2010). Bushmeat Hunting in Serengeti, Tanzania: An Important Economic Activity to Local People, *International Journal of Biodiversity and Conservation*, 2(9), 263–72.

Miller, J. (1995). Struggles Over the Symbolic: Gang Style and the Meanings of Social Control, in J. Ferrell and C.R. Sanders (eds), *Cultural Criminology*, Boston: Northeastern University Press, 213–34.

Monahan, J. (2002). Cruel Harvest, *Times Educational Supplement* (London), 21 June, at 18–19.

New York Zoological Society (1992). *The Wild Bird Trade: When a Bird in the Hand Means None in the Bush*, Bronx, NY: Wildlife Conservation International.

Nurse, A. (2003). *The Nature of Wildlife and Conservation Crime in the UK and its Public Response, Working Paper No 9*, Birmingham: University of Central England Birmingham, Faculty of Law and Social Sciences.

Nurse, A. (2011). Policing Wildlife: Perspectives on Criminality in Wildlife Crime. *Papers from the British Criminology Conference*, 11, 38–53, London: British Society of Criminology.

People for the Ethical Treatment of Animals (2011). *A Shocking Look Inside Chinese Fur Farms*. Norfolk, VA: PETA. Available at http://features.peta.org/ChineseFurFarms/ [accessed 20 January 2012].

People for the Ethical Treatment of Animals (2010). *Exotic Skins: The Animals*. Norfolk, VA: PETA. Available at http://www.peta.org/issues/animals-used-for-clothing/exotic-skins-animals.aspx [accessed 20 January 2012].

Redmond, I., Aldred, T., Jedmamzik, K. and Westwood, M. (2006). *Recipes for Survival: Controlling the Bushmeat Trade*, Ape Alliance Report, London: WSPA.

Reid, S. (1997). Getting Under Their Skin, *The Sunday Times* (London), 16 February.

Revill, J. (2002). Rare Animals Trade is New Sideline to Drugs, *Birmingham Post*, 22 August.

Reuters (2012). Poachers Slaughter 200 Elephants in Cameroon National Park in Six Weeks, *The Guardian* Online, 17 February. Available at http://www.guardian.co.uk/environment/2012/feb/17/poachers-slaughter-200-elephants-cameroon [accessed 17 February 2012].

Robinson, J.G. and E.L. Bennett. (2004). Having your Wildlife and Eating it Too: An Analysis of Hunting Sustainability across Tropical Ecosystems. *Animal Conservation*, 7, 394–408.

Royal Society for the Protection of Birds (RSPB) (1991). *The International Trade in Wild Birds*, Sandy: RSPB.

Ruggiero, V. (2002). Service Providers and Criminals, in Ruggiero, V. *Crime and Markets: Essays in Anti-Criminology*, Oxford: Oxford University Press, 90–105.

Schendal, W. and Abraham, I. (2005). *Illicit Flows and Criminal Things: States, Borders, and the Other Side of Globalization*, Bloomington: Indiana University Press.

Schneider, J.L. (2008). Reducing the Illicit Trade in Endangered Wildlife: The Market Reduction Approach. *Journal of Contemporary Criminal Justice*, 24(3), 274–95.

South, N. and Wyatt, T. (2011). Comparing Illicit Trades in Wildlife and Drugs: An Exploratory Study. *Deviant Behavior*, 32, 538–61.

Suri, S. (2002). Environment: Organized Crime Muscles in on Wildlife Trade, International Press Service, 17 June.

Tomkins, K. (2005). Police, Law Enforcement and the Environment. *Current Issues in Criminal Justice*, 16(3), 294–306.

US Department of State (2009). *Against Wildlife Trafficking: Working Together to End the Illegal Trade in Wildlife*, Washington, DC: US Department of State (Bureau of Oceans and International Environmental and Scientific Affairs).

Varese, F. (2010). General Introduction. What is Organized Crime? in F. Varese (ed.), *Organized Crime*, 1. London and New York: Routledge, 1–33.

Veash, N. (1999). In Brazil, Web Weaves Illegal Trade; Animal Dealers Find a Home on the Internet, *Boston Globe*, 31 October.

Wall, D. (1999). Getting to Grips with Cybercrime. *Criminal Justice Matters*, 36, 17–19.

Webster, D. (1997). The Looting and Smuggling and Fencing and Hoarding of Impossibly Precious, Feathered and Scaly Wild Things, *New York Times*, 16 February, § 6 (Magazine), at 27.

White, R. (2008). *Crimes Against Nature: Environmental Criminology and Ecological Justice*, Cullompton: Willan.

Williams, P. (2001). Transnational Criminal Networks, in J. Arquilla and D.F. Ronfeldt (eds), *Networks and Netwars: The Future of Terror, Crime, and Militancy*, Washington, DC: Rand Corporation, 61–97.

Williamson, D.F. (2004). *Tackling the Ivories: The Status of the US Trade in Elephant and Hippo Ivory. TRAFFIC North America*. Washington, DC: World Wildlife Fund.

Woodiwiss, M. and Hobbs, D. (2009). Organized Evil and the Atlantic Alliance. *British Journal of Criminology*, 49, 106–28.

Wright, A. (2006). The Magical Roundabout: Traffic in the Global Village, in A. Wright, *Organised Crime*. Cullompton: Willan Publishing, 73–99.

Wu, J. (2007). World Without Borders: Wildlife Trade on the Chinese-language Internet. *TRAFFIC Bulletin*, 21(2), 75–84.

Wu, J. (2010). Wildlife Trade on the Internet. *CITES World: Official Newsletter of the Parties*, 19, February.

WWF (2011). *Promoting Alternative Remedies*. Washington: WWF/American College of Traditional Chinese Medicines. Available at http://www.tcmwildlife. org/300EnPromotiing.htm [accessed 22 January 2012].

Wyatt, T. (2009). Exploring the Organization in Russia Far East's Illegal Wildlife Trade: Two Case Studies of the Illegal Fur and Illegal Falcon Trades. *Global Crime*, 10(1 and 2), 144–54.

Wyatt, T. (2011). The Illegal Trade in Raptors in the Russian Federation. *Contemporary Justice Review: Issues in Criminal, Social and Restorative Justice*, 14(2), 103–23.

Zimmerman, M.E. (2003). The Black Market for Wildlife: Combating Transnational Organized Crime in the Illegal Wildlife Trade. *Vanderbilt Journal of Transnational Law*, 36, 1657–89.

Chapter 9
Animal Harm and Public Policy

Given the variety of animal harm offences and differences in criminal behaviour involved in animal harm any legal system aimed at dealing with animal harm faces a challenge: how can the disparate nature of animal harm be adequately reflected in public policy? Schaffner (2011) identifies that legislative policy is dependent on the drafting entity and its function as well as the manner in which legal rules are interpreted or implemented by regulatory authorities. Thus the importance given to animal harm within legal systems is dependent on a number of factors; beyond the basic text of any legislation the scope and jurisdiction of the regulatory bodies responsible for animal harm are factors and this reflects the social construction of animal harm and its place within public policy. Such attitudes change over time so that animal harm may become an issue of core importance in public policy when the public demands that it should be, or is considered to be a fringe issue at other times (Arluike and Sanders 1996). However given the wide-ranging scope of animal harm and its links with other types of crime there is an argument for it to be considered alongside mainstream criminal justice policy.

This chapter assesses the current public policy approach to animal harm and initiatives aimed at dealing with animal harm. It argues that the current public policy approach is primarily one of detection and punishment rather than being based on early intervention where animal harm is known to occur or crime prevention measures to prevent it from happening. The chapter argues that animal harm, whether abuse or wildlife crime, should be seen as part of an overall criminal profile rather than being dealt with separately as an environmental or animal welfare issue. The chapter considers the links between animal abuse/wildlife crime and other types of offending and how these crimes are currently dealt with by global crime control/criminal justice policy and in national policies.

Consideration of animal welfare by social, political and public policy theorists also informs the assessment of its benefit to society. Green criminology's concern with the study of crimes against the environment and animals, accepts that it is often difficult to disentangle environmental harms from the abuse of non-human animals. Beirne and South argue that 'animals live in environments, and their own well-being – physical, emotional, psychological – is absolutely and intimately linked to the health and good standing of their environments' (2007: xiii–xiv). Effective animal welfare policies thus provide for both tangible and intangible public benefits through the improvement of the environment and integration of policy initiatives that could protect the public.

Animal Harm and Social Policy

A general perspective from the animal rights literature is that violence towards animals harms human beings by making us more violent and prone to a more violent type of society. In his controversial book *Eternal Treblinka*, Patterson theorizes that 'since violence begets violence, the enslavement of animals injected a higher level of domination and coercion into human history by creating oppressive hierarchical societies and unleashing large-scale warfare never seen before' (Patterson 2002). The book argues that better treatment of animals, which is frequently achieved through robust, effective animal welfare laws, is necessary to minimize breakdowns in society and continue the development of enlightened society. Wise makes a similar point in relation to the case for legal rights for animals, arguing that 'as our domestication of wild animals served as an unprincipled model for our enslavement of human beings, so the destruction of human slavery and all its badges can model the principled destruction of chimpanzee and bonobo slavery' (2000). Like Regan (1983), Wise argues that legal recognition of the harm caused by animal abuse and the development of statutory rights for animals contributes to the development of society, a view supported by Connelly and Smith in a broader sense in their philosophical arguments that protecting the environment (and animals) is for the common good and should be a core part of public policy (1999). Yet a more compelling argument is made when exploring the links between animal abuse and violence towards humans. While not all theorists go as far as Patterson's provocative query as to whether human 'enslavement' of animals was the first step on the road to the Holocaust, it is now becoming accepted that animal abuse may be a precursor of violence towards humans and should be the subject of attention by the criminal justice agencies. Yet the reality is that animal harm, while the subject of attention from green criminologists, NGOs and some in law enforcement, continues to remain outside of the criminological mainstream. This fact means that its implications for other offending and its overall impact on crime rates and offending behaviour are not always adequately considered.

Animal Harm and Criminal Justice Policy

As the causes of crime vary, policies needed to deal with their causes may also vary and need to change over time. The political ideology promoted by and influencing a particular government's policy determines the nature of their criminal justice policies and also determines criminal justice priorities. Thus in reality animal harm is subject to two main political ideologies: conservative perspectives which are generally tough authoritarian approaches which emphasize discipline, deterrence and punishment; and social-democratic (or radical) approaches which tend to accept that economic, social and cultural deprivation are the causes of crime. While these are generalized descriptions of the two main political ideologies that dominate in the UK and the United States, analysis of policy documents issued by the main political parties (Conservatives and Labour in the UK, and Republican and Democrat in the United States) demonstrate how these policies are implemented in practice. In the UK in the run up to the 2010 general election the Conservatives (2007) announced that the focus of their criminal justice policy is the criminal, suggesting a belief in radical choice theory. The Conservatives' policy document, *It's Time to Fight Back*, proposed a more punitive law enforcement regime based on increased discipline in schools, the end of the early release scheme for prisoners, an increased prison building scheme, more police officers and an extension of stop and search powers. Introducing the report, party leader (now Prime Minister) David Cameron asserted family values and the need for discipline by saying that 'widespread minor crime is the direct product of a broken society, including the failure or inability of the police to assert control of the streets' (Conservatives 2007). Both the Conservatives and Republicans believe in a smaller role for government with a broadly authoritarian approach to crime as being determined by rational choice, but also incorporating law enforcement perspectives that emphasize personal choice and free enterprise in keeping with liberalism as their dominant ideology. Thus, under the conservative perspective government generally refrains from imposing regulation that stifles private enterprise and impacts on business owners. This extends to environmental regulation which conservative perspectives might consider to be burdensome on business (Cabinet Office 2011), preferring self-regulation as a route to compliance.[1] As a result environmental regulation is generally weaker under conservative perspectives, allowing business to continue operating under a lighter regulatory regime and generally permitting the killing of animals to protect business interests.

Social-democratic approaches attempt to address the conditions that cause crime. In the UK, Labour Party policies are based on creating 'strong vibrant communities' (Labour Party 2008) using neighbourhood policing considering the causes of crime and developing a culture of respect. Labour policies thus favour education and collaborative working with NGOs in order to address animal harm issues and encourage the public to become involved in reducing animal harm. Both approaches, however, tend to rely heavily on the use of imprisonment as a primary means of addressing the crime problem once detection and prosecution has occurred. Bright explains that:

---

1   Within the UK the Coalition Government currently has a policy initiative called the 'Red Tape Challenge' which argues that there is 'too much' environmental regulation (which includes conservation and species protection regulation). As a result during 2011 the government consulted on reducing and simplifying the amount of environmental regulation and abolishing what it considers to be obsolete regulations, and an overly complex natural environment and wildlife protection regulatory regime. Details can be found at: http://www.redtapechallenge.cabinetoffice.gov.uk/home/index/ [accessed 29 June 2011].

> In the UK, it is generally believed that the criminal justice agencies have a
> significant crime prevention effect, that if the police detect crime, the courts
> sentence offenders and the prisons and probation service discharge those
> sentences, crime will be prevented. (Bright 1993: 63)

In the United States, the existence of a federal enforcement agency for wildlife
crime provides a means through which both social-democratic and conservative
policies can be incorporated within the law enforcement perspective. This allows
for the use of a dedicated enforcement agency to target action at the individual
offender and implement detection and prevention as the core focus of policy. But
the remit of the US Fish and Wildlife Service and the EPA also allow for some
educational work aimed at the causes of wildlife and environmental crime within
a law enforcement perspective. However, Bright argues that the evidence does
not substantiate the perceived effectiveness of the law enforcement perspective
and faith in imprisonment given that substantial increases in expenditure have
been 'rewarded' by increases in crime rates and by high rates of re-offending by
those given custodial sentences. Home Office figures for the UK regularly show
re-offending rates in excess of 50 percent (Cuppleditch and Evans 2005) and
repeat offending is hardly unknown in the United States. Various sets of figures
are used to assess reoffending rates. In the UK the Prison Reform Trust concluded
that 47 percent of all adults released from prison were reconvicted within one
year 'rising to 57% for those serving sentences of less than 12 months and almost
70% for under 18 year olds' (Prison Reform Trust 2012: 3). While there may be
some fluctuation in the annual reconviction rates, the reliance on custody may be
misplaced if at least half of those offenders incarcerated as a result of their entry
into the criminal justice system simply re-offend.

Given that animal harm can have many different causes, policies intended
to reduce such crime and prevent further offending will need to address each
of the different causes. Policies aimed at providing good housing, education
and low unemployment, diverting people from crime by increasing their life
chances and providing a healthy society where there are alternatives to crime
and by also reducing opportunities for committing crime are the proposed social-
democratic responses to mainstream crime. There is, however, evidence of failure
in employing this 'common sense' approach to crime. James Q. Wilson (1985),
a former presidential crime advisor, explains that in the 1960s United States the
Kennedy and Johnson administrations embarked on aggressive programmes
aimed at addressing the social causes of crime and that the United States entered
its greatest and longest sustained period of prosperity that, at time of Wilson's
writing in 1985, it had ever seen. The expected result was a radical decline in
crime levels but, as Wilson explains, the reality was somewhat different and,
in fact, 'crime soared. It did not increase a little; it rose at a faster rate and to
higher levels than at any time since the 1930s and, in some categories than any
experienced in this century' (Wilson 1985: 14). Young called this the aetiological
crisis, explaining that the conventional wisdom on how to address crime failed

and that the dominant paradigm of social-democratic positivism which believed that crime could be addressed by political intervention needed to be reconsidered. Young (1999) argued that the challenge for criminology was to find an integrated approach that involved intervention at all levels, the social cause of crime, social control exercised by the community and the formal agencies and on the victim. But the three policy perspectives outlined by Bright remain at the core of public policy on crime prevention (Grimshaw 2004) and the perceived wisdom that bad behaviour by individuals can be theoretically controlled remains the basis of most policy decisions concerning crime. Whether that behaviour is controlled via direct action aimed at the motivation of the offender, action aimed at making it harder or less desirable for the offender to commit crime or wider social measures aimed at making it unnecessary for the offender to commit crime varies from time to time and with the political persuasion of the policymakers (Grimshaw 2004).

However in the case of animal harm there are other factors to be considered. As earlier chapters have outlined, animal harm is the cause of a variety of offender motivations and behaviours, not all of which consider the animal as the focus of the crime. Thus the idea that all animal offending is a product of rational choice can be directly challenged and policy needs to also consider the reality of animal offending as being an indicator of other criminality (discussed in more detail later in this chapter) and influenced by factors other than the offender's desire for profit. An understanding of the different aspects of animal harm and various factors that determine whether it will take place is important in developing appropriate policy. Research into the psychology of animal abuse has demonstrated that individuals who are abusive towards others, including animals, are characterized by low empathy and low impulse control. Beirne (1999) argues that animal cruelty should be drawn into the realm of criminological inquiry as it has importance on multiple levels:

1. animal cruelty may signify other actual or potential interpersonal violence;
2. animal cruelty is, in many forms, prohibited by criminal law;
3. violence against animals is part of the utilitarian calculus on the minimization of pain and suffering (the public good);
4. animal cruelty is a violation of rights; and
5. violence against animals is one among several forms of oppression that contribute, as a whole, to a violent society.

Beirne's arguments (1999) reflect the emergence over the last 30 years or so of the view by many law enforcement and social welfare professionals in the United States (and increasingly in other countries) that there is a link between animal abuse and violence to humans or antisocial behaviour (see for example Ressler and Schachtman 1993, Arluke et al. 1999, Ascione and Arkow 1999, Arluke 2006). An FBI study into the childhoods of serial killers identified a history of juvenile animal abuse in most cases suggesting that serial killers such as Ted Bundy and Jeffrey Dahmer started by killing animals and then graduated to people (Lockwood 1997). As a result, a history of cruelty to animals is a trait looked for by the FBI and law enforcement professionals when investigating serial killers and has become a diagnostic trait used in the treatment of psychiatric and emotional conduct disorders (Goleman 1991). As a matter of policy, there is an argument for the precise nature of an offender's animal harm to be considered not only as a factor in determining the required law enforcement response but also in considering what an offender's animal harm indicates about their potential for other offending or antisocial behaviour and their level of risk to society.

Dealing with Animal Offenders

While the evidence is that animal harm is caused by a range of factors and involves offenders with different motivations (see Chapter 3 and subsequent) the public policy approach to animal harm is primarily based around deterrence through detection and punishment. One of the main problems with deterrence theory is that it assumes that offenders are rational and responsible individuals who calculate the risks associated with crime before deciding whether to commit an offence. This is a questionable conclusion to come to in animal harm as many offences will not achieve sufficient widespread publicity to achieve a deterrent effect and it is unlikely that offenders conduct a full assessment of their offending behaviour before the commission of an offence. Although it should be noted that exemplary cases of animal abuse (i.e. those demonstrating excessive or unusual cruelty) or significant seizures in wildlife crime routinely appear in the press. Such stories are considered newsworthy as they allow for graphic depictions of crime and discussion of the aberrant nature of offending behaviour and are suitable for media commentary which demands a firm deterrent and retributive response (Chibnall 1977). However, Martin Wasik explains that 'a burglar sufficiently well-informed to have read the sentencing reports will also have read the criminological literature which tells him that the police detection and clear-up rate for burglary is less than 15 per cent' (Wasik 1992: 123). The deterrent effect is therefore limited if a rational offender concludes that his chances of being caught and receiving the punishment are minimal. This is especially so in animal abuse (and particularly in wildlife crime) where prosecution rates generally remain low due to the lack of sufficient enforcement resources (Nurse 2003) and where a well-informed offender would certainly know that a significant proportion of the law enforcement activity in is carried out by NGOs with limited resources, police officers sometimes acting in a part-time capacity or statutory agencies who lack the resources (and sometimes powers) of their mainstream criminal justice colleagues.

   White (2008) identifies three main perspectives as the desired approach to environmental crime:

1. the socio-legal approach;
2. the regulatory approach;
3. the social action approach.

While reliance on a socio-legal (law enforcement) approach as the main public policy response to animal harm is a potentially flawed perspective one clear advantage of this approach is its emphasis on use of the criminal law as it is presently constituted (White 2008: 182). Thus the law enforcement approach is consistent with the definition of animal harm as offences under current law and provides for an approach that improves the quality of investigation and law enforcement with a goal of greater prosecution and conviction of offenders. Thus the socio-legal approach provides for incarceration of offenders at the end of the criminal justice process and despite the problems of re-offending and the limited effectiveness of prison regimes in addressing this, this at least prevents offenders from committing offences for a set period of time (i.e. whilst in prison). This does not, however, address the problems of what should be done with offenders whilst in prison and Sutherland's theory (1973) provides a compelling explanation for how prisons may simply become universities of crime where individuals learn new and more sophisticated techniques for committing crime. In addition, given the evidence that some forms of animal harm are a precursor to more serious forms of crime or are associated with other forms of antisocial behaviour, a public policy approach solely based on punishment and incarceration fails to consider the wider social implications of animal harm or the emergence of new offenders, some of whom are victims as well as offenders (see Chapter 4).

The regulatory approach relies on social regulating incorporating a range of different means to address environmental harm. In practice this approach is employed in animal harm as an adjunct to the public policy law enforcement approach because of the active involvement of NGOs as part of the regulatory process. The regulatory approach is arguably successful in utilizing the vigilance of bodies like the ASPCA and RSPCA as active investigators, although arguably their role has developed, and in some cases increased, as a result of failures in public enforcement (discussed later in this chapter). However the regulatory approach recognizes that a constellation of measures may be required to address animal harm (White 2008: 182) and that a pure law enforcement approach is only a partial solution. It thus provides for intervention from, for example, animal welfare professionals in companion and domestic animal abuse (see Chapter 4) and the use of NGOs as specialist advisors.

The social action approach emphasizes the need for social change and attempts to address environmental harm through social transformation driven by 'deliberative democracy and citizen participation' (White 2008: 182). In effect the animal rights and species justice movements pursue this agenda, although as Donaldson and Kymlicka observe (2011), they have met with limited success in their goal of achieving legal rights for animals. However, where social action has been successful is in developing the integration of NGO perspectives into law enforcement, albeit in a limited way. One aspect of social action is to challenge the traditional domination of nation states in setting the environmental agenda. Increasingly it is NGOs through campaigning that influence public policy while their practical law enforcement activities also highlight inadequacies in public enforcement. (This is discussed in more detail later in this chapter.)

The law enforcement perspective can, however, have an effect in disrupting crime even if only temporarily. James Wilson's work is influential in arguing that action should be taken to increase the costs of offending so that the benefits of leading a law-abiding lifestyle are more obvious to the potential offender. White (2008) identifies the role of the police as integral to environmental law enforcement while Wilson argues that the role of the police is not just detection and prevention of crime but is also one of order maintenance. Young, writing and describing Wilson's position in the *Oxford Handbook of Criminology* (1994), explains that the police role is:

> to jump-start the informal control system back into action in those areas where it has broken down and which are, of course, ipso facto, high crime areas. Effective police work per se, in the traditional mode of detection, should be directed to the high-risk repeat offenders. Similarly, the courts and prisons should give high sentences to this small group of offenders in order to incapacitate them. (Young 1994: 101)

However White identifies that while environmental crime is gaining public and political attention as a category of crime it is still something of an unknown for many police both individually and collectively (White 2008: 196–7). Thus policing perspectives and knowledge are factors in determining how individual crimes are dealt with and where animal harm is concerned the effectiveness of police action and willingness of police to engage with such offences varies considerably from jurisdiction to jurisdiction. Police officers are generally accepted as having a specific view of the social world and their role in it and to have a specific cultural ethos – cop culture – that informs the way in which they behave. Reiner explains that:

> there are differences of outlook within police forces, according to such individual variables as personality, generation or career trajectory, and structured variations according to rank, assignment and specialisation. (Reiner 1992: 109)

Thus the conceptualization of environmental crimes (Carrabine et al. 2004, Beirne and South 2007) and animal harm in particular by criminal justice policy, operational policing practices and individual officers may influence the importance attached to animal harm and whether it is seen as a policing priority or a matter for the police at all. It is also true that the organizational styles and cultures of police forces vary between different places and periods, much of which is dictated by individual police managers and which reflects their attitudes towards particular crimes. Informal rules, embedded in specific practices and nuances might dictate, for example, that in some inner-city police areas most animal harm (except possibly wildlife crime and the trade in endangered species) is seen as being a low priority for police investigation whereas in rural areas (such as Scotland where rarer birds such as the golden eagle and the osprey are seen as being part of Scotland's heritage or those parts of the United States where California condors or bald eagles hold special cultural significance) considerable police and criminal justice resources may be directed at those offenders who seek to exploit wildlife resources. Reiner further explains that 'cop culture has developed as a patterned set of understandings which help to cope with and adjust to the pressures and tensions which confront the police' (1992: 109). Each new generation of police officers is socialized into 'cop culture' but not in any structured way so that the interactional processes of each encounter reinforce what is expected of officers. As a result, 'cop culture' survives because it is a suitable fit with the psychological physical and social demands of rank and file policing.

One central factor of cop culture is the manner in which police officers classify the types of work that they do. Skolnick's (1966) account of the policeman's working personality is a primary work in discussing police culture. Successive writers (Holdaway 1977, Shearing 1981, Graef 1989, Reiner 1992) have commented on the machismo inherent in policing and the problems caused by it. A body of literature also exists on the manner in which the police assess the legitimacy of some aspects of crime and police work while dismissing other aspects. For example, murder and other forms of serious violent crime are seen as being worthwhile, challenging and rewarding involving 'good-class villains' (Reiner 1992: 118) and crimes that are considered to be solely the responsibility of the police. Domestic violence, however, is often seen as not being something that the police should be involved in as it is a private matter and in some areas officers may feel the same towards animal harm, considering that it is not a priority for them, particularly where the nature of animal harm might be seen to be a property matter which should be dealt with by private law.

Morley and Mullender's research into domestic violence (1994) highlighted what Reiner (1992) called the 'rubbish' phenomenon, essentially people who make calls on the police who are seen as being unworthy of attention, or victims of crimes which are the complainant's own fault. Studies undertaken during the 1970s and 1980s showed that in domestic violence cases during this period rarely did the police arrest the assailant, even where the victim requested it and the violence was severe. In a small number of cases the police failed even to arrive at the scene (Morley and Mullender 1994: 13). But the classification of 'rubbish' and 'worthwhile' crime does not necessarily mean that only the more traditional 'serious' crimes are enforced by the police. As indicated earlier, those who exploit certain aspects of wildlife seen as being integral to national identity and representing important aspects of national heritage find themselves the subject of disproportionately high police (or other statutory agency) attention.

Although there have been considerable advances in police responses to domestic violence there are still a wide variety of possible criminal justice and public policy responses to animal harm. Crimes seen as being victimless or of low priority, or which can be dealt with as private law matters, are unlikely to be seen as candidates for police resources whereas those crimes seen as being of local (i.e. force) importance, as being politically important or high-profile crimes, will be allocated resources. For efficient crime prevention and crime control the allocation of those resources is crucial and for those crimes considered as fringe areas of policing or low priority, this is unlikely to happen. However developing understanding of the importance of animal harm in relation to mainstream criminal justice has the potential to significantly increase its priority within public policy.

Animal Abuse and Violence towards Humans

There are a number of studies (mainly US) linking animal welfare offences (particularly cruelty) to further offending.[2] Animal abuse and interpersonal violence towards humans have a number of common characteristics, both types of victim are living creatures, can experience pain and distress, can display physical signs of their pain and distress (with which humans can empathize) and may die as a result of the injuries inflicted in cruelty such as torture. For law enforcement professionals, therefore, the tendency of some individuals to inflict pain and suffering on animals is an important factor in predicting future violent offending. Increasingly law enforcement professionals and psychologists are researching how the tendency towards violence against non-human animals may be used as 'practice' for offenders who then escalate towards interpersonal violence towards humans. The public benefit of such research is obvious, if it is possible to identify violent offenders early in their 'careers', the escalation might be prevented and the fear and harm caused to society by serious violent offenders might be prevented. Brief details of some key studies are discussed below.

In a 1985 study, Kellert and Felthous found that violent, incarcerated men reported higher rates of 'substantial cruelty to animals' in childhood (25 percent) than the comparison group of non-incarcerated men (0 percent). The findings indicating that cruelty towards animals in childhood may be a factor in the development of violent offenders. A similar difference had emerged in an earlier study of violent women offenders (Felthous and Yudowitz 1977) where 36 percent of the incarcerated group reported cruelty to animals compared with 0 percent of the non-incarcerated group. In a study of 28 convicted male sexual homicide offenders Ressler et al. (1988) examined self-reports of cruelty to animals among dangerous sex offenders. Childhood animal abuse was reported by 36 percent of the offenders, 46 percent admitted to abusing animals as adolescents and 36 percent of the men admitted they had also abused animals in adulthood.

---

2 See, for example: Flynn (2002), Henry (2004) and Sunstein and Nussbaum (2006).

Tingle et al. (1986) also surveyed 64 convicted male sex offenders and discovered that animal abuse in childhood or adolescence was reported by 48 percent of the rapists and 30 percent of the child molesters.

Miller and Knutson's 1997 study of self-reports of animal abuse by 299 American inmates incarcerated for various felony offences compared their offending with 308 introductory psychology class undergraduates. The results showed higher levels of animal abuse among the inmates than undergraduates reporting the following types of animal abuse:

- 'hurt an animal?' – 16.4 percent inmates, 9.7 percent undergraduates;
- 'killed a stray animal?' – 32.8 percent inmates, 14.3 percent undergraduates; and
- 'killed a pet?' – 12 percent inmates and 3.2 percent undergraduates.

Arluke et al. (1999) carried out research comparing convicted animal abusers with other offenders. They found that the animal abusers were significantly more likely than the comparison group participants to be involved in some form of criminal behaviour, including violent offences. The different types of offending are of relevance in assessing the propensity of animal abuse offenders towards interpersonal violence. While the limitations of these studies must be acknowledged, the higher incidence of animal abuse among extremely violent offenders such as serial killers and sexually violent offenders (e.g. rapists and child molesters) indicates that animal abuse may be characteristic of the developmental histories of violent offenders. Attitudes towards animal welfare and the adoption by these offenders of animal abuse as a form of criminal behaviour are, thus, a factor.

More recently a study by Verlinden (2000) of nine school shootings in the United States (from Moses Lake, WA, in 1996 to Conyers, GA, in 1999) revealed that five (45 percent) of the 11 perpetrators had histories of alleged animal abuse. Ascione (1999) points to the well-documented case of Luke Woodham who, in the April before his October 1997 murder of his mother and two schoolmates, tortured and killed his own pet dog to illustrate animal abuse as an indicator of future violence or a precursor to interpersonal violence. From a common-sense point of view an individual who has killed an animal and either enjoyed doing so or has gained some form of cathartic release from the killing will be more likely to commit other forms of violence or need to escalate to larger animals and eventually people in order to continue receiving 'benefits' from their killing. However, as Chapter 4 illustrates, juvenile killing of animals is a complex phenomenon which requires consideration of juvenile offending within its social and domestic context. Juveniles cannot be seen solely as potentially serious offenders but must also be seen as victims or witnesses to other crimes within the home. Public policy in the United States is beginning to appreciate this fact although the UK lags somewhat behind.

In September 2001 the US Department of Justice (DOJ) issued a special issue of its Juvenile Justice Bulletin on *Animal Abuse and Youth Violence*, commenting that 'the forms of abuse to which animals may be subjected are similar to the forms of abuse children experience, including physical abuse, serious neglect, and even psychological abuse' (Ascione 2001: 1). The DOJ bulletin recommended that 'parents, childcare providers, teachers, others who play care giving roles for children (e.g., clergy, coaches), and young people themselves should be informed that animal abuse may be a significant sign of a tendency to violence and psychological disturbance and should not be ignored' (Ascione 2001: 7). Acceptance that animal abuse is a social problem that affects wider society was part of the DOJ's conclusions; they also accepted that animal welfare organizations have a role to play in reducing the problem, commenting that the expertise of animal welfare organizations could help develop a typology for children who abuse animals. However there was also acknowledgement that animal welfare organizations have been actively developing educational and therapeutic efforts that incorporate 'animal assisted' or 'animal-facilitated' components (Duel 2004). The DOJ gave recognition to research which shows that lack of empathy is a factor in offending (Bavolek 2000, Beetz 2009) and that effective youth violence prevention and intervention programmes that taught young people 'to train, care for, and interact in a nurturing manner with animals' might reduce their propensity towards aggression and violence (Ascione 2001: 10). Bavolek (2000) indicated that caring for animals may be a way to restore or develop empathy compromised by, for example, years of neglect or maltreatment at the hands of parents or other carers. In addition, identification with animals in a therapeutic setting may engender respect for or identification with animals as sentient beings making it more difficult to view them as objects suitable as an outlet for aggression and thus making violence towards them less likely (Ascione 2001).

Increasingly the link between animal abuse and interpersonal human violence has begun to be recognized by other policy professionals. In the UK, the Royal College of Veterinary Surgeons (RCVS), for example, has noted that veterinary surgeons are among a number of professionals who may see and hear things during the course of their professional activity which arouse suspicion of animal abuse and/or domestic violence and child abuse (see Chapter 4). The RCVS's professional conduct guidance notes that 'given the links between animal and child abuse and domestic violence, a veterinary surgeon reporting suspected animal abuse to the relevant authority should consider whether a child might be at risk' (RCVS 2003). In addition Hawksworth and Balen (2009) identify that health visitors tend to have close contact with deprived families and are in a position to observe animal abuse but note that the UK does not as yet have a cross-disciplinary mechanism through which animal abuse and other forms of abuse could be identified and information shared among public policy professionals. Thus while veterinarians have professional guidance which advises them to report animal abuse or child abuse and provides a mechanism for either form of harm to be considered as an indicator of problems in the home, health professionals in the UK currently lack the same clear guidance. As a result the current system is one in which unlike the developments in the United States (see Chapter 4) public policy in the UK still primarily views domestic animal harm in isolation of other forms of abuse. There is, thus, a need to develop the good practice of the veterinary profession into other areas, linking animal welfare to other forms of offending and ensuring that professionals are both alert to the signs and implications of animal abuse and take action to address them.

Preventing Animal Harm

The importance of animal welfare and health professional intervention in animal harm is the potential for a preventative approach to be implemented as part of public policy. Much animal harm 'policing' is reactive, dealing with animal harm incidents once they have happened. Yet, as White indicates, environmental law enforcement poses challenges 'especially from the point of view of police interagency collaborations, the nature of investigative techniques and approaches, and the different types of knowledge required' (2008: 197). The problem is compounded when viewing animal harm holistically as there are distinctions between animal welfare and wildlife crime or wildlife and game offences. Thus a range of jurisdictional, legislative and policy approaches may combine, compounding the difficulties of the enforcement task.

These problems notwithstanding, public policy needs to move beyond reactively policing animal harm to proactively preventing animal harm. Mainstream criminology has recognized that there may be limited rationality on the part of offenders and hold that much crime is opportunistic, being committed where situations arise that makes crime possible. This being the case, administrative and environmental criminologies might be employed to reduce crime through environmental design or the use of situational crime prevention policies (Bottoms 2007, Newburn 2007). Where limited rationality exists, crime may be seen as a combination of opportunism and some rationality on the part of offenders but does not necessarily have its roots in social conditions or family influences. Nor are offenders necessarily 'conditioned' towards being criminal. Because crime is opportunistic, Young explains that 'it can be deterred by structural barriers, for example steering locks in cars, better locks and bolts on houses, greater surveillance from, for example, Neighbourhood Watch schemes or ticket inspectors' (Young 1994: 93). This also has the effect of reducing opportunities for crime and will prevent offences by those offenders who react to opportunities to commit crime. What situational crime prevention policies can do is to reduce the incidence of crime by simply making it harder to commit crime. In mainstream crime, target hardening can address some of the vulnerable areas outlined above (cars, domestic windows, etc.).

While situational crime prevention measures are used only selectively in animal harm there have been some attempts to apply situational crime prevention to wildlife crimes recognizing that while the public has a major role to play in the policing and detection of this type of crime, practical crime prevention measures might be taken in some places. CCTV cameras have been placed at rare bird breeding sites (the ospreys at Loch Garten in Scotland, the peregrine falcons at Simmonds Yat in Herefordshire, and hen harriers in Northumbria in the north of England) and at deer or animal sanctuaries owned by LACS, where hunting with dogs is not permitted and hunts do not have rights of access. But little other crime prevention is employed, although this is largely due to the nature of the offences and the fact that much of the countryside in which wildlife crimes take place is not 'owned' in a way that would allow the police or individual landowners to take responsibility for initiating target hardening measures. Where this has been done in the UK, it is often on RSPB, Wildlife Trust or LACS owned nature reserves where the charity also has the resources to monitor the cameras, pursue any incidents with the police and, if necessary, pursue a private prosecution as the aggrieved landowner. One problem with situational crime prevention is that it does little to address the problem of displacement, i.e. the possibility that crime prevented in one area might simply move to another area where opportunities are easier to realize (such as areas where no Neighbourhood Watch scheme or camera monitoring of wildlife exists). However what situational crime prevention does is to focus on those areas that are considered to be vulnerable and where target hardening or greater enforcement activity might have some effect. Arguably, the perspective results in an escalating programme of CCTV installations, local crime prevention initiatives, and increased police patrols and so on with area after area being subject to more aggressive crime prevention policies. At the extreme end of the aggressive crime prevention spectrum, conservationists and NGOs engaged in combating wildlife trade have resorted to dehorning rhinos as an alternative to costly law enforcement monitoring and interventions (Milner-Gulland 1999). The justification for such crime prevention action is its elimination of the rhino as a target of poaching by reducing the value of the dehorned rhino to poachers. As an extreme form of target-hardening, Daly et al. (2011) argue that dehorning has proved to be a cost-effective deterrent to poaching and thus effective as a crime prevention tool. NGOs conservationists and law enforcement agencies have, thus in certain circumstances used creative yet extreme situational crime prevention techniques to address problems of non-compliance with wildlife poaching rules. Such measures might be accompanied by increased patrols and other preventive policing approaches (Kahler and Gore 2012).

In animal harm, clear-up of crimes is dependent more on the public witnessing crimes and providing evidence that crime has taken place than on police detection of crimes given that animal harm is frequently outside of the experience of most operational police officers. However in wildlife crime, for example, much crime takes place in remote areas that fall outside police patrol areas and where observation of offences by the public is vital to ensuring they are reported. Thus, in the UK, birds of prey are monitored by volunteer raptor study group members, badgers are monitors by badger survey workers and illegal hunting activities are monitored by LACS Hunt Monitors. Similarly, in the United States, observation by Sierra Club members (and their regional affiliates), Defenders of Wildlife and Earthjustice members and activists and PETA, HSUS and ASPCA officials together with the many regional animal protection bodies and members of the public who report incidents to them is essential in identifying that animal harm crimes have taken place. Public co-operation in animal harm crime prevention is vital, and also helps to provide some of the informal controls that may inhibit animal harm from occurring in the first place. This does not, however, address any of the social causes of crime (unemployment, poor housing, family circumstances, etc.), instead it favours informal methods of control and situational crime prevention with an emphasis on target hardening.

Social Crime Prevention

Given generally positive social attitudes towards animals as companions and growing social awareness of the need for improved standards of animal welfare, social crime prevention offers scope for introducing animal harm crime prevention through social action (White 2008). Law enforcement and situational crime prevention perspectives generally aim to catch offenders to prevent further crime, and make it difficult for offenders to commit crime. Social crime prevention, however, aims to prevent crime from taking place by addressing the factors that lead to crime and criminal behaviour, offering the possibility that crime can be prevented rather than being punished after it occurs. Young makes the observation that 'it is difficult to prevent crime if one does not know the underlying force behind the commitment of crime by the actors involved' (1994: 96). Yet a criminological approach to animal harm which is primarily based around a belief that offenders fail to recognize animals as sentient beings perpetuates this failure by ignoring the underlying causes. Animal harm, encompassing as it does a variety of different types of crime, incorporates a variety of different forces that lead individuals towards crime or provide circumstances where crime is likely to occur. Crimes take place within communities where there is scope for the social action approach to bring benefits although, as previous chapters indicate, offenders often lack incentives (whether social, moral or financial) to avoid animal harm and integrate ethical practices into their behaviour.

If the push towards crime is greater among the poor, the lower working class and certain ethnic minorities who are marginalized from the rewards of society (Lea and Young 1993, Young 1999), crime prevention policies need to address the inequalities that make certain parts of society more likely to commit crime. Treatment of animals frequently reflects their position of powerlessness and lower social status. Citizens who feel marginalized within society and who lack appropriate life chances or are under economic or social pressure to harm animals, will do so unless they are provided with alternatives. Within mainstream criminological discourse Lea and Young argue that good jobs, good housing, community facilities and a reduction in inequalities and uneven distribution of wealth 'all create a society which is more cohesive and less criminogenic' (1993: 116). However, as previous chapters illustrate, within animal harm some offences are committed as a direct result of employment, particularly offences involving the killing of protected wildlife to ensure higher levels of game for shooting or in industries which rely on the exploitation of animals to produce saleable products. It is, of course, arguable whether those involved in the game-rearing or (lower end) animal fashion industry are employed in 'good jobs' and receive 'good housing'. Certainly there is an uneven distribution of wealth here as the bulk of the economic power in the game-rearing industry rests with the estate owners and the consumers that pay thousands of pounds for a day's shooting and in the fashion industry designers and retailers have considerable economic power over producers and suppliers. Egg collectors, badger-diggers and badger-baiters and some of those involved in hunting with dogs (perhaps with the exception of the senior huntsmen) may also suffer from inequalities that create the circumstances that might cause crime and which dictate that even in an era of strong environmental and animal welfare awareness, wildlife crimes continue to be committed.

But while the police and other statutory agencies should have primary responsibility for enforcing animal legislation, for those communities where crime is given either covert or overt approval, action should also be taken to ensure that the community considers animal crime to be unacceptable. Social crime prevention includes not just criminal justice policy but also education programmes and community action so that offenders are unable to operate with the consent of their community. Disadvantaged areas become the subject of regeneration schemes aimed at improving the community and increasing opportunities so that citizens feel less marginalized and disadvantaged. In areas where it is known that wildlife crime is being or is likely to be committed (for example game-rearing and fishing areas) measures that involve the community in providing informal social controls by making sure that offenders know that wildlife crime is unacceptable may be required.

While the role of the urban offender (and particularly the travelling offender) should be considered, social crime prevention in animal harm would need to be tailored to its environment. In companion animal abuse, this means considering an environment rife with secrecy and where much offending is deliberately concealed from criminal justice agencies. Given the intimate nature of violence within the home there is not only a reluctance on the part of the victim to report abuse (Morley and Mullender 1994) but also unwillingness on the part of neighbours and family members to become involved. As a result achieving effective social crime prevention where companion animal harm occurs is problematic and is further compounded where cultural attitudes towards animals dictate that their abuse is a private matter. In the case of wildlife crime, social crime prevention can require consideration of the demands of a rural environment and wild areas where community attitudes towards and knowledge of animal harm may require considerable effort to overcome ingrained beliefs and practices.

For example in game-rearing areas education of game employees to ensure understanding of wildlife legislation and conservation priorities might be pursued. This was attempted by the RSPB in the UK by speaking at gamekeeper training courses during the 1990s; the policy continues and several UK-based conservation organizations currently produce some educational material on wildlife crime aimed at the wider community. Measures that also enhance the value of wildlife to an area so that it becomes a resource valued by all in the community (such as in the green tourism programmes employed in African and Asian countries) might also be attempted, with an emphasis on putting in place social protection of animals and awareness of the conservation and biodiversity value and importance of wildlife. This might create positive conditions in which offenders do not continue to see wildlife crime as a soft option or victimless crime and are encouraged both personally and by their community to value wildlife as a benefit. This might be combined with more traditional programmes that aim to turn offenders away from committing any type of crime. Such approaches have mostly been trialled by NGOs who seek to use education and public campaigning as a tool to address animal harm and to help communities develop positive approaches towards animals. However while some NGOs pursue social action, others adopt the regulatory or socio-legal approach to animal harm particularly where failures of public enforcement and policy is perceived.

Perspectives on 'Green' NGOs and Environmental Justice

The approach taken by NGOs in dealing with animal harm is significantly influenced by the ideology of the NGO and their precise focus as animal rights, conservation, animal welfare or environmental justice NGO. Green criminology incorporates a range of perspectives (Beirne and South 2007) and within green criminology discourse, debates about the nature of environmental justice and social justice combine with perspectives on environmental responsibility and the operation of the 'green movement'. However, the behaviour of NGOs within the environmental field and within the sphere of wildlife crime differs according to the nature of the organization, the policies they intend to pursue and the focus of their campaigning or fundraising activity. Far from there being one coherent 'green movement', environmental NGOs (both within a nation state and in different jurisdictions) occupy a range of different disciplines and policy perspectives and seek to achieve a range of different objectives. While some organizations may pursue wildlife and environmental issues from a moral or theological perspective, others approach wildlife crime from a conservation or law enforcement perspective and the underlying motivation of specific organizations dictates both the policies employed and the manner in which the NGO might pursue those policies.

Before any assessment of the required policy perspectives relevant to policing animal harm can be achieved, consideration should be given to the basis on which NGOs in different jurisdictions operate. Pressure groups and campaigning organizations operate within a specific institutional framework with interests of their own that shape their activities and policies. Particularly for those NGOs that have a single species focus (e.g. the RSPB is concerned mainly with birds and the Badger Trust is concerned solely with badgers while Earthjustice pursues a much broader ecological justice remit) their policies are designed to achieve greater legal protection for the species that the organization was originally created to protect and to ensure that any current threats to that species are addressed and, where possible, reduced. Such policies may, therefore, not address wider conservation issues and might conflict with the policies of other NGOs.

The UK, for example, is considered to be a nation of animal lovers but complex attitudes to animals persist in the UK resulting in a situation where animals are generally protected but are still reared specifically for shooting and where resistance to legislation to control fieldsports continues (see Chapter 5). The campaign against the *Hunting Act 2004* was often characterized as 'town versus country' and discussions of traditional fieldsports and hunting activities that become subject to legislation often contain debates concerning perceptions that affluent sections of society seek to impose their will on poorer rural members of society. Lowe and Ginsberg (2002) concluded that the animal rights movement (in the United States) has a disproportionately well-educated membership reflecting what Parkin (1968) called 'middle class radicalism'. Certainly the NGOs involved in wildlife crime in the UK, while not all pursuing policies from an animal rights perspective, represent a professional movement comprising large professional organizations (comparable with medium to large businesses) rather than being a grassroots or 'activist' movement. For example the RSPB's accounts for 2006–7 show expenditure of £82 million and with total charitable expenditure of £67 million. The RSPCA's accounts for 2006 show running costs of £82 million with over 1,500 staff employed (18 percent part-time). The public support that these organizations have (the RSPB has over a million members) together with the resources available for campaigning (including political lobbying discussed below) allows these two organizations to take the lead in promoting wildlife crime as an issue of importance. It also places the organizations in a position to employ expertise, for example, specialist investigators and political lobbyists, to promote their policy objectives. The organizations adopt a position of being expert in their chosen field and their socio-economic position allows them to exploit that perceived expertise. Kean (1998) assessed attitudes towards animal rights in the context of political and social change in Britain since 1800. She explains how following the introduction of Martin's 1822 animal protection legislation the Society for the Prevention of Cruelty to Animals (which became the RSPCA in 1840) was set up. She explains that 'the Society did not come into being to campaign for new legislation as such, but rather to ensure that the law which had been passed would be implemented' (Kean 1998: 35). NGOs primarily achieve their objectives through public campaigning to raise awareness of an issue, commonly commissioning or carrying out their own research to prove the case for a particular issue and using this research to lobby for legislative change or to convince the public of the need for a particular policy, change to the law or the need for government intervention.

The objective of ensuring that legislation is effectively enforced, however, is pursued by some organizations by way of taking on practical law enforcement of legislation as a means of ensuring that legislation is used effectively and prosecutions taken where the statutory agencies might not do this. Jasper (1997), in discussing 'postmaterial' social movements, explained that these are comprised mainly of people already integrated into their society's political, economic and educational systems and who by virtue of their affluence did not need to campaign for basic rights for themselves but could pursue protections and benefits for others. His arguments could certainly be applied to the animal rights and animal protection movements in the UK which from their activist roots have certainly grown to embrace animal protection and conservation corporations with considerable economic and political power. These organizations are often placed at the upper end of the NGO scale both in terms of their income and their position within the UK NGO establishment. The RSPB and RSPCA, for example, are both incorporated under Royal Charter giving them considerable legitimacy within the policy environment and providing them with a middle-class social position as indicated by Jasper (1997) for many successful campaigning organizations. In addition the economic power of these organizations and others like LACS, the Wildlife Trusts and the Badger Trust (which have smaller support groups throughout England and Wales) and WWF and Greenpeace allows for campaigning on a national scale ensuring widespread saturation of the campaigning message through mass market mailing, advertisements and editorials in national magazines and newspapers and the provision of campaigning materials to television news programmes and documentary film makers.

The author's examination of the different NGOs involved in wildlife crime carried out for the field research stage of the wildlife crime project (Nurse 2003 and 2011) identified that the following different types of NGO are involved:

1. campaigning NGOs;
2. law enforcement NGOs;
3. political lobbying NGOs.

This model can be broadly apply to this book's wider definition of animal harm, recognizing that it is possible for an NGO to operate in more than one of these areas, although in relation to their activities concerning animal harm, NGOs generally adopt one of these functions as a primary role (e.g. law enforcement) which dictates how the issue of animal harm is pursued, even though a secondary objective (e.g. political lobbying) may be pursued alongside this. A theoretical model can be produced that places each NGO in one of the categories as follows:

Campaigning NGOs are those organizations whose primary concern in relation to animal harm is one of raising public awareness. As a result, the organization's primary activity is public campaigning, which may involve generating news stories on a particular campaign (e.g. the Badger Trust raising the profile of badger culling through the news media), raising support for a particular campaign (e.g. the Whale and Dolphin Conservation Society's petition to protect dolphins on the Moray Firth) or to raise funds on an issue (e.g. Friends of the Earth pursuing fundraising for specific activities). Campaigning organizations may also undertake some direct action (for example the WSPCA has worked with governments and member societies to build bear sanctuaries as a practical way of protecting bears) but the primary aim of the organization is to raise public awareness on an issue and subsequently to convert that public awareness into public support for changes in policy or the adoption of protective measures for wildlife. WWF (2011), for example, have campaigned to change the behaviour of British travellers in a bid to reduce the illegal imports of endangered wildlife and their derivatives into the UK and have also run direct action programmes which encourage members of the public to 'adopt an animal' by themselves giving funds that can be directly used for the conservation of various species. NGOs fitting into this category include WWF, Friends of the Earth, IFAW, the Whale and Dolphin Conservation Society and the World Society for the Protection of Animals (WSPA).

Law enforcement NGOs are those organizations whose primary function in relation to animal harm is a law enforcement one. In effect the NGO is concerned with ensuring that animal laws are properly and rigorously enforced and in the absence of effective statutory enforcement activity it has adopted the responsibility for carrying out this function itself. This means that the NGO carries out practical casework to investigate animal harm itself and to assist the police (and other statutory agencies in the investigation of animal harm offences (or to encourage them to do so) employing specialist investigative staff able to gather evidence, give evidence at court and to prosecute cases where necessary. The prime examples would be the ASPCA (and regional equivalents), Earthjustice and the Sierra Club in the United States, and the RSPCA and SSPCA, both of whom retain a uniformed inspectorate and undercover or plain-clothes officers for investigations work in the UK. The RSPB also maintains a full-time investigations section although in contrast to the RSPCA it does not routinely prosecute cases, instead preferring to work with the Crown Prosecution Service (CPS) to ensure that cases are dealt with by the public prosecutor. However, this does not alter the fact that the RSPB's focus in wildlife crime cases is to ensure efficient investigations and prosecution of cases which are routinely reported to its officers by members of the public. Indeed, members of the public are more likely to report wild bird crime and animal cruelty offences to the RSPB and RSPCA respectively reflecting the high profile that both organizations have achieved for this aspect of their practical law/policy enforcement work.

While publicity about animal harm and increasing the importance of the issue in the political agenda are secondary objectives pursued by the RSPB, the continued existence of its investigations section despite a significant decrease in the number of prosecutions taken by the society over the years indicates that the law enforcement function remains an important one. Similarly despite having achieved success in its long-running campaign to ban hunting with dogs LACS continues to monitor the activities of hunts and takes prosecutions for breaches of the *Hunting Act 2004*. Its monitoring and prosecutions functions are, however, secondary to its political activities (discussed below). NGOs falling into the law enforcement category include the ASPCA, RSPCA, SSPCA (and RSPCA Australia), RSPB, EIA, Sierra Club, Earthjustice and the Bat Conservation Trust.

Political lobbying NGOs are those organizations whose primary function is to influence the legislative and political agenda to ensure that the animal harm issue of concern to the NGO is raised up the political agenda and is seen as a priority for government. Wildlife Link, for example, as an umbrella organization for various wildlife and conservation NGOs in the UK, does not carry out any of its own law enforcement activities or carry out public campaigning in the way that say the NSPCC does in relation to child abuse. Instead the focus of its work is on policy research and development and using this policy expertise to actively pursue legislative change or changes to policy. In this regard, Wildlife Link can be thought of as an environmental 'think-tank' or policy institute drawing on the expertise of its members to conduct policy analysis and research and to pursue environmental advocacy and political strategy in the area of wildlife crime. Individual members of the public cannot become members of Wildlife Link but membership is open to national and international voluntary and non-profit organizations within the UK involved in the protection of wildlife and the countryside. What Wildlife Link does is to provide a coalition through which policy initiatives and changes to wildlife and conservation legislation can be pursued and best practice and critical thinking on wildlife issues can be disseminated. Link also provides for a co-ordinated response to government and other consultations on the environment and legislative change or policy initiatives that might affect the environment.

NGOs operating from a political lobbying perspective see the enforcement of animal law and conservation legislation as being primarily a matter of public policy and the responsibility of public authorities rather than being an issue for action by individual NGOs. The purpose of political lobbying activity is to influence policy ensuring that animal harm and animal protection is accepted as mainstream policy whether by a government's environment department or its criminal justice agencies (or both). NGOs fitting into this category include Wildlife Link, Greenpeace, the Campaign to Protect Rural England (CPRE), the UK Environmental Law Association, LACS and the Badger Trust. As mentioned above, LACS does carry out an enforcement role but this is in support of its research and lobbying activities designed to ensure that wildlife crime is seen as an issue of policy importance. For example, in September 2007 it sponsored an interdisciplinary conference on the links between animal abuse and human violence at Keble College, Oxford, as a means of establishing this issue in the policy debate within the UK. In addition to academics and members of NGOs, delegates included representatives from the Ministry of Justice and the Police and covered issues such as the links between domestic violence and wildlife crime, the responsibilities of veterinary professionals in identifying animal abuse and the extent to which animal abuse can be taken as an indicator of a propensity to violence and future offending.

Having considered the types of NGO involved in animal harm a further classification for the ideological basis on which their policies are produced can be developed. In his analysis of the animal rights movement Beirne (2007) argues that the animal protection movement and environmental movements are two distinct entities that 'often think and act at best in parallel and, at worst, in vehement opposition to each other' (Beirne 2007: 72–3). However, NGOs involved in animal harm in both the UK and United States include both animal protection and environmental organizations and the movement is not exclusively a pro-animal one as the literature often suggests. Some largely conservation organizations such as the RSPB, for example, rigorously pursue wildlife crime policies not solely from an animal rights or animal welfare perspective but from a conservation one, considering that crimes against birds or animals are indicative of wider environmental harms such as habitat destruction. There is also a distinction to be made between animal welfare and cruelty prevention policies which seek to prevent offences against animals and policies intended to manipulate the law enforcement agenda by influencing the extent to which animal harm is considered to be a policing or core criminal justice priority, and legislative change to achieve greater protection for animals is enacted. Analysis of the available literature on NGO policies and discussion with NGOs (Nurse 2003, 2011) reveals that NGOs operating in the field of animal harm develop their policies from the ideological positions of:

1. moral culpability – censuring activities that they believe are morally wrong;
2. political priorities – censuring activities that they consider should be given a higher profile in public policy (which may include issues that they consider are worthy of being a higher law enforcement priority or those which should be the subject of law enforcement activity and/or legislative change); and

3. animal rights – a belief in rights for animals which includes policies that demonstrate either the case for animal rights or which demonstrate breaches of the existing rights which animals are said to have.

There is inevitably some overlap in these policy objectives but discussion of each provides some background to understanding how NGOs develop their policies.

Moral culpability policies are employed where NGOs consider that an activity is morally wrong and should not be allowed to continue. There is some overlap here with utilitarianism and green criminology's species justice perspective (South 1998, Rollin 2006, Linzey 2009) in which the issue of human action in relation to other sentient beings (non-human animals) is questioned. In particular NGOs embrace as a core part of policy development questions concerning whether it is morally right to inflict pain and suffering on animals including the killing or taking of animals for sport. For example, LACS's long-running campaign to ban hunting with dogs actively discussed the cruelty involved in hunting animals, ethical issues in hunting, and whether it was right to chase and terrify the animals if the intention of fox-hunting was fox control. The question of necessity and the concept of 'fair chase' were integral to such debates informed by moral perspectives and the right of animals not to suffer cruelty (see Chapter 5).

Such campaigns identify the manner in which NGOs can influence the social construction of animal harm and the public policy that deals with it. A central feature of the campaign to end fox-hunting and other forms of hunting with dogs was, therefore, a moral objection to a form of animal control that was considered unnecessary and which could not be justified in terms of its apparent objective. But this was arguably a secondary objective and the primary objective was social condemnation of an activity considered to have no place in contemporary society, and through this condemnation the change in the law that ultimately occurred when legislators accepted that a change in legislation was needed to ban hunting with dogs what needed to be agreed was the precise manner of the ban. Thus the political and social campaigning by NGOs was instrumental in forcing the government to consider the issue and to 'officially' consider evidence from conflicting viewpoints that had been publicly aired for many years previously. In achieving this stage, modification of the message by NGOs in order to achieve a legitimate aim became possible and in some submissions on the draft *Hunting Bill*, advocates of a ban on hunting with dogs accepted that if foxes, mink or deer needed to be controlled this should be done, but via a humane method of control and not by first chasing and arguably terrifying the animal. This potentially represented a shift from the animal rights position widely associated with the campaign (and dismissed by its opponents) that there should be no killing of animals.

Political priorities dictate that a primary objective for some NGOs (pursued by way of their policies) is to increase the importance of animal harm in political discourse and policy debates. For some NGOs the lack of importance paid to animal harm (or their specific area of interest within it) by governments and policymakers is the central issue to be addressed. In particular, NGOs engage in political lobbying to seek changes to legislation, to ensure that animal harm is considered as a priority in government policies and to register it as an area of public concern. For the NGO this means taking action and pursuing policies designed to ensure that animal harm is a policing priority, that there is consistency in animal law and that new legislation is enacted where inadequacies are identified. From this ideological position, law enforcement policies might be pursued where NGOs consider that an issue is worthy of enforcement activity by the statutory agencies and should be an enforcement priority. Although NGOs will sometimes undertake law enforcement activities themselves as a means of ensuring that enforcement action is taken (particularly where statutory action is considered to have failed or secured an inadequate remedy) policy objectives aimed at placing animal harm at the centre of the law enforcement agenda and as a 'policing' priority are also promoted. The intent of such policies is to ensure that enforcement of legislation is carried out by statutory authorities and that it is effective. This requires that the police and other statutory authorities regularly investigate and prosecute animal harm and that sufficient pressure and encouragement is in place to ensure that they do so. NGOs will, therefore, comment on the manifestos of the main political parties and publish their own manifestos and policies for legislative and policy change and will actively engage with MPs, government committees, agencies and departments to pursue particular agendas and will also encourage their supporters to do so.

Within NGO animal harm discourse much campaigning activity (in the UK at least) is less concerned with ensuring or obtaining legal rights for animals and more concerned with effective animal protection and the prevention of animal abuse. Thus while green criminologists debate the theoretical importance of animal rights, the practicalities of NGO policy and enforcement work are such that NGOs are more concerned with practical tools that exist within current legislative frameworks. This is not to suggest that NGOs ignore the animal rights perspective but that practical law enforcement can already be achieved without relying on animal rights and for many NGOs there is a distinction between social activism that will result in a fundamental change in legislative regimes and socio-legal or regulatory action (White 2008) that could achieve animal protection. Even within the RSPCA there is a distinction between cruelty (animal welfare) offences which are generally investigated by the uniformed Inspectorate (e.g. cruelty and harm to domestic and wild animals and neglect of animals such as horses) and the 'organized' crimes dealt with by the undercover unit SOU (badger-baiting, badger-digging, etc.) which are dealt with more in terms of the conduct of criminal gangs exploiting animals than as offences that impact on the rights of animals and which demonstrate the need for legislation such as the *Animal Welfare Act 2006* to protect the rights of animals.

While utilitarianism and questions of whether animals can suffer (see Bentham 1789, Singer 1975) are often factors in campaigning or public policy material, the focus on moral principles and legal animal rights is often downplayed in NGO activity on animal harm given that much US and UK legislation already provides basic protection for animals generally making it an offence to kill, injure or take wild animals or to deliberately inflict cruelty (with some exceptions). To a certain extent, therefore, animals already have some legal rights given that legislation provides that once in captivity animals are protected from cruelty such as 'unnecessary suffering', from being kept in cages that are too small and are protected from being removed from their wild habitat (again with some exceptions). NGO policies aimed at protecting animals and enforcing animal protection legislation are, therefore, not aimed at increasing animal rights or establishing new rights for animals but aim to uphold existing legislation and to extend the established principle that causing suffering to animals is contrary to law either to a wider range of species or to particular activities that constitute cruelty. Animal protection polices also aim to directly address animal welfare issues to the extent that they are intended to prevent human interference with animals or violence towards animals.

Case Study: *First Strike* and the *First Strike Scotland* Campaign

The *First Strike* and *First Strike Scotland* campaigns are aimed at addressing the links between animal cruelty and family violence through education and activism. Duel (2004) identifies that programmes fall into three broad categories:

- primary programmes aimed at educating the general public about violence-related issues;
- secondary programmes intended to change the attitudes and behaviour of high-risk individuals. These programmes provide mentoring and assistance aimed at developing non-violent skills;
- tertiary programmes providing direct intervention or treatment for individuals already identified as having antisocial behaviour or violence problems.

First Strike represents an attempt to deal with animal harm by integrating animal abuse into social policy. As a result it combines social intervention with socio-legal approaches (White 2008) to recognize that a range of enforcement and social justice bodies are required to deal with animal harm and its consequences. *First Strike* originated with HSUS; its Scottish equivalent is run by the SSPCA. The Scottish programme works with the juvenile justice system and established the UK's first cross-reporting system (Carpentieri 2001). The Scottish programme also provides training in the links between animal abuse and violent crime to recruits going through the police college in Scotland. In its US programme, the HSUS provides a variety of materials to assist law enforcement and communities and organizes workshops on coordinating communities' responses to animal cruelty, family violence and community violence (Humane Society 2008). HSUS programmes address and support a range of professions such as law enforcement, teachers and social services who deal directly with animal abuse and human violence.

The *First Strike* campaign combines several different aspects of NGO activity to achieve its goals. Direct engagement with law enforcement bodies is combined with campaigning and educational activity in order to address NGO concerns and integrate animal abuse into other aspects of policy. In addition, some lobbying takes place through informing law enforcement, judicial systems and policymakers of the importance of animal abuse, furthering the goal of having courts and policymakers appreciate the seriousness of animal abuse and its implications for their policy and practice.

Summarizing the Policy Issues

Public policy on animal harm is predominantly concerned either with animal protection or welfarism rather than animal harm as an aspect of criminal justice. Although recent developments have taken place which begin to view animal harm as having implications for mainstream criminal justice (Ascione 2001, Linzey 2009) for the most part the efforts of green criminologists and NGOs have had little effect on public policy regarding animal harm. NGOs may however have influenced practical law enforcement efforts either by providing advice and assistance to statutory enforcers, taking their own practical educational or enforcement activity or conducting and publishing research or developing policy initiatives aimed at addressing animal harm problems.

Criminal epidemiology, criminal aetiology and criminalists provide mechanisms for analysing and dealing with crimes while criminological research and past experience of dealing with crime provide a basis for assessing the likely effectiveness of criminal justice policy. Crime has no single definition or simple cause and animal harm, an under-researched area of criminology, has only recently emerged as an area attracting the attention of law enforcement and policy practitioners and professionals. In animal harm, the actions of the individual are a factor but social conditions when combined with the role of the individual also need to be considered as an explanation for crime. There is, however, no single type of offender and animal harm crimes are committed by the poor and lower working classes as well as the comfortable middle classes and even the rich and powerful. Criminal justice policy, therefore, needs to consider these different types of offender and the different circumstances that cause them to commit crime if it is to be effective.

Although the general aim of criminal justice policies may be to reduce crime and make society a safer place, individual policies can have specific goals. Separate from the goal of punishing offenders for behaviour that society considers unacceptable, criminal justice policies employed in both mainstream criminal justice and in animal harm may have as a secondary aim any of the following motives:

1. repressing deviation from the accepted norms in society;
2. protecting society from wrongdoers;
3. providing restitution for the wronged (including the environment);
4. rehabilitating offenders to protect society by preventing future offences;
5. retribution, revenge and 'just desserts';
6. general (as opposed to individual) deterrence to keep the bulk of society law-abiding.

An effective criminal justice policy may have to combine several of these intentions to effectively address crime problems in society and prevent offending and re-offending. Public policy on animal harm needs to therefore incorporate measures that range from those that target the offender to those that deal with minimizing the opportunities for offences to be committed and attack the conditions that cause animal harm.

As a result, there is no simple policy that will address animal harm but in the menu of options employed in mainstream criminal justice, policies aimed at reducing poverty, racism (other discrimination or disadvantage and speciesism), unemployment and improving education need to be implemented. Unfortunately, while some policies that address these issues have been considered and implemented, the focus of criminal justice policy in animal harm is still predominantly the law enforcement perspective that relies on action by the police (supported by NGOs) and the courts to address crime. The use of sentencing remains largely punitive rather than rehabilitative which fails to address problems of repeat offending, instead relying on temporary incarceration as a means of addressing the crime problem. This means that little attention is paid to crime prevention and that policy is over-reliant on the effectiveness of detection, apprehension and subsequent punishment.

Animal harm policies should take account of what is known and what has been tried in dealing with 'mainstream' crime as well as the emerging green criminology scholarship and should apply the appropriate policies to the specific crime (and individual offender) under consideration.

What the available literature on animal harm policing in the UK, United States and transnationally identifies is that although the enforcement of animal harm has developed from its ad-hoc and voluntary beginnings to being carried out in a more structured (albeit still largely voluntary) way, there are still problems to be addressed. Over the years NGOs in their policy documents have highlighted inadequacies in the current legislative and practical enforcement regime for animal crime and have also made the case for a stricter enforcement regime.

References

Arluke, A. (2006). *Just a Dog: Understanding Animal Cruelty and Ourselves*, Philadelphia: Temple University Press.

Arluke, A. and Sanders, C. (1996). *Regarding Animals*, Philadelphia: Temple University Press.

Arluke, A., Levin, J., Luke, C. and Ascione, F. (1999). The Relationship of Animal Abuse to Violence and Other Forms of Antisocial Behavior. *Journal of Interpersonal Violence*, 14, 963–75.

Ascione, F.R. (1999). The Abuse of Animals and Human Interpersonal Violence: Making the Connection, in F.R. Ascione and P. Arkow (eds), *Child Abuse, Domestic Violence, and Animal Abuse: Linking the Circles of Compassion for Prevention and Intervention*, West Lafayette, IN: Purdue University Press, 50–61.

Ascione, F.R. and Arkow, P. (eds) (1999). *Child Abuse, Domestic Violence and Animal Abuse: Linking the Circles of Compassion for Prevention and Intervention*, West Lafayette, IN: Purdue University Press.

Ascione, F.R. (2001). Animal Abuse and Youth Violence. *Juvenile Justice Bulletin*, September, US Department of Justice, Office of Juvenile Justice and Delinquency Prevention.

Bavolek, S.J. (2000). *The Nurturing Parenting Programs*. Bulletin. Washington, DC: U.S. Department of Justice, Office of Justice Programs, Office of Juvenile Justice and Delinquency Prevention.

Beetz, A. (2009). Empathy as an Indicator of Emotional Development, in A. Linzey (ed.), *The Link Between Animal Abuse and Human Violence*, Eastbourne: Sussex Academic Press, 63–74.

Beirne, P. (1999). For a Nonspeciesist Criminology: Animal Abuse as an Object of Study. *Criminology*, 37(1), 1–32.

Beirne, P. (2007). Animal Rights, Animal Abuse and Green Criminology, in Piers Beirne and Nigel South (eds), *Issues in Green Criminology: Confronting Harms against Environments, Humanity and Other Animals*, Cullompton: Willan Publishing, 55–86.

Beirne, P. and South, N. (eds) (2007). *Issues in Green Criminology: Confronting Harms against Environments, Humanity and Other Animals*, Devon: Willan Publishing.

Bentham, J. (1789[1970]). *Introduction to the Principles of Morals and Legislation*, edited by J.H. Burns and H.L.A. Hart, London: Athlone Press.

Bottoms, A.E. (2007). Place, Space, Crime and Disorder, in M. Maguire, R. Morgan and R. Reiner (eds), *The Oxford Handbook of Criminology*, 4th edn, Oxford: Oxford University Press, 528–74.

Bright, J. (1993). Crime Prevention: The British Experience, in K. Stenson and D. Cowell (eds), *The Politics of Crime Control*, London: Sage, 62–86.

The Cabinet Office (2011). *Red Tape Challenge*. Available at http://www.redtapechallenge.cabinetoffice.gov.uk/home/index/ [accessed 29 June 2011].

Carpentieri, J.D. (2001). Cruelty Connection. *Cats Today*, August/September.

Carrabine, E., Iganski, P., Lee, M., Plummer, K. and South, N. (2004). *Criminology: A Sociological Introduction*, London: Routledge.

Chibnall, S. (1977). *Law-and-Order News: An Analysis of Crime Reporting in the British Press*, London: Tavistock.

Connelly, J. and Smith, G. (1999). *Politics and the Environment: From Theory to Practice*, London: Routledge.

Conservatives (2007). *It's Time to Fight Back*, London: The Conservative Party.

Cuppleditch, L. and Evans, W. (2005). *Re-offending of Adults: Results from the 2002 Cohort*, London: Home Office.

Daly, B.G., Grayling, A., Friedmann, Y., Downie, S., du Toit, R., Emslie, R., Eustace, M., Malan, J., Nghidinwa, K., O'Criodain, C. and Trendler, K. (eds) (2011). *Perspectives on Dehorning and Legalised Trade in Rhino Horn as Tools to Combat Rhino Poaching*. Proceedings of a workshop assessing legal trade in rhino horn as a tool in combating poaching as well as a detailed assessment of the efficacy of dehorning as a deterrent to poaching. Johannesburg: Endangered Wildlife Trust.

Donaldson, S. and Kymlicka, W. (2011). *Zoopolis: A Political Theory of Animal Rights*, New York and Oxford: Oxford University Press.

Duel, D.K. (2004). *Violence Prevention and Intervention: A Directory of Animal-Related Programs*, Washington, DC: The Humane Society of the United States.

Felthous, A.R. and Yudowitz, B. (1977). Approaching a Comparative Typology of Assaultive Female Offenders. *Psychiatry*, 40, 270–76.

Flynn, C.P. (2002). Hunting and Illegal Violence Against Humans and Other Animals: Exploring the Relationship. *Society & Animals*, 10(2), 137–54.

Goleman, D. (1991). Experts See Parallels Between Dahmer, Previous Serial Killers. *New York Times* News Service, 11 August.

Graef, E. (1989). *Talking Blues: The Police in their Own Words*, London: Fontana.

Grimshaw, R. (2004). *Whose Justice? Principal Drivers of Criminal Justice Policy, Their Implications for Stakeholders, and Some Functions for Critical Policy Departures*, London: British Society of Criminology.

Hawksworth, D. and Balen, R. (2009). Animal Cruelty and Child Welfare: The Health Visitor's Perspective, in A. Linzey (ed.), *The Link Between Animal Abuse and Human Violence*, Eastbourne: Sussex Academic Press, 281–94.

Henry, B.C. (2004). The Relationship between Animal Cruelty, Delinquency, and Attitudes toward the Treatment of Animals. *Society & Animals*, 12(3), 185–207.

Holdaway, S. (1977). Changes in Urban Policing. *The British Journal of Sociology*, 28(2), 119–37.

HSUS (2008). *First Strike: The Violence Connection*, Washington, DC: Humane Society of the United States.

Jasper, J.M. (1997). *The Art of Moral Protest: Culture, Biography, and Creativity in Social Movements*, Chicago: University of Chicago Press.

Kahler, J.S. and Gore, M.L. (2012). Beyond the Cooking Pot and Pocket Book: Factors Influencing Noncompliance with Wildlife Poaching Rules. *International Journal of Comparative and Applied Criminal Justice*, 36(2), 103–20.

Kean, H. (1998). *Animal Rights: Political and Social Change in Britain since 1800*, London: Reaktion Books.

Kellert, S.R. and Felthous, A.R. (1985). Childhood Cruelty toward Animals among Criminals and Noncriminals. *Human Relations*, 38, 1113–29.

Labour Party (2008). *Labour's Policies on Crime and Justice*. Available at www.labour.org.uk/crime_and_justice [accessed 17 May 2008].

Lea, J. and Young, J. (1993 Revised edition), *What Is To Be Done About Law & Order?*, London: Pluto Press.

Linzey, A. (ed.) (2009). *The Link Between Animal Abuse and Human Violence*, Eastbourne: Sussex Academic Press.

Lockwood, R. (1997). *Deadly Serious: An FBI Perspective on Animal Cruelty*, Washington, DC: The Humane Society of the United States.

Lowe, B.M. and Ginsberg, C.F. (2002). Animal Rights as a Post-citizenship Movement. *Society & Animals*, 10(2), Washington, DC: Society & Animals Forum Inc., 203–15.

Miller, K.S. and Knutson, J.F. (1997). Reports of Severe Physical Punishment and Exposure to Animal Cruelty by Inmates Convicted of Felonies and by University Students. *Child Abuse and Neglect*, 21, 59–82.

Milner-Gulland, E.J. (1999). How Many to Dehorn? A Model for Decision-making by Rhino Managers. *Animal Conservation*, 2(2), 137–47.

Morley, R. and Mullender, A. (1994). *Preventing Domestic Violence: To Women*, London: Home Office.

Newburn, T. (2007). *Criminology*, Cullompton: Willan Publishing.

Nurse, A. (2003). *The Nature of Wildlife and Conservation Crime in the UK and its Public Response, Working Paper No 9*, Birmingham: University of Central England Birmingham, Faculty of Law and Social Sciences.

Nurse, A. (2011). Policing Wildlife: Perspectives on Criminality in Wildlife Crime. *Papers from the British Criminology Conference*, 11, 38–53, London: British Society of Criminology.

Parkin, F. (1968). *Middle Class Radicalism*, New York: Praeger.

Patterson, C. (2002). *Eternal Treblinka: Our Treatment of Animals and the Holocaust*, New York: Lantern Books.

Ponder, C. (2001). The Missing Link. *Cats Today*, August/September.

Prison Reform Trust (2012). *Bromley Briefings Prison Factfile*, London: Prison Reform Trust.

RCVS (2003). *Guide to Professional Conduct*, London: Royal College of Veterinary Surgeons.

Royal Society for the Protection of Birds (2010). *The RSPB Annual Review 2009–2010*, Sandy: RSPB. Available at http://www.rspb.org.uk/Images/Annual_review_tcm9-261508.pdf [accessed 30 August 2011].

Regan, T. (1983). *The Case for Animal Rights*, Berkeley: University of California Press.

Reiner, R. (1992). *The Politics of the Police*, Hemel Hempstead: Harvester Wheatsheaf.

Ressler, R.K., Burgess, A.W. and Douglas, J.E. (1988). *Sexual Homicide: Patterns and Motives*, New York: Lexington Books.

Ressler, R.K. and Schachtman, T. (1993). *Whoever Fights Monsters: My Twenty Years Tracking Serial Killers for the FBI*, New York: St Martin's Press.

Rollin, B.E. (2006). *Animal Rights And Human Morality*, New York: Prometheus.

Schaffner, J. (2011). *An Introduction to Animals and the Law*, New York: Palgrave Macmillan.

Shearing, C.D. (1981). *Organizational Police Deviance: Its Structure and Control*. Toronto: Butterworth.

Singer, P. (1975). *Animal Liberation*, New York: Avon.

Skolnick, J. (1966). *Justice without Trial: Law Enforcement in Democratic Society*, New York: Wiley.

South, N. (1998). A Green Field for Criminology? A Proposal for a Perspective. *Theoretical Criminology*, 2(2), 211–33.

Sunstein, C.R. and Nussbaum, M.C. (eds) (2006). *Animal Rights: Current Debates and New Directions*, New York: Open University Press.

Sutherland, E.H. (1973). *On Analysing Crime*, edited by K. Schuessler, Chicago: University of Chicago Press (original work published 1942).

Tingle, D., Barnard, G.W., Robbins, L., Newman, G. and Hutchinson, D. (1986). Childhood and Adolescent Characteristics of Paedophiles and Rapists. *International Journal of Law and Psychiatry*, 9, 103–16.

Verlinden, S. (2000). Risk Factors in School Shootings, unpublished doctoral dissertation. Pacific University, Forest Grove, OR.

Wasik, M. (1992). Sentencing: A Fresh Look at Aims and Objectives, in E. Stockdale and S. Casale (eds), *Criminal Justice under Stress*, London: Blackstone, 118–41.

White, R. (2008). *Crimes against Nature: Environmental Criminology and Ecological Justice*, Cullompton: Willan.

Wilson, J.Q. (1985). *Thinking about Crime*, 2nd edn, New York: Vintage Books.

Wise, S.M. (2000). *Rattling the Cage: Towards Legal Rights for Animals*, London: Profile.

WWF (2011). *Wildlife Souvenir Guide*, Godalming: WWF.

Young, J. (1994). Incessant Chatter: Recent Paradigms in Criminology, in M. Maguire, R. Morgan and R. Reiner (eds), *The Oxford Handbook of Criminology*, Oxford: Oxford University Press, 69–124.

Young, J. (1999). *The Exclusive Society: Social Exclusion, Crime and Difference in Late Modernity*, London: Sage.

Chapter 10

Conclusion

This book began by asking the question:

> What makes people harm, injure, or kill animals?

Its analysis of animal harm and animal offending concludes that applying green perspectives to the behaviours, legislation and policy involved in animal harm reveals a complexity to the question and to the behaviours involved that is often ignored. So perhaps a better question would be:

> What makes people harm, injure, or kill animals in those specific circumstances in which the law makes their activities unlawful?

Animal harm criminality reveals much about the attitudes of individuals and groups towards animals as well as their attitudes towards wider society. But so too does the public policy response to animal harm and the manner in which legislators, prosecutors and the courts deal with this area of criminality. The question is not solely whether animal harm can be resolved by providing additional legal protection (or even rights) for animals, but why those harms already made unlawful continue to be committed, particularly in those circumstances where those harming animals know or ought to know that their actions are unlawful. In the formulation of their policy and campaigning responses, it may be convenient and comforting for both animal rights activists and policymakers to think of animal offenders as being simply evil (Linzey 2009, Rowlands 2009) or inherently cruel. Such perspectives allow for the demonizing of offenders and the promotion of policies that assert ideological perspectives on offending that can be easily understood by the public, fit comfortably into digestible media narratives, and which reflect a 'common sense' logic of offending compatible with mainstream rational choice criminological narratives (Francis and Soothill 2005). But the simplistic assessments of animal harm and its associated criminality revealed by such policies are inadequate to deal with or explain the reality of animal harm; which is a complex phenomenon. As the analysis in this book has shown, animal harm encompasses a variety of behaviours, motivations, influences and criminality that defy simplistic explanations. As a result, a more detailed analysis of animal harm is required in order to develop an understanding of its complexity, varied societal effects and the manner in which it is dealt with by law enforcement agencies. Yet public policy on animal harm consistently treats all offenders as if they were rational, free-thinking individuals who choose to commit offences against animals and are primarily motivated by cruelty, profit, or some other form of personal benefit. But the evidence suggests otherwise and thus animal harm requires deeper examination.

This final chapter concludes that animal harm has a range of causes and consists of several different types of criminality which need to be specifically considered in its public policy, legislative and law enforcement response, rather than treating all animal abusers, wildlife offenders and different aspects of animal harm as the same (Nurse 2011, South and Wyatt 2011). Public policy, enshrined in a legislative and law enforcement perspective that predominantly considers animal harm as homogenized cruelty containing uniform or common characteristics, generally treats animal harm as an animal rights, welfare or animal management issue divorced from other forms of criminality. As a result, animal laws fall predominantly within the agricultural, conservation or environmental sphere of policy rather than the criminal justice one; albeit links are sometimes (and inconsistently) made between animal offending and other crimes. White's assessment of the socio-legal approach, for example, identifies an emphasis on use of the criminal law as presently constituted (2008: 182). In its simplest terms, a reliance on investigation, law enforcement and prosecution of offenders as rational actors dominates policy responses to environmental and animal crimes. Thus, public policy fails to adequately address the complexity of animal harm, treating it as activity that can be addressed through improved animal welfare standards or via legislative measures that still consistently consider animal interests as secondary to human ones (Linzey 2009) especially where the two conflict. Alternatively it treats animal harm as wildlife crime (which predominantly means wildlife trafficking) which is primarily dealt with via trade regulation or social regulation (White 2008: 182) on the principle of sustainable use, and is generally subject to an enforcement approach of search and seizure despite consistent evidence of the problems and animal harm associated with CITES and national wildlife trade legislation (Zimmerman 2003, Schneider 2008) and the failure of this approach to effectively deal with animal harm problems.

As the previous chapters have shown, there is scope to integrate animal harm into mainstream public policy and in doing so consider the impacts of, and behaviours associated with, animal harm within the broader context of criminal law enforcement and environmental justice initiatives. Green criminology's focus on ecological justice and aspects of species justice provides for critical analysis of the interaction between human behaviour and the environment (Jasper and Nelkin 1992, Garner 1993, Benton 1998, South 1998, White 2007, Beirne 2007) in a way that positively informs criminal justice policy. While green criminology has predominantly discussed animal issues within the context of animal rights and species justice discourse, a green perspective can be applied to the subject of animal harm within the context of current animal law enforcement perspectives to provide a means through which animal law enforcement can be improved and criminal justice policy developed. This should be the case even if animals are not given any greater legal protection by virtue of being given legal rights.

Applying the green criminological perspectives (White 2007) discussed throughout this book and incorporating White's notions of different approaches to environmental harms and species justice (White 2008), this final chapter recommends a policy agenda for dealing with animal harm. In doing so, it recognizes the remoteness of legal rights for animals becoming a reality in either the short or medium term. However, it also argues that legal animal rights are not a prerequisite to addressing animal harm as a criminal justice issue, despite the desirability of such a development (Singer 1975, Wise 2000, Francione and Garner 2010). Indeed several existing animal law regimes provide a mechanism for dealing with animal harm notwithstanding persistent enforcement problems and inconsistency in the level of protection provided. However, the widespread acceptance of the need for anti-cruelty statutes across different jurisdictions (Kean 1998, Radford 2001, Schaffner 2011) and the existence of national and international enforcement initiatives provide a framework through which animal harm can be detected, investigated and prosecuted.

In asserting that animal harm is a global problem, this book proposes an agenda for dealing with animal harm as a mainstream criminal justice problem, recognizing that:

1. animal harm should be considered as social harm;
2. animal harm should be considered as part of an overall criminal career rather than as isolated animal offending;
3. animal law should be enforced via the criminal law and as animal protection law and species justice, rather than as conservation or animal management law;
4. animal harm prevention should be regarded as a public good;
5. animal harm should be integrated into public policy as part of a holistic approach to crime and criminal justice.

This agenda acknowledges Donaldson and Kymlicka's arguments that 'the animal advocacy movement is at an impasse' (2011: 1) but argues that this need not be the case if an appropriate anti-animal harm agenda is adopted within green criminology and environmental justice discourse. The focus on animal rights, even within species justice discourse, is potentially misleading and a distraction from the reality of animal harm as a breach of *current* legislation in many countries. Given the existence of legislative regimes which already outlaw animal harm there are compelling arguments for first improving the enforcement of current legislation (Nurse 2003, White 2008), before developing a further set of legislation that provides for additional animal protection through the granting of legal rights for animals. Thus the anti-animal harm agenda set out above is developed further below as a *precursor* to any suggested new legal animal rights regime. While this does not in any way marginalize or ignore the justifications put forward for legal animal rights, it argues that a system of animal protection in many ways comparable to legal rights already exists but is failing for a variety of reasons, not least an over-reliance on a socio-legal approach rather than regulatory or social action approaches (White 2008). Improvement of this position such that active animal protection becomes integral to the criminal law is not only possible but falls squarely within the remit of green criminology.

Animal Harm as Social Harm

A basic perspective dictating the reduction of animal harm is that man's dominant position in nature provides dominion over animals and thus provides man with a duty of care to protect animals and the environment in which we and they live (Wise 2004, Rollin 2006). There are conflicting perspectives on whether this obligation should be a legal, moral or ethical obligation albeit the legal obligation has been clearly developed in UK legislation and in the anti-cruelty statutes of other countries (Schaffner 2011). Radford explains that over the course of two centuries (leading up to the twenty-first century) animal welfare law in Britain 'has been developed to provide for greater protection for individual animals because society at large and public policy makers have recognized that the way in which each is treated matters' (2001). Nussbaum further argued that 'utilitarianism has contributed more than any other ethical theory to the recognition of animal entitlements. Both Bentham and Mill in their time and Peter Singer in our own have courageously taken the lead in freeing ethical thought from the shackles of a narrow species-centred conception of worth and entitlement' (2004: 302). However while these ethical considerations have greatly informed public debate and have undoubtedly developed the animal rights movement in ways that would have probably have seemed unthinkable when Singer first wrote of the need for animal rights, the reality is that the legal conception of animal rights and of animals as legal persons has yet to be achieved and remains unlikely.

However what has already been achieved is a wide acceptance of the need for anti-cruelty and wildlife trade statutes and their associated enforcement regimes; and it is here that a practical conception of animal rights by virtue of legal protection and the prohibition on specific activities already exists, with potential to be developed further. As a practical measure, anti-cruelty statutes already codify activities that are prohibited in relation to animals. They recognize that inflicting unnecessary harm, cruelty or illegally trading in protected wildlife should not be allowed, and that those which carry out these activities should be punished, in some cases through public law and the imposition of prison sentences (Nurse 2011, Schaffner 2011). CITES, for example, explicitly requires that all nation states which are parties to the convention must put in place a system of enforcement, penalties and sanctions for those who illegally trade in wildlife and provide for public enforcement of CITES provisions (Zimmerman 2003), while various anti-cruelty statutes also impose criminal sanctions on animal abusers and recognize the criminality inherent in their actions. Thus the first step in recognizing that those who commit offences against animals are a threat to wider society and contribute to social harm has already been achieved. The existence of public enforcement bodies such as the US and Canadian Fish and Wildlife Services, dedicated police wildlife crime officers in the UK, the animal police service in the Netherlands, and the various CITES management and enforcement authorities across the globe together with the involvement of Interpol in wildlife trafficking and environmental crime, also shows animal harm to be an issue of public interest and, more importantly, public policy. Further recognition of the social harm caused by animal offending is the next step in developing an effective anti-animal harm agenda.

Animal harm *is* social harm; offenders have negative impacts not just on the animal populations that they adversely affect but also on their wider community, local and national economies, and on social cohesion. Situ and Emmons argue that 'in a variety of cultures, jurisdictions, and eras, criminal law has served as an agent of social control and an instrument of social change' (2000: 20). The criminal law attempts to control unacceptable behaviour through a system of punishment, defining what is illegal and providing for behavioural correction as a system of social control. Much (but admittedly not all) animal harm involves violence towards those less powerful than the perpetrator and thus involves socially undesirable characteristics, sometimes exhibited in public. In addition, the influence of masculinities as a factor in crime (Groombridge 1998) and in animal harm in particular (Nurse 2011) identifies animal harm as an aspect of societal violence inextricably linked to the marginalization of women, children and other vulnerable citizens (Donaldson and Kymlicka 2011). Men who become used to exerting power over the vulnerable, whether non-human animals or other humans, may begin to see power and violence as legitimate tools to be used in their interpersonal relationships and to consider their use of such violence as an acceptable social norm. Criminal justice generally seeks to minimize violence within society on the grounds that exposure to violence is harmful and the presence of violence in society usually leads to an escalation beyond its original focus (Levi 1994, Shepherd and Lisles 1998). Thus violence towards animals and the deliberate inflicting of cruelty represents a social harm that should be controlled as part of society's overall aim of reducing violence and its harmful effects.

Animal harm's social harm effects also extend to the impact on both the immediate and wider community. Companion animals are now an integral part of most human societies and are protected as such (Budiansky 1999, Schaffner 2011) while attachment to animals is widely recognized as having beneficial or therapeutic effects (Crawford et al. 2006, Barker et al. 2010). Animal harm involving cruelty is therefore capable of causing great distress to a range of people in society beyond those immediately involved (Bekoff 2007) and of contributing to societal anxiety about the compassionate nature of society, inherent levels of cruelty in society and the possibility of escalating violence and a lack of compassion (Franklin 2005). In respect of wildlife, the negative impact of animal harm on wildlife populations by hastening the extinction of various species in the wild prevents future generations from viewing wild animal populations and arguably conflicts with the right to enjoy the environment (Stookes 2003, Stech 2010). In addition, wildlife trade has a negative impact on ecosystems which, in some cases, has the potential effect of causing ecological damage that may not be felt for several years. Animal harm thus has a negative effect on the social environment of future generations and represents a long lasting form of social harm that extends beyond short-term impacts to potential long-term environmental and social impacts (White 2008).

While discussion of the benefits of animal welfare to society can be found throughout the animal welfare and animal rights literature, animal harm in its widest sense (as discussed by this book) has negative consequences for society and represents a significant form of social harm. At the heart of arguments concerning animal welfare are perceptions that society increasingly considers animal welfare to be important and a matter of public concern; but while utilitarianism argues that human interests and animal interests coincide, arguably it is in the direct area of protecting human interests that controlling animal harm becomes most important. The negative consequences of some aspects of animal harm include direct human harm and thus the anti-animal harm agenda needs to consider animal harm not in the isolated, yet worthy, context of legal animal rights, but as a gateway to further human harm.

Animal Harm and Criminal Careers

Theorists from different perspectives within animal rights debates have identified that the reduction of animal cruelty, prevention of animal abuse and provision of equal consideration for animals and humans alike benefits society by creating a society that is increasingly cruelty free and where cruelty towards both non-human animals and humans is less likely to occur and is not tolerated when it does. White (2008) identifies that the response to environmental and ecological problems (including species justice concerns) varies according to the nature of the harm being caused. Control theory arguments suggest that crime can be prevented due to the formal and informal controls that operate within a community, so that crime which harms the community is not tolerated and the community actively engages with law enforcement agencies to prevent crime (Lea and Young 1993, Peelo and Soothill 2005). Criminologists and law enforcement professionals are increasingly becoming interested in animal welfare issues (specifically animal abuse and animal cruelty) as a potential risk factor in violence towards humans and as a means of identifying future offenders (Linzey 2009). A variety of studies have identified that those who commit interpersonal violence are more likely to have previously abused animals (see Chapters 3, 4 and 9). The link between animal abuse and interpersonal violence has been accepted in the United States by the FBI, Department of Justice and social welfare agencies, so that in some states, professional agencies have begun to intervene with juvenile animal abusers on the grounds that those who abuse animals are more likely to escalate to interpersonal violence towards human. Increasingly the link is also becoming accepted within the UK and other jurisdictions; in 2001 the RSPCA and NSPCC held their first joint conference in over 100 years to explore the links between child abuse and animal abuse, and subsequently the *First Strike Scotland* campaign was initiated to explore and address the links between animal abuse and family violence. In 2003 the UK's Royal College of Veterinary Surgeons provided guidance for vets on reporting animal abuse, and in 2009 Sussex Academic Press published a book on the links between animal abuse and violence towards humans following an international multi-disciplinary conference on the subject held at the Oxford Centre for Animal Ethics in 2007 (Linzey 2009). Criminal justice and social welfare agency intervention with animal abusers thus provides the tangible benefit of potentially protecting the public from violent offenders and the harmful effects of crime. While this is currently an intangible benefit due to the lack of co-ordinated intervention or policy initiatives within the UK, there is considerable evidence that animal abuse is one of the risk factors in serious crime which should be considered in dangerousness assessments and crime prevention (Brantley et al. 2009).

As a proposal for an anti-animal harm green criminological agenda, therefore, this book argues that animal harm should be considered as part of a criminal career along a continuum of offending that may begin with animals and end up with humans. But it may also be either an indication of other criminality and antisocial behaviours, or a reaction to other forms of crime and antisocial behaviour such that the offender may be involved in other forms of crime against their will or may be reacting to their own abuse by harming those more vulnerable than themselves. Definitions of criminality vary according to the ideological, theoretical and disciplinary perspectives of academic theorists, theologians, social scientists, criminologists and animal rights activists. However, analysis of the varied types of offending involved in animal harm illustrates that animal offenders' do not all share the same motivations or operate within similar communities or control mechanisms. Chapter 2 defines animal harm as being more complex than just cruelty or commercial trading in animals, while Chapter 3 develops models that show the different types of offender, discussing five different types and the motivations of each based on research analysis of literature, the views of NGOs and activists and extensive assessment of case and court records. Chapter 8 further identifies that within the broad description of organized crime there are, in fact, different types of offender involved in wildlife trafficking and a range of motivations and behaviours involved. This being the case there is little point in treating all animal harm offenders as if they were the same. Indeed, one conclusion that can be drawn from investigating the characteristics of animal harm is that a blanket animal harm policy, legislative or law enforcement approach based on the presumption of all animal harm as being rational choice offending is unlikely to be successful. The enforcement regime for animal harm thus needs to be adapted at both an international and national level to provide for appropriate action that fits the circumstances of the offender and allows the specific nature of the offence to be taken into account. In addition, there is an urgent need to view animal harm as part of an overall criminal career rather than solely as an isolated environmental or animal rights/welfare issue.

The varied nature of animal harm means that for some offenders their behaviour should be evaluated to determine the extent to which their behaviour constitutes part of an overall criminal career. The importance of animal harm to an offender's other criminal activity or their tendency towards anti-social or other criminal behaviour provides a means through which future offending or at least risk of offending can be assessed. An enforcement and rehabilitative approach that considers specific offender types should be at the core of the criminological and public policy approach which addresses animal harm. White identifies clear 'social differences in the ability of the powerful, in relation to the less powerful, to protect and defend their interests' (2008: 194). He identifies that the powerful can frustrate investigations, manipulate evidence and forestall prosecution by appearing to comply with record-keeping procedures. Thus prosecution of environmental offences committed by corporations becomes difficult while small businesses and individuals become the focus of state intervention. This book argues that state intervention and prosecution of animal harm needs to recognize the varied nature of both individual and corporate animal harm, tailoring its response accordingly. Chapter 3 provided preliminary conclusions on dealing with the different types of animal offender identified as being involved in animal harm. South and Wyatt's (2011) typology of wildlife trade offenders (see Chapter 8) complements Chapter 3's offender models and provides further explanation of the varied nature of offending, particularly by organized groups. Thus the perspectives on dealing with offenders can be developed further as follows.

For **traditional criminals** financial penalties may work as a means of negating any benefit they derive from their activity but the same approach is unlikely to work with economic criminals or stress criminals. An argument can also be made that increased sentencing and use of prison has been unsuccessful in mainstream criminal justice (Wilson 1985) and so the evidence that it will be effective in reducing or prevent animal harm is lacking. For traditional criminals, greater efforts should be made to attempt situational crime prevention, making the physical cost of committing the crime prohibitive as well as increasing the actual cost and removing the perception that their distinct form of animal harm may be seen as a soft option. South and Wyatt (2011) indicate that for some offenders wildlife trafficking is an incidental or secondary business and that crimes are committed only where specific opportunities to do so arise. Increasing the cost of pursuing such opportunities together with eliminating minor opportunities provides a means through which the casual or secondary offender might be prevented from committing wildlife crime where this is not integral to their business. However, there is also a clear link with the more serious forms of organized crime where major wildlife trafficking operations are also involved in people or drug trafficking and use violence, intimidation and interference in legitimate government institutions as tools to facilitate their business. Thus the law enforcement approach needs to be compatible with that used in other forms of organized crime and reflect the seriousness of this particular aspect of animal harm, its links to other forms of crime and its transnational nature and association with crimes of violence and disregard for both law enforcement and the animals it uses as commodities. Increased integration of this form of crime into the criminological mainstream is thus a necessity.

For **economic criminals**, the source of their offending behaviour is their employment and so any approach to these offenders must include pressure on and penalties for the employer as well as action which prevents them from continuing with employment that provides opportunities for animal harm or is related to animals whether directly or indirectly. Legislative regimes may also require amendment to provide for culpability of employers for the actions of their staff. Accepting the notion of much environmental crime as crimes of the powerful (Pearce and Tombs 1998, Tombs and Whyte 2003, Walters 2007, White 2008) there is scope to ensure that abuses of power by employers that force their staff to either cut corners on welfare, health and safety and human animal handling and despatch processes, causing animal harm in the process, are punished. There is scope also to make the economic costs of ignoring or being negligent of the realities of environmental and animal law compliance costly to businesses committing such animal harm. This could be achieved either through implementing a restorative regime that routinely requires offenders to provide for and meet the costs of redress for the animal harm that they have caused or through increasing the stigma attached to animal harm as serious crime. The difficulty in dealing with economic criminality is currently exhibited by the failure of environmental justice regimes to effectively impose penalties or preventative measures. Situ and Emmons identify that only a small proportion of environmental violations are prosecuted and that fines, which can be incorporated into an economic offender's operating budget or be paid by an employer, tend to dominate corporate wrongdoing. Thus in the case of animal harm committed by an employee there remain difficulties not only in securing convictions and identifying the responsible individual (i.e. whether employee or corporation) but also in providing an appropriate penalty. Fortney (2003) and White (2008) suggest that for corporation offending an enforcement approach based on firm-type rather than offence committed should be introduced with particular attention paid to fine-multiples for repeat offenders. White also suggests a combination of criminal, alternative sentencing options and civil penalties being used. Thus as a practical means of dealing with these offenders any conviction for animal harm offences should carry with it the threat of being banned from animal related employment for those involved in the countryside, game rearing, fieldsports or animal trading industries as well as significant penalties for the employer.[1]

---

1 Bans exist in some legislation so that pet store owners, for example, who are convicted of cruelty offences, can be banned from running such a business in the future. But these provisions are not uniformly applied across different jurisdictions and in some cases can be easily bypassed by registering a business in a family member's name.

For the masculinities offender, the effectiveness of prison or high fines is also questionable. For these offenders, their crimes are situated in notions of what it means to be male and the associated stereotypical masculine behaviours that are integral to their identity. Thus criminalization through minor criminal measures like the UK's ASBO scheme, community service, or other lesser criminal penalties may simply reinforce the perception of their masculinity and any perceived male status which is linked to their offending. However, the importance of recognizing the role of masculinities and identification with a self-image that is reinforced by societal condemnation of their behaviour is important.

Masculinities offenders who commit their crimes within the home and intimate relationships require both a situational crime prevention approach and a social one. Social work intervention at an earlier age, e.g. when domestic animal abuse is being committed or when signs of antisocial behaviour begin to manifest, are important and may prevent young male offenders from escalating into serious offenders at a later stage. However, given the 'group' nature of much offending and the association of like-minded individuals in, for example, dog-fighting rings, a law enforcement approach that embraces the 'serious crime' techniques of surveillance and infiltration may be essential in order to detect and gather evidence of some crimes (Hawley 1993, Saunders 2001). There is, however, a need to also consider rehabilitation alongside law enforcement approaches. Masculinities offenders frequently commit their animal offending as part of a continuum of offending and where the causes of their behaviour are not addressed they may well simply go on to commit interpersonal violence or indeed may already be doing so (Linzey 2009). Thus, where the causes of their animal harm are not addressed it is likely that not only will they continue to offend when given an opportunity to do so even if apprehended and sentenced (Cuppleditch and Evans 2005), but their abuse of others may well go undetected or escalate within the home. Thus a wider range of offending may occur. There are, however, potential problems in dealing with a group of offenders that already see themselves as marginalized, or misunderstood by society and which is resistant to law enforcement intervention in its activities. The social approach adopted with other delinquent groups such as youth offenders (Utting 1996) and which emphasize identification of risk factors and development of supportive environments and disrupting the negative impacts of high risk peer groups has potential for success but requires early intervention of a type only sporadically attempted in animal abuse enforcement (Clawson 2009).

Hobby offenders as a group may be the most difficult offenders to deal with. The drive to collect and the obsessive behaviour of such offenders cannot easily be overcome by fines and prison sentences which could even strengthen the desire to commit offences by activating the drive to replace lost items such as a confiscated egg collection or collection of taxidermied animals. While prevention and detection of crimes should continue to be employed for these offenders, treatment to address the issues of collecting as well as education in the effects of animal harm, considering both the societal costs of animal harm and the impact on animal populations, should be considered. As Chapter 3 identifies, collecting can become an obsession, thus some hobby offenders are themselves victims of their compulsion, committing animal harm in the home or the wild as a result of this. Again, a strong situational crime prevention element could be attempted (at least in the case of wild animal hobby offending) and sentencing provisions need to contain measures that will prevent future offending, for example by imposing bans on keeping animals or prohibitions on visiting wildlife sites, as well as measures that attempt to address the causes of these crimes.

For **stress offenders**, there is a need to situate their offending within the context of the harm being caused to them. In particular, their offending needs to be seen in the context of the wider sources of distress or abuse within their family or social environment that may be contribute to their distress and any policy response may need to also consider other victims within the environment. In the case of animal hoarders, for example (Chapter 4), their crimes are often indicative of personal issues such as stress, unresolved personal issues or mental illness such that an individual unwittingly commits animal harm. Stress offenders are victims of crime as much as they are perpetrators of animal crime and like other abused individuals who go on to themselves commit abuse (Ascione 2001) there is a need for a criminal justice and therapeutic response that identifies the cause of their activities and provides a means for dealing with it.

Central to the notion of animal harm as part of a criminal career is active consideration of the extent to which animal harm is linked to other forms of offending. While the link between animal abuse and violence towards humans is becoming established within criminological discourse (Linzey 2009) the link between animal harm and other forms of offending is not yet fully realized in criminal justice policy. In part this is due to animal harm's location within the environmental or animal welfare arena of policy rather than it being a core concern of justice departments. As a result, animal harm remains marginalized within criminal justice policy notwithstanding the efforts of criminologists and activists to raise its profile as an area of concern and the emergence of green criminology as a recognized area of study (South 1998, Beirne and South 2008, White 2008). The next step in developing the anti-animal harm agenda to provide for effective animal harm policy and enforcement is to locate animal harm within the remit of the criminal law and to see its importance recognized by justice departments as a core criminal justice issue.

Animal Law as Criminal Law

The reality of animal harm is that much of its enforcement activity takes place outside of mainstream criminal justice, given that the focus of much animal law is based on animal management or control, property rights, or anti-cruelty as an animal welfare issue rather than a species justice one (Nurse 2011, Schaffner 2011). As a result, enforcers and activists are frequently in the position of trying to apply criminal law principles to legislation not designed for that purpose, even where animal law forms part of a state's criminal code. While there are notable exceptions, particularly in US law which contains criminal penalties alongside civil ones or animal crimes which are intended to be subject to federal enforcement such as the *Marine Mammal Protection Act of 1972* (see Chapter 6), much animal law is not intended as criminal law and so fails to adequately deal with the types of animal harm criminality discussed throughout this book.

In addition animal harm offences are poorly enforced with a lack of dedicated resources for the task being reported in a variety of jurisdictions (Lowther et al. 2002, Nurse 2003, Zimmerman 2003, Damania et al. 2008). Indeed in the UK the majority of wildlife crime law enforcement activity takes place on a voluntary basis (Kirkwood 1994, Nurse 2003, 2011) so that many of the problems that exist are due to the lack of dedicated resources and a co-ordinated enforcement regime. Central to this problem is the enduring perception among policymakers and governments that animal harm is an environmental issue (wildlife crime) or property or ethics issue (animal abuse) rather than a criminal justice one. Thus, the efforts of many dedicated professionals notwithstanding, a fundamental problem exists in that animal harm is generally not seen as a national policing or criminal justice priority in many jurisdictions and this impacts on the resources available for law enforcement, educational or crime prevention measures and the manner in which investigations are conducted and any penalties are applied. The location of wildlife crime within the remit of DEFRA, the UK's Environment Department, rather than the Ministry of Justice or Home Office (who have responsibility for crime and criminal justice), is a factor from which it can be concluded that UK police chiefs are not directed to allocate resources to animal harm and will only do so where an individual chief constable considers it necessary to do so or where it is considered to be politically expedient to do so for that force. In the absence of a federal investigations and prosecutions unit like the US Fish and Wildlife Service, this means that UK wildlife law enforcement is largely ad hoc and subject to different levels of enforcement and resource allocation dependent on the priorities existing in different parts of the UK. However, even where dedicated enforcement or an appropriate regulatory regime is provided for, it may be subject to political control such that the efforts of environmental organizations may be required to intervene to ensure appropriate protection is provided.[2]

Separate from the resource issue is the specialist knowledge required to carry out animal harm investigations and the lack of this knowledge among mainstream justice professionals. White identifies that for many police, dealing with environmental (and animal) crime is 'basically dealing with the unknown' (2008: 197). While the US Fish and Wildlife Service employs specialist investigators, such knowledge is unevenly distributed across enforcers with a lack of centralized expertise in animal harm issues among enforcers in many jurisdictions.

---

2   See, for example, lawsuits filed by bodies such as Defenders of Wildlife to force the US Fish and Wildlife Service to take appropriate action to protect rare species under the US *Endangered Species Act 1973*.

For example in discussing the enforcement problems facing tiger anti-poaching policy Damania et al. commented:

> Wildlife agencies frequently lack the very basic resources needed for effective management – personnel, communication equipment, and transport – while the legal institutions needed to convict offenders are often overstretched and under resourced. Economic pressures have overwhelmed the virtuous intent of policy. (2008: 2)

This picture is replicated across the animal harm policy and enforcement world. Although enforcers who remain in post for long enough will inevitably develop a level of expertise, the reality is often that many statutory enforcement agencies continue to rely on the expertise of NGOs and others. In some cases this is because statutory bodies assigned animal harm duties are enforcement specialists and not animal crime (or law) professionals. In such cases there is a need for centralized resources to be made available for statutory agencies in the fields of animal identification, animal handling, scientific and forensic analysis, animal habitats, populations and behaviours and threats to wildlife legislation and conservation priorities. Often such services are only provided where NGOs such as the ASPCA, RSPB or RSPCA (and their equivalents in other countries) are available or where specialist animal investigators are able to work alongside mainstream criminal justice agencies. In other cases, enforcers are the conservation bodies who, while expert in conservation and animal management techniques, simply lack appropriate criminal justice enforcement skills. Damania et al. (2008) and others have also identified that conservation and animal management bodies lack appropriate resources for their enforcement activities while they may have them for conservation activities, and are often working in isolation of other law enforcement activities despite the fact that the criminality involved in the wildlife trade aspects of animal harm 'transcends countries and cannot be resolved by unilateral national actions' (2008: 3). As a result, co-ordinated action that recognizes the transnational elements of the animal harm involved is required.

The voluntary and 'fringe' nature of animal harm enforcement means that resources to detect, investigate and prosecute offences are scarce and vary between different aspects of animal harm, jurisdictions and even species. Given this fact it is unrealistic to expect all crimes to be given the same level of attention by the statutory agencies and in any case it is perhaps not desirable that they should do. There should, thus, be a system for prioritizing enforcement action on animal harm so that enforcement resources are not expended on 'minor crimes' or those for which there is no immediate threat to the target species where other mechanisms might be used to deal with the immediate problem. A model exists for this in road traffic legislation where the use of on-the-spot fines/fixed penalty notices and the use of speed cameras has reduced the need for lengthy detection, investigation and sentencing procedures. Such a model could be adapted for certain animal harm offences, for example fixed penalty notices for registration or technical offences (for example administrative breaches of documentation such as a failure to properly complete the required returns on the number of CITES species sold, where no other offence has been committed and no actual injury to animals is present or likely). While such a notion may offend some notions of species justice, international wildlife legislation generally makes a distinction between 'specially protected' wildlife and others (CITES listed species are grouped according to their conservation status and the perceived level of threat from trade as are different species of whales and cetaceans under the *International Whaling Convention*) so that a higher level of protection is afforded to endangered species than the 'ordinary' level of protection provided to other species. This is also replicated in national legislation so that the species can go on or off the 'endangered list' of the US *Endangered Species Act 1973* or the relevant schedules to the UK's *Wildlife and Countryside Act 1981*. Enforcement priorities should be developed along these lines so that the primary enforcement activity is directed towards the more threatened species and more serious types of offence, or those offences with more serious social consequences. Enforcement action also needs to be proactive rather than reactive as currently a disproportionate amount of animal harm enforcement attention is reactively directed at individual wildlife traders and animal abusers rather than at preventative or situational crime measures or at the major wildlife traders and organized gangs involved in the wildlife trade (South and Wyatt 2011).

In relation to wildlife trade Damania et al. suggest that 'on the supply side, immediate actions are needed to break the supply chain by preventing poaching and through global efforts to control cross-border trafficking' (2008: 4). Where offenders have been able to take advantage of jurisdictional differences or cross-jurisdictional issues to evade prosecution and enforcement, the co-operation of states to address their shared problems of animal harm may be required, including action at an international level that recognizes the failure of states to deal with animal harm as a global issues and also recognizes the international nature of the organized crime involved. In addition to addressing the supply side there is also a need for 'vigorous efforts to tackle the root cause of the problem – the demand' (Damania et al. 2008: 4). While NGOs such as WWF and PETA are heavily involved in action aimed at encouraging tourists not to buy products (illegally) made from animals, and to especially avoid products made from endangered species, the demand for live animals for falconry, in zoos, circuses, safari parks and elsewhere persists. Where large sums can be made in providing animals as commodities, traders will always seek to fulfil that demand even where they need to transcend legislation and regulatory regimes to do so.

In the case of animal cruelty, the problem is not one of demand as much as it is desire. As previous chapters identify, exercising control over animals and vulnerable family members is often an expression of power where animals, and especially companion animals, are simply a tool to be used by offenders in a variety of ways. Such activities should clearly be brought within the remit of criminal law so that rather than animal cruelty and other forms of animal harm being dealt with as animal law offences they are considered to be criminal law ones and explicitly treat the offender within the remit of the criminal law. Some measures to do so already exist in US and UK legislation as well as in other jurisdictions and others are being proposed. At time of writing in 2012, Michigan's House Judiciary Committee is considering a bill to introduce an animal abuse registry in Michigan. If passed, the bill (H.B. 5403) would require convicted animal abusers to register with state law enforcement, paying a $50 fee to do so. This proposal is complemented by H.B. 5402 which would require shelters and pet stores to consult the registry before allowing individuals on the register to adopt or buy cats, dogs and ferrets. UK law already allows for those convicted of certain animal offences to be banned from owning animals for a period of up to seven years subject to the discretion of the courts. Such provisions attach the stigma of criminal conviction to animal abuse and crucially link it to future action in a way that considers past animal harm as relevant to the possibility of future offending, and explicitly considers the possibility of animal harm as being part of an overall criminal profile rather than as an isolated activity.

This book has considered the evidence of the link between animal abuse and other forms of interpersonal violence. While it cannot be said that all those involved in animal harm are violent offenders, the evidence is that some forms of animal harm crime contain a violent element which involves not only violence towards the target animal but violence towards others. Animal harm sentencing policy should reflect this, taking into account the need to protect vulnerable individuals, domestic animals and spouses who may come into contact with such offenders. In the United States, such offences are increasingly seen as an indicator of future violent behaviour and evidence of past animal abuse can be a factor in sentencing decisions. Such considerations are not yet the norm in all jurisdictions but combined with measures to ensure that all animal harm incidents are appropriately recorded by criminal justice agencies one recommendation for developing an appropriate animal harm criminal justice agenda is that the recording of all animal harm incidents (wildlife crimes and animal abuse) should take place as an indicator of possible future offending. Public policy should also consider measures to divert individuals from animal harm and to rehabilitate particularly those offenders involved in the more violent forms of animal harm so that they do not escalate their behaviour towards human violence. In doing so, animal harm policy may be able to achieve additional public benefits beyond those that arguably already exist.

Animal Harm and the Public Good

A number of jurisdictions recognize the public benefit of having good standards of animal welfare and thus by implication consider animal welfare to be a public good. By extension, measures to address animal harm and to eliminate it by effective enforcement of animal laws could also constitute a public good. Notwithstanding continuing debates around the legal personhood of animals and legal animal rights, public policy that positively provides for the elimination of animal harm has the potential to achieve public benefits.

Changes in the importance afforded to animal welfare and animal protection reflect not just the growth and influence of a protectionist animal welfare movement but growing acceptance of the 'public benefit' served by animal welfare. For example the public benefit 'test' is an important factor in defining charitable activity in UK charity law.[3] The test generally consists of two strands: the activity must be of a public character and be of some benefit to the public generally. The latter strand requires that there must be some benefit to public beneficiaries (i.e. the wider public) rather than favouring a recipient on the basis of a private, professional or other relationship. For an animal welfare charity to meet the public benefit 'test', therefore, its actions must extend beyond its membership or traditional supporter base.

The UK courts have long established that a public benefit derives from animal welfare by virtue of the moral improvement derived from the promotion of feelings of kindness towards animals. The UK High Court in *Re Wedgwood, Allen v. Wedgwood [1915]1 CH 113* stated that a gift held for the benefit of the protection of animals provided public benefit to the wider community through the promotion of 'feelings of humanity and morality'. English courts have further developed the tests of public benefit in relation to animal welfare concluding that animal welfare is a legitimate charitable purpose. In *Wedgwood*, the Master of the Rolls had accepted that a trust that promoted public morality by checking the innate tendency towards cruelty to animals was a charitable purpose. The Court accepted that cruelty to animals was degrading to man and thus it was beneficial to society to teach justice and fair treatment towards animals. While this relates to a distinct aspect of UK law, and to satisfy the requirements of charity law the activities of an animal welfare charity would need to fall within a category specified in the relevant charities legislation, in essence the Court provided legal backing for the view that animal cruelty is harmful to society and eliminating such activities constitutes a public good. However what is regarded as charitable or for the public good is inextricably linked to prevailing social values and contemporary cultural norms. The UK's *Charities Act 2006* specifies 'the advancement of animal welfare' as a charitable purpose, subject to the charities concerned being able to meet the public benefit criteria contained within the legislation. As earlier chapters of this book indicate, criminologists (e.g. Benton 1998, Beirne 1999, White 2007) have also recognized the link between environmental and animal protection laws and the development or improvement of society. Criminological research indicates a link between animal cruelty and violence towards non-human animals

---

3   The UK's legal framework provides that charities must be registered with a regulatory body called the Charity Commission and that certain criteria must be met before a body can lawfully call itself a charity. One such criterion is that the charity must specify its charitable purpose according to a predetermined set of criteria. Advancing animal welfare is a permissible category.

and violence towards humans. Promoting good standards of animal protection and welfare and preventing animal harm thus benefits society not only by preventing possible violence towards humans, but also in protecting and improving society by improving the way we protect and live in harmony with the environment and create a strongly institutionalized protection of universal civil liberties.

The definition of the 'advancement of animal welfare' in the UK's *Charities Act 2006* also allows for discussion of the scope of what constitutes a public benefit in relation to animal harm. The *Charities Act 2006*'s animal welfare definition includes any purpose directed towards the prevention or suppression of cruelty, or the prevention or relief of suffering by animals. This broad definition thus encompasses not just the 'common sense' view of animal welfare (e.g. adopting minimum welfare standards for farm animals or other livestock) but also the prevention of cruelty towards wild and domestic animals, the investigation of animal cruelty offences, and enforcement of animal welfare and wildlife legislation. Arguably most action aimed at the majority of animal harm activities which involve cruelty or suffering, and are discussed within this book, would be caught by this definition, with the exception of political activity which is specifically exempted under UK law owing to the historical prohibition on political bodies also being charitable ones. However, the legislative and campaigning activities of such US bodies as Defenders of Wildlife or Earthjustice, if applied to the UK setting, would fall within this definition and thus a body such as the RSPCA, which investigates and prosecutes a range of animal harm activities, is a charity able to operate under the animal welfare category, and does so. This model could, therefore, be adapted to other jurisdictions.

The UK has developed its animal welfare legislation over 200 years, culminating in the *Animal Welfare Act 2006* and associated codes of practice which actively provides for the protection of companion animals and promotion of good standards of animal welfare. Animal welfare is also a concern for the EU such that there are European Directives on animal welfare harmonizing animal welfare across the EU's 27 member states. Animal welfare is thus now accepted as an issue on which governments legislate in the public interest and, as the UK's case law on charitable gifts demonstrates, promoting animal welfare is considered a public good through the promotion of feelings of humanity and morality. The prevailing social conditions in the UK are, thus, those in which since at least the early twentieth century and animal welfare's recognition as being charitable in *Re Wedgwood, Allen v. Wedgwood [1915] 1 CH 113*, the UK courts have accepted the benefit to society from animal welfare; this social context has been enhanced rather than diminished through the further development of animal welfare law and the growth and political acceptance of the animal welfare movement.

As Jasper (1997) observed, some NGOs occupy a position within the political and social establishment which allows them to positively engage with the political realities of public policy life. In the case of the major US environmental and animal protection bodies such as the ALDF, Earthjustice and Defenders of Wildlife who (among others) litigate on behalf of animals and the environment and have achieved a political legitimacy within the legislative and judicial arenas, their ability to challenge the law and government policy and litigate against animal harm is considerable when compared to the restrictions placed on their UK colleagues by their legal system. With such bodies campaigning, developing policy and litigating regularly on their respective sides of the Atlantic with considerable public support, the promotion of animal welfare thus satisfies widespread public concern and broad social interests that go beyond a specialist interest group.

The existence of anti-cruelty statutes in a range of jurisdictions reflects the acceptance by contemporary governments and legislatures that they should (and indeed must) legislate to either improve animal protection to achieve higher levels of animal welfare, or do so to punish excessive animal cruelty. There is, thus, scope for legislators and policymakers to benefit society through promoting animal protection and the elimination of animal harm as a core part of public policy. For example, good standards of animal welfare in livestock and the food industry benefit consumers wishing to buy ethically sourced goods by providing them with the choice to buy according to their tastes and conscience, the psychological well-being that arises from doing so, and knowing that in their buying choices they have not contributed to animal cruelty or abuse. There are also possible health benefits from buying goods with reduced levels of pathogens and chemicals. While such benefits may be difficult to measure, the established market share for such foods indicates that there is sufficient public interest that needs to be satisfied and positively embracing animal welfare meets this need. The question of what constitutes a 'sufficient' proportion of the community to achieve this form of tangible benefit is one that may need to be determined by each jurisdiction. Public benefit arising from addressing animal harm may well be different in the United States, Canada and the UK and will undoubtedly be subject to conflicting measurements across the different states of the EU according to cultural imperatives.

O'Halloran (2000) explains that the 'public benefit test' in UK charity law requires that 'it must be both of a public character and be of some benefit to the public generally' and that in theory the test offers a simple yardstick for identifying, measuring and comparing charitable activity. However in practice applying the test to animal harm across different jurisdictions presents some problems. Legislative definitions (such as that in the *Charities Act 2006*), while perhaps being a prerequisite for considering certain activities to be beneficial, may not *by themselves* be taken as evidence that a particular activity is for the public benefit. Thus while species justice considerations would contend that eliminating animal harm or reducing animal suffering are clearly in the interests of society (Singer 1975, Rollin 2006), O'Halloran explains that the UK charity law test defines an activity as being charitable or not relative to 'contemporary social circumstances' (2000). Thus the legal conception of the benefits from reducing animal harm differ from ethical conceptions and this implies that the same animal welfare activity may acquire or lose charitable status dependent on the prevailing social circumstances within a country or between countries. O'Halloran also explains that 'another more specific problem is that jurisdictional differences exist in relation to the application of this test: a difference between subjective and objective judicial approaches; and between judicial and legislative determination' (2000). The difficulty in defining the public benefit of an animal harm control measure therefore may be in *proving* that the measure benefits the public according to the judicial determination applied to a particular instance. While there are compelling arguments for reducing or eliminating animal harm both in terms of reducing the suffering, exploitation and negative impact on animal populations and in reducing the negative impacts on human societies, not all animal harm control activities will demonstrably provide both a public benefit and serve the public good in a manner that passes judicial scrutiny.

However, public benefits can be direct and/or tangible benefits, or can be intangible or indirect and thus there is a wider consideration to be applied to reducing animal harm. For intangible benefits a common understanding that there is a benefit, perhaps derived from prevailing public opinion, could suffice. This raises the possibility of only commonly accepted benefits being accepted as 'intangible' benefits and the courts having to clarify the matter where there is dispute. In UK law, guidance from the UK's Charity Commission helps to assess the elements involved in the (charitable) public benefit test. The guidance clarifies that:

- a benefit may be recognized where it is capable of having demonstrable effect and is regarded as such by the law;
- the benefit need not be obvious (but its existence should be capable of being determined by a court if need be);
- the form of the benefit can take many different shapes and forms; and
- what is capable of being recognized as a benefit must be assessed in light of modern conditions.

This final condition dictates that in determining the public benefit of a particular charitable activity account should be taken of the current general law, social habits and social and economic circumstances. The Foveaux case (referred to in Chapter 2) clarified that, for example, the anti-vivisection cause is not always accepted as being charitable and thus it would not always be for the public good to pursue such a policy. However, contemporary circumstances are such that an activity like wildlife trafficking is now a matter of public concern allowing anti-animal harm activity aimed at reducing or eliminating wildlife trafficking through campaigning, education and direct law enforcement to be seen as being of public benefit. Similarly in the context of species decline and increased threats to wild animals' survival, Defenders of Wildlife's wolf protection initiative might meet public good criteria. The Charity Commission guidance also clarifies that a benefit cannot be recognized where the overall or net benefit cannot be established, where the benefit relies on the intention, opinions or beliefs of the charity where there is no prospect of proof of evidence being laid before the court and also for those activities which simply may be of some benefit to the community. The Charity Commission's recent assessment guidance suggests that benefits available to the general public (whether or not they actually take them up) are public benefits so that a charity that freely provides, for example, educational material for all members of the public or provides an animal rescue service available to all members of the public would be providing a (tangible) benefit to the public.[4]

However, geographically restrictive animal welfare organizations or those that provide their services to only part of the community or a specified subsection (e.g. members only) within a state may find it difficult to demonstrate the 'public' benefit. Geographical restrictions can, however, be overcome by making information and advice publicly available in the way that many NGOs do by using the Internet and making their publications, campaigning material and expertise available to supporters in other countries and encouraging supporters across the globe to share in the benefits of their activities.

While this discussion of the public good and public benefits from reducing animal harm is based on a discussion of UK charity law, it provides a basis on which anti-animal harm policy might be developed as a public good within public policy. From a common sense point of view, the definition of the 'advancement of animal welfare' contained within the *Charities Act 2006* seems to incorporate an acceptable definition of animal welfare activities carried out by mainstream animal welfare charities like the RSPCA and SSPCA in the UK and the ASPCA (and state equivalents) and the HSUS in the United States. Mainstream animal welfare charities are generally involved in educational and campaigning work to enhance public awareness of animal welfare issues, promote humane treatment of animals and reduce animal harm. Such a definition also incorporates practical work such charities are engaged in, aimed at preventing the suffering of animals, for example animal cruelty investigative work and the provision of rescue and treatment services for suffering animals and the victims of cruelty or neglect. In keeping with this book's definition of animal harm the prosecution of animal abusers would meet the definition due to the deterrent effect generally relied upon by enforcers within the criminal justice system. Detecting and prosecuting animal abusers has the dual benefit of preventing further offending by the individual offender by punishing him for his actions, and the wider benefit of deterring other members of the public by publicizing the likelihood of apprehension and the penalties for offences. There is also the further benefit of identifying offenders likely to escalate to interpersonal violence which could serve the benefit of protecting the public. The availability of public helplines, web addresses and email reporting points for members of the public to use in reporting animal harm may help to demonstrate that an animal welfare charity is providing a public service.

UK courts have accepted that the feeling of goodwill generated by reducing animal cruelty is a charitable purpose and benefits the community. Thus, animal

---

4   See for example Charity Commission (2009), where the Commission indicated that the provision of services open to all the public met the aim of advancing the Buddhist faith.

welfare charities that make their educational, information and animal rescue or treatment services available to all are likely to 'pass' the UK's public benefit test and be able to demonstrate that their anti-animal harm activities are a public good. While legislative differences do not guarantee that this perspective will easily translate to other jurisdictions this serves as a basis on which an anti-animal harm policy agenda can seek to have animal harm integrated into public policy, separate from the issue of animal rights.

Some aspects of public policy already accept this. In the UK, DEFRA's consideration of farm animal welfare (McInerney 2004) concluded that animal welfare was an externality (an economic value not considered by normal market processes) but considered that people not involved in the production or consumption of a livestock product can nevertheless feel unease (a loss of benefit) if animals are not treated well. Debates about the public good (whereby everybody is potentially affected) are generally accepted as a role for government policy. McInerney's report for DEFRA suggested that:

> There is a (conceptual) scale on which the level of animal welfare can be measured. Below a certain point on this scale the welfare outcomes would be regarded as totally inconsistent with the ethical values of a civilized society, and all reasonable people would feel a distinct loss of benefit if farm animals were treated in such fashion. The element of animal welfare up to this threshold is therefore in the nature of a 'public good', a benefit that all wish to gain and government policy has a responsibility to ensure. At the upper end of the scale are levels of animal welfare that only a small minority of people would feel are important; the economic value attached to such increments in welfare can be treated as a private good which government has no responsibility to provide. (McInerney 2004)

While McInerney did not conclude that good standards of animal welfare *must* be applied across the board, he did conclude that 'because animal welfare is evidently a "public good" externality there is an obvious role for government policy in establishing and enforcing standards' (2004). There is a question mark over how widely animal welfare concerns are felt such that while some individuals are conscious of welfare characteristics in their food purchases, and collectively society looks to government to protect their concerns by ensuring adequate standards are enforced in livestock agriculture, there may be some who do not accept that they should (or indeed can afford to) pay a premium for higher standards of animal welfare in food protection. However, the 'public benefit' test is only that 'sufficient' numbers of society will feel the benefit and the wide availability of ethical foods and organic food options which implement high standards of animal welfare suggests that there is widespread consumer interest in animal welfare. The RSPCA has said that in a poll, consumers shopping for better produced food (i.e. higher welfare standards) felt increased psychological benefit and also that consumers may experience increased health benefits as, for example, chickens reared with higher welfare have been reported to be more resistant to infection from harmful pathogens that can lead to food poisoning (RSPCA 2006). This view is also replicated in European research on attitudes towards animal welfare carried out on behalf of the European Commission which monitors public opinion and behaviour on animal welfare standards; identifying positive attitudes towards animals on the part of citizens and a belief that animal protection should form part of public policy.

Animal Harm and Criminal Justice Policy

Criminological theory, past experience of implementing criminal justice policies and analysis of the characteristics of animal harm shows that there is no single cause of crime (Peelo and Soothil 2005). Some crimes have a basis in individual or group criminal activity and behaviour, while a range of social conditions such as poverty, relative deprivation, poor parenting and tradition can also cause some crime. The role of masculinities is also a factor, especially given that the majority of animal abusers are male (Nurse 2003, 2011) and so animal harm should be considered in line with the influences and motivations that cause men to turn to crime. However, no one aspect can be put forward as a definitive explanation for all crime and so criminal justice policy needs to consider the different causes of animal harm in order to determine where resources should be concentrated, and the precise policies needed to prevent or reduce animal harm. Several different approaches to law and order exist as well as conflicting perspectives on how to deal with crime, and there are also different objectives behind animal laws (see Chapters 1 and 3), thus specific policies such as 'target hardening', the 'short, sharp, shock' of harsh punitive regimes and the use of non-custodial and community sentences or restorative justice go in and out of fashion. However, western criminal justice policy is mainly centred around a law enforcement perspective that is based on ideas of deterrence and punishment relying on the police as the main detection and apprehension tool to deal with crime even though NGOs play a significant role in dealing with animal harm offences. While initiatives to address the social causes of crime have been, and continue to be tried, mainstream criminal justice policy continues to rely heavily on enforcement action by the police, sentencing in the courts and the use of custodial sentences.

Policies promoted by animal rights activists and in the species justice literature primarily argue that animal harm offences are treated leniently and that there are flaws in animal protection and wildlife legislation and a fundamental lack of rights for animals. In line with this perception, it has been concluded by NGOs and activists that animal harm is not taken seriously and that a stricter enforcement regime comprising stiffer sentences and a more punitive approach to offenders is needed to provide an effective deterrent (Nurse 2003, 2009). While NGO documents, campaign materials and the failures of prosecutorial efforts may identify inadequacies in legislation and weak sentencing by the courts as problematic factors in animal harm, the author's research into wildlife crime, through interviews and detailed analysis of case materials, revealed an enforcement regime which contains significant problems in the practical enforcement of animal legislation and the detection, investigation and prosecution of offences. This picture is replicated across the animal harm literature such that other commentators (Zimmerman 2003, Damania et al. 2008, Schaffner 2011) raise the same concerns in relation to different aspects of animal harm. The evidence uncovered during the author's wildlife crime research and applied to animal harm suggests, therefore, that rather than animal suffering being perpetuated by an inherently weak legislative regime, considerable problems exist in the practical implementation of animal harm legislation and in operational enforcement of legislation even where legislation is considered to be strong and potentially effective (Damania et al. 2008, Nurse 2003, 2009). Thus it is in enforcement and in directly addressing the specific behaviour of animal offenders that attention is needed if efforts to reduce animal harm are to be successful.

That is not to say that cultural and policy considerations that allow animal harm to continue are unimportant. Indeed, despite the considerable efforts of a number of dedicated officers and a global animal rights and animal protection network, animal laws are still enforced in a predominantly ad-hoc manner and across many jurisdictions the resources allocated to this area of crime are inadequate to the task. This is in part due to the relatively low priority that animal harm has within criminal justice systems, being primarily seen as an environmental issue rather than a mainstream criminal justice one. However the evidence suggests that practical enforcement problems exist in almost all areas of animal harm crime, meaning that even where sufficient legislation exists, it is poorly and inconsistently enforced and fails in achieving adequate animal protection.

Situ and Emmons (2000) and Rackstraw (2003) identify that prosecutorial discretion is a significant factor in environmental and animal harm cases. Rackshaw suggests that lack of empathy on the part of prosecutors, misplaced understanding of the seriousness of animal crimes and lack of resources are all factors determining that animal crimes are sometimes not prosecuted (2003). Situ and Emmons concluded that in environmental cases prosecutorial discretion can have the effect of reducing a criminal offence to a civil one where the prosecutor's decision on how to charge and prosecute has the effect of downgrading an offence and dealing with it by administrative means (2000: 16). A variety of research suggests an inconsistency in the way that animal harm offences are dealt with. Rackshaw's analysis of prosecutorial discretion in the United States identified wide discrepancy in the way that animal crimes were dealt with by different states. However the research generally showed that a low percentage of reported cases were prosecuted (Lord and Wittum 1996, Arluke and Luke 1997) and problems with the enforcement of animal cruelty laws. This perception is replicated in the UK with NGOs routinely reporting that the courts do not take animal crime seriously (RSPB 1990, 1996, Nurse 2003) and describing sentencing for animal offences as haphazard with courts routinely handing out minimum sentences and failing to address or recognize the seriousness of offences (Nurse 2003, 2009).

The reality is that animal harm offences are distributed across civil and criminal justice systems such that animal harm carries with it a range of differing sentences, police powers and offences. Thus treatment of animal harm as a matter of public policy varies and the enforcement of animal legislation is inconsistent, in part because it is also true to say that the legislation itself is inconsistent and does not adequately protect those species that it purports to protect. Moore (2005) identifies that while animals should be afforded the same level of protection as other crime victims this is not the case. The species justice perspective might have it that this is because of a lack of legal rights for animals (Wise 2000, Rollin 2006) and this is true in part given animals' exclusion from the definition of 'crime victim' in the United States (Beloof 1999, Moore 2005) and status as property elsewhere. Thus animal crimes are often seen as victimless crimes except where a human victim (i.e. an 'owner') is involved. However, different conceptions of victimhood apply to animals and humans not solely because of their ability to articulate the effects of victimization on them but in respect of the perceived seriousness of the crime. The gravity of an offence dictates not only whether it will be prosecuted but also *how* it will be prosecuted, and the general attitude to environmental and animal offences on the part of prosecutors is that these are 'lesser' offences frequently capable of being dealt with through the civil law system, notwithstanding the violence that occurs in many animal abuse cases. The construction of the law aids in this perception such that analysis of animal law reveals that:

- some animal law offences carry a power of arrest, some do not;
- the level of fines differs between animal laws within and across jurisdictions such that some animal offences provide for serious criminal penalties while many do not. The logic behind the differences is not always clear but is largely socially constructed;
- the option for prison sentences exists for some animal harm offences (in particular the more serious wildlife crime offences) but not others;
- some species that are protected under animal law may still be killed or taken under certain exemptions. The nature of the exemptions varies according to the legislation and the jurisdiction; and
- some legislation provides that individuals convicted of an offence are subsequently banned from keeping or controlling animals or from carrying out activities related to the offence and continued interaction with animals, whereas other legislation does not.

Moore argues that to achieve consistency, animals should be recognized as crime victims and the recipients of criminal behaviour that is an offence against the state (2005). Thus animal legislation should be reviewed to ensure that police powers and sentencing options are applied in a uniform manner, at least across the various pieces of legislation within a state, so that animals are protected as crime victims within a state's criminal justice system. This being the case, it makes sense that there should be a power of arrest for all animal offences commensurate with the power of arrest provided to other crime victims and sentencing powers for animal crimes should also be consistent with those for other offences such that the criminal justice system recognizes criminality in respect of its effect on all crime victims whether human or non-human animal.

Animal Harm: A Conclusion

In answer to its core question, this book concludes that individuals commit crimes against animals in part because they can, in part because in some cases it is profitable for them to do so, but also in part because other strains – social, socio-economic and psychological or emotional – cause them to do so. As a result, animal offending needs to be seen as the complex phenomenon that it is with some offenders choosing their actions, some unaware of the full nature or consequence of their actions and others forced either into action or inaction that causes animal harm.

What should be done with animal offenders? Calls for legal rights for animals and a more punitive regime for animal harm by animal activists and animal rights theorists can certainly be justified on moral and campaigning grounds. In terms of campaigning, it is relatively easy to explain to the public that existing animal protection legislation and the current enforcement regime are ineffective in reducing animal harm. This being the case, it can be argued that it is time to recognize that current legislation fails to recognize the sentient nature of animals and so needs to be replaced with a more punitive and protective regime providing legal rights for animals. The argument that persistent crime and repeat offenders are a consequence of weak legislation and ineffective sentencing reflects the 'common-sense' approach to crime often portrayed in tabloid newspapers and other media. It therefore represents an easy 'sell' to the public. It would be far harder to campaign for community sentences, target hardening, rehabilitative regimes and increased education and to promote the often complex arguments and reasoning behind persistent animal crime problems. Instead policies that appear to represent a 'get tough' policy on animal cruelty and wildlife crime and offer stiffer punishment for offenders that are considered to be wilful in their actions and offensive to the normal morals of society are often promoted by NGOs; these are policies that the public can easily identify with and which can easily be sold to policymakers.

However given the varied nature of offending outlined in this book it can be questioned whether such policies and the persistent reliance on an animal rights agenda are effective. As Donaldson and Kymlicka (2011) imply it is possible that the animal rights movement has become inextricably bogged down in a worthy, fully justified, yet ultimately stilted campaign that seeks a level of legal change governments are unable to accept and will remain unwilling to do so for the foreseeable future. This book suggests that the campaign for legal rights for animals can succeed and that a legal framework exists that may achieve these rights by building on existing criminalization of animal harm and developing the effectiveness of legislative and enforcement responses through multi-agency co-operation and greater integration of animal harm into criminal justice systems. This approach is one of evolution, not revolution.

In practice, the evidence does not support the view that a more punitive regime or legal rights for animals would lead to a reduction in animal harm. While the perception of animal rights theorists is rightly that animal law is inadequate in many fundamental respects, the reality is that in many jurisdictions animal protection is already provided for but it is in the enforcement of legislation and the nature of the criminal justice or law enforcement response that problems occur. The evidence is that even where the available penalties are considered to be sufficient, they are inconsistently applied, penalties are often at the lower end of the available scale and enforcement is carried out on an ad-hoc, largely voluntary basis which relies on NGOs or poorly resourced conservation and welfare professionals rather than the dedicated law enforcement response that is applied to other forms of crime. Analysis of a range of examples across the entire spectrum of animal harm shows this to be the case, whether discussing wildlife trafficking in Russia, illegal bushmeat hunting in Africa, egg collecting in the UK or animal cruelty in the inner cities of the United States. In all jurisdictions, the chances of animal harm being detected and an offender being apprehended, prosecuted, and receiving a sentence that has either a deterrent effect or contains sufficient rehabilitative elements to prevent further offending is slight. In addition there is evidence that some animal harm offenders are fully cognizant of their actions, the illegality of their actions and the harm they are causing to animals. This being the case, a more punitive regime or wholesale change to animal laws by providing legal animal rights is unlikely to be effective unless the enforcement problems are also addressed as it is doubtful that providing legal rights for animals will significantly alter such criminal behaviour or manifestly impact on the vast majority of animal harm.

But effective anti-animal harm public policy and its enforcement has scope to develop an animal protection regime that makes best use of existing animal protection and wildlife crime law to provide actual rather than theoretical animal protection. This could provide for animal rights in practice if not in fact by developing an effective criminal justice response to the different types of criminality inherent in animal harm. White (2008) identifies that contemporary police studies identify that a problem-solving rather than policy-prescribed model of intervention is required to address environmental and species justice issues. In the case of animal harm, a specific approach to animal offending incorporating harm-based and place-based specific policies that directly address the animal harm at issue are required.

While animal rights may remain a distant hope for green criminology and species justice, animal protection is achievable through recognition of specific animal-harm criminality and the links between animal harm and other crimes within an enforcement regime that punishes animal harm wherever it occurs, and which seeks to prevent animal harm from occurring in the first place or escalating into other forms of violence or social harm. While animals may not be recognized in law as being as sentient beings deserving of legal rights there is scope through enforcement of law and investigating animal harm criminality for them to be recognized and protected as victims of crime. This book proposes such an agenda.

References

Arluke, A. and Luke, C. (1997). Physical Cruelty Toward Animals in Massachusetts, 1975–1976. *Society & Animals*, 5(3), 195–204.

Ascione, F.R. (2001). Animal Abuse and Youth Violence. *Juvenile Justice Bulletin*, Washington, DC: U.S. Department of Justice, Office of Juvenile Justice and Delinquency Prevention, September 2001.

Barker, S.B., Knisely, J.S., McCain, N.L., Schubert, C.M. and Pandurangi, A.K. (2010). Exploratory Study of Stress Buffering Response Patterns from Interaction with a Therapy Dog. *Anthrozoos*, 23(1), 79–91.

Bekoff, M. (2007). *The Emotional Lives of Animals: A Leading Scientist Explores Animal Joy, Sorrow, and Empathy – and Why They Matter*, Novato, CA: New World Library.

Beloof, D.E. (1999). The Third Model of Criminal Process: The Victim Participation Model. *Utah Law Review*, 289, 328–9.

Beirne, P. (2007). Animal Rights, Animal Abuse and Green Criminology, in P. Beirne and N. South (eds), *Issues in Green Criminology: Confronting Harms against Environments, Humanity and Other Animals*, Cullompton: Willan Publishing, 55–86.

Beirne, P. and South, N. (eds) (2007). *Issues in Green Criminology: Confronting Harms against Environments, Humanity and Other Animals*, Devon: Willan.

Benton, T. (1998). Rights and Justice on a Shared Planet: More Rights or New Relations? *Theoretical Criminology*, 2(2), 149–75.

Brantley, A.C., Lockwood, R. and Church, A.W. (2009). An FBI Perspective on Animal Cruelty, in A. Linzey (ed.), *The Link Between Animal Abuse and Human Violence*, Eastbourne: Sussex Academic Press, 223–7.

Budiansky, S. (1999). *The Covenant of the Wild: Why Animals Chose Domestication*, New Haven: Yale University Press (first published by William Morrow, 1992).

Charity Commission (2009). *Tara Mahayana Buddhist Centre: A Public Benefit Assessment Report by the Charity Commission*, London: The Charity Commission.

Clawson, E. (2009). The New Canaries in the Mine: The Priority of Human Welfare in Animal Abuse Prosecution, in A. Linzey (ed.), *The Link Between Animal Abuse and Human Violence*, Eastbourne: Sussex Academic Press, 190–200.

Crawford, E.K., Worsham, N.L. and Swinehart, E.R. (2006). Benefits Derived from Companion Animals, and the Use of the Term 'Attachment'. *Anthrozoos*, 19(2), 98–112.

Cuppleditch, L. and Evans, W. (2005). *Re-offending of Adults: Results from the 2002 Cohort*, London: Home Office.

Damania, R., Seidensticker, J., Whitten, A., Sethi, G., Mackinnon, K., Kiss, A. and Kushlin, A. (2008). *A Future for Wild Tigers*, Washington, DC: The International Bank for Reconstruction and Development / The World Bank and Smithsonian's National Zoological Park.

Donaldson, S. and Kymlicka, W. (2011). *Zoopolis: A Political Theory of Animal Rights*, Oxford: Oxford University Press.

Fortney, D. (2003). Thinking Outside the 'Black Box': Tailored Enforcement in Environmental Criminal Law. *Texas Law Review*, 81(6), 1609–30.

Francis, B. and Soothill, K. (2005). Explaining Changing Patterns of Crime: A Focus on Burglary and Age-Period-Cohort Models, in Moira Peelo and Keith Soothill (eds), *Questioning Crime and Criminology*, Cullompton: Willan Publishing, 102–19.

Francione, G.L. and Garner, R. (2010). *The Animal Rights Debate: Abolition or Regulation?*, New York: Columbia University Press.

Franklin, J.H. (2005). *Animal Rights and Moral Philosophy*, New York: Columbia University Press.

Garner, R. (1993). The Politics of Animal Protection: A Research Agenda. *Society and Animals*, 3(1), Washington, DC: Society & Animals Forum, 43–60.

Groombridge, N. (1998). Masculinities and Crimes against the Environment, *Theoretical Criminology*, 2(2), London: Sage, 249–67.

Hawley, F. (1993). The Moral and Conceptual Universe of Cockfighters: Symbolism and Rationalization. *Society and Animals*, 1(2).

Jasper, J.M. (1997). *The Art of Moral Protest: Culture, Biography, and Creativity in Social Movements*, Chicago: University of Chicago Press.

Jasper, J. and Nelkin, D. (1992). *The Animal Rights Crusade*, New York: The Free Press.

Kean, H. (1998). *Animal Rights: Political and Social Change in Britain since 1800*, London: Reaktion Books.

Kirkwood, G. (1994). *The Enforcement of Wildlife Protection Legislation: A Study of the Police Wildlife Liaison Officers' Network*, Leicester: De Montfort University.

Lea, J. and Young, J. (1993 revised edn). *What Is To Be Done About Law & Order?*, London: Pluto Press.

Levi, M. (1994). Violent Crime, in M. Maguire, R. Morgan and R. Reiner (eds), *The Oxford Handbook of Criminology*, Oxford: Oxford University Press, 295–354.

Linzey, A. (2009). *Why Animal Suffering Matters*, Oxford: Oxford University Press.

Lord, L.K. and Wittum, T.E. (1996). *1996 Ohio Survey of Animal Care & Control Agencies*. Ohio State University. Department of Veterinary Preventative Medicine.

Lowe, B.M. and Ginsberg, C.F. (2002). Animal Rights as a Post-citizenship Movement. *Society & Animals*, 10(2).

Lowther, J., Cook, D. and Roberts, M. (2002). *Crime and Punishment in the Wildlife Trade*, Wolverhampton: WWF/TRAFFIC/Regional Research Institute (University of Wolverhampton).

McInerney, J. (2004). *Animal Welfare, Economics and Policy*, London: DEFRA.

Moore, A.N. (2005). Defining Animals as Crime Victims. *Journal of Animal Law*, 91(2005), 91–108.

Nurse, A. (2003). *The Nature of Wildlife and Conservation Crime in the UK and its Public Response, Working Paper No, 9*, Birmingham: University of Central England.

Nurse, A. (2009). Dealing with Animal Offenders, in A. Linzey (ed.), *The Link Between Animal Abuse and Human Violence*, Eastbourne: Sussex Academic Press, 238–49.

Nurse, A. (2011). Policing Wildlife: Perspectives on Criminality in Wildlife Crime. *Papers from the British Criminology Conference*, 11, 38–53.

Nussbaum, M.C. (2004). Beyond 'Compassion and Humanity': Justice for Nonhuman Animals, in C.R. Sunstein and M.C. Nussbaum (eds), *Animal Rights: Current Debates and New Directions*, New York: Oxford University Press, 299–320.

O'Halloran, K. (2000). *Charities, the Law and Public Benefit: Ireland as a Case Study for the Use of Charity Law to Promote Social Capital*, International Society for Third Sector Research, Fourth International Conference, Dublin.

Pearce, F. and Tombs, S. (1998). *Toxic Capitalism: Corporate Crime and the Chemical Industry*, Aldershot: Dartmouth Publishing Company.

Peelo, M. and Soothill, K. (eds) (2005). *Questioning Crime and Criminology*, Cullompton: Willan Publishing.

Rackstraw, J.H. (2003). Reaching for Justice: An Analysis of Self-Help Prosecution for Animal Cases. *Animal Law*, 243, 246.

Radford, M. (2001). *Animal Welfare Law in Britain: Regulation and Responsibility*, Oxford: Oxford University Press.

Rollin, B.E. (2006). *Animal Rights And Human Morality*, New York: Prometheus.

Rowlands, M. (2009). The Structure of Evil, in A. Linzey (ed.), *The Link Between Animal Abuse and Human Violence*, Eastbourne: Sussex Academic Press, 201–5.

Royal Society for the Protection of Birds (RSPB) (1990). *Crime Justice and Protecting the Public, Home Office White Paper The Government's Proposals for Legislation, Submission by the Royal Society for the Protection of Birds*, Sandy: RSPB.

Royal Society for the Protection of Birds (RSPB) (1996). *Proceedings of the 1995 National Police Wildlife Liaison Officers' Conference*, Sandy: RSPB.

RSPCA (2006) *Everyone's a Winner: How Rearing Chickens to Higher Welfare Standards can Benefit the Chicken, Producer, Retailer and Consumer*, Horsham: RSPCA.

Saunders, T. (2001). *Baiting the Trap: One Man's Secret Battle to Save Our Wildlife*, London: Simon & Schuster.

Schaffner, J. (2011). *An Introduction to Animals and the Law*, New York: Palgrave Macmillan.

Schneider, J.L. (2008). Reducing the Illicit Trade in Endangered Wildlife: The Market Reduction Approach. *Journal of Contemporary Criminal Justice*, 24(3), 274–95.

Shepherd, J. and Lisles, C. (1998). Towards Multi-Agency Violence Prevention and Victim Support: An Investigation of Police-Accident and Emergency Service Liaison. *British Journal of Criminology Delinquency and Deviant Social Behaviour*, 38(3), 351–70.

Singer, P. (1975). *Animal Liberation*, New York: Avon.

Situ, Y. and Emmons, D. (2000). *Environmental Crime: The Criminal Justice System's Role in Protecting the Environment*, Thousand Oaks: Sage.

South, N. (1998). A Green Field for Criminology? A Proposal for a Perspective. *Theoretical Criminology*, 2(2), 211–33.

South, N. and Wyatt, T. (2011). Comparing Illicit Trades in Wildlife and Drugs: An Exploratory Study. *Deviant Behavior*, 32, 538–61.

Stech, R. (2010). *Human Rights and the Environment: Understanding Your Right to a Healthy Environment*, London: Environmental Law Foundation.

Stookes, P. (2003). *Civil Law Aspects of Environmental Justice*, London: Environmental Law Foundation.

Tombs, S. and Whyte, D. (2004). *Unmasking the Crimes of the Powerful: Scrutinizing States and Corporations*, New York: Peter Lang Publishers.

Utting, D. (1996). Reducing Criminality among Young People: A Sample of Relevant Programmes in the United Kingdom? *Home Office Research Study 161*, London: Home Office.

Walters, R. (2007). Crime, Regulation and Radioactive Waste in the United Kingdom, in P. Beirne and N. South (eds), *Issues in Green Criminology: Confronting Harms against Environments, Humanity and Other Animals*, Devon: Willan, 186–285.

White, R. (2007). Green Criminology and the Pursuit of Social and Ecological Justice, in P. Beirne and N. South (eds), *Issues in Green Criminology: Confronting Harms against Environments, Humanity and Other Animals*, Devon: Willan, 32–54.

White, R. (2008). *Crimes Against Nature: Environmental Criminology and Ecological Justice*, Devon: Willan.

Wilson, J.Q. (1985). *Thinking about Crime*, 2nd edn, New York: Vintage Books.

Wise, S.M. (2000). *Rattling the Cage: Towards Legal Rights for Animals*, London: Profile.

Wise, S. (2004). Animal Rights, One Step at a Time, in C.R. Sunstein and M.C. Nussbaum (eds), *Animal Rights: Current Debates and New Directions*, New York: Oxford University Press, 19–50.

Zimmerman, M.E. (2003). The Black Market for Wildlife: Combating Transnational Organized Crime in the Illegal Wildlife Trade. *Vanderbilt Journal of Transnational Law*, 36, 1657–89.

Glossary

Biodiversity – the shortened and commonly used form of 'biological diversity' which refers to the community formed by living organisms and the relations between them. The phrase reflects the diversity of species and diversity of genes within species.

Blood Sports – any activity (sport or other form of entertainment) which involves violence towards animals. This includes activities where drawing the blood of the animal is integral to the activity and the death of an animal is a frequent outcome, and sometimes the goal, of blood sports. This includes coursing (chasing) animals and combat sports such as badger-baiting, cock-fighting and dog-fighting.

Bushmeat – the term 'bushmeat' is used to refer to wildlife and the meat derived from it. The phrase's origins are in the meat obtained from hunting indigenous wildlife in the forest areas of Africa which are often referred to as 'the bush', although the common usage of the phrase now extends to meat from a range of most indigenous wild species. Thus the term 'bushmeat' now extends to a wide range of wildlife species although in the context of the illegal bushmeat trade it most commonly refers to those species specifically hunted for their meat, including: elephant, gorilla, chimpanzee and other primates, forest antelope (duikers), crocodile, porcupine, bush pig, cane rat, pangolin, monitor lizard and guinea fowl.

Common Law – a system of law that has developed through judicial decisions and precedents to arrive at a common understanding of law. Common law incorporates the system of case law where judges use the precedent from previously decided cases to decide how the law should be applied in current cases.

Criminal aetiology – the analysis of the causes of crime, and the nature of criminals.

Criminal epidemiology – the incidence and social, temporal and geographical distribution of crime, criminal acts and criminal behaviour.

Deforestation – in its negative sense the phrase has come to mean destruction of forests although its correct technical usage is the permanent removal of forest cover which is not then replaced either by replanting or natural regeneration of trees.

Ecosystem – used to describe the interdependent community of plants, animals and other organisms and their interaction with the natural world and habitats on which they depend.

Egg Collecting – form of wildlife crime in which the eggs of wild birds are collected from nests. Egg collectors drill a small hole in one end and either blow out the contents using a tube or dissolve the contents using embryo solvent or some other caustic substance without harming the shell. The egg minus its contents is then retained for inclusion in a personal collection.

Endemic Species – species native to the geographical area.

Exotic Species – species not native to the geographical area.

Indigenous Peoples – refers to ethnic groups that are considered to be the original dwellers of a region and who retain some connection to their historical, cultural and/or spiritual way of life outside of mainstream society. While strictly speaking there is no universally accepted definition of the term, the United Nations' definition of indigenous people as 'the descendants of groups, which were in the territory at the time when other groups of different cultures or ethnic origin arrived there' has been broadly accepted. This definition is incorporated into the United Nations Declaration on the Rights of Indigenous Peoples.

Non-Governmental Organizations (NGOs) – are usually created by individuals or companies with no participation or representation of government. The term is increasingly used to refer to think-tanks and voluntary sector areas who carry out functions beyond pure fundraising and charitable concerns to include some aspects of a policy development or law enforcement role. NGOs vary in their methods. Some act primarily as lobbyists, while others conduct programmes and activities primarily to raise public awareness of an issue and actively carry out functions that the statutory sector are perceived as failing to carry out effectively (e.g. species protection or wildlife law enforcement).

Ooology – scientific name given to the study of birds' eggs.

Private Law – the law and legal system which governs relationships for the good of society and deals with resolving disputes between individuals (or individuals and companies). Private law can be further divided into contract law, family law and tort law (civil wrong).

Public Law – the law and legal system governing the relationship between citizens and the state. Public law is divided into administrative law, constitutional law and criminal law. Public law is usually introduced by the government and applies to all citizens whereas private law only applies to certain individuals and circumstances.

Universal Declaration on Animal Welfare (UDAW) – is a proposed treaty on animal welfare currently being promoted by the WSPA and other NGOs with a view to having the treaty adopted by the United Nations.

Wildlife Trafficking (Illegal Wildlife Trade) – the phrase used to describe the illegal trade in wildlife which can include illegal trade, smuggling, poaching, capture, or collection of endangered species or protected wildlife or derivatives. The terms wildlife trafficking or illegal wildlife trade are used interchangeably within green criminology and criminal justice discourse to refer to trading in animals whether alive or dead, primarily in contravention of CITES regulations and/or any national legislation which implements CITES.

Further Reading

As this book identifies, animal harm is a wide subject which has been the subject of a variety of academic and popular writing, especially on the aspects of animal abuse and animal cruelty. There are many excellent books on the subject of animal harm and its different constituent parts, but recent academic and campaigning interest means that now a number of online sources provide useful information on the subject. Recent years have seen a growth in online law and human–animal studies journals which cover issues relating to animal harm and provide a forum for academics, activists and students to discuss animal harm topics. In addition to the sources listed below, animal harm articles also now regularly appear throughout the mainstream criminological press and journals such as Sage's *Theoretical Criminology* and the *Journal of Law Culture and Humanities* have published themed issues on animal topics. A selection of the key established journals and news services follows.

Animals

http://www.mdpi.com/journal/animals [accessed 28 January 2012]
International open access journal with a wide remit across the field of animal studies including zoology, ethnozoology, animal science, animal ethics and animal welfare. Published online quarterly by MDPI of Switzerland.

Animal Law Review

http://law.lclark.edu/law_reviews/animal_law_review/ [accessed 28 January 2012]
A student-run law review based at Lewis & Clark Law School in Portland, Oregon, and published bi-annually. Each volume includes two issues: a fall/winter issue and a spring/summer issue.

Animal Legal and Historic Centre

http://animallaw.info/ [accessed 28 January 2012]
Substantial online repository of animal law cases and legal articles housed at Michigan State University College of Law. The site contains both US and UK case law and over 1,400 US statutes.

Anthrozoology

www.anthrozoology.org [accessed 28 January 2012]
Online resource of research into human–animal interaction encompassing several different fields of research, including: psychology, psychiatry, political science, the social sciences, medical science, allied health sciences, behavioural science and veterinary science and veterinary medicine.

British and Irish Legal Information Institute

http://www.bailii.org/ [accessed 28 January 2012]
Free online searchable database of British and Irish case law and legislation, European Union case law, Law Commission reports, and other law-related British and Irish material.

Environmental News Network (ENN)

www.enn.com [accessed 28 January 2012]
An online resource for environmental news stories, contains a dedicated wildlife section, a peer news sharing network and an email newsletter that delivers environmental news stories from around the globe free to its subscribers.

Environmental Protection Agency (US)

www.epa.gov [accessed 28 January 2012]
United States governmental agency with a remit to ensure that the US's federal laws protecting human health and the environment are enforced fairly and effectively. Details of US legislation and enforcement activities are published on the site.

Journal of Animal Welfare Law

http://alaw.org.uk/publications/ [accessed 28 January 2012]
The journal of the UK's Association of Lawyers for Animal Welfare (ALAW), two main editions are currently published each year. Back issues of the journal from May 2005 (Issue 1) can be downloaded free of charge from this site.

Journal for Critical Animal Studies

http://www.criticalanimalstudies.org/journal-for-critical-animal-studies/ [accessed 28 January 2012]
The journal of the Institute for Critical Animal Studies is a peer-reviewed interdisciplinary academic (yet readable) journal published online by the Institute. The journal promotes academic study of critical animal issues in contemporary society.

Journal of International Wildlife Law and Policy

http://www.tandfonline.com/loi/uwlp20 [accessed 28 January 2012]
Quarterly journal on wildlife law and policy issues published by Taylor & Francis. The journal has published special issues on large mammal conservation (2012), new research ideas for human–animal interactions (2010), the fortieth anniversary of the Ramsar Convention on Wetlands (2011) and human–wildlife conflict and peace-building strategies (2009). Selected articles from the journal can be downloaded free of charge from the journal website at Taylor & Francis' online journal platform.

Society and Animals Forum

www.societyandanimalsforum.org [accessed 28 January 2012]
The forum provides a number of resources relating to the field of human–animal studies, including a calendar of events for the Animals and Society Institute, links to *Society and Animals*, the Institute's journal, its book series and the *Journal of Applied Animal Welfare Science*.

Stanford Journal of Animal Law and Policy

http://sjalp.stanford.edu/ [accessed 28 January 2012]
Online animal law journal covering a range of animal law and policy topics, articles and scholarship from around the world. The website includes access to past volumes.

Useful Organizations

A number of organizations are actively involved in advocacy, campaigning or litigation aimed at reducing or eliminating animal harm. The precise nature of the organization's activity is defined by whether its focus is on particular animals or types of animal harm, or on general animals and species justice concerns. A list of some of the key players involved in addressing animal harm follows. By necessity this list is not exhaustive nor is it intended to be. Instead its focus is on those organizations that are either firmly established within the field or which derive from the efforts of established academics or previously existing organizations within the field of animal harm and human–animal studies.

Animal Defenders International (ADI)
Millbank Tower
Millbank
London
SW1P 4QP
United Kingdom
Website: www.ad-international.org
ADI is a campaigning and investigative group of organizations working for animal protection. ADI campaigns for long-term protection and appropriate standards of animal welfare for farm animals, animals in entertainment, an end to animal experimentation and to end animal suffering at fur farms and in the entertainment industry. ADI has offices in London, Los Angeles, Bogota and also representatives and partner organizations in a number of other countries.

Animal Legal Defense Fund
170 East Cotati Avenue
Cotati
CA 94931
United States
Website: www.aldf.org
The Animal Legal Defense Fund (ALDF) campaigns within the US legal system to end animal suffering. A number of resources are available on its website including details of US animal abuse case law bulletin boards and current news.

Association of Lawyers for Animal Welfare (ALAW)
PO Box 67933
London
NW1W 8RB
United Kingdom
Website: www.alaw.org.uk
ALAW is a UK based organization of lawyers and legal academics with interest and experience in animal protection law. ALAW members provide advisory services and research on effective implementation of animal protection law and developing a better legal framework for the protection of animals. ALAW also campaigns for better animal protection law and publishes the *Journal of Animal Welfare Law*, a legal journal dedicated to animal welfare topics.

British Union for the Abolition of Vivisection (BUAV)
16a Crane Grove
London
N7 8NN
United Kingdom
Website: www.buav.org
The BUAV campaigns to end animal suffering linked to animal experimentation and challenges the need for and legality of animal experimentation. Originally a charity, the BUAV's status changed in 1947 when UK courts ruled that anti-vivisectionist organizations could no longer be regarded as charitable. The BUAV provides expert advice on animal experimentation to governments, media, corporations and official bodies and also conducts campaigning, investigative work, political lobbying and research. The BUAV publishes reports and campaign material on animal experimentation and has also conducted legal work on animal experimentation issues.

Centre for Animals and Social Justice (CASJ)
PO Box 4823
Sheffield
S36 0BE
United Kingdom
Website: www.casj.org.uk
The CASJ is a UK registered charity and independent think-tank who's core strategic aim is to embed animal protection as a core policy goal of the UK Government, international governments and intergovernmental organisations, using and developing applied research as a primary tool to achieve this. The CASJ seeks to develop academic capacity in the field of applied animal protection to ensure that high quality research informs policymaking. It engages with specific issues directly affecting the wellbeing of animals, and seeks to foster the political reorientation that is required to embed animal protection as a core value of social justice.

Centre for the Expansion of Fundamental Rights (CEFR)
5195 NW 112th Terrace
Coral Springs
FL 33076
United States
Website: www.nonhumanrights.org
UK-based organization founded in 2007 by attorney and former President of the
Animal Legal Defense Fund Steven M. Wise in order to campaign and lobby for
legal rights for animals. The organization's primary focus is to change the US legal
system to establish legal personhood for non-human animals.

Centre for Public Integrity
910 17th Street, NW, Suite 700
Washington
DC 20006
United States
Website: www.iwatchnews.org
US-based non-profit organization to investigate, analyse and disseminate
information on national issues of importance to policymakers, academics and
news organizations. The Centre investigates environmental issues and was
co-author/publisher of Alan Green's investigation into the black market for rare
and exotic species.

Coalition Against Wildlife Trafficking (CAWT)
Website: www.cawtglobal.org/
International coalition of government partners and NGOs working together
to eliminate wildlife trafficking and ensure the effective implementation and
enforcement of CITES. UK-based organization NGO partners include IFAW,
IUCN, Save the Tiger Fund, the Smithsonian Institution, WCS, the Wildlife
Alliance and WWF (among others).

Defenders of Wildlife
1130 17th Street NW
Washington
DC 20036
United States
Website: www.defenders.org
US-based not-for-profit organization founded in 1947 with a remit to protect and
restore America's native wildlife and safeguard wildlife habitats. Defenders' main
focus is restoring wolves to their surviving former habitats in the lower 48 states of
the United States and to challenge efforts to reduce the protection afforded to wolves
under US law. It also works to prevent the extinction of other North American
wildlife and to prevent cruelty to wildlife. Defenders of Wildlife have offices in
nine US states and Mexico, in addition to its Washington, DC headquarters.

Department for Environment, Food and Rural Affairs (DEFRA)
Nobel House
17 Smith Square
London
SW1P 3JR
United Kingdom
Website: www.defra.gov.uk
The UK government department with responsibility for environmental issues, including: climate change, wildlife crime, sustainable development and rural communities. DEFRA's website contains a wildlife crime section covering aspects of UK wildlife crime and links to the website for its Partnership for Action on Wildlife Crime (PAW), the body that co-ordinates UK wildlife crime policy via a partnership between government and NGOS.

Earthjustice
50 California Street, Suite 500
San Francisco
CA 94111
United States
Website: http://earthjustice.org/
Earthjustice is a not-for-profit public interest law firm originally founded in 1981 as the Sierra Club Legal Defense fund. Earthjustice lawyers litigate on behalf of US citizens in environmental cases, in particular litigating in cases involving the Endangered Species Act, Clean Air Act, Clean Water Act and Natural Environment Policy Act. In addition, Earthjustice campaigning work highlights current threats and details of campaign work. In addition to its San Francisco headquarters, Earthjustice has regional offices across the United States in Anchorage, Bozeman, California, Denver, Florida, Honolulu, New York, Seattle and Washington.

The Environmental Investigations Agency (EIA)
62–63 Upper Street
London
N1 0NY
United Kingdom
Website: www.eia-global.org
EIA is an international campaigning organization which investigates and exposes environmental crime primarily through the use of undercover investigations using the evidence gained in investigations in advocacy and lobbying campaigns. EIA has published investigative reports and policy documents on various wildlife and environmental crime issues and has also produced documentaries on various aspects of animal harm. In addition to its London office EIA has a US office in Washington.

Environmental Justice Foundation (EJF)
1 Amwell Street
London
EC1R 1UL
United Kingdom
Website: www.ejfoundation.org
The EJF is a registered charity that works on the protection of the natural environment and combating environmental abuses. EJF provides film and advocacy training to individuals and grassroots organizations (primarily in the global south) and campaigns internationally to raise awareness of environmental issues facing its grassroots partners and vulnerable communities. EJF publishes a range of environmental research reports and campaign materials and in addition to its team of campaigners and film-makers based at its headquarters in London also works with partners in Brazil, Vietnam, Mali, Sierra Leone, Uzbekistan, Mauritius and Indonesia.

Environmental Protection Agency US (EPA)
Ariel Rios Building
1200 Pennsylvania Avenue, N.W.
Washington
DC 20460
United States
Website: www.epa.gov
The EPA is a US governmental agency with a remit to protect human health and the environment. The EPA is responsible for enforcing federal environmental laws, developing and enforcing these laws by writing regulations that states and tribes enforce through their own regulations. The EPA also publishes information on environmental crimes and its regulatory activities. The EPA has 10 regional offices across the United States, each of which is responsible for several states and territories.

European Commission Environment Directorate
1 Amwell Street
London
EC1R 1UL
United Kingdom
Website: www.ejfoundation.org
The Environment Directorate of the EU publishes information on European wildlife trade regulations, threats to wildlife and wildlife trade issues in the EU.

Exxpose Exxon
Exxpose Exxon Campaign
218 D Street
SE Washington
DC 20003
United States
Website: www.exxposeexxon.com
Campaigning coalition formed by several environmental and public advocacy groups intending to highlight Exxon's activities in relation to denying the effects of global warming and the company's support for proposals to drill for oil in the Arctic National Wildlife Refuge. The campaign also seeks to force Exxon to pay all of the punitive damages awarded to fisherman, Alaskan natives and others in respect of the harm caused by the 1989 Exxon Valdez oil spill. Exxpose Exxon's founding organizations are: Defenders of Wildlife, Greenpeace, the Natural Resources Defense Council (NRDC), the Sierra Club, the US Public Interest Research Group, and the Union of Concerned Scientists.

Humane Society of the United States (HSUS)
The Humane Society of the United States
2100 L St., NW
Washington
DC 20037
United States
Website: www.humanesociety.org
American animal protection organization with approximately 10 million members and a network of regional offices across the United States.

Institute for Critical Animal Studies (ICAS)
PO Box 4293
Ithaca
NY 14852
United States
Website: www.criticalanimalstudies.org
The Institute for Critical Animal Studies (ICAS) is an interdisciplinary scholarly non-profit animal protection centre which provides education policy, research and analysis. The ICAS was originally formed in 2001 as the Center on Animal Liberation affairs and changed its name to the ICAS in 2007. In addition to publishing the *Journal for Critical Animal Studies*, the ICAS organizes annual critical animal studies conferences in the United States and Europe.

International Fund for Animal Welfare (IFAW)
290 Summer Street
Yarmouth Port
MA 02675
United States
Animal Advocacy group based in the UK, originally formed to protest against the culling of seals in Canada but now working globally on animal welfare and animal cruelty issues. IFAW works to prevent the elephant ivory trade and the extinction of whales. In addition to its US international office there is a UK office based in London.

International Union for the Conservation of Nature (IUCN)
IUCN Conservation Centre
Rue Mauverney 28
1196, Gland
Switzerland
Website: www.iucn.org
The IUCN is a global environmental network and democratic membership union with more than 1,000 government and NGO member organizations, and some 10,000 volunteer scientists in more than 160 countries. Its priority work areas are biodiversity, climate change, sustainable energy, the development of a green economy and helping governments to understand the link between nature conservation and human well-being.

Oxford Centre for Animal Ethics
The Ferrater Mora Oxford Centre for Animal Ethics
91 Iffley Road
Oxford
OX4 1EG
United Kingdom
Website: http://www.oxfordanimalethics.com/
The Oxford Centre for Animal Ethics is an academic research centre based at the University of Oxford and specializing in ethical treatment of animals. The Oxford Centre for Animal Ethics are the publishers of the *Journal of Animal Ethics* in partnership with the University of Illinois Press, and also publishes the Palgrave Macmillan *Animal Ethics* book series. The Centre has previously organized an international conference on the links between animal abuse and human violence. Papers from that conference were subsequently developed into a book published by Sussex Academic Press in July 2009.

Partnership for Action against Wildlife Crime (PAW)
PAW Secretariat
Zone 1/14
Temple Quay House
2 The Square
Temple Quay
Bristol
BS1 6EB
United Kingdom
Website: www.defra.gov.uk/paw
PAW is a UK based multi-agency body comprising representatives of statutory agencies and NGOs involved in UK wildlife law enforcement. Its secretariat is hosted by DEFRA (see above) and maintains the PAW website, the distribution of PAW's email bulletins and publicizes PAW's activities.

People for the Ethical Treatment of Animals (PETA)
501 Front St.
Norfolk
VA 23510
United States
Website: www.peta.org
PETA is one of the largest animal rights organizations in the world with a global support base in excess of three million (members and supporters). PETA predominantly campaigns against animal cruelty on factory farms, in the clothing trade, in laboratories, and in the entertainment industry. Its work includes high-profile campaigning, advocacy, public education, cruelty investigations, animal rescue and legislative work aimed at changing animal protection laws.

The Royal Society for the Prevention of Cruelty to Animals (RSPCA)
Wilberforce Way
Southwater
Horsham
West Sussex
RH13 9RS
United Kingdom
Website: www.rspca.org.uk
A UK-based charity that works to prevent cruelty to, the causing of unnecessary suffering to and the neglect of animals in England and Wales. Uniformed Inspectorate investigates cruelty offences, while a plain-clothes and undercover unit called the Special Operations Unit (SOU) deals with more serious offences and low-level organized animal crime like dog-fighting and badger-baiting. The RSPCA has a network of branch offices across England and Wales.

The Royal Society for the Protection of Birds (RSPB)
The Lodge
Sandy
Bedfordshire
SG19 2DL
United Kingdom
Website: www.rspb.org.uk
The RSPB is a conservation charity that campaigns for the protection of wild birds and their environment. An in-house investigations section carries out investigations into wild bird crime and advises the police and others as well as publishes annual reports on bird crime in the UK and a quarterly investigations newsletter on bird crime problems, sometimes with an EU slant. The charity is UK based but has international offices and is part of Birdlife International, a global network of bird conservation organizations.

The Scottish Society for the Prevention of Cruelty to Animals (SSPCA)
Kingseat Road
Halbeath
Dunfermline
KY11 8RY
Website: www.scottishspca.org
The SSPCA is the Scottish counterpart to the RSPCA. The SSPCA works to prevent cruelty to, the causing of unnecessary suffering to and the neglect of animals in Scotland.

Sierra Club
National Headquarters
85 Second Street, 2nd Floor
San Francisco
CA 94105
United States
Website: www.sierraclub.org
The Sierra Club is a US-based grassroots environmental organization with a remit to protect communities and wild places and to restore the quality of the natural environment. In addition to its national headquarters in San Francisco the Sierra Club has a legislative office in Washington, DC and regional offices across the United States. In addition to campaigning and publishing research and policy documents on wildlife and environmental issues the Sierra Club has also employed strategic legal action and regulatory advocacy to protect US wildlife and the environment.

TRAFFIC
TRAFFIC International
219a Huntingdon Rd
Cambridge
CB3 ODL
United Kingdom
Website: www.traffic.org
TRAFFIC is the wildlife trade monitoring arm of the World Wide Fund for Nature (WWF) and the International Union for the Conservation of Nature (IUCN). It mainly investigates compliance with CITES and related trade in endangered species, TRAFFIC has regional offices in Africa, Asia, the Americas, Europe and Oceania supported by a Central Secretariat based in the UK.

The Whale and Dolphin Conservation Society (WDCS)
Brookfield House
38 St Paul Street
Chippenham
Wiltshire
SN15 1LJ
United Kingdom
Website: www.wdcs.org
WDCS is a global charity dedicated to the conservation and welfare of all cetaceans (whales, dolphins and porpoises). It has regional offices in the UK, Latin America, Germany, North America and Australasia. In addition to its campaigning work WDCS conducts investigations work to expose abuses of wildlife regulations and advises governments and regulatory bodies on the working of conventions and other mechanisms needed and intended to protect cetaceans.

Wildlife Alliance
909 Third Avenue, Fifth Floor
New York
NY 10022
United States
Website: www.wildlifealliance.org
Wildlife Alliance began life in 1994 as the Global Survival Network. The organization works with governments and other partners to implement direct protection programmes for forests and wildlife, particularly to stop the illegal trade in wildlife by directly protecting wildlife in its habitats and reducing consumer demand for wildlife.

World Society for the Protection of Animals (WSPA)
WSPA International
5th Floor
Grays Inn Road,
London
WC1X 8HB
United Kingdom
Website: http://www.wspa-international.org/
The World Society for the Prevention of Cruelty to Animals is an animal welfare and anti-cruelty charity with a global remit. WSPA campaigns for the protection of companion animals, against commercial exploitation of wildlife and against intensive farming, long distance transport and slaughter of animals for food. It has regional offices in the United States (Boston), Australia (Sydney), Asia (Thailand), Brazil (Rio de Janeiro), Canada (Toronto), Sweden, South America (Colombia), New Zealand (Auckland), the Netherlands, India (New Delhi), Germany (Berlin) and China (Beijing).

The World Wide Fund for Nature (WWF)
WWF International Gland (Secretariat)
Av. du Mont-Blanc 1196 Gland
Switzerland
+41 22 364 91 11
+41 22 364 88 36
Website: www.wwf.org
The World Wide Fund for Nature is an independent conservation network working in more than 90 countries. A registered charity in the UK with campaigning interests in wildlife trade, threats to endangered species and their habitats. Its main regional offices are in the United States (Washington, DC), Australia (Sydney), China (Beijing), Brazil (Brasilia), Canada (Toronto), France (Paris), Germany (Frankfurt), India (New Delhi), Japan (Tokyo), Sweden (Solna), South America (Colombia), New Zealand (Wellington), the Netherlands (Zeist), Pakistan (Lahore), Spain (Madrid), Switzerland (Zurich) and the United Kingdom (Godalming).

Index

Snares 50, 54, 114, 121; *see also* traps
souvenirs (wildlife) 173, 183
species 1–5, 7–12, 14, 17–19, 22–4,
    26–8, 30, 35–6, 38, 40, 42–3, 47–8,
    50–52, 55–7, 66, 70–71, 73, 79,
    81, 91, 92, 109–12, 121–3, 132,
    139, 142–3, 148–9, 155–63, 165,
    170–77, 180, 82, 184–6, 189–90,
    199, 203, 205, 214, 216, 219, 221,
    223, 230–34, 239–42, 246–7, 250,
    252, 254, 261–3, 269, 271–2,
    278–9
speciesism 223
species justice 1–3, 11–12, 14, 18, 22,
    26–8, 30, 35–6, 38, 40, 47, 91, 109,
    139, 143, 158, 162, 165, 203, 219,
    230, 231, 234, 239, 242, 246, 250,
    252, 254, 269
Sport tourism 121, 155–62, 173
spousal abuse 66, 82, 84, 91, 93–5,
    100–101, 243
Strain theory 39, 98, 253
stress 41, 42, 63, 93, 96–7, 99, 166, 236,
    239
stress offender 63, 70, 83, 85, 93, 97, 239
subsistence hunting 65, 109, 111–12, 119,
    121, 127, 138, 140–46, 149–50,
    156–7
sustainability 160, 165
Sutherland, Edwin 64, 73, 98, 203
Sykes, G.M. 20–21, 64–5, 67, 68–9, 75,
    77, 117, 121, 139, 140
Symbolic interactionism 98, 105

Tannenbaum, J. 13, 32
taxidermy 53, 78, 79, 81
theology 4, 27, 59
therapeutic
    benefits of animals 208, 233
    policy response 86, 239
torture 1, 14, 37, 82–3, 96–7, 99, 206–7
TRAFFIC 56, 17–178, 185, 190, 278
trafficking (illegal trade) 24, 46, 71–2, 79,
    164, 169, 178–88, 190–92, 230,
    233, 235–6, 242, 247, 254, 263
transportation 8, 181–3
traps 42, 53; *see also* snares

treaty (treaties) 7, 9, 14, 128, 142–3, 149,
    263
tourism 121, 158–9, 162–3, 166–8, 213;
    see also sport tourism
trophy hunting
    canned hunts 175–6
    commercial 156, 163–5
    conservation 156, 160–63, 166; *see
        also* sport tourism
    exploitation 109, 111, 121, 155, 159,
        163
    sport 155–6
    violence and dominion over animals
        155, 157–9, 163
turtles 170, 184, 193
typology of offending 69–86, 186, 208,
    236

United Nations 9, 151, 193, 262–3
United Nations Declaration on the Rights
    of Indigenous Peoples 262
United Nations World Charter for Nature
    8–9
United States
    animal protection 17, 18, 25, 43,
        49–50, 76, 126–7
    Criminal justice policy 15, 37, 66, 73,
        75, 85
    environmental protection 18, 26
    Legislation and legislative provisions
        5, 7, 9, 17, 18, 37, 43, 48, 49–50,
        52
United States Department of Justice 86,
    208, 224, 234, 255
United States Environmental Protection
    Agency (EPA)
United States Fish and Wildlife Service 12,
    19, 81, 164, 168, 179, 200, 233,
    240
Universal Declaration on Animal Welfare
    (UDAW)
underground activities 44, 54, 109, 177
unnecessary suffering
    avoidable pain and suffering 91, 129,
        177, 251
    concept 35, 91–2
    elimination and reduction 4, 9, 11, 14,
        22, 246–8, 269–70, 276–7

Made in the USA
Middletown, DE
14 January 2020